SPANISH CINEMA AGAINST ITSELF

NEW DIRECTIONS IN NATIONAL CINEMAS

Robert Rushing, editor

SPANISH CINEMA AGAINST ITSELF

Cosmopolitanism, Experimentation, Militancy

Steven Marsh

INDIANA UNIVERSITY PRESS

This book is a publication of

Indiana University Press
Office of Scholarly Publishing
Herman B Wells Library 350
1320 East 10th Street
Bloomington, Indiana 47405 USA

iupress.indiana.edu

Manufactured in the United States of America

Library of Congress Cataloging-in-Publication Data

Names: Marsh, Steven, [date-] author.
Title: Spanish cinema against itself : cosmopolitanism, experimentation,
militancy / Steven Marsh.
Description: Bloomington : Indiana University Press, 2020. |
Includes bibliographical references and index.
Identifiers: LCCN 2019011399 (print) | LCCN 2019012412 (ebook) |
ISBN 9780253046345 (ebook) | ISBN 9780253046307 (hardback : alk. paper) |
ISBN 9780253046314 (pbk. : alk. paper)
Subjects: LCSH: Motion pictures—Spain—History—20th century. |
Motion pictures—Spain—History—21st century. | Motion pictures—Social
aspects—Spain—History and criticism.
Classification: LCC PN1993.5.S7 (ebook) | LCC PN1993.5.S7 M29395 2019 (print) |
DDC 791.430946—dc23
LC record available at https://lccn.loc.gov/2019011399

1 2 3 4 5   25 24 23 22 21 20

For Tatjana

CONTENTS

ACKNOWLEDGMENTS

Tʜɪs ʙᴏᴏᴋ ʜᴀs ʙᴇᴇɴ ᴀ ʟᴏɴɢ ᴛɪᴍᴇ ɪɴ the making and would not have been possible without the help, support, and enthusiasm of many people who have contributed to its gestation over the years. In Spain, many filmmakers were among the first to understand the nature of the project and help shape it in productive conversations. I would like to express my gratitude to the members of the Collective Los Hijos: Luis López Carrasco, Natalia Marín Sáncho, and Javier Fernández Vázquez. I thank Flavio G. García, Miguel Llansó, Ramiro Ledo Cordeiro, Carlos Serrano Azcona, Cecilia Barriga, Antoni Padrós, Pere Portabella (and Films 59), Adrián Onco, Anna Petrus, Virginia García del Pino, Gonzalo de Pedro Amatria, Raya Martín, Sylvain George, Guillermo G. Peydró, Andrés Duque, Victor Moreno, Óskar Alegría, and Gonzalo García Pelayo—all of whom generously shared their work with me. I thank David Varela Alvarez and Samuel Alarcón for inviting me to participate in a roundtable discussion on the filmic dialogue between Ramon Ledo Cordeiro's *VidaExtra* and Portabella's *El sopar* during a cycle of militant cinema in Spain. Diego Rodríguez Blázquez at Márgenes cine has consistently backed my work, as has Marta Sánchez from Pragda.

Many of my academic colleagues in Spain have proved stimulating interlocutors and have helped me access films and other material. I thank Elena Oroz, Albert Alcoz, Joan M. Minguet Batllori, Josetxo Cerdán, Miguel Fernández Labayen, Román Gubern, Sonia García López, and Lidia Mateo Leivas.

Preliminary sections and early drafts of this book were presented as lectures in Spain, the United Kingdom, and the United States. Among those who invited me to deliver such talks are Jill Robbins of the University of Texas, Austin, Juan Egea of the University of Wisconsin–Madison, Sara Nadal-Melsió of New York University, Bryan Cameron of the University of Cambridge, John Kraniauskas and Mari Paz Balibrea of Birkbeck College, London, and Eduardo Ledesma of the University of Illinois at Urbana-Champaign. Vicente Benet of the Universitat Jaume I in Castellón kindly invited me to give a talk to his seminar. Elena Oliete and Beatriz Oria hosted me at the University of Zaragoza. I had the honor to be the keynote speaker at the Hispanic Studies graduate student conference at Indiana University and at the conference "Aquí y Ahora" that Rosi Song and Adrián Gras-Velázquez organized at Swarthmore. The first time I spoke publicly about this project was at the Chicago Film Seminar at the invitation of Sara Hall.

Over the years, I have benefited from being able to teach successive generations of extraordinary graduate students who are too numerous to name here. I want, though, to single out for gratitude Yanire Márquez, Dag "Sasha" Lindskog, Lorenzo Gattorno, Daniel Sánchez Bataller, and Susana Domingo Amestoy.

I have had the privilege of receiving rich feedback on my work from colleagues such as Belén Vidal, Tom Whittaker, Oscar Cabezas, Alberto Moreiras, Elixabete Ansa Goicochea, Karen Benezra, Pablo Pérez Wilson, Brad Epps, Marvin D'Lugo, Carmelo Esterrich, Palmar Álvarez, and Sebastiaan Faber. Anna Cox and Rob Trumbull generously shared their work with me. I have also worked intensely over the last few years with a group of colleagues that promises to continue its work of making waves in the rather moribund field of Spanish film studies. These collaborators are Teresa Vilarós, Patty Keller, Cristina Moreiras Menor, Sarah Thomas, Julián Gutiérrez Albilla, and Camila Moreiras.

Carl Good and Sam Steinberg invited me to participate in the *Discourse* issue they coedited, and the result was an early version of what would become chapter 7 of this book. Iván Pinto invited me to contribute to the important online journal *La Fuga* in Chile—a contribution that was a fragment of what in time would be chapter 9. Earlier versions of chapters 8 and 3 appeared in the *Journal of Spanish Cultural Studies* and *Hispanic Review,* respectively.

I am fortunate to work at an institution with a vibrant intellectual community at the University of Illinois at Chicago. I owe a special debt to my colleagues Margarita Saona, Rosilie Hernández, Imke Meyer, and Heidi Schlipphacke. I benefited from a fellowship in 2010 at the Institute for the Humanities at UIC that allowed me time away from teaching and enabled me to lay the foundations of the project. Dan Streible, Susan Courtney, Ina Rae Hark—the original members of the Film and Media Studies Program at the University of South Carolina—were there when I first began to think about this book. As ever, Jo Labanyi has consistently believed in and encouraged my work.

This book is dedicated to my wife and *compañera,* Tatjana Gajic, who, together with my daughter, Jana, means more to me than anything in the world.

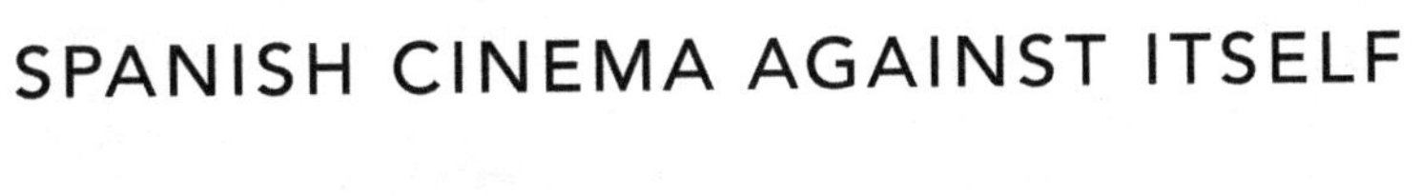

SPANISH CINEMA AGAINST ITSELF

INTRODUCTION

Différance. *Otherness. Experiment.*

EXPERIMENTATION WITH FORM—ALL THAT DETERMINES, CONDITIONS, AND disciplines formal filmic practice—is what defines this book. *Spanish Cinema against Itself: Cosmopolitanism, Experimentation, Militancy* explores, within that framework, the concept of Spain's national cinema from the margins that outline both the nation and the discipline of film studies. This work is an attempt to mobilize, in ways hitherto unexplored in Spanish film studies, the politics of global filmic practice and its materialities beyond the sterile confines of the nation. The aim is to theorize the terrain on which such discourse is constructed by focusing on largely neglected experimental and independent film produced within the boundaries of the nation-state but that exceed the national narrative. Part of this book's critical intervention is to disentangle films produced within a specific geographical space from the baggage of identity. Indeed, the title, *Spanish Cinema against Itself*, points to the plurality of affiliations at work within the territorial space known as Spain, the otherness that dwells within its frontiers as well as that which seeps beyond them. The book's title also hints at the idea of transmission—analogic and electronic—contained within the complex, alternating wavelengths of moving-image technology. It points to a displacement or translation suggestive of a sense of movement, of the ground itself seismically shifting, and of the yawning abyss of the conflictive and productive void. And it posits, within that transit or passage, a notion of *allos*, the *alter*, alterity, the other, the alternative.

Cosmopolitan *Teleiopoiesis*

Spanish critics and commentators have recently coined the phrase the "other Spanish cinema" to define a new era in the history of independent filmmaking in Spain that has emerged in the wake of the popularization of digital technology and the new (often online) formats for the distribution and exhibition of films.[1] The phrase has since been adopted by British and North American critics and commentators as well. While acknowledging the honest intentions behind the usage of the term, this book argues against such classification, and any other. It disputes the emphasis on naming, periodization, and historicity that has determined and limited much study of national cinema, and particularly that of Spain. Instead it argues for a disruptive otherness lurking within, beneath, and against such historical formulations and for a heterogeneity or "spectral duplicity"[2] that interrogates claims to origins and undermines efforts to forge an autochthonous canon.

By mapping a genealogy of underground film that harkens back to the surrealists to draw out its traces, this book seeks to disrupt the temporal certainties that conventional historiography defines. The proposal here is to read film and its history *otherwise*—to create a counterhistory via a live, mobile, unruly, and overflowing archive and to disorder chronology (as María Blanco and Esther Peeren put it). It is this *teleiopoiesis*—the play on words that Jacques Derrida conjures by combining *telos*, *poiēsis*, and *tele* (the poetic effects of transformation produced in transmission and telecommunication; the pun on dispatch, distance, and sending; and the impossibility of closure, completion, or arrival at a final destination)—that defines the cosmopolitanism to which I refer in the book's subtitle. I propose here a critical cosmopolitanism in film influenced by Jean-Luc Nancy's theorization of international cultural and human movement across borders as *mondialisation*, an alternative to economic globalization, and a politicized worldliness. It is a cosmopolitanism marked by the heterodox, or difference, rather than the Kantian universality with which cosmopolitanism is traditionally associated. It is a cosmopolitanism characterized by transference, discordance, and displacement over origin, equivalence, and correspondence. It is an abrasive cosmopolitanism of ill-fitting hybrids over assimilation.[3]

At the paradoxical heart of this book is the idea of an outsider cinema at work within, a filmmaking at the periphery that inflects the center. *Spanish Cinema against Itself* analyzes the film production connected with a single territory but only insofar as that territory is singular by virtue of its conflicting regional, national, and transnational elements that, in turn, exceed their own definitions. It examines a cinema that is worldly in ways that are indifferent to identification with a nation-state and exceptional to the interests implicit in such identification. As we will see in chapter 3, this book proposes an emergent productive space, or *khôra*, in the face of teleological claims to a national origin. It posits the unfamiliarity of experimentation against the reassurance of home. This is not to deny the specificity of place, nor the sense of belonging associated with it. Of interest here are questions of how film can disturb location while still acknowledging the placeness of place and how film can provoke awkward surprises in the quotidian and generate discomfort in that sense of belonging. Contrary to dominant discourse and traditional ways of thinking, this sense of belonging has nothing intrinsically to do with origin or an arbitrary birthplace.

But this book also maps a counterhistory, though inevitably a selective one. It is a spectral historiography, a subterranean history, and a history of interruption written in the spirit of Walter Benjamin. It is not so much an untold history (though it is that, too) as it is a different way of conceiving and writing history. The book offers a critique of traditional historiography and particularly of the historicist approach to national cinema that has distinguished and diminished criticism within Spain (see chap. 4). More specifically, however, it is a book about time—to which history, of course, is central. It explores how time affects, configures, and constitutes film. Interruptions in temporal flows, the exceptions that disturb efforts to shape and define time, are the points, I will argue, at which filmmaking becomes interesting.

Temporality is both a discourse of power—the codification and modulation of time for particular interests—and a key feature of the processes involved in film's diegetic components. Film makes use of time in ways that few other cultural modes are capable of, and in a manner that is uniquely convincing. Flashbacks, rhythm, fast-forwards, slow motion, simultaneity (split screen effects, superimposition, and cross-cutting), and instantaneity are but a few of these filmically specific time effects. More than that, though, film can elongate time through the creation of pauses, intervals, interludes, and temporal parentheses. The recent critical interest in "slow cinema" is a clear symptom of this, as is the marginal experimentation that haunts mainstream film, which is analyzed in detail in chapter 5. If temporality is governed by and shaped discursively into manageable units, film can undo that regulation, and it can divide the instant. A key argument of this book is that it is precisely otherness that undoes such efforts to shape time. The field of operations of film, I propose, is found in the other of time, or, more specifically, in what Patricia Keller, invoking Derrida, has dubbed "now and other," the other of now.[4]

The paradox of filmic time is that, despite cinema's characteristic freeze-frame, the film still, and the photogram, it never stands still in the present. The single most visible aspect of time is that of change—backward and forward, past and future, alternation and alteration. The condition of film is that of the untimely. The final chapter of this book homes in on the relation of time to change and to form itself to focus on and propose a filmmaking practice whose very gesture is able to per*form* a trans*form*ation. Part of the project of this book is to argue, in this spirit, for a new definition of the term *performative film. Performativity,* in the sense of the word as Derrida conceived of it, as radical speech act, is a particularly apt tool of film analysis in the age of digital filmmaking.

As a discourse of power, temporality establishes a regime of order that I seek to question. This book's interrogation of systemization passes through the prism of temporality to other such regimes of normativity, categorization, and genre. It proposes a critique of the concept of identity (and "national cinema" as a concept both assumes a univocal identity and interpellates the spectator as the subject of that assumption) as disjunctive rather than as the key element in classificatory discourse. In my view, the phrase "other Spanish cinema" is frequently reduced to a fetishized slogan that disregards its potential for disruption and establishes yet another criterion for forging the kind of identity that this book seeks to challenge.

In the chapters to follow, I emphasize the self as the proper, or *propio* (to employ the Spanish word), with its authoritarian connotations of property and propriety. With Derrida, I am interested in the *propio* not so much in opposition to the other as the self *as* other, as the means by which the self is destabilized from within. I highlight this instability in discussions about authorship and, later, in the writing of the self, or *autography* (most explicitly in chap. 6 but throughout the book), of the encounter within the *propio* of interior and exterior movement, of the aporias of the self that unfold in the word *propio*.

An insistence on identity runs counter to these movements, because identity requires an origin. Origin, of course, similarly requires an end point, a destination. Origin suggests, in turn, whether we like it or not, a telos, an order, a beginning and an end, an aperture and a closure. This book questions such ideas through a series of theoretical paradigms, from the linguistic sign, to the citation, to the concept of legacy or inheritance, the prosthetic, and the postal motif. Identity, of course, also requires an ontology, a defining essence (or being). These theoretical terms are mobilized throughout this book to question such an ontology. Moreover, the evolution of the technologies of the moving and the sonic image has cast doubt on identitarian discourses, as testified to by the onset of the so-called digital revolution. Among other things, the ontology of the photographic image (the title of André Bazin's hugely influential 1945 essay) is what I seek to engage with in this book. The resurgence of critical interest since the 1990s in Bazin as a theorist as well as a return to auteurism in the context of transnationalism, slow cinema, and queer studies are but a few of the many symptoms of the shifts happening now in film and in its academic study. My contribution to such debates is to argue throughout this volume for a theoretical lineage that connects Benjamin with Bazin and then with Derrida.

Questions of filmic and theoretical legacy or heritage—what constitute them and what they are constitutive of—are, then, key elements in this book's interrogation of the construction of tradition but also in the opening up of a new theoretical lineage within film studies. In an interesting essay titled "Deconstruction avant la letter" that appeared in a 2011 collection on Bazin, Louis-Georges Schwarz boldly compares Derrida's seminal essay "Différance" with Bazin's "The Ontology of the Photographic Image" (one of the founding texts of modern film theory) in an exercise Schwarz terms "reverse philology." The notion is apt to this book's guiding principles, which seek to upturn conventional lineage. Schwartz reads Bazin as if he were writing *after* Derrida and points out—again the question of *being*—their common interest in the funereal rituals of ancient Egypt (the figure of the mummy as primitive representation in Bazin's essay, the pyramid-like shape of the letter *A* in Derrida's) and what Derrida calls "the economy of death."[5] I will return to this idea later in this book, but for now it is worth noting that early in his essay, Schwartz observes that Bazin writes in the conditional, "within the state of the virtual being indicated by this conditional, a massive 'perhaps.'"[6] Although the subjunctive mode, with all its connotations of an uncertain future, might be a more accurate and more appropriate grammatical formulation, it is this conditional "perhaps" that marks the present work, as we will see in chapter 7.

Schwartz's essay, while an exception, suggests a turn in theoretical approaches to film. Deconstruction, the body of work associated with the thought of Derrida, has not habitually or historically been deployed in film theory (a rare exception being Peter Brunette and David Wills's 1989 volume *Screen/Play: Derrida and Film Theory*). Recently, though, and in the wake of Akira Mizuta Lippit's books, journals such as *Discourse* and a special issue of the *Journal of Spanish Cultural Studies* that I edited have begun to close this gap in the theoretical corpus of film studies. In part this absence has to do with a suspicion toward theory within Anglo-American film studies since the 1980s, coinciding with the advent of cultural studies and the shift of interest toward reception theory, production values, and the film industry itself. This suspicion is also possibly, however, an adverse reaction to the highbrow debates of previous decades that dominated the pages of *Cahiers du Cinema* and *Screen*.

Just as I pose theoretical questions about history and identity in the film studies of Spain, I also seek to mobilize deconstruction to consider the constituent elements of representation; this is at the center of the book's spectral interpretation of Spanish film. What Hubertus von Amelunxen, in conversation with Derrida, has referred to as the "division of the instant" points to the doubled quality of the photographic image—that element produced at the very moment of its emergence that haunts it.[7] The "instant" is the temporal difference between liveness and its ghostly other that marks the difference between the actual and the virtual, the here and the elsewhere, the shadow and its subject. This book deploys an array of concepts and terms from the lexicon of deconstruction originally coined by thinkers such as Derrida, J. Hillis Miller, Jean-Luc Nancy, Philippe Lacoue-Labarthe, Lippit, and others whose work has grappled with these concepts. Such constellations of theoretical references extend from the sense of paradoxical impasse, the tension or tautness at the point of encounter contained in the word *aporia*, to the destabilizing potential of the supplement, to the use of ex-appropriation to capture the aporetic notion of simultaneous interior-exterior movement. That said, and despite its recourse to philosophical writing, this book is not a work of philosophy. It is, rather, an attempt to reconfigure certain theoretical paradigms in the field of film studies.

While the book's critique of historicist teleology is central, its intimately related critique of representation as traversed by temporality returns it again and again to the work of Fredric Jameson. Jameson has consistently maintained that there is a correspondence between representation and the political reality of its production. He has argued that this link is manifested through allegory and through coherent temporal patterns in a process he calls periodization. My point is not the argument often leveled at Jameson by scholars of Asian, African, and Latin American cultures—that such a position is generalizing and ignores specific conditions—but rather that it seeks closure and it conceives of representation as a correlation to social reality, not a means by which to challenge it or of being discordant with it. Jameson's work (which, despite my reservations, I admire) seeks to classify, define, pigeonhole, and enclose within periods. My doubts concerning periodization as the codification or shaping of temporality for the purposes of analysis emerge at several points throughout this book as part of its broad conceptualization of the otherness of time and its proposal for a spectral time.[8] Regarding allegory, as described in detail in chapter 1, I follow Benjamin's outline of the concept as fragment or ruin, as metonym, rather than Jameson's more conventional use of the term as extended metaphor corresponding to a defined, objectified entity.

Ghostly Antecedents

The history of experimental film in Spain stretches back almost to the beginning of cinema itself, but the focus of this book is to map a genealogy from the 1930s to the present day with an emphasis on the period from the 1960s to today.[9] The enduring legacy of surrealism is found in the work of contemporary Spanish filmmakers from Ramiro Ledo to Isaki Lacuesta, from José Luis Guerín to Jacinto Esteva, and from Pere Portabella to Óskar Alegría. This legacy, though, is not only that of Luis Buñuel and Salvador Dalí—the most celebrated of the Spanish surrealists. As explored in this book, non-Spanish surrealists Antonin Artaud, Germaine Dulac, Man Ray, Marcel Duchamp, and others have left their mark on subsequent generations of filmmakers. However, it should be noted that this is not a book about surrealism; rather, it follows the ripples that surrealism has left in its wake, its traces and its spirit.

Surrealism is only one of the antecedents of contemporary experimental filmmaking in the Spanish state, albeit an important one. The latter years of the Francoist dictatorship witnessed a number of avant-garde initiatives. These include the 1967 Jornadas Internationales de Escuelas de Cine, a conference in Sitges that provided the stage for fierce cultural and political debates among the opposition and several emerging experimental and independent filmmakers discussed in this volume,[10] and the Encuentros de Pamplona in 1972 (attended by, among other celebrities, John Cage). In addition, several gatherings, exhibitions, and publications took place in Catalonia, notable among them being those promoted by the conceptualist circle called the Grup de Treball, which included filmmakers such as Pere Portabella and Carles Santos, whose work is analyzed in detail in chapter 3. Similar groups existed in Madrid, among them the Grupo Zaj, with whom the celebrated performance artist Esther Ferrer collaborated. Other artists working in this experimentalist milieu (and making experimental films) included Isidoro Valcárcel Medina in Murcia and Jorge Oteiza in the Basque Country.[11] Several links exist between Salvador Dalí and the 1960s Catalan filmmakers—most notably, Jacinto Esteva, the leading figure of the Barcelona School filmmakers. Likewise, Pilar Parcerisas has extensively documented Duchamp's lifelong fascination with Catalonia.[12]

In this genealogy, one of the most significant legacies is the fascination with the "primitive" and with ethnography. The coincidence between the anthropological filmmaking of some Spanish cineastes of the 1960s and that of ethnographer Jean Rouch (in West Africa) or Maya Deren (in Haiti) is remarkable, as I suggest in chapter 1. Whether the Spaniards were aware of the work of their counterparts is another topic, but the connection to surrealism in this haphazard and incidental lineage might be conceived as stretching backward in time from Esteva to Deren to Rouch and to the work of 1930s surrealist poet Michael Leiris, whose travel diary of the "Mission Dakar-Djibouti" expedition has recently been translated into English under the title *Phantom Africa*.[13] In the Spanish state, anthropologist Julio Caro Baroja exercised a significant influence on some of the filmmakers discussed in this book.

Aside from formal experimentation and the surrealists, there is a long-standing tradition of politically committed cinema in Spain that flourished during the 1930s and whose connections with subsequent filmmaking have been neglected by both critics and film historians. The term *militant film* only enters the parlance of film studies in the 1960s and largely as a result of anticolonialist filmmaking in the Third World, yet there is a case to be made that the politically committed cinema of the 1930s set a precedent for future filmmakers both in the 1960s and for the present day, as I argue in chapter 9. Nonetheless, this book is concerned more with the theoretical configurations presented by militant film than with documenting its different historical development and evolution. There is important work currently being undertaken by scholars in Spain and the United States in the field of Spanish political film and cultural memory (during the late stages of the dictatorship and the Transition),[14] from which my work differs in its emphasis on the notion of spectral distance. It is important to draw attention to the early predecessors of political filmmaking in Spain as they emerge in the 1930s. In large part this emergence is a consequence of the Second Republic's Misiones Pedagógicas, the state-sponsored initiatives designed to take culture to the "people" that Jordana Mendelson has written extensively about,[15] but it also owes much to the work of several leftist filmmakers prior to the Spanish Civil War, of whom Buñuel was only one. The documentaries of Carlos Velo (both in 1930s Spain and during his lengthy exile in Mexico) are exemplary in this respect, and, as I explore in the final chapter of this book, his work features ghost-like in that of certain contemporary filmmakers. That militancy also has a formally experimental, disjunctive character that emerges more explicitly in the productions of filmmakers such as Buñuel, Velo, and José Val del Omar.

However, perhaps surprisingly, it should be noted that among the least adventurous political cinema of the 1930s, in formal terms, is that produced by the anarchist federation CNT-FAI (Confederación Nacional del Trabajo–Federación Anarquista Ibérica). While the Anarchist newsreels of the Civil War period provide interesting and dramatic documents of the conflict, the fiction films are largely mediocre melodramas. Film served the Anarchists as a means of social and moral pedagogy that they conceived of as contributing to raising political consciousness. *Barrios bajos* (1937) is a Rousseau-like disquisition about a community of the lumpen proletariat in the port district of Barcelona and the figure of a sacrificial noble savage, a character dubbed "El Valencia." In its hackneyed course, the film counsels against the evils of alcohol and the exploitation of women trafficked into prostitution by organized crime. Likewise, the musical *Nosotros somos así* (1937)—one of the more formally innovative Anarchist-produced films, at least in terms of its Soviet-like montage—is earnestly simplistic in its message. Almost entirely populated by child actors, the film offers an austere lesson in popular democracy. Against a background of the war and the repressive measures taken by the Anarchists against the wealthy, the children establish an assembly that votes in defense of the arrested bourgeois father of one of their classmates, who, dazzled by this display of solidarity, renounces his father's class values. This film is an exception among the Anarchist productions of the period in that, unlike most of the others, the war is actually mentioned.

Two of the few Anarchist films made outside Barcelona and, in my view, the most interesting pieces of the group were *Carne de fieras* (1936) and *Nuestro culpable* (1937). Directed by Armand Guerra, *Carne de fieras* was shot in Madrid during the very early days of the Civil War (shooting commenced on July 16, 1936, and the war began two days later).[16] Because of the conflict, filming was interrupted on several occasions, rationing threatened the food supply of the circus lions that feature in the film, and it was never completed. Because Guerra was keen to make documentaries that recorded events in the trenches, *Carne de fieras* remained unedited, and the film reels were lost until the late 1980s, after which the film was restored and edited by Ferrán Alberich of the Filmoteca Española (the Spanish national film archive). Coincidentally, this latency, the temporal folds in the film's extradiegetic history—its time lag— reflects its own narrative twist, which turns on a stopped watch in the screen action. It is a film that, like Benjamin's revolution (in the "Theses on History"), hinges on the untimely, the interruption or telescoping of time, and the truncation of the seemingly inexorable, forward movement of progress. What is remarkable, though, is how an on-screen temporal shift was reproduced in real historical time off-screen (with the film's loss and subsequent rediscovery). Indeed, seeing the film in hindsight reveals other spectral elements, not the least of which are several of the actors whose existence in this film is their only remaining trace.

Erotic spectacle is one of the distinctive elements of *Carne de fieras*. Each of the protagonists is in some way a public performer: Marlene Grey—"La Venus Rubia" (the blonde Venus)—dances naked with a group of lions; Pablo, her lover, is a boxer; Aurora, his unfaithful wife, is a dancer; and her lover is a singer. A large section of the film is shot at a cabaret, and much of the rest is Marlene Grey's show as filmed at the zoo in Madrid's major park, the Retiro. The film is strikingly transgressive in that central to its discourse is a notion of sexual freedom amid questions of adultery, divorce, and jealousy. This sense of taboo is most graphically exemplified by the daring nudity of Marlene Grey's dance sequences.

Nuestro culpable (made the following year) is an urban comedy that was criticized not only by the Communist Party press for its frivolity but also by the Anarchist media outlets for its indebtedness to the sophisticated liberal filmmaker Benito Perojo. Directed by former set designer Fernando Mignoni, the film is indeed reminiscent of the deliciousness that Perojo specialized in during the 1930s, in worldly films such as *Rumbo al Cairo* and *El negro que tenía el alma blanca*. Mignoni's film, though, is also a celebration of the same working-class *castizo* (that is, purportedly "authentic") culture that Perojo sought to represent in *La verbena de la Paloma* (1934): the culture of the distinctive (and cramped) living quarters of central Madrid, the patio or *corrala*, and the figure of the *chuleta madrileño* (the lovable Madridian wag). The quick-witted protagonist of this film is reminiscent of many of the roles later played by popular actor Tony Leblanc in the 1950s and 1960s. Within this hybrid of registers, social anarchism shapes the film's discourse. *Nuestro culpable* inverts the moral order regarding crime as it makes heroes out of "El Randa," the happy-go-lucky thief, and his accomplice, Greta, while simultaneously lampooning the assembled crew of dim-witted and doltish bankers, judges, state functionaries, and other class enemies.

Spectrality

Spectral time is that of the untimely; it is the temporal connection between what is impossible to connect. Or, once again in Derrida's terms, it is the other of now. The disjoining of the present from the contemporary means that time is always already fraught with its own sense of the untimely and its out-of-joint condition between the not yet and the no longer. Spectrality is the virtual other that makes its presence felt. "We always have to do with spectrality, not simply when we experience ghosts coming back or when we have to deal with virtual images," writes Derrida.[17]

While film's virtuality defines it as spectral, spectrality manifests itself in different ways within film. *Vida en sombras* (1948), the only full-length feature directed by Lorenzo Llobet-Gràcia, is a work of mourning that turns on the ghostly quality of the filmic image and its spectral transmission. Obsessed by the possibilities afforded by cinema, Carlos Durán (Fernando Fernán Gómez) leaves his wife, Ana, at home while he goes to film a gun battle in the street during the war. Upon his return, Carlos discovers that Ana has been shot and killed by a stray bullet that has entered the house. Remorseful, Carlos blames Ana's death on his passion for filming, and he abandons his camera. Later, he is persuaded by his friend Luis to return to filmmaking, but only after watching his former self and Ana on-screen, ghost-like and postmortem in the home movies he made years before. The effect is similar to Derrida's description of the sensation of uncanniness he experienced on seeing himself and the actor Pascale Ogier during a screening of Ken McMullen's 1982 film *Ghost Dance* in Texas.[18] In the interim since the shoot, Ogier had died, and yet here she was—undead and speaking to a phantasmagoric Derrida discussing ghosts— on-screen. What confirms for Carlos that he can finally return to filmmaking is when Ana smiles affirmatively from the old photograph perched on his desk. It is, of course, the ghost of Ana who smiles from beyond the grave.

The film's first sequence takes place in a photography studio. The film undertakes a review—in the movie theater—of the history of film, from the cinema of the attractions, the cinematograph, and the Lumière brothers to Hitchcock's *Rebecca*. This history parallels but does not overlap or correspond thematically with Carlos's biography or tribulations. It is a spectral history of the virtual.

Tom Gunning, in his essay "To Scan a Ghost: The Ontology of Mediated Vision," draws attention to the technology of visibility to highlight another aspect of filmic spectrality: the role of the materiality of the apparatus itself. In his analysis of Murnau's *Nosferatu*, Gunning writes—in ways that chime, albeit indirectly, with the discussion of intermediality in chapter 2—that the film "explored the play between the visible and the invisible, reflections and shadow, on- and off-screen space that cinema made possible, forging a technological image of the uncanny."[19] Drawing on the work of Giorgio Agamben, Gunning uses the figure of the "phantasm" "to focus on the term *medium . . .* its very materiality and its paradoxical aspiration to immateriality."[20] He notes that the transparency of the ghostly body is like that of the strip of film, the very material of the moving image, "a filter of light, a caster of shadows, a weaver of phantoms."[21] Furthermore, the techniques of montage bring forth optical effects and make visible the invisible in the same way as other materialities of film do (with lighting, lenses, mirrors, sound equipment, and so on).

The exact verisimilitude of the object filmed and the projected film image—its capacity to represent reality—that led Bazin to insist on its ontology also establishes an uncanny distance between the profilmic event and the image projected in the public auditorium. Its present is deferred in time (its "now" is "other"), and its presence is illusionary. Additionally, the effects of film beyond its extraordinary capacity to play on time by means such as ellipsis, doubling, and distortions of sound give film a particularly ghostly resonance. Given film's intangible materialities (such as light and shadow) and capacity for reproducing reality, it is ideal for hauntological analysis. In the same vein, filmic mise en abyme, seen particularly in the kind of experimental film that comprises much of the work discussed in this book, with its frames within frames and mirroring effects—like the ghost itself—marks the shimmering threshold space that blurs the border dividing life from death, absence from presence.

This is a book about that limit and about the legacies that arise from it. It is an essay on films shot, produced, and distributed from the margin, but it is also a book about that frontier, the dividing line from the edges of the frame or screen to the fringes of Europe or the nation-state. It is a book about spectral genealogies and the kind of film that is an exergue, a space beyond, an excess, and a surfeit that is both a part of and separate from the national legacy, or, to quote Lippit, "between, beside and outside" the totality.[22]

Sergio Caballero's experimental *Finisterrae* (2010) is a film populated by ghosts while also having a spectral predecessor in Jean Epstein's *Finis Terrae* (1929). As their titles suggest, both films focus on the historical end of the known world, the limits of Europe. Both films play around the imprecise edges of the European continent. Each also, in very different ways, resorts to the rich and mixed legacy whose vestiges are to be found at the very margins of European culture. Caballero's film inherits a geographical eschatology from Epstein's and, arguably, also from Buñuel's *La vía láctea* (1969). While Epstein's film is an example of a poetic cinema of nature, Caballero's is a film about ghosts who speak Russian and travel the route of the historical pilgrimage of the Way of Santiago in Galicia in northwestern Spain. Such a haunted genealogy is never a straightforward or linear matter; its legacy resounds like an echo and leaves its imprint in the form of a residue, or afterimage, or glow fading on the horizon. Film, to paraphrase Derrida, is a ghost that comes back from the future. As Blanco and Peeren indicate, spectrality for Derrida is both *revenant* and *arrivant*. Futurity, as embedded within history, is central to this volume, as we will see in the discussion of the future anterior in chapter 8 and the gesture to the future to come in chapter 9.

The opening up of these fields by interruption—the spatial pauses, the stuttering hesitations, the apertures, the parentheses in time—all combine to disrupt the smooth coherence and operation of the official archive. The spatialization of time and the temporalization of space, the deferrals and differences of Derridean *différance*, are elements that return again and again throughout this book. Indeed, the neologism *différance* is perhaps the most significant of all the key words deployed throughout this volume. It defines the procedures of the text—the spacing that divides and holds together in abeyance its aporias like celluloid itself—and the terms of its argument.

I conclude this introduction with a contemporary example that serves as a metonym for the entire volume. The contrasting images—dividing lines between the materiality and immateriality to which Gunning refers—the porous or the translucent and the opaque, and the screen and the ground that distinguish the filmic aesthetic are important features of this book. Such images of doubling pervade the work of Isaki Lacuesta, a leading figure of the younger generation of contemporary filmmakers in Spain. Lacuesta's films suggest another important encounter intimate to the filmmaking process: that between surface and depth. A filmmaker of traces and historical fragmentation, of unearthing the buried and concealed, Lacuesta is also a cineaste of apostrophes (that turn away) or *revenants* (that return, turn back, turn toward). This material filmic disjoining—like the motif of the ground disturbed, which is present throughout Lacuesta's work—is illustrated in the complexity of one of the final sequences from his 2010 film *La noche que no acaba* (Not to sleep all night long), based on the years US actor Ava Gardner lived in Spain. Using footage from Gardner's films shot in Spain from different periods, the montage generates an unanchored encounter in a wavering disjunction between surface and depth—the visual and the aural—between the younger and the older actor. It is enacted through the overlaid spectral voices of the two most emblematic Spanish women actors of their respective generations (Charo López and Ariadna Gil), who alternate reciting the text of Robert Graves's poem "Not to Sleep," which is dedicated to Gardner and from whose first line the film takes its title. The invisibility of the two actors generates visibility, a translucent presence to the ghost, and amid the acoustic mix, the spectral figure of Ava Gardner emerges—a flickering transparent apparition whose voice is in the mouths of others—from beyond the grave and from the depths of the archive to extend and float ethereal through the space and the ground of the image, without origin or destination.

Notes

1. See, for example, Carlos Losilla, "A favor de este cine español," *Transit: cine y otros desvíos* (July 31, 2013), http://cinentransit.com/a-favor-de-este-cine-espanol/; and "Otro cine español," coord. Carlos Losilla Alcalde, special issue, *Caiman: cuadernos de cine*, no. 19 (September 2013). A number of pieces concerning the "other Spanish cinema" have appeared in *Sight and Sound*, among them Mar Diestro-Dópido, "Hidden Visionaries: 50 Years of the 'Other' Spanish Cinema," *Sight and Sound* (February 7, 2014), https://www.bfi.org.uk/news -opinion/sight-sound-magazine/features/hidden-visionaries-50-years-other-spanish-cinema. Many of the filmmakers discussed in this book—including Andrés Duque, Los Hijos, and Isaki Lacuesta—fall within the appropriative category.

2. María Blanco and Esther Peeren, *The Spectralities Reader: Ghosts and Haunting in Contemporary Cultural Theory* (London: Bloomsbury Academic, 2013), 8.

3. A turn to cosmopolitanism in film theory in recent years has complicated the concept of transnational approaches. I refer to, for example, the Screen conference of 2011 and "For a Cosmopolitan Cinema," ed. James Mulvey, Laura Rascaroli, and Humberto Saldanha, special issue, *Alphaville: Journal of Film and Screen Media*, no. 14 (Winter 2017). My conceptualization of cosmopolitanism and its politics is greatly indebted to Pheng Cheah and Bruce Robbins, eds., *Cosmopolitics: Thinking and Feeling beyond the Nation* (Minneapolis: University of Minnesota Press, 1998).

4. Patricia M. Keller, *Ghostly Landscapes: Film, Photography and the Aesthetics of Haunting in Contemporary Spanish Culture* (Toronto: University of Toronto Press, 2016), 5.

5. Jacques Derrida, "Différance," in *Margins of Philosophy* (Chicago: University of Chicago Press), 8.

6. Louis-Georges Schwartz, "Deconstruction *avant la lettre*: Jacques Derrida before André Bazin," in *Opening Bazin: Post-war Film Theory and Its Afterlife*, ed. Dudley Andrew and Herve Joubert-Laurencin (Oxford: Oxford University Press, 2011), 97.

7. Jacques Derrida, *Copy, Archive, Signature: A Conversation on Photography*, ed. Gerhard Richter, trans. Jeff Fort (Stanford, CA: Stanford University Press, 2010), 1.

8. Jameson is, of course, not alone in periodizing. In a significantly different way, it is characteristic of the work of Michel Foucault. See, in particular, Foucault, *The Archaeology of Knowledge* (Paris: Gallimard, 1969).

9. Segundo de Chomón is the best known early Spanish filmmaker. A contemporary of Melies, he is considered a pioneer in filmic animation techniques. Isaki Lacuesta refers to him in the work discussed in chapter 7.

10. The Sitges conference was notable for the interventions of groups associated with the far left beyond, and critical of, the Communist Party (PCE), many of whom were Anarchists (among them Antonio Artero, whose work is discussed in chap. 1). Often contrasted to the Conversaciones de Salamanca (1955), the radicals at Sitges called for a "rupture" over the "reformism" or "*posibilismo*" of Salamanca and its conclusions as they were promoted by the PCE. The Sitges conference ended in chaos, with arrests and an inflammatory final manifesto sequestered by the Civil Guard. See, too, chapter 4.

11. The documentary filmmaker Óskar Alegría, one of whose films is discussed in chapter 4, in 2016/2017 made a montage film using Oteiza's own footage and simultaneously published a book based on the time he spent in the sculptor's library collecting the notes Oteiza wrote in the margins of books. Óskar Alegría, *Oteiza al margin* (Punto de Vista/Gobierno de Navarra, 2017).

12. Pilar Parcerisas, *Duchamp en España: las claves ocultas de sus estancias en Cadaqués* (Barcelona: Siruela, 2009).

13. Michael Leiras, *Phantom Africa* (Chicago: Chicago University Press, 2017). Although not discussed in this book, Isaki Lacuesta's African films *Los pasos dobles* (2011) and *El cuaderno de barro* (2011), both with painter and sculptor Miquel Barceló, bring this genealogy to the present day.

14. I am thinking here particularly of Pablo La Parra-Pérez and Lidia Mateo Leivas.

15. Jordana Mendelson, *Documenting Spain: Artists, Exhibition Culture, and the Modern Nation, 1929–1939* (University Park: Pennsylvania State University Press, 2005).

16. Armand Guerra (a pun that while literally meaning "arming war," might be translated as "causing trouble") was the pseudonym of José Estívalis Cabo (1886–1939).

17. Jacques Derrida, *Deconstruction Engaged: The Sydney Seminars*, ed. Paul Patton (Urbana-Champaign: University of Illinois Press, 2001), 44.

18. Jacques Derrida and Bernard Stiegler, *Echographies of Television: Filmed Interviews* (Oxford: Polity Press, 2002), 119–20.

19. Tom Gunning, "To Scan a Ghost: The Ontology of Mediated Vision," in *The Spectralities Reader: Ghosts and Haunting in Contemporary Cultural Theory* (London: Bloomsbury Academic, 2013), 209.

20. Ibid., 211.

21. Ibid., 212.

22. Akira Mizuta Lippit, *Ex-cinema: From a Theory of Experimental Film and Video* (Berkeley: University of California Press, 2012), 4.

1

INTERROGATIONS OF THE NATIONAL ALLEGORY

Trance Film and Ethnography

I BEGIN THIS INTERROGATION WITH TWO IMAGES FROM the introductory sequence of Jacinto Esteva's *Lejos de los árboles* (Far from the trees) (1963–1971). In the first image, a raw egg left in a glass of water overnight, on the summer solstice, gyrates slowly; its white lingers and elongates in the fluid, and the strands of albumen delineate a seeping aquatic cartography caught in the light and in the glass. The bulbous yolk mutates, deforms, expands, shrinks, distends, and spreads, viscous and affecting. The other image is acoustic and precedes the visual image. Off-screen, we hear the unidentified and disembodied voice-over of two people—first a woman and then a man. They both utter the same words: "Erase una vez" (Once upon a time).

The dissonance between these two images highlights a disjunction that defines the entirety of this book. The egg swirling in slow motion contrasts with the pure speech act of the first words. The performative convention of fairy-tale openings is delivered anonymously in what purports to be a documentary film. The two images are defined by their liminal differences; by the permeable borders between sight and sound, between different genders, between the optical and the auditory, between claims to truth and falsehood, between the death of the old and new life, a rebirth. Also in this first sequence, the film cuts in scenes of young people in a nightclub who burst into frenetic dance, stop as if frozen, and then repeat their wild movements. The moments when the dancers stop are the only times then when the film stills, when the action slows, and we see the distension of the egg. It is a rhythm that sets the pace for the film.

Walter Benjamin famously writes in *The Origin of German Tragic Drama*, "In allegory the observer is confronted with the *facies hippocratica* of history as a petrified primordial landscape."[1] The image is like an X-ray; like a

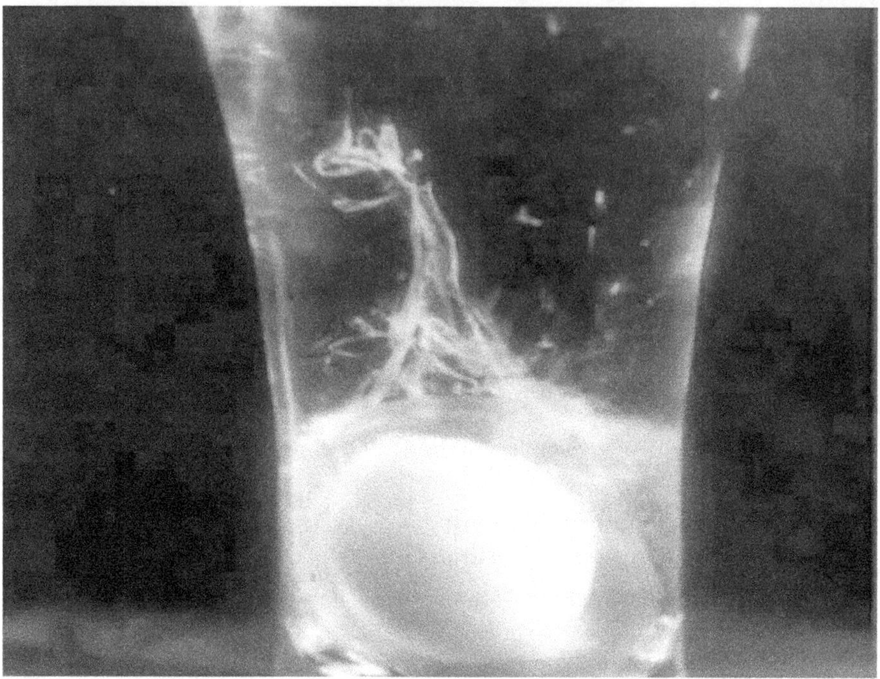

Fig. 1.1 The distending, hypnotic egg left in the glass on Midsummer Night in the opening sequence of *Lejos de los árboles*.

stark, dried outline left behind or like skin drawn tight over bones. Allegory, Bainard Cowan writes, is "veiled language"—*allegoria*, or other-discourse in its derivation from the Greek *allos*.[2] Benjamin's image stresses the excess, the washed-out, stretched, and death-like flesh of the face of history as seen and experienced from the sidelines.

This chapter introduces what will be a consistent conceptual theme throughout this book, evidenced by the initial sequence of *Lejos de los árboles*: that of the limit. *Limit* here refers to the interstitial zones between life and death, Eros and Thanatos, interiority and exteriority, self and other, and many more. I am interested in allegory as a form of writing rather than as an extended metaphor to be unpicked by an exegesis in search of correspondence. Allegory is customarily associated with depth of meaning; yet Benjamin's image is telling in that it suggests an allegory as surface, as effect rather than explication. The Benjaminian theory of allegory as fragment—or the ruin that was later taken up by Paul de Man—is a significant element of this book, and particularly in contrast to the theory of national allegory posited by Fredric Jameson. Benjaminian allegory is, in my view, more apt for the reading of film. Vulgar interpretations of the work of André Bazin have generated a theory of cinematic montage—arguably a matter of the management of filmic time—in opposition to mise-en-scène, which is often concerned with the distribution of screen space. But recent work by Adrian Martin has facilitated a more complex use of Bazin.[3] And Benjaminian montage techniques also contribute to the erosion of such a questionable dichotomy. Montage—the dialectical counterpoising of images in the editing process, according to Sergei Eisenstein's formulation— was key to Benjamin's method. As is well known, Benjamin sought to write in a way that reflected dialectical montage, fragmentation, and the spatial disturbance of time. The classical example of this approach in his work is the *Arcades Project*, with its amassed juxtaposed quotations and literary bricolage style.

In this chapter, I propose first a tentative inversion of the categorization that pairs surface against depth and space contra time. Benjamin insists that in allegory, form and content are the same thing within the movement he traces. Cowan, glossing Benjamin, writes, "Transforming things into signs is both what allegory does—its technique—and what it is about—its content."[4] Appearance and meaning are indivisible, and this leads to Benjamin's—and Eisenstein's—interest in the hieroglyph. Peter Brunette and David Wills, in their book on Derrida and film, draw attention to the similarity between Eisenstein's interest in the hieroglyph and Derrida's description of the same form, which is constituted by—to quote Derrida—"the organized cohabitation within the same graphic code, of figurative, symbolic, abstract, and phonetic elements."[5] Indeed, for Eisenstein, the hieroglyph is emblematic in montage of not only the conflicting dialectic between images but also that which relates to the distribution of elements within the assemblage of the individual image. Allegory as effect suggests an abrasive proximity to that which it claims an equivalence, a disturbance at the heart of representation that disrupts that equivalence. To this end, the hieroglyph might be conceived of as both trace and performance, an expressive form of writing that takes the unmoving shape of a seal, imprint, or stamp. It is the taut, paradoxical connection that holds together incompatible and impossible differences that Derrida calls the "spectral bond."

The word *bond* is etymologically linked to *boundary*—the demarcation or enclosure of space (generic or national) in a framing that binds affiliation, and yet, as spectrality, that bond is rendered unstable. A boundary encloses an archive and stakes out a discrete, identifiable (and identitarian) territory—one imagines a national archive—but it also defines its outer edges and margins. The word *archive* here relates to the concept of supplement—both as a central repository of information and as surplus that seeps beyond the threshold of containment. Significantly, in Freud's *Beyond the Pleasure Principle*, the word *binden* (*gebunden*) is translated as "annexed." An annex is, of course, supplementary to the main text, as an appendix. In this context, it is no coincidence that all the films discussed in this chapter touch on the subject of death, or, at the very least, on the no-man's-land that marks the meeting place of life and death.

The limit defines and reveals the topography of difference: of the shoreline, the border, gender, and genre. It is the brink, the cusp, the frame itself, the parergon. I am interested here in the overlap and excess that such an encounter produces, creating a tension that recalls not only Derrida's hauntings—of historiography by historicity—but also his and Maurice Blanchot's notion of spacing, the aperture in the graphology of the filmic text itself, and the relation between such spacing and filmic materiality. There is in spacing, as we will see, an additional connection between the hieroglyph and the freeze-frame. And there is, as Laura Mulvey has suggested, a further relation between this latter technique and death itself (and the death of cinema as a medium). Once more, death, in different ways, links all the films analyzed in this chapter.

If allegory is the discourse of the other, then ethnography is its field of study, its writing, and its documentation. Part of the purpose of this chapter is to query the term *document,* with its claims to truth and connotations of veracity and the verifiable. Early in his book on German tragic drama, Benjamin pens a striking description that resonates with a certain performativity (that is, surface effect) and has particular relevance to this chapter's concern with what has come to be known as trance film: "Truth," Benjamin writes, "bodied forth in the dance of represented ideas, resists being projected . . . into the realm of knowledge."[6] The checkered history of documentary cinema is littered with claims to truth. It is now quite commonplace to refer to Dziga Vertov's coinage *Kino-Pravda* (Cinema-truth) as having a huge influence on ethnographer and filmmaker Jean Rouch, who, in turn, adopted the term *cinema verité.* There is also a long tradition of false documentaries— the genre's counterfeits—that tell or seek to tell countertruths. Indeed, the parody of ethnography that imbues Luis Buñuel's celebrated short film *Las Hurdes: Land without Bread* (1933) serves as a national precedent for several of the films discussed in this chapter (including *Lejos de los árboles*). The relation between documentary and allegory suggests a fictionalization and overlapping of contradictory signifying practices garnered through the modes of realism, ethnography, and filmic abstraction that characterized Spanish independent cinema of the 1960s to shed light on a subterranean avant-garde tradition. These spectral linkages connect the experimentalists of the 1960s with their predecessors of the 1930s. Such ghostly antecedents, figures from the past embedded within the strata of the filmic texts and whose persisting legacy suggests a temporal simultaneity, exceed empirical historiography's capacity for representation.

The disturbance of representation generated by this kind of underground history returns us to the question of what Tom Gunning once called "truth claims" and the question of indexicality. It returns us to the Bazinian notion of the photographic image as the most faithful representation of the original object that it purports to represent. Mulvey, meanwhile, echoes Raymond Bellour, linking indexicality in the digital age with pre-cinema and the frozen filmic image—the photogram's or the still's uncanny "shudder"—with death itself. "In cinema," Mulvey writes, "the blending of movement and stillness touches on this point of uncertainty so that, buried in the cinema's materiality, lies a reminder of the difficulty of understanding passing time, and ultimately of understanding death."[7]

Trance Film

The trance film is usually associated with ethnographic filmmakers Margaret Mead, Gregory Bateman, Jean Rouch, and Maya Deren. P. Adams Sitney uses the term specifically in reference to Deren, and its invention as a genre is sometimes attributed to him. However, it is noticeable that the term *trance*, used with respect to film, was deployed as early as 1928 by Antonin Artaud in his text "Sorcery and the Cinema." Surrealism would prove important to Rouch and to Esteva (who befriended Salvador Dalí and visited him at his home in Cadaqués). Artaud writes, "Cinema in its raw state [*le cinema brute*] emits something of the atmosphere of trance conducive to certain revelations."[8] In the same text, Artaud refers directly to Germaine Dulac's *La Coquille et le Clergyman* (1928), a film for which he wrote the scenario and that some two decades later would prove influential in the work of Deren.[9] Decades later, Derrida, in a passage that resonates with the thrust of this book, would write: "The trance is that kind of limit (trance/partition), of unique case, of singular experience where nothing comes about, where what surges up collapses 'at the same time,' where one no longer can cut through to a decision between the more and the less."[10]

Jacinto Esteva-Grewe was the founding member and central figure of the avant-garde group of filmmakers dubbed (by critic and producer Ricardo Muñoz Suay, in a deliberate promotional echo of the New York School) La Escuela de Barcelona (the Barcelona School). Aside from Esteva (whose family financed the initial project and the production company behind it, Films Contact), the principle members of the Barcelona School were Gonzalo Suárez, Joaquim Jordà, José María Nunes, Carlos Durán, and Vicente Aranda.[11] Although he maintained friendly relations with the group, Pere Portabella, the doyen of Spanish experimental filmmaking whose work is discussed in chapters 2 and 3, declined to formally join the Barcelona School. Portabella's refusal owes much to his political differences with the group. Although he originally collaborated on *Lejos de los árboles* as associate producer, Portabella, a fellow traveler of the Communist Party, quickly withdrew from the project when he detected a lack of serious political critique in the film.

Trance, as filmic mode, constitutes the space of undecidability, a critical zone apt to the films of the Barcelona School. Rosalind Galt has highlighted the double bind the members of the Barcelona School found themselves trapped in by the national question. They were marginalized by the Spanish state for their formal experiments and by Catalan nationalism for their failure to reference the aspirations of the underground independence movement.[12] Members of the Barcelona School were labeled wealthy apolitical dilettantes whose overly intellectual and abstruse work clashed with the dominant realist aesthetic and the emphasis on the auteur that prevailed among the Madrid-based New Spanish Cinema. Meanwhile, the major Catalan historian and film critic of the 1960s Miquel Porter i Moix ridiculed them as not "a real Barcelona school but a neighborhood one: [complete] . . . with Mao suits, money in their pockets or in the bank, a provincial Europeanism. The Barcelona of these films is that of its authors. And its authors fantastically represent the smallest minority."[13] While none of these criticisms is completely fair (not all the filmmakers of the Barcelona School shared Esteva's privileged background, for example), none of them were so absurdly misguided as Jean Narboni's. Following the film's 1967 screening at Pessaro, Narboni described Esteva and Jordà's *Dante no es únicamente severo* (often held to be the manifesto film of the Barcelona School) in *Cahiers du Cinéma* as "un beau film franquiste" (a beautiful Francoist film).[14]

Although the national question is not my main interest with regard to the Barcelona School, these attempts at enclosure by the critical arbiters of the day (and later) are striking. In this chapter and throughout this book, I argue that such claims to proprietorial ownership, property rights, and propriety all generate their own perforating surplus. The cleavage that developed between different nationalist aspirations produces in these filmmakers a status similar to that identified by Gilles Deleuze and Felix Guattari in their book on Kafka as "minority." Theirs is a cinema shot in an alien language, the language of the other (Castilian rather than Catalan). It is a language on the margins, sandwiched between two competing discourses that, in combination with filmic experimentation, was located at the extreme outer limit of definition and identity.[15] Neither Catalan nor Madridian, these filmmakers inhabit an unfolding, bifurcating space that radiates out from the central districts of Barcelona to the wider Spain. But it also extends beyond national frontiers. The Barcelona School is characterized by a cosmopolitanism (contrasting with the parochial aspirations of the dominant sector of Catalan nationalism) that extends to the rest of Europe and beyond, to Brazil and Mozambique, and back again in a worldly mapping that emerges from a confined locality that politicizes cinema itself. Despite the disavowal of politics by the members of the Barcelona School, Deleuze and Guattari suggest that such a "cramped space forces each individual intrigue to connect immediately to politics. The individual concern thus becomes all the more necessary, indispensable, magnified because a whole other story is vibrating in it."[16]

Lejos de los árboles (Jacinto Esteva)

Throughout the 1960s, Esteva made a series of documentaries, the longest and most striking of which was *Lejos de los árboles*. The film was finally released in 1972, after eleven years of intermittent shoots, problems with the censorship board, and several despairing editors (one of whom was José María Nunes). In 2011, at the behest of Esteva's daughter, Daria, the "original" film was reedited by Portabella and released with a new montage that shortened the film to just over ninety minutes. An ethnographic feature shot in different parts of Spain, *Lejos de los árboles* documents the rites and rituals of death cults, the ludic and religious uses (and abuses) of animals, and the pervasive recourse to popular superstitious belief (often manifesting as what appears to be mass hysteria). The film follows a period marked by the Iberian festive cyclic year, from one summer solstice to the next. In this structure, preference is given to temporal re-creation over mimetic representation. The film combines verité with surrealism, harking back to Buñuel's tongue-in-cheek ethnographic film *Las Hurdes: Land without Bread*.

For all its claims to ethnographic verisimilitude, however, at least three of the film's episodes are falsified or staged for the purposes of cinematic spectacle. In this staging (which Jean André Fieschi on Jean Rouch, one of the great pioneers of anthropological filmmaking, terms the "slippages of fiction"), we see a particular interest in mise-en-scène.[17] The staging not only differs from what James Naremore has described as the "untendentious uses of the camera" and the purported "ethics of *mise en scène*"; it also disrupts such concepts.[18] Fieschi enumerates a series of rich descriptions ("truant ethnology," "contraband," or "double-agent cinema") that define Rouch's working practices and that, in turn, challenge claims to the objective truth of the camera.[19] Filmic style (to mobilize Martin's term) becomes more meaningfully politicized (in discursive ways that Portabella could not have foretold). Fieschi could be referring to Esteva when he quotes Rouch's own justification for invention in his anthropological films: "If young ethnographers," he writes, "are well advised to favour rituals and techniques as subjects for filming, it is because rituals and techniques incorporate their own *mise en scène*."[20]

In an essay about *Lejos de los árboles*, Manuel Delgado identifies what is, to my mind, a false differential at the heart of the film. He maintains that the film focuses not on *lo ancestral* (the ancestral) or *lo atrasado* (the backward) but rather on *lo alterno, lo otro* (the alternative, the other).[21] Clearly, though, the two aspects are not necessarily incompatible. The destabilizing quirks of time are precisely what undergird the film's fascination with otherness. The untimeliness of atavism facilitates the coexistence of differences, the encounter with alterity. Indeed, the title of Delgado's essay, "El arte de danzar sobre el abismo" (The art of dancing over the abyss), with its resonance of Georges Bataille, is suggestive of the limit, crevice, or abyss that the spatialization of temporality and the temporalization of space open up. It also hints, in conjunction with bodily movement, at trance.

The following discussion serves to exemplify various aspects of *Lejos de los árboles*'s encounter with alterity. Each sequence, in different ways, concords with Fieschi's analysis of Rouch's notorious short film *Les maître fous* (1955), about which Fieschi writes, focusing specifically on the limit: "With *Les maîtres fous* comes a first, though still hesitant, edging towards more open forms, more disturbing structures: structures in which the disturbing element the frontier crossed somewhere, is integral to their functioning."[22]

The first of these sequences in Esteva's film, and one of the most celebrated of *Lejos de los árboles*, is that of the *endemoniados* (the possessed), pilgrims who believe they have been taken over by the devil and flock to the Romería de O Corpiño in Lalín, Pontevedra, from all over Galicia in northwestern Spain to be cured by the Virgin. These remarkable scenes feature a soundscape of screams and moans of agony. We see people being held by their arms as they lash out wildly, supposedly resisting being forced into the church, and it seems they are contaminating others with their delirium. Notable is the absolute loss of individual control in the face of state and institutional coldness. The ghoulish members of the Guardia Civil (attired in cloaks with distinctive three-cornered helmets) protect the Virgin on her podium, and a line of priests administers open-air confession and hastily dispatches the anguished faithful with ill-disguised indifference. A secular variation on trance is depicted in the wine battle at the annual celebration of the grape harvest in Haro, in the region of La Rioja. Here, drunken rather than religious intoxication prevails. A collective inebriation leads to a wholesale breakdown of inhibitions and to a liquid exchange. It is a saturation and an incontinent ludic dissolving of barriers, including those that divide the filmmakers from the object of the film. In the screenshot shown in figure 1.2, Esteva himself, drenched in wine, fills the frame as he drinks on set.

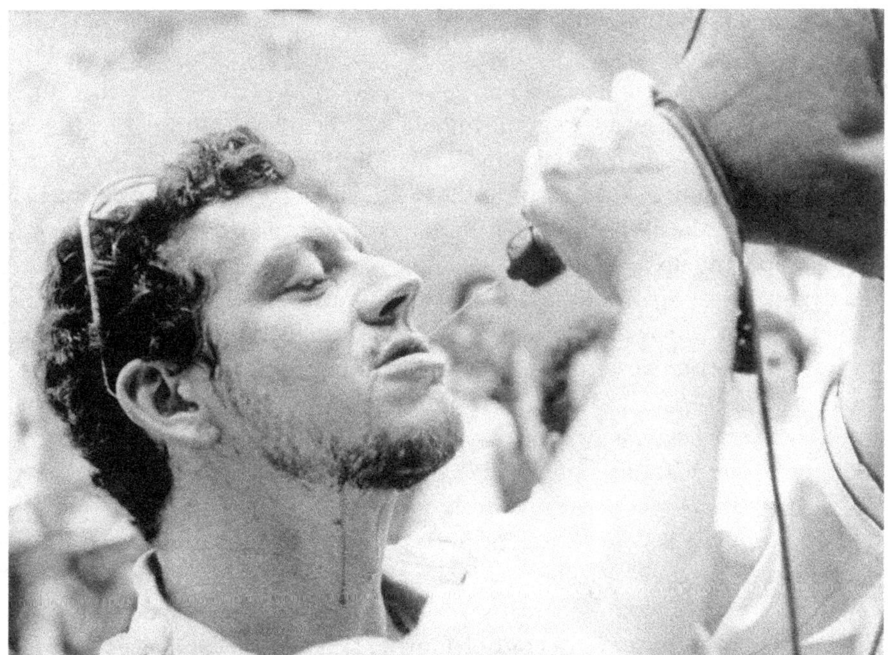

Fig. 1.2 Jacinto Esteva on set at La Rioja grape festival.

Esteva's attempts at national allegory (to judge by the original choice of title, *Este país de todos los demonios* [This accursed country]—a line from a poem by Jaime Gil de Biedma)[23]—are undone by the on-screen action and the filming itself. Trance disrupts form in both filmic practice and the totality that is nation. This disruption becomes clearer in the efforts to map the traces and rituals of rural primitivism as they emerge in the city. The collapse of the urban-rural dichotomy is shown in the film's first sequence. As discussed at the beginning of this chapter, prior to the sequence of the egg in the glass, young people dance as a collective mass of rhythmic bodies at a discotheque on the Costa Brava.[24] A flimsy line is drawn between the ludic and the lethal. The potential for cruel savagery is explicitly revealed in an attack on a transvestite dancer in a bar in cosmopolitan Barcelona. The frontiers here between the sane and insane, or those marked by drunkenness and religious intoxication, breach the rural-urban/barbaric-civilized divide.

Alrededor de las salinas

Esteva's interest in experimenting with the mise-en-scène of ethnography became apparent the year before he commenced work on *Lejos de los árboles* when he made the short documentary *Alrededor de las salinas* (Around the salt flats). Again produced by Portabella, and purporting to document the work and conditions of laborers on the salt flats of Ibiza, it is a film that turns enigmatically on Esteva's own anthropological or directorial intervention as an ethnographic experiment conducted within the cinematic text. To contextualize its location, the film hints at the future of an Ibiza (where Esteva had a house) in the wake of the Spanish economic recovery plan of 1959 and the consequent opening up of Spain to foreign investment. The early 1960s witnessed the beginning of Spain's enduring tourist boom (particularly in the Balearic archipelago to which Ibiza belongs)—an era that this film seems to recall as an atavistic alternative (a reminder of Spain's uneven incorporation within the modern project). The transition to the body of the film—in a foretaste of what would come in *Lejos de los árboles*—consists of scenes of a local religious festivity complete with an authoritative travelogue-style narrator whose stilted delivery is reminiscent of the newsreels of the day.

Alrededor de las salinas starts, however, with an uncommented introduction of what appears to be raw footage of a series of street scenes shot in apparent objective Italian neorealist documentary style: whitewashed houses, the occasional murmur or sound of footsteps, fishermen and their families repairing nets in doorways, unpaved streets. This footage comes to an abrupt halt with the appearance of a young girl at a doorway, posing for a photograph to be taken by the film's director. Esteva coaxes the girl into adopting a suitable facial expression ("Smile, please"). Once the picture is taken, he announces: "Good. With that image we will begin the film." The photographic image of the girl is held frozen in the frame in a scorched, overexposed negative that stands as a material epigraph—an instantaneous hieroglyphic imprint—to the subsequent film.

A series of extraordinary shots captures the uncanny landscape of mountains of salt glistening beneath the baking sun—reminiscent of the 1959 Venezuelan film *Araya*.[25] These shots are followed by a lengthy series of medium shots that frame workmen in overalls and broad-brimmed hats toiling in the sweltering heat. The dramatic contrast of light and shadow emphasizes the white salt and the silhouetted darkness of the laborers. The narrator's voice informs us of the history of the salt deposits, their past ownership and workforces, and the centrality of salt to the local community and its economy. All this is articulated in the register of a conventional instructional documentary.

The film's twist—its exploration of truth—permits it to take flight into the realm of fictive speculation. The island's extraordinary natural light (in a technological overlap with the overexposure of the earlier portrait photographic image that forms a chain of supplements implicit in the prefix *over-*),

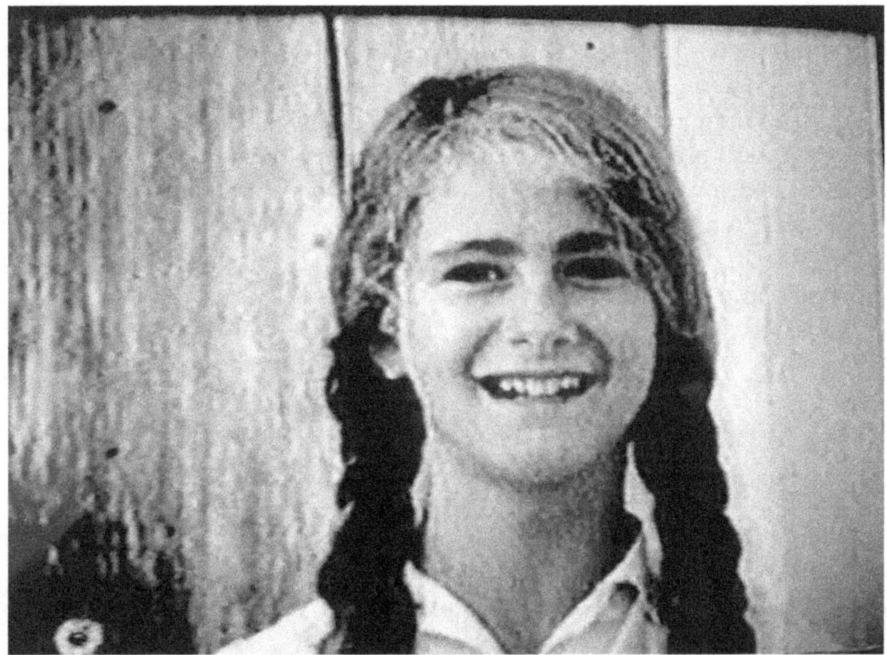

Fig. 1.3 A young girl in Ibiza poses for a photo in the introductory sequence of *Alrededor de las salinas.*

the Mediterranean sun and its dramatic contrasting shadows that eclipse the features of the workers, points to a philosophical-conceptual association with truth. The camera is absorbed by the brightness. Derrida has expounded on the figure of light, and particularly sunlight, as a metaphor for truth in the Platonic tradition.[26] Here, light emphasizes the film's concern with the *physis-technē* relation, or that between nature and artisanship, which will be explored later in this book.

The narrator informs us that the film crew plans to feign the death of one of the workers (whose complicity they count on) and film the reaction of the other workers. The scenario is described by the narrator as a serious filmic experiment that seeks to highlight "the difference between objective reality and cinematographic reality." We are then privy to the staged illness of the laborer and a brief and muted exchange of opinions as the false information is relayed to his workmates. The shadows cast from the brims of the workmen's hats and their sunglasses render them anonymous. But one man removes his hat to reveal his identity and insists that he does not believe the man is dead. "None of this is true," he says. Here, light and truth are seemingly correlated. But this same man is seen in the next sequence leading the funeral cortege, and the correlation is undone. We suspect the dissenting voice was in on the plan all along.

From that moment, the controlling voice-over is abandoned in favor of a staccato soundtrack alternating between the diegetic murmuring of the horse-drawn funeral procession's ascent to the hilltop church and the extradiegetic jangling of drums and cymbals punctuating scenes of rural mortuary customs and death rituals. Amid this improvised clamor (or *glas,* to use the title of one of Derrida's most celebrated books), the somber chime of church bells tolls out the film's false message.

In a match shot that translates and transports us from the false grave filmed from above to a cockfight elsewhere on the island, the discursive apparatus assumes in the final sequences of the film a kind of quotidian naturalism. In a quite literal dance of death, light and shadow once more alternate as the camera shifts in rhythm with the roosters. In a Bazinian vein, the film returns to its ontological relation to reality. Except, of course, we have already been made jarringly aware of the fictionalization involved in the filmmaking process. The narrator—Esteva himself—as the interlocutor of the fiction, is made unreliable. As the Bazinian speaker-witness, the disappearance of the voice-over from the filmic text in favor of the image strengthens the film's claim to authenticity (its neorealist mise-en-scène) while questioning its formal premises on the basis of what has gone before.[27]

What is remarkable about this film—aside from its social experiment and supposed depth—is its raw aesthetic surface quality. It has a number of truly beautiful moments that owe much to its purported naturalism—the apparent (and false) nonintervention of the filmmaker and the striking landscape. The final sequences of two boys racing through the town with their victorious rooster, their figures silhouetted against the beach, are exemplary of the film's paradoxical lyricism. The paradox lies in the fact that these sequences are also reminders of the film's materiality. The final shot of this last sequence (filmed as if to emphasize the film's anthropology and concern with atavism but also the incommensurability of these elements) returns to the question raised by the photograph of the film's prologue. The culmination of this sequence is achieved, once again, by means of a rapid series of freeze-frames—pointedly phantasmagorical—of the older boy casting the rooster triumphantly into the air in a set of staggered, stammering images that capture in a conceit the convergence of artifice with nature, the confusion of light and shadow.

Among Esteva's other frustrated ethnographic projects was the footage he shot and never edited in different African countries in the early 1970s.[28] These anthropological shards are paradigmatic of the Barcelona School's capacity to exceed the discursive corset of the nation-state.[29] What was originally conceived

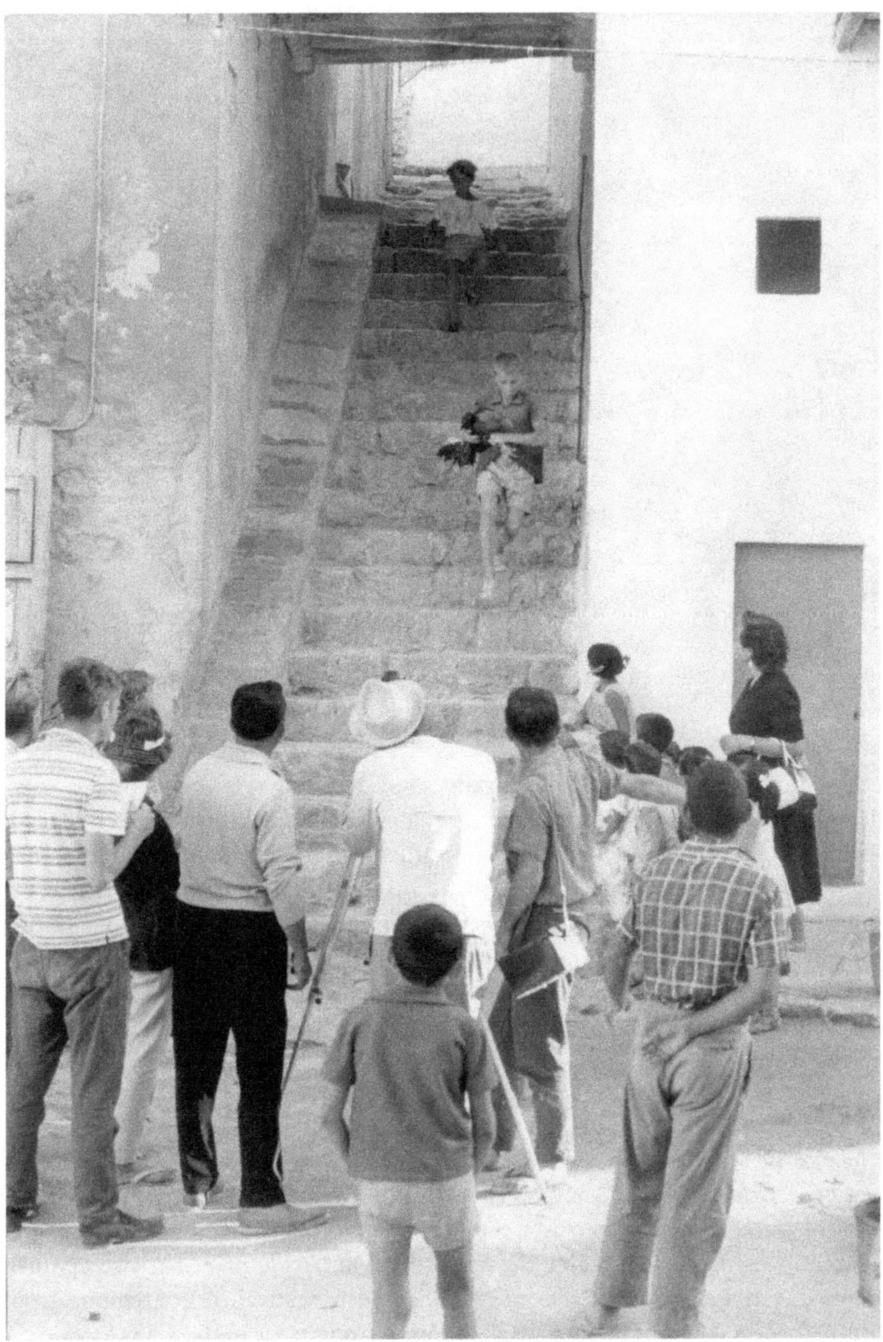

Fig. 1.4 The young boys with their victorious rooster. A still image from the set of the shoot of *Alrededor de las salinas*.

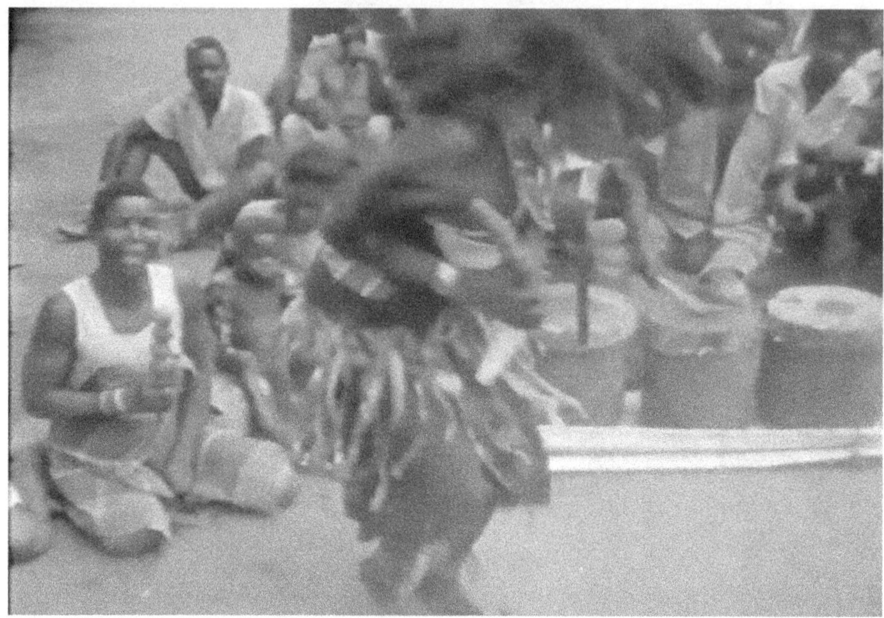

Fig. 1.5 A tribal dance sequence from the raw footage of one of Esteva's African films.

of as a piece of militant cinema at the service of the Mozambique national liberation movement FRELIMO has disappeared. Nothing remains of this footage, if, indeed, it was ever shot.[30] What has survived from Esteva's many African jaunts is an amassed collection of soundless fragments that are suggestively evocative of the same kind of ritualistic material that so fascinated the director in earlier films. As in the Spanish films (and as in the work of Rouch), this unedited footage foregrounds the funeral rites, animals, ceremonial healing, and rhythms of dance. The African work poses a challenge to the accusations of parochialism often leveled against the Barcelona School filmmakers.

Fuego en Castilla (José Val del Omar)

If *Lejos de los árboles* and *Alrededor de las salinas* owe much, in their half-serious ethnography, to the precedent of Buñuel, José Val del Omar's genealogical connection is even closer. Shot between 1959 and 1960, *Fuego en Castilla* (Fire in Castile) accompanied the better-known *Viridiana* as the two Spanish representatives present at the 1961 Cannes Film Festival. A contemporary of Buñuel, Val del Omar had begun his filmmaking career in the 1930s as a documentarian. In 1936, he made a film—now lost—about the same remote western Spanish region where Buñuel had shot his 1932 film *Las Hurdes*. Val del Omar is one of the few avant-garde filmmakers who either survived the Spanish Civil War or was not forced into exile. His work spans almost the entirety of different waves of cinematic innovation, from the surrealist period of the 1930s to the experiments of expanded cinema and structural film of the 1960s. Val del Omar provides a rare direct link in Spain between (to appropriate Peter Wollen's term) "the two avant-gardes."[31]

Perhaps, though, Val del Omar connects with a third avant-garde—that of contemporary Spain. As if to emphasize its spectral character, Val del Omar's work has continued posthumously (he died in 1982) in the recuperation of his unedited and often unfinished films. Eugeni Bonet, in *Tira tu reloj al agua: Variaciones sobre una cinegrafía intuida de José Val del Omar* (Throw your watch in the water: Variations on an intuited *Cinegraphy* of José Val del Omar; 2002–2003), has used Val del Omar's legacy and material shot by Val del Omar himself to resurrect and actualize his work. Not only futuristic in its ambition, Val del Omar's corpus has proved productive postmortem, auguring a dislocating projection beyond the boundaries of his own life.

Fuego en Castilla (1958–1960) is the second of what Val del Omar dubbed his "elemental trilogy"—a triptych of short films that focuses on elements that function as metonyms for three different regions of Spain. The first is about the southern Andalusian city of Granada and deploys the figure of water, and the final one is about Galicia and is articulated around the motif of earth or clay. Each of these films is remarkable in its own way, both because of their extraordinarily adventurous experimental quality and because, despite their insistence on "elements"—the *essential* element—each proves in practice to be the opposite of that claim. Although Val del Omar himself vehemently rejected the term, it is useful to consider the word *abstraction*, derived, as Stephen Heath reminds us, from the Latin *abstrahere*, the "drawing away from representation."[32]

Val del Omar's project—with the legacy of surrealism in its inventiveness and incongruence, its atonal discrepancy between sound and image, its texture and tactile quality—is located precisely in an engagement with the limits of representability. Such representability is important for two reasons. First, the self-reflexive significance of techne to this filmmaker is evident in his concern with the materials of filmmaking and their effects (both optic and haptic) and in his indifference to representing reality. Second, and once again, the very experimentation undoes claims to national allegory. Allegorical interpretations of *Fuego en Castilla* exist (concerning its place, for example, within the historical context of the Francoist dictatorship as a counterdiscourse), but these interpretations seem to be attempts to extrapolate a message from the film and reduce it to an explanation at the expense of the politics of its form—or, rather, its radical experiment as film.

This film commences with an on-screen epigraph—once more about death—taken from a poem written by Buñuel's friend Federico García Lorca ("En España, todas las primaveras viene la muerte y levanta las cortinas" / In Spain, each spring, death comes and lifts up the curtains); and in a very real sense the poet Lorca haunts the film. The epigraph is a citation and an exergue, a supplementary element beyond, between, and in excess of the textual frame of the film. Shot at the national sculpture museum in the Castilian city of Valladolid, *Fuego en Castilla* takes as its point of departure Lorca's youthful prose travelogue *Impresiones y paisajes* (Impressions and landscapes), written in 1918, in which the future poet bemoans the cold immobility of the religious statues. It is that coldness, the icy stasis of sculpture, that Val del Omar brings to life (according to the film's press book) and seeks to set alight through film. Val del Omar turns the filmic apparatus inside out by superimposing light and shadow on the statues to produce a kinesthetic alchemy of light in movement. In doing so, the film expands and exceeds the internal limits of cultural memory and national historiography. As in Benjamin's description of the structure of allegory based on what Michael Löwy has described as correspondence between theology and politics, *Fuego en Castilla* combines fragments of the primordial and the technological, the sacred and the profane, the archaic and the modern, and religious mysticism and cinematic montage.[33]

The film's architectonics—crosses, Christs, pietàs, gargoyles, and stone stairwells—are given ghostly force by the flicker of flames and the luminosity that bring fantasy skulls to life, generate concentric circles of light, and create cat's cradles of the cloister and the confessionals' wicker barriers. Indeed, if Esteva's ersatz ethnography is to be found in the naturalistic (albeit staged) mise-en-scène, the key elements of Val del Omar's filmic investigation make a spectacle of national religious culture out of artifice, montage, and experimental illumination in the shards of pulsating light that enflame the monuments. The film's juxtaposing of images, technical transformations, and sizzling, cacophonic soundtrack produces a different kind of ethnographical commentary that is unspoken in a shimmering, saturated hail of sparks. While Esteva plays with the camera's possibilities of realistic depiction, Val del Omar exploits the poetry of special effects in what he terms a "cinegrafía libre," a free filmic form of writing.

Marie-Claire Ropars-Wuilleumier (and others, such as David Wills, Thierry Kuntzel, and David Rodowick) has written about film *écriture*, or writing, in ways that are relevant not only to the discussion of Val del Omar but also to this book as a whole. The term refers to an intermediality "always already" existing in film. I will address this idea in more detail in the next chapter but

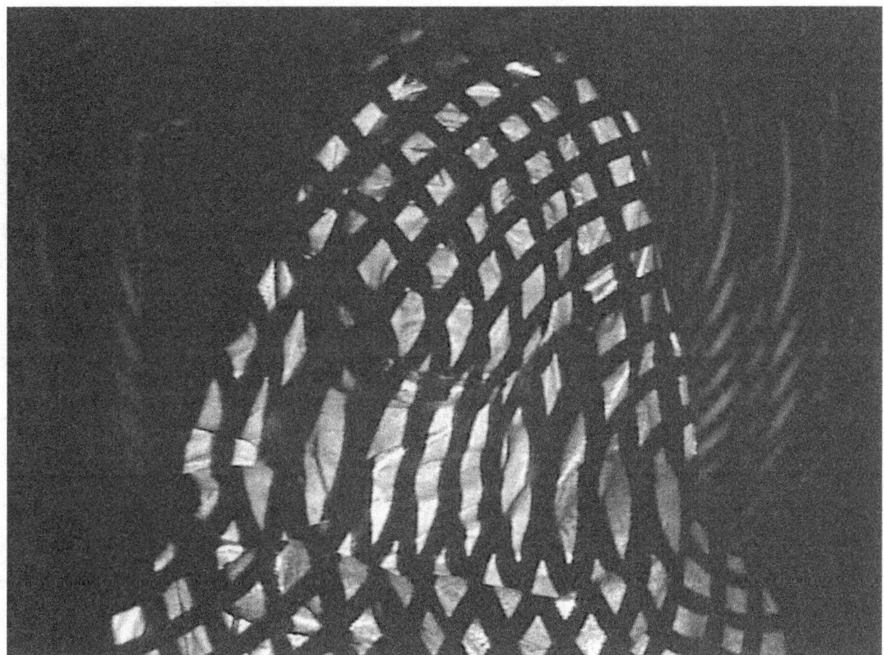

Fig. 1.6 The illuminated stone Virgin behind bars in *Fuego en Castilla*.

note for now that on-screen writing, etched in a sort of *graphic grafting* within the frame, is significant to Val del Omar's aesthetic and semantic surplus that exceeds any indication or clarification provided by intertitling.

As a non-narrative film, *Fuego en Castilla*'s abstraction offers a distorted, asymmetrical mirror image of the conventional documentary. In this, it is similar to the overexposed photograph at the beginning and end of Esteva's film. But whereas the negation is diegetic in *Alrededor de las salinas*, in Val del Omar's case, it is formal. Both films, though, play on technological specificity. *Fuego en Castilla*'s employment of lighting effects and its experimentalism are like Benjamin's "primordial landscape." The lighting is radiographical; it exposes realism's inner excess and is the phantasmagoric underbelly to Lorca's youthful travelogue. Again, *écriture* has a significance beyond conventional literary adaptation. The effect is one of dislocation. Place is as important to this film's diegesis—Valladolid, Castile—as Ibiza is to Esteva's. However, it is only significant in order to *dis*place it, to dislodge its centrality by the deployment of its specific technology. The abstraction of place—its "drawing away from representation" and the singularity of its montage—fractures the representational notion of place, and this fragmentation is Benjaminian rather than Jamesonian. Like the written word, it trespasses into other terrains.

Such a fracture points to the particular ghostliness of *Fuego en Castilla*. Not only is the film haunted by the austere historical-political legacy of Castile, by Lorca, and by a tradition of literary-pictorial mysticism (San Juan de la Cruz and El Greco, among others) that enshrouds it; the film's own technology, its *experiment* with the filmic material, renders such a legacy disjunctive and discontinuous. This, too, might be considered a form of trance cinema (particularly given its religious-mystical overtones), albeit notably different from Esteva's work and work produced by Rouch or Deren. Fracture, rupture, spatial disturbance, and, above all, the excess or overflow of the limits marked by the filmic apparatus (the screen, the frame) in time would lead to expanded cinema or *paracinema* (to use a term employed by Esperanza Collado Sánchez) that Val del Omar described in "Desbordamiento apanorámico de la imagen" (Apanoramic overflow of the image), an essay he wrote shortly before commencing the filming of *Fuego en Castilla*.[34]

Desbordamiento (overflow) also lent its name to a major exhibition of Val del Omar's work at the Reina Sofía Museum in Madrid in 2010. The word overflow suggests exceeding barriers or frontiers. Ostensibly a text about the relationship between vision, projection, and screen, with a proposal for a three-dimensional, all-embracing spectatorial experience, the intriguing premises of Val de Omar's essay are clearly extendable to the nation itself. One feature of *Fuego en Castilla* that is often commented on (occasionally to highlight the telos of "the national," an idea from which I dissent)[35] is the enigmatic text that appears in the final shot (both here and in the other films in the trilogy). "Sin fin" (without end) is seemingly a parody of the "Fin" that often brings films to an end. It is also, though, a gesture toward the infinite, a sense of boundlessness and open-endedness; a repudiation of the limits of national teleology or heritage; and a signal toward endless technical possibility and the overflowing capacity of experimentation.

Los Monegros (Antonio Artero)

With this idea of place as a charged constellation, a configuration shot through by splintering time, I conclude this chapter with a brief discussion of *Los Monegros*, Antonio Artero's twenty-five-minute short that seeks ostensibly to portray the quasi desert of the Aragonese hinterland from which the film takes its name. Aragón, the birthplace of several celebrated Spanish filmmakers and the site of one of the first films shot in Spain (*Salida de la misa de doce de la Iglesia del Pilar de Zaragoza* [Leaving the twelve o' clock mass at the Church of Pilar in Zaragoza] 1896), is often considered the cradle of Spanish film. Shot in the region where Buñuel was born, Artero's 1969 documentary is perhaps the most faithful of those discussed here to the Buñuelian legacy. However, *Los Monegros* also departs somewhat from that legacy and differs from the other films discussed in this chapter in that its critique of representation is clearly influenced by Bertolt Brecht's distancing effect and, through Brecht, by the work of Jean-Luc Godard.

Artero, a professed anarchist, had been a significant dissenting voice at the Sitges conference (see the introduction), the 1967 gathering that sought to promote independent filmmaking in Spain. *Los Monegros* provided an opportunity for him to put his ideas into practice. It is no accident that the only book devoted exclusively to this filmmaker (and it is more a biographical than a critical or theoretical work) is titled *Yo filmo que . . . Antonio Artero en las cenizas de* representación (I film that . . . Antonio Artero in the ashes of representation). Artero's cinema is one constructed from the ruins, the embers of representation. This becomes even more evident in Artero's 1974 full-length feature, whose title *Yo creo que . . .* (I think that . . .) is echoed by the book's title.[36] The latter film constitutes a wholesale assault on filmic semiotics.

Artero, who, like others of his generation, combined experimentation with commercial filmmaking, has been largely overlooked by critical writing. But it is worth noting the fertile coexistence and overlap of different tendencies of independent cinema throughout the late 1960s and the first half of the 1970s in Spain. The coincidence is between Artero, who sought to lay bare the materiality of film production, on the one hand, and the structural-materialist filmmakers who experimented with the language of film within (often abstract) diegeses on the other.

In the case of *Los Monegros*, Artero, like Buñuel thirty-five years before him, purports to conduct a serious study of a region devastated by poverty, depopulation, and a lack of infrastructure in the face of the scarcity of natural resources—namely, the region's lack of water. This is indeed a very real historical problem, which gives an unwittingly surreal tint to the film when Artero's shoot was disrupted by the largest amount of rain to fall in the region since record keeping began. Some of the early sequences show crew members standing around holding umbrellas amid the deluge in one of Spain's most notoriously arid regions. The film is structured as a collage with a multiplicity of registers. As if they were real ethnographers, members of the crew interview some of the more eccentric residents of the Monegros villages; on other occasions, intertitles appear in the frame with no further explanation. Scenes from what seem like a photo story (or *fotonovela*) provide an incongruous commentary to the on-screen activity. Local men are recorded reciting poetic romances. A

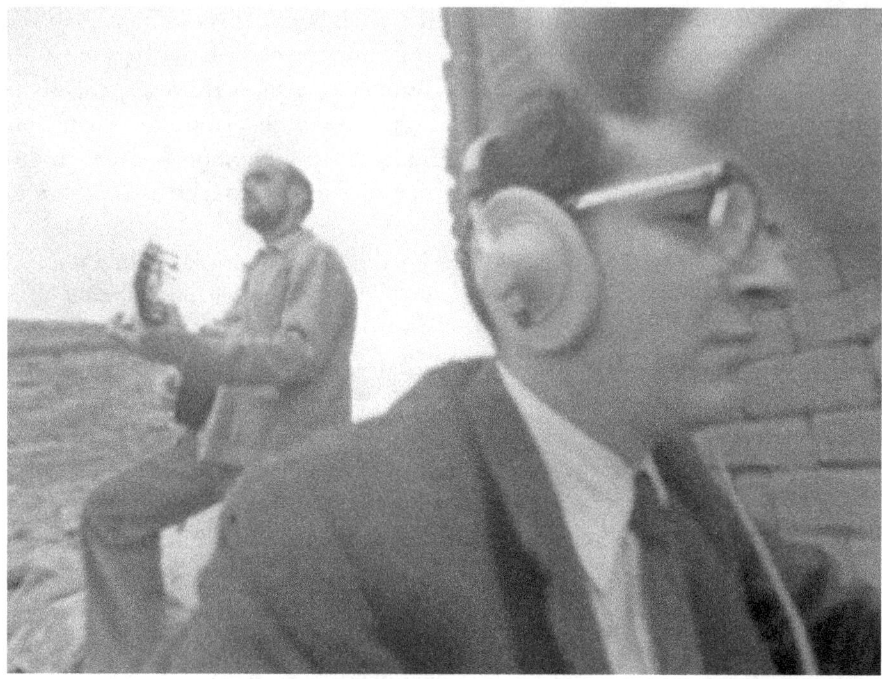

Fig. 1.7 José Antonio Labordeta plays the guitar in *Los Monegros.*

sequence of a worker filling up his water supply truck from the primitive reservoir is interrupted by underwater shots of a naked snorkeler. A single insert grafted into the text (a still, photogram, or hieroglyph of sorts in the arrest of what Benjamin calls "empty time") presents a tableau of the traditional reenactment of the Moros y Cristianos festivities.

The materiality of film and its processes is reiteratively impressed on the spectator: the testing of the sound equipment, a single camera standing forlorn in the desolate landscape, a diagram of Kodak color scales inserted on the screen. But not everything is Buñuelian playfulness or Godardian politics. The soundtrack, provided by the folk singer and future parliamentarian José Antonio Labordeta, gives the film a troubadour-like quality (similar to that of the "contraband" or double-agent filming that Fieschi identifies in Rouch).[37] The film is structured around a set of *jotas*, a traditional song form that originates in Aragón and whose revival is largely attributed to Labordeta.[38] The folksinger stands amid the ruins of a castle surrounded by recording apparatus and the film crew, or he wanders like a nomad across the barren, forsaken plains.

Among the fictive inventions, the formal experimentalism, the imperative to reveal the workings of film, and the region's culture of ruins, a certain

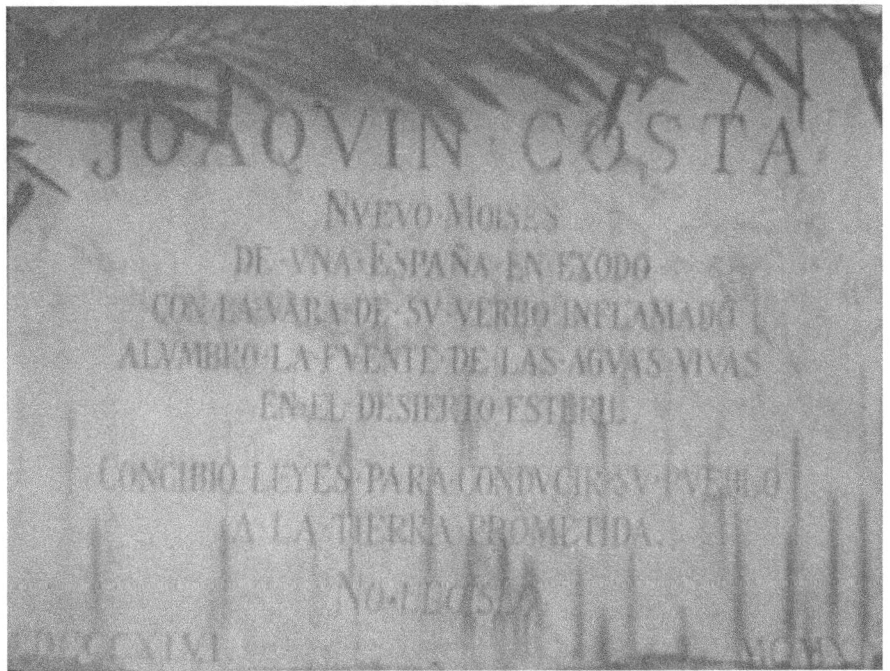

Fig. 1.8 The tombstone of Joaquín Costa.

recursiveness amid the mass of buried history that Benjamin, in his discussion of hieroglyphs, terms the "sepulchral" emerges quite literally, albeit with a hint of irony. *Los Monegros*'s final shot is of the tombstone and monument to Joaquín Costa in the cemetery at Zaragoza, the capital of the province. Costa was a late nineteenth-century campaigner for agrarian reform (who failed in successive attempts to win election to parliament). The text that is carved in stone on the grave—again, a grafting, quite literally an en*graving*—casts Costa in a religious aura as a "Nuevo Moisés de una España en éxodo con la vara de su verbo inflamado alumbró la fuente de las aguas vivas en el desierto esteril" (New Moses, of a Spain in exodus, who with his fiery verbal rod illuminated the fountain of living waters in the sterile desert). The final line of the epitaph reads: "No legisló" (He never legislated).

Conclusion

The latter films discussed in this chapter are connected thematically in their concern with place and their fascination with death. Val del Omar's film begins with a quote from Lorca. Artero's film ends in a cemetery with Costa's epitaph.

Both films use the written word on-screen. The graphic presence of writing is grafted within the filmic text as diegesis, and its visuality functions as hieroglyph. In this graphology—cinematography or ethnography—other figures leave or stamp their imprint on the conflictual national space.

Just as Buñuel's film owed its origins to a serious ethnographic study of the region (Maurice Legendre's 1927 work[39]), Esteva's *Lejos de los árboles*, the first of the four filmic texts analyzed in this chapter, is indebted to the work of the leading Spanish anthropologist of his generation, Julio Caro Baroja. Val del Omar was a contemporary of and clearly influenced by both Buñuel and Lorca. These skewed legacies—truncated and haunted by the trauma of civil war, dictatorship, and exile—facilitate a spectral counterreading of Spanish film that succeeds precisely because of their rejection of a direct correspondence with nation and its narration.

I end this chapter by returning once more (albeit anecdotally) to the figure of Walter Benjamin, whose theses on history feature the kind of nonlinear approach I propose (like his interest in montage as a form of writing). Although a matter of pure coincidence, we might recall, in the context of place and spectral linkage, or as lingering aftereffect, that Benjamin was living in Esteva's Ibiza at exactly the same time in April and May 1932 that Buñuel was filming *Las Hurdes* on the other side of the country. Moreover, the ethereal presence of Benjamin haunts in other ways. His "Ibizan Sequence" pieces, some of which were written under the intoxicating influence of hashish, are themselves ethnographic and foresee the social changes that tourism would bring to the island. Benjamin later committed suicide in the Catalan town of Port Bou, not far from Salvador Dalí's residence. Dalí's collaborations with Buñuel opened up new possibilities for filmic representation, and Dalí himself would later make ethnographic film and befriend his neighbor on the Costa Brava, the young Jacinto Esteva.

Notes

1. Walter Benjamin, *The Origin of German Tragic Drama*, trans. John Osborne (London: Verso, 1977), 166.

2. Bainard Cowan, "Walter Benjamin's Theory of Allegory," *New German Critique*, no. 22 (1981): 113.

3. See Adrian Martin, *Mise-en-Scène and Film Style: From Classical Hollywood to New Media Art* (Basingstoke, UK: Palgrave, 2014).

4. Cowan, "Walter Benjamin's Theory," 110.

5. Peter Brunette and David Wills, *Screen/Play: Derrida and Film* (Princeton, NJ: Princeton University Press, 1989), 129; Jacques Derrida, *On Grammatology*, trans. Gayatri Chakravorty Spivak (Baltimore: Johns Hopkins University Press, 1976/2016), 88.

6. Benjamin, *Origin of German Tragic Drama*, 29.

7. Laura Mulvey, *Death 24x a Second: Stillness and the Moving Image* (London: Reaktion Books, 2006), 32.

8. Paul Hammond, *The Shadow and Its Shadow: Surrealist Writings on the Cinema* (San Francisco: City Lights, 2001), 104.

9. http://www.filmoteca.cat/web/programacio/cicles/fantasmagories-del-desig/sessio -triple-la-coquille-et-le-clergyman-linvitatin-au.

10. Jacques Derrida, *Glas*, trans. John P. Leavey Jr. and Richard Rand (Lincoln: University of Nebraska Press, 1990), 22.

11. Filmmakers Ricardo Bofill, Jorge Grau, Jaime Camino, Carlos Durán, Roman Gubern, and others were also associated with the group.

12. Rosalind Galt, "Missed Encounters: Reading, *Catalanitat*, the Barcelona School," *Screen* 48, no. 2 (2007): 193–210.

13. Quoted in Esteve Riambau and Casimiro Torreiro, *La Escuela de Barcelona: el cine de la "gauche divine"* (Madrid: Anagrama, 1999), 182.

14. Ibid., 303.

15. Although they met and began their careers in Barcelona, not all the members of the Barcelona School were Catalans. Aranda was from Valencia, and Suárez was from Cantabria. Nunes was born in Portugal and moved to Barcelona when he was twelve.

16. Gilles Deleuze and Felix Guattari, *Kafka, Towards a Minor Literature* (Minneapolis: University of Minnesota Press, 1986), 17.

17. Jean-André Fieschi, "Slippages of Fiction," in *Anthropology-Reality-Cinema: The Films of Jean Rouch*, ed. Mick Eaton (London: British Film Institute, 1979).

18. James Naremore, *An Invention without a Future: Essays on Cinema* (Berkeley: University of California Press, 2014), 22.

19. Fieschi, "Slippages of Fiction," 67, 71.

20. Ibid., 68.

21. Manuel Delgado, "El arte de danzar sobre el abismo," in *Imagen, memoria, fascinación: Notas sobre el documental en España*, ed. J. M. Català, Josetxto Cerdán, and Casimiro Torreiro (Madrid: Ocho y Media/Festival de Cine español de Malaga: 2001), 227.

22. Fieschi, "Slippages of Fiction," 71.

23. The poem, "Apología y petición," appears in Gil de Biedma's collection *Poemas póstumos*, 2nd ed. (Madrid: Poesía Para Todos, 1970).

24. This celebrated nightclub was called Tiffany's and was in the resort town of Plaja D'Aro.

25. I am not, however, suggesting that Esteva had seen *Araya*. Indeed, I think it is unlikely.

26. "In Plato's Republic (Books VI–VII), before and after the Line, which expounds an ontology by analogies of proportion there appears the sun. Only to disappear. The sun is there but as the invisible source of light in a kind of insistent eclipse. It is more than essential: it produces essence, being and appearing: the essence of that which is. One may not look upon it on pain of blindness and death. Beyond that which is, it portends the Good, of which the sensible sun is the offspring: source of life and visibility, seed and light." Jacques Derrida and F. C. T. Moore, "White Mythology: Metaphor in the Text of Philosophy," *New Literary History* 6, no. 1 (Autumn, 1974): 43.

27. André Bazin, *What Is Cinema*, trans. Hugh Gray (Berkeley: University of California Press, 1967), 1:156.

28. I am indebted to Riambau and Torreiro, who are unique in having written about these films. Esteva indulged in a number of ill-fated schemes in the course of his adventures in Africa, such as organizing safaris and big-game hunting (Joaquim Jordà goes into more detail about this phase in his posthumous documentary about Esteva titled *El encargo del cazador*, 1990). Esteve Riambau and Casimiro Torreiro, "Más allá del diluvio: El cine africano de Jacinto Esteva," Biblioteca Virtual Miguel de Cervantes, 1993, http://www.cervantesvirtual .com/obra-visor/mas-alla-del-diluvio-el-cine-africano-de-jacinto-esteva--0/html/ff8b86c4 -82b1-11df-acc7-002185ce6064_2.html.

29. There is a global filmic circuit that emphasizes the theme of cosmopolitanism, a chain for which the Barcelona School provides a key link. Esteva's initial idea came from an encounter with Mozambican filmmaker Ruy Guerra (who was living in exile and later settled in Brazil). At the same time, Ricardo Muñoz Suay met Brazilian director Glauber Rocha and persuaded him to shoot a film in Catalonia. That film, produced by Films Contact, was called *Cabezas cortadas* (1971).

30. It is interesting to note that some forty years later, another Barcelona-based filmmaker, Andrés Duque (whose work is discussed in chap. 8), would make use of real FRELIMO propaganda films from the period of the anticolonial war. As I will argue later, Duque's work is also related to trance cinema.

31. Peter Wollen, "The Two Avant-Gardes," in *Readings and Writings: Semiotic Counter-Strategies*, 92–104 (London: Verso, 1982).

32. Stephen Heath, "Keywords: *Representation*," *Critical Quarterly* 50, nos. 1–2 (Spring/Summer 2008): 92.

33. Michael Löwy, *Fire Alarm: Reading Walter Benjamin's "On the Concept of History"* (London: Verso, 2005).

34. "La pantalla cinematográfica es una gran retina apanorámica con perspectiva de conjunto esférica, cóncava, envolvente. Las líneas de movimientos que el espectador puede perseguir libremente sobre su área son mínimas" (The cinema screen is a great apanoramic retina with the perspective of a spherical ensemble, concave and enveloping. The lines of movement that the spectator can follow freely across its space are minimal). José Val de Omar, "Desbordamiento apanorámico de la imagen": Intervention in the IX Congress of Cinematographic Technique, Turín, September 29 through October 1, 1957, http://www.valdelomar.com/pdf/text_es/text_6.pdf, 3.

35. See Santos Zunzunegui, "Lo popular en el cine español durante el franquismo. Diálogo entre Jo Labanyi y Santos Zunzunegui," *Desacuerdos* 5 (2009): 103.

36. Javier Hernández Ruiz and Pablo Pérez Rubio, *Yo filmo que . . . Antonio Artero en las cenizas de la representación* (Zaragoza, Spain: Ayuntamiento de Zaragoza, Servicio de cultura, 1998).

37. Labordeta was a member of parliament for the Chunta Aragonesa party. He died in 2010.

38. Javier Hernández Ruiz and Pablo Pérez Rubio quote Artero: "Cuando el alcalde de un pueblo escuchó cantar Labordeta, dijo que eso no era una jota y que debíamos ir a su bodega aquella tarde para enterarnos de cómo se entonaba como Dios manda. Una vez allí, el alcalde, que ya estaba bastante borracho, se había rodeado de unos jóvenes joteros a los que hacía gritar como energúmenos mientras la troupe de la película so moría de vergüenza (When a village mayor heard Labordeta sing he said that that was not a jota and that we should go to his bar that evening to find out how to sing one in the way that it should be sung. Once there, the mayor who was already quite drunk, had surrounded himself with young joteros

who he ordered to screech like morons while the film crew were dying of embarrassment). Hernández Ruiz and Pérez Rubio, *Yo filmo que . . . Antonio Artero en las cenizas de la representacion* (Zaragoza, Spain: Servicio de Cultura, 1998), 106–7.

39. Maurice Legendre, *Las Hurdes: Estudio de geografía humana*, trans. Enrique Barcia Mendo (Merida, Spain: Editora Regional de Extremadura, 2006; originally published as *Las Jurdes: étude de géographie humaine*, 1927).

2

INTERMEDIALITY, INTOXICATION, AND THE *INFRATHIN*

THE COUNTERHISTORY OF SPANISH CINEMA IS LOCATED AWKWARDLY at the intersection of popular film, the everyday, and the avant-garde. This is the juncture where the trace of surrealism that commenced in the late 1920s reemerges insistently in future periods, but with a particular density in the late 1960s. As we will see later in this book, this iteration or trace structure continues in other forms to the present day. In the formal context of this surrealist genealogy, I consider in this chapter the paradox of the specificity—the materiality—of film in the context of the fashionable term *intermediality* (with its suggestion of, to quote Lúcia Nagib, "contaminating" influences of other media at work within film).[1]

I focus here on the idea of experimentation and the avant-garde at a watershed moment in historical time in a particular place. The emblematic nature of the year 1968 suggests a central point of an uncontrollable turbulence like the eye of a whirlwind or a wild displacement that also interrogates the notion of hybridization in ways that distinguish intermediality from intertextuality. Intertextuality is more readily applicable to literature than to film for reasons that concern the disciplines' very different procedures and specificities. Intertextuality tends to seek dialogic fusion rather than the kind of cacophonic confusion and discord that is explored in the next chapter on the cinema of Pere Portabella. Intermediality is connected to the void of the in-between or the emergence of something new and difficult to classify. Significant differences that exist between written texts and visual media also affect ongoing debates within the discipline and pose a challenge to the current hostility to theorizing new critical spaces.

My interpretation of intermediality concerns an encounter, often a discordant encounter, with and between different media that results in ill-fitting formulations rather than the telos of assimilation by one of the others. It is an irresolvable and immeasurable encounter that occupies the liminal space—an otherwise, elsewhere—where ingress and excess meet. It is where we might say, with Georges Perec, the *infra* lurks imperceptible to the naked eye or ear. Marcel Duchamp—who practiced a form of intermediality *avant la lettre* throughout his life—calls this the *infrathin* or *inframince*. It is the indescribable differences between things that one can only discern implicitly beyond the senses and one can define only by example (one of the most celebrated of which is the following: "When the tobacco smoke smells also of the mouth which exhales it, the two odors marry by infrathin").[2] According to Duchamp, the effect is as follows: "The possible, implying the becoming—the passage from one to the other takes place in the infrathin."[3] This, to me, infers a kind of politics that flies under the radar (*infra*, after all, means below or beneath), a clandestine politics that demands a labor of theoretical connectivity. Here I attempt that linkage by reading two films both made in the politically charged year of 1968.

Intermediality is today a term very much associated in visual culture (and particularly that of the photographic image) with the transformations produced in the context of contemporary globalization and the philosophical consequences of digitalization. Indeed, in an age of the proliferation of screen culture, media interacts with our lives at almost every juncture. However, Jens Schöter reminds us that in the wider field of art, the term has a long history that dates back at least to the 1960s.[4] Schöter disagrees with the influential art critic Rosalind Krauss's critique of the relation between the image and the market in the current period—the reduction of art to the spectacle culture at the service of capitalism. Schöter points out that the break with artistic purity (that defended by Krauss's former teacher Clement Greenberg) has its origins much earlier. Intermediality, Schöter says, dates back to the 1960s, when conventional notions of medium-specific art were already under attack by the rise of new forms of expression such as happenings, installation art, performance, and video. In any event, one might argue (and it has been argued) that film was always intermedial from its origins. The earliest films involved theatrical or circus-like effects and spectacle, and several artists who in the 1920s would defend a so-called *pur* cinema were also visual artists in other media whose influence they brought with them to film (notably, Fernand Léger and Man Ray). The advent of sound cinema, which was criticized in its day for diluting the purity of the image, gave film a new language and an oral element with which to function beyond the exclusivity of the visual track.[5]

Much of this debate (detailed exhaustively by Schöter) turns on interpretations of Marxism by art historians over the forty-year period that predated the advent of digital technology in all forms of cultural production but particularly (or at least most visibly) in film. It is notable that the tenor of this debate is far more concerned with matters of the division of labor, alienation, defamiliarization, or the function of art in an evolving class society than it is about fragmentation, the rupture of the sign, unruly discharge, or the technological developments that cast doubt on all kinds of ontologies (cultural, photographic, and human). It is equally clear that the resurgence of interest in intermediality in recent years turns precisely on these latter questions as they have emerged as responses to the onset of digital media and the constituent elements of filmic materiality. Related to both of these developments are the unstable functions and processes of mediation. This is the historical conjuncture within which we might view intermediality.[6]

In the spirit of Duchamp's infrathin, this chapter considers intermediality as transference—and transference as adaptation, translation, or intoxication, among other terms. Whereas *media* means measure, *to mediate* signifies to intervene and maintain equilibrium between two elements or parties. There is the hint of a paradox here—an incommensurability—of media not so much as a moderator but as a field of taut, potentially electric tension between opposites, each transmitting sparks that ignite and activate the other. I am more interested, however (as suggested in this chapter's first reference to the infrathin), in the immeasurable.

If we think in terms of the Spanish word *desmesurado*, meaning unmeasured (or perhaps actively *demeasured*), we are faced with the swirlingly unbalanced, the excessive, the supplementary, or the surplus. The idea of excess here might be conceived of as a form of intoxication. The margin between measure and demeasure produces a relation not dissimilar to the infrathin. It is this implausible, nigh impossible, *between* generated by transference that interests me. It is the aporetic space between elements or concepts corresponding to something like Jacques Derrida's *différance*. The lingering, in-between residue produced by the passage from one field to another is found not so much in the displacement from one cultural form to another as in the transference through a porous skein from one language to another, from one discipline to another, from one country to another, from one mental state to another, from wakefulness to sleep, from life to death, and—a point particularly important to philosophers—from truth to falsehood and/or vice versa. These shifts and transfers leave traces in their wake.

Connected to this chapter's focus on the *trans* of displacement is its preoccupation with its homonym *trance* of the previous chapter. In this connection I seek to highlight the delicate, almost imperceptible (but nonetheless disruptive) differences at work in the hybrid filmic process; that is to say, the infrathin. I also explore here the category of that kind of transfer that we call metaphor—the "carrying across," "transportation," or "transfer" of the original Greek. Among other things, I register the particular significance of Pedro Calderón de la Barca's seventeenth-century play *La vida es sueño* for thematic reasons and as an inspiration for certain dramatic elements of the films I will discuss. Calderón deals with the semblances of sleep to death and dream to virtual life: the *trans* as trance.[7] *La vida es sueño*, moreover (like much baroque theater), is built on the classical metaphoric structure concerning light and darkness, day and night, and sun and moon that I am interested in disturbing. As the following quote, part of a celebrated speech delivered by Segismundo, the protagonist of Calderón's play, suggests, metaphor indicates the hiatus that emerges between reality and its representation. Confusion arises from the void that opens between the *propre* (proper) and its substitute.[8]

> ¿Tan semejante es la copia
> al original que hay duda
> en saber si es ella propia?
>
> Is the copy so similar
> to the original that doubt arises
> as to which is which?[9]

Beyond its function as a common metaphor, light, as I alluded to in chapter 1, is also the key materiality of film. The word *photology* means the study of light.[10] "Light," writes cinematographer Henri Alekan in terms that recall the infrathin, "does not adhere to its surroundings; it leaves no heir to its luminous actions. To put it another way, it is only passing through, its host environment, unable to retain it, is always ontologically at its mercy. Heat is different, despite the fact that it is a secondary effect of that which produces light. Heat takes root in its environment, progressively penetrating and then leaving it; its surroundings become its subject of inherence, albeit imperfect."[11] This quote, which appears in an essay included with the DVD of *Ici et maintenant* (a film Alekan worked on), directed by Serge Bard, one of Jackie Raynal's collaborators in the short-lived Zanzibar project (discussed below), is coined in intriguing terms. It confirms the widely held view that light's compatibility with form is subject to question; or rather, to paraphrase Marshall McLuhan's celebrated work on the medium of electricity, it has an "unfixed form" or a formlessness.[12] Tellingly, McLuhan says of the electric light that it is "pure information": "It is a medium without a message, as it were, unless it is used to spell out some verbal ad or name. . . . Whether the light is being used for brain surgery or night baseball is a matter of indifference . . . because it is the medium that shapes and controls the scale of human association and action."[13]

The "unfixedness" of light invoked by McLuhan connects to Alekan's allusive vocabulary. Just as the word *inhere* is related to *inherent* and *inheritance*, *adhere* and *heir*—the operative words in the Alekan quote—suggest a similar legacy, a kindred affiliation, and the notion of trace. The idea of unfixed form—infrathin—suggestively undoes that of metaphor.

Jackie Raynal's *Deux fois* and Pere Portabella's *Nocturno 29* emerged as the results of two obscure avant-garde initiatives: the Paris-based experimental collective Zanzibar Films in Raynal's case and (albeit indirectly) the Barcelona School in Portabella's.[14] If light is the constitutive materiality of photography, then luminosity and darkness are not only central to the thematic of the two films (a fact emphasized in the title of *Nocturno 29*) but also their key formal properties. Likewise, both pieces emerged from the obscurity of the underground in 1960s dictatorial Spain. Both are non-narrative films—incantatory, dreamlike experiments—that have at their center a singular and never explained enigma. Both films also possess a formal rigor with a particular structure that overrides their common rejection of conventional narrative. They are both political films in a specific, rupturing way—though not in the discursive sense of political rupture. But it is precisely for that reason, I suggest, that these films are more effectively political.

It is notable that the two groups of filmmakers (which were more loose associations of individuals who came together with the financial backing of wealthy allies than they were formal organizations) were reactions against the French Nouvelle Vague (in the case of Zanzibar) and the Nuevo Cine Español, or New Spanish Cinema (in the case of the Barcelona School). Likewise, the two groups had in common the fact that several of the actors (Nico and Caroline de Bendern in Zanzibar, Romy and Teresa Gimpera in the Barcelona School) had previously worked as fashion models.[15] There is an additional overlap between Zanzibar Films and the Barcelona School: *Deux fois* is a film mainly featuring Raynal, but she frequently appears on-screen in the company of Spanish actor Francisco Viader, who also played an important role in the direction and production of the piece. Viader was a friend and collaborator of Jacinto Esteva, the central figure of the Barcelona School and the lead actor in Esteva's *Después del diluvio*, made the same year as *Deux fois*.[16]

Both *Nocturno 29* and *Deux fois* are also what might be called late modernist films in the tradition of Chris Marker, Jacques Rivette, and Alain Resnais. By modernist, I mean, above all, a self-reflexive cinema whose acting is often theatrical and whose diegesis is highly referential and conscious of its condition as film.[17] To this end, both films address questions of voice, narration, and vision in ways that are specifically cinematographic or that can be addressed only as such, with flashbacks, montage, sound effects, and the materiality of the footage. Interestingly, such specificity is demonstrated in dialogue with other fields of artistic production. These two films are clearly linked in terms of place and time—both were shot in 1968 in Barcelona—and I reflect here on that context together with their experimental form—their *media*—as constitutive of a constellation of political transformation.

In 1976, the Camera Obscura collective, in what would be the first major analysis of *Deux fois*, foregrounded "the material processes of film" in terms of the film's formal structure and its sequences and shots. *Deux fois* is marked by an initial geographical displacement. Raynal leaves Paris for Barcelona to make the film in a week. But its diegesis is largely about other displacements of all kinds: filmic, personal, professional, and corporeal. The *Camera Obscura* article notes the film's preoccupation with "sexuality, subject, narration, representation."[18] And indeed, there is in both films a deliberate drawing away from representation, an interrogation of the medium. When Raynal solemnly pronounces at the end of the film's first sequence, "This evening will be the end of signification," her declaration of intentions could equally apply to *Nocturno 29*. While the apparent abstraction of these two films—their unresolved enigma—is grounded in history, it is also a self-conscious comment on the question of the impossibility of representation (or mediation, or media itself) *as* communication. This, in turn, leads to a productive sense of ambiguity, an undecidable doubt that lingers suspended in the air like the infrathin itself, together with the proliferation of mazes and mirrors. Amid the experimentation and political discourse, both films deploy the ambivalent tensions surrounding the symbolic figure of the romantic couple as a secret unit at their common heart.[19]

Nocturno 29

An early shot in *Nocturno 29* (similar to another in Portabella's 2007 film *Silencio antes de Bach*) shows the naked body of the protagonist framed in the transparent door of a shower, her mottled image fused with the frosted glass in a blurred yet revealing barrier to vision. Via frame and fuzziness, the anonymous woman is indexed as object of the erotic gaze. Poised on the threshold of the 1970s, the decade that (as discussed in chap. 5) heralds what is generally held to be the most important period in experimental filmmaking (in Spain and elsewhere), these films also reveal subtle signs of the year of their production. They exhibit symptoms of the seismic shifts taking place around the year 1968. As will become clear, the title of *Nocturno 29* contains an oblique reference to the year of its production. On the face of things, then—and, almost inevitably, it has been interpreted in this way—*Nocturno 29* possesses certain elements of national allegory. Portabella, albeit somewhat cryptically, has alluded to this and has insisted on the film's "realistic" properties.[20] In a film that is indebted to surrealism and to the Catalan avant-garde (the influence of Joan Brossa is particularly pronounced),[21] Portabella is arguably being disingenuous. While the Catalan director identifies the specificity of the filmic medium and what has determined the history of writing on the film—that is, its relation to "real life"—I suggest that it is precisely the formal experimentation of this film rather than the thematic indicators that brings into question the notion of allegory.

Michel Mardore, writing in *Le Nouvel Observateur* in 1969, proclaimed *Nocturno 29* "the first political Spanish film." Although this is certainly not the case—many earlier films are conceivably political—it is nonetheless true that the film's title refers to the twenty-nine years that had passed since the end of the Spanish Civil War. (The same kind of explicit intervention in history is also explored in chap. 3, which is devoted exclusively to Portabella.) The allegorical aspects of the film have been emphasized and exhaustively outlined by Josep Torrell, who, while appropriating Mardore's term, focuses on the film's title, the cryptic references to the war, and the depiction of the bourgeoisie that financed the regime (the exclusive club, the Círculo Ecuestre, the golf course, the Banco Hispano Americano). Torrell also highlights a singular sequence (one of only two shot in color) in which a visual gag alludes to the red, yellow, and purple of the national flag of the defeated Spanish Second Republic (1931–1939), together with the pointed suggestion of exile in Lucia Bosé's departure by airplane at the end of the film.[22]

Although there is little doubt that these references to the regime are deliberate and that, in this sense, *Nocturno 29* is unquestionably a political film, such an interpretation tends to relegate its formal innovation to that of conventional political discourse in the spirit of Portabella's later (and decisive) work of the mid-1970s. Here, though, I am more interested in how the politics of *Nocturno 29* emerge in the film's formal practice and via the interstices of filmic composition in ways that extend beyond the limits and limitations of a univocal interpretation as allegory, as *only* anti-Francoist discourse. Indeed, to employ the central trope of the next chapter, the two aspects—form and politics—complement and supplement each other. Rather than functioning as an extended metaphor of Francoism, I argue, the film shadows the regime. It is its other, its ghost.

Cowritten with Brossa, with poet and novelist Pere Gimferrer's translation of Brossa's original text from Catalan to Castilian, the film also features, in discordant choral form composer Carles Santos (who, in time, would become Portabella's most consistent longtime collaborator), who vehemently punctuates the film with a fiercely emphatic and violent piano intervention. *Nocturno 29* is thus structured musically and poetically rather than narratively. It is, in its initial composition, an intermedial work, and that intermediality—that is, the film's formal properties—marks its relation to the political conjuncture. The film's soundtrack—not just the music but the array of noise (the clatter of dishes, typewriters, footsteps on gravel, lengthy silences)—generates a spectrum of virtual sound. It forms a spectral sonic backdrop to the dictatorship, with an agonized, haunting melody and screeching, groaning, and gasping that are often at odds with the placid visual images. The *no* of nocturne, its negative—both as denial and as filmic material—reinforces this sense of the ghost. The film's title, furthermore, evokes a musical form ironically. The stark black-and-white photography that dominates the film holds suggestive echoes of the horror genre, whereas the musical nocturne is an ensemble piece devised for light evening entertainment.

Torrell observes that the film is composed of twenty-nine sequences, reflecting the twenty-nine years of the dictatorship. However, while the twenty-nine sequences shape the film formally, they also draw attention to the filmic apparatus, its artifice, and the nature of its experimentation. The rejection of narrative order is also a rejection—paradoxically—of chronological order, which would suggest an undoing or at least a questioning of the twenty-nine-year period since the onset of the dictatorship or, indeed, of the importance of the year 1968. Time in this film is set off against itself, putting in doubt the significance of its historical moment. This is the spectral paradox, the elusive quality of *Nocturno 29*, by which time and measurement (temporality, the year, the order of filmic sequences) interrogate themselves. While the significance of the emblematic year can only be reckoned with retrospectively, its putative intent might best be understood performatively rather than allegorically. History becomes charged and destabilized by the discordance between experimentation and experience, sound and image, structure, rhythm, and time. The following shots from a sequence in *Nocturno 29*—a tour de force of editing and mise-en-scène—are exemplary of this disturbance of hermeneutic equivalence.

Despite the film's languid tone, it contains few long shots in any spatial sense of the word *long*, as in a long distance. The film does, however, contain many lengthy shots in the temporal sense, with detailed close-ups that, bolstered by the high-contrast sound-negative stock, give the film's texture a particular graininess. Throughout the film there is an interesting tension between movement through space and temporal (dis)continuity. Such discontinuity is both compositional and diegetic. In a film that has a disengaging couple at its center, the decoupage editing technique of cutting within the frame is symptomatic of the ongoing decoupling that plays out across the film. These shots are paradigmatic of the surfaces, sensuality, and circularity that prevail throughout *Nocturno 29* in a deceptively continuous discontinuity. The contrasting

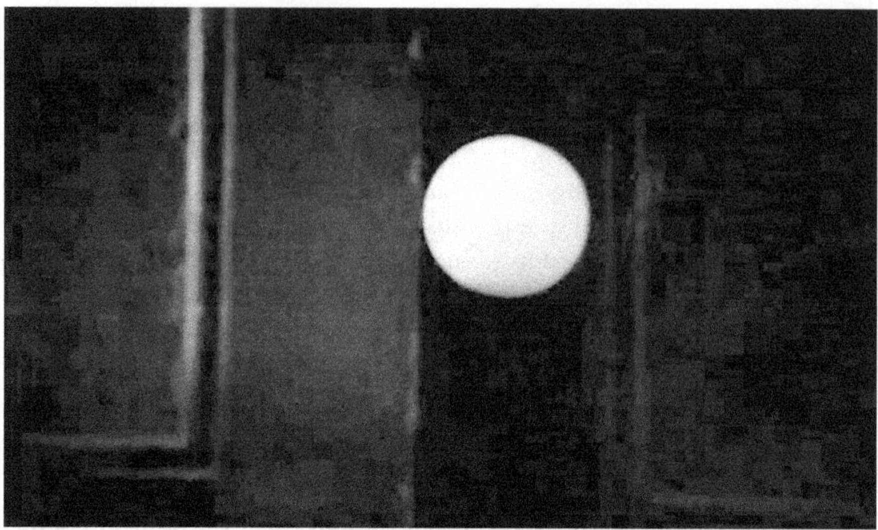

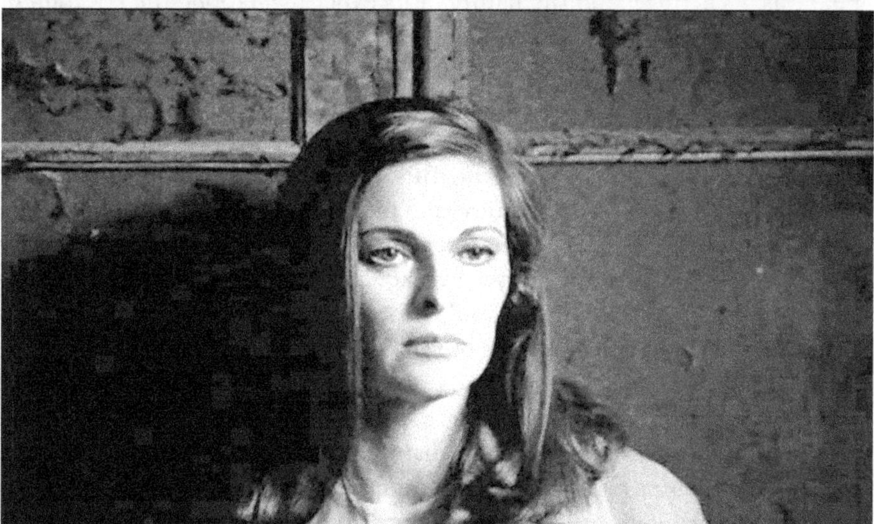

Fig. 2.1 a–h From a doorknob to the hub of a car wheel, a tour de force of circularity and editing in Portabella's *Nocturno 29* as Lucia Bosé wanders through the factory.

editing foregrounds the relation between light and surface, of elision, ellipsis, and eclipse.

The series of photograms presented here (figs. 2.1a—2.1h) hints at the influence of Eisensteinian montage.[23] The first shot, a close-up of the doorknob, is suggestive of the nocturne of the film's title. At first sight, it resembles a full moon at night, the raw element to be eclipsed. The moon, of course, is also an

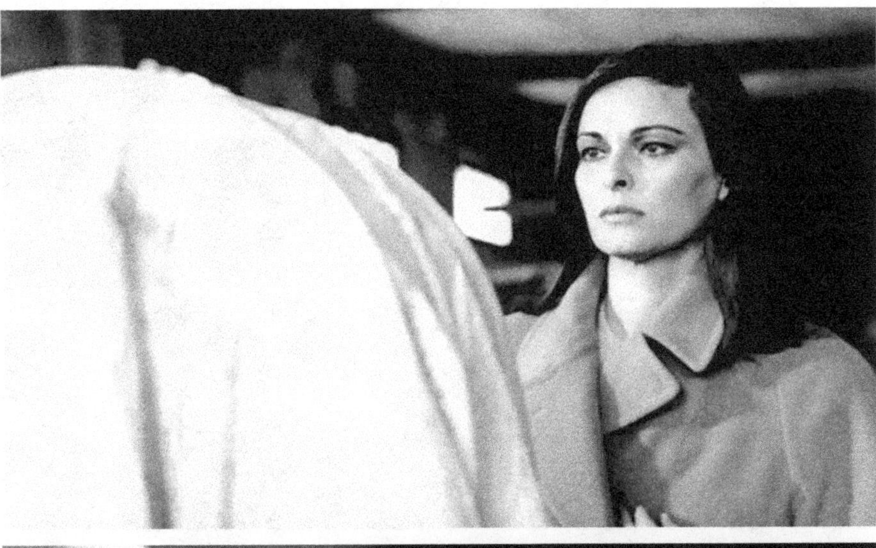
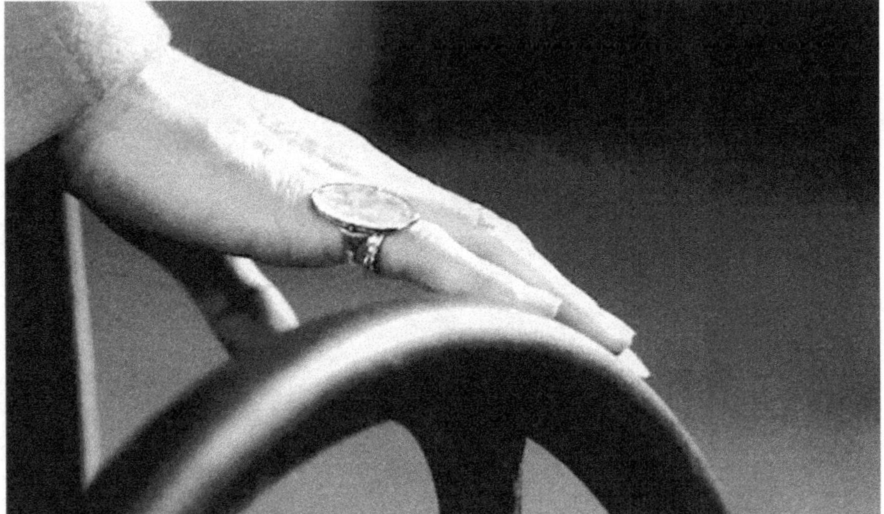

Fig. 2.1 a–h (*continued*)

erotic symbol whose mythological associations are with the feminine. Critical writing's focus on the political allegory of *Nocturno 29* has been at the detriment of the film's erotic mode. Not only is the erotic present in the amorous triangle of the film's incidental and erratic narrative; it is also there in the sensuality of almost every sequence, and, significantly, it is connected to the surrealist spirit that pulsates throughout *Nocturno 29*. This erotic charge forms

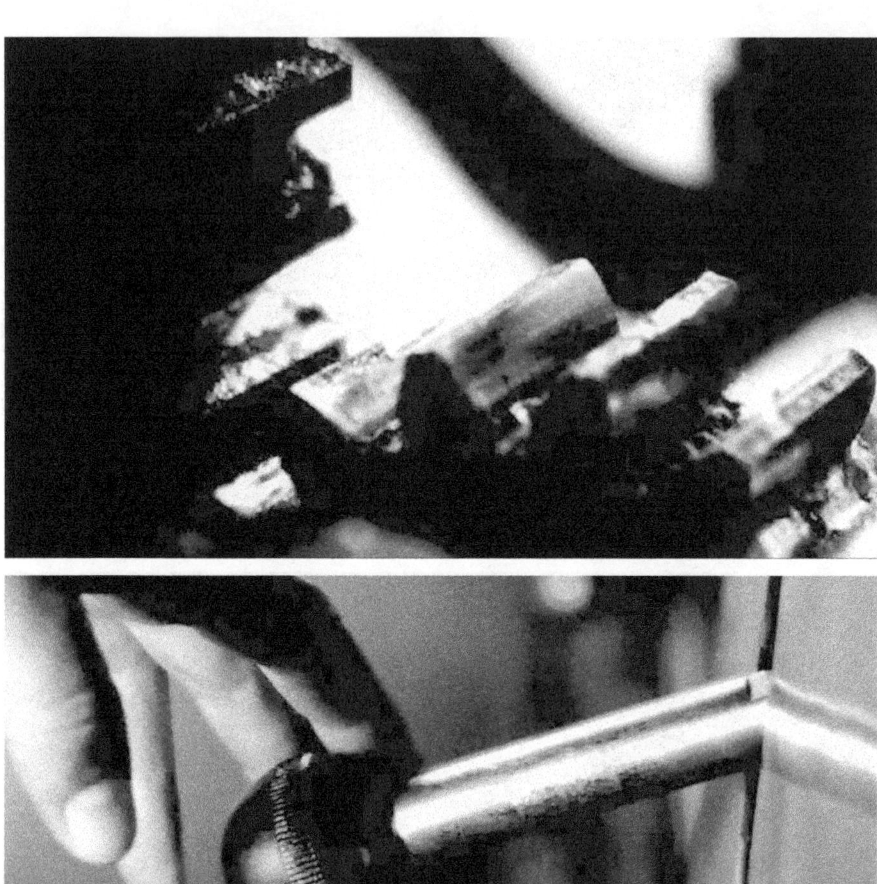

Fig. 2.1 a–h (*continued*)

part of the haunted quality of both films discussed in this chapter, and in both instances it proves to be an eroticism closely allied with the filmic apparatus—or, at the very least, juxtaposed with it in a tension between the disordered effusiveness of eros and the regulatory logos of the apparatus (including the frame itself) or the time period—the twenty-nine years of Francoism. The erotic *is* political.

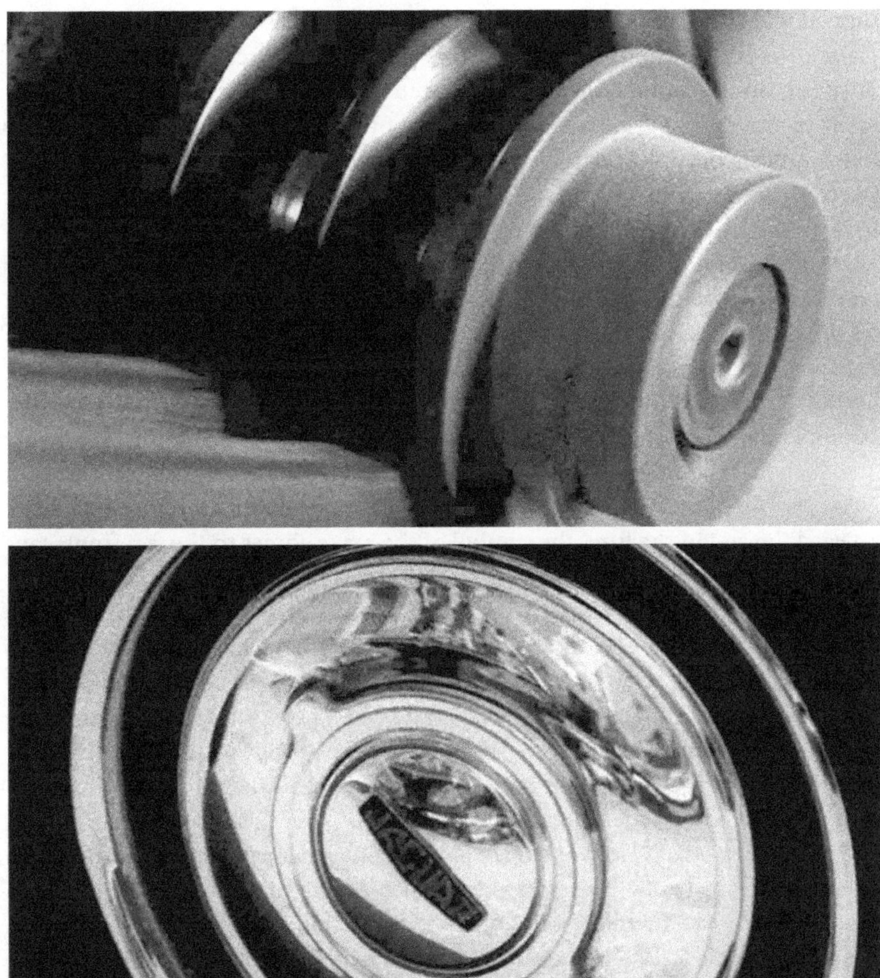

Fig. 2.1 a–h (*continued*)

The photograms from the sequence of *Nocturno 29* suggest an erotic encounter with the machinery itself, a relation between the caressing and rotating fluency of the camera in its engagement with other mechanical artifacts (the factory equipment, the car wheel, the viewfinder, and the aspect ratio). They highlight a disturbance of logos by eros with an uncoupling and a set of uncouplings revolving around the thematic couple of the film itself. Technological supplements and nature—hard metal and human flesh—are engaged on the plane of the filmic and the erotic, while the star presence of the iconic Lucia Bosé is mobilized in counterpoint to spectorial expectations.[24] Surface movement in the swirling, sensual circularity both of Bosé in the delicacy of her touch and of the rounded objects her character encounters—from the doorknob to the teeth of the rotary mechanical device, from the phallic control stick to the wheel of the car—parallel her movements through the city within an economy of desire. This free-flowing, revolving camera movement, the play on distances, the detailed shots, the reframings, the mirroring and reflections on shiny surfaces, the film work, and the editing all combine in dense silence to produce an intoxication with the filmic process itself. This spinning, swirling hint of turbulence suggests eddying interruptions in a flow, a turmoil, a maelstrom, and a sense of vertigo and of displacement or disorientation.

Such disorientation and circularity are also present in the urban confines of *Nocturno 29.* Barcelona is a subtle but pervasive presence throughout the film. Toward the end of the film, the symbol of the maze comes to the forefront, captured in a long take at the city's Laberinto de Horta. This sequence is marked by a set of formal ruptures. Initially shot in color, the focus of the artificial lighting beating down from beneath a shade on the green card table and anonymous hands distributing playing cards is on the sharp edges of concentrated space. Filmed at shoulder height of the card players, their faces are concealed amid the shadows. The startling color is reinforced by the rigorous quadricularity of the cards and table in contrast not only to the black and white but also to the circularity that has dominated the film to this point. Only Bosé's face—round, full, and curvaceous—becomes apparent in the sequence, her porcelain complexion emerging from the swirl of cigarette smoke. She is the sole woman among a group of men. Meanwhile, a kind of sonic regulation imposes itself in the form of a metronomic ticktock of a clock followed by the sound of winding-up time mechanisms. Bosé is summoned away by her lover's secret sign, and suddenly, in a match shot triggered by the doorway (she is associated with entrances and exits throughout the film), she steps across the threshold into the black-and-white exterior high above the fuliginous city.

The abrupt transition here is akin to an awakening. Bosé steps out of the Tardis-like otherworldly and nocturnally bounded space of the color sequence and into the open panoramic and monochrome city of daylight.[25] The staircase leads her down from the pavilion of the card game toward the cypress labyrinth whose entrance is marked by a marble bas-relief with a verse inscription that reads: *Entra, saldrás sin rodeo, / el laberinto es sencillo, / no es menester el ovillo / que dio Ariadna a Teseo* (Enter, you will leave without detour, / the labyrinth is simple / the ball of thread that Ariadne gave Theseus is not necessary).[26] In the center of the labyrinth is a statue of Eros, and at its exit another bas-relief with the inscription: *De un ardiente frenesí, / Eco y Narciso abrazados, / fallecen enamorados, / ella de él y él de sí* (In ardent frenzy / Echo and Narcissus embraced / die in love / she with him and he with himself).

The labyrinth and the stories of Ariadne and Theseus and Narcissus and Eco, wrapped in a register of the erotic and the adulterous that is articulated through poetic inscriptions in stone, highlight a different way of conceptualizing the politics of intermediality. This is a politics that transcends the discourses of temporality and metaphor. I discuss this in more detail in the later section on *Deux fois*, but as an aside, we might note as exemplary of the play of representation throughout the film, of intermedial politics—the excess, the residue, or politics as infrathin—the incongruous appearance of Mario Cabré (Lucia Bosé's character's distant husband) dressed as Pierrot. Pierrot is the figure of the sad clown, the cuckold of commedia dell'arte (whom, paralleling the on-screen action, Columbine abandons for Harlequin). Likewise, we witness the burlesque and Buñuelesque inserts of papier-mâché *gigantes* of Spanish popular festivities in footage of a solemn religious ceremony.[27] And an extraordinary sequence portrays a man (Ramón Julia), apparently Bosé's lover—the same man who later accompanies her in the Eco-Narcissus game of hide-and-seek or silent call and response in the labyrinth[28]—as he climbs a spiral staircase, enters his modernist apartment, and sits before a television set (foreshadowing the effects of technological visuality that Portabella would return to more than twenty years later in *Puente de Varsovia*). On the television is the military parade that the man has just passed on the street below. And then we see the man, silhouetted from behind, remove his prosthetic eye (see fig. 2.2).

The false eye here coincides thematically with the roundness of the machinery sequence discussed earlier and makes explicit the centrality to the film of the combination of artifice, the erotic, and the visual. This ludic intermedial play, more of which is described later, takes place within the Spanish pictorial tradition represented in this film by the physical presence of celebrated artists Antoni Tapiés, Antonio Saura, and Joan Pons in the card-playing sequence. Connected to the painters and the eye is the explicit reference to Buñuel and Dalí's collaborative films of the 1920s and 1930s.

Nocturno 29 commences with an ostensibly lyrical and naturalistic sequence of an anonymous young couple on a misty mountainside at the point of making love amid the undergrowth. The image is overtracked by the prosaic cranking rhythms of a film camera. Once more the process of naturalization is undone by the artificial mechanism of the apparatus, and the visual is subverted by the sonorous.

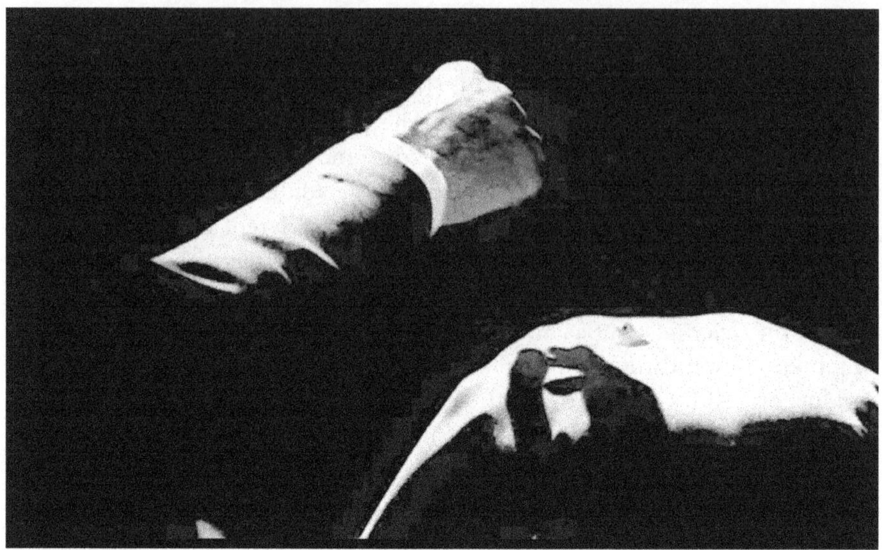

Fig. 2.2 The false eye on the table.

In another link in the metonymic chain connecting surrealism, this introductory sequence—itself supplementary and seemingly disconnected from the diegesis of the body of the film—was shot in Port Lliget, the area where Dalí lived in the early 1930s, having been banished by his father from the family home in nearby Cadaqués. Duchamp, who died the same year that both *Deux fois* and *Nocturno 29* were made, was also very much associated with Catalonia (an area he visited many times throughout his life), with the surrealist tradition, and with Dalí (who fascinated him) in particular. Port Lliget is close to Cap de Creus, where Dalí and Buñuel shot some of the famous sequences of *L'age d'or* (1930). Man Ray also took well-known photographs at Cap de Creus during a visit in 1933, and the spectacular rocky outcrop provides the backdrop to Dalí's 1934 painting *Espectro del sex-appeal*. The area is also the site of several films from the late 1960s and early 1970s that are associated with the Barcelona School—most notably the unfinished *Hortensia-Beancé*, directed by Spain's singular cineaste *maudit* of the 1960s, Antonio Maeza, and produced by Portabella. Meanwhile, Glauber Rocha's chaotic *Cabezas cortadas* (1970), produced by Esteva's company Films Contact, was shot nearby in the Empordà region and at the Sant Pere de Rodes Monastery, a shoot that, according to Augusto M. Torres's *Diario de Rodaje* (Film shoot diary), Portabella visited.

This trace structure—of personalities, films, paintings, and places—forms a locus around a surrealist genealogy haunted, in turn, by the figure of the Gradiva. The Gradiva so fascinated Dalí that it became his pet name for his wife, Gala. André Breton appropriated the name for his Parisian bookshop, the door of which was designed with a double aperture by Duchamp. The Gradiva is there in the enigmatic, muted figure of Lucia Bosé—the naked figure framed in the shower sequence mentioned earlier. She is the "walking woman" who traverses the labyrinthine city, silent and sculptural, set in frozen, flowing motion (the flare of her trouser suit mirrors the sweep of the Gradiva's gown) in the bas-relief of the filmic frame—as in a freeze-frame—against domestic alienation and the urban landscape of Barcelona. The sense of movement in the frieze-like sequentiality[29] of the bas-relief form and the framing of the original is in Portabella's version also a reframing. Bosé passes through as a transient captured briefly in her seemingly estranged husband's gaze from the other side of a delineating threshold (another "enframing," a Heideggerian *Gestell*). This is a gathering together of all the elements of the filmic text in an image that quite literally produces a standing out. If the image of the Gradiva is impressed in the stone (like the inscription at the Laberinto de Horta), that of Lucia Bosé—a flaneuse gliding through the streets of Barcelona—is reflected fleetingly in the mirror on the wall (see fig. 2.3). The Gradiva is exemplary of indexicality, of the material relation between the thing and its representation, of the other.[30] This impression of a doubled woman—an inscription and engraving of sorts—leads, in turn, directly to a discussion of *Deux fois*.

Deux fois

Serge Daney famously wrote in *Cahiers du cinema* of Jackie Raynal's film *Deux fois* that "She [Raynal] put in her film the visionary crazed coldness of major paranoiacs."[31] The idea of paranoia resonates aptly with Dalí's "paranoiac-critical" method, which was influential in the cinema of the late 1960s. In a film about doubles, repetitive iterations, mirrors, and dreams, the self-contained psychic circuit that constitutes paranoia might be conceived of as a kind of autobiographical imprint, a fractured writing of the self, an autography. It hints at a genealogy of women's experimental cinema from Maya Deren to Barbara Loden to Chantal Akerman,[32] who share a common interrogation of fragmented subjectivity.[33] It is significant that if the first of these filmmakers is a historical pioneer of trance cinema, the others form a global nucleus of women filmmakers clustered together in a singular moment in the history of feminism. We might add to this list Germain Dulac as one of the key precedents in avant-garde women's filmmaking and the surrealist tradition.

One of the earliest images of *Deux fois* (see fig. 2.4) focuses on at least three of the central features of Raynal's remarkable film: autobiography (Raynal herself appears in almost all the film's sequences), the filmic process in the form

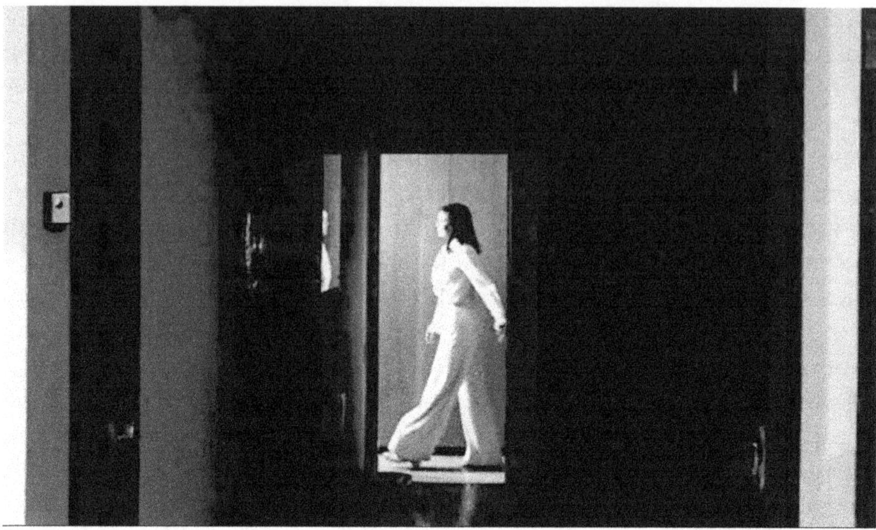

Fig. 2.3 Flaneuse Bosé framed in imitation of the Gradiva.

of photographic material (the film consistently draws attention to its own cinematic practices), and luminosity (the flash of a small mirror). Light illuminates, blinds, obscures, and distracts vision. Pure light is here unmediated and dazzling; it is blinding at the very moment when Raynal confronts (as she will on other occasions throughout the film) her virtual image in a mirror, her double, her spectral other.

In *Deux fois*, Raynal, who spent most of the 1960s working as an editor for the Nouvelle Vague directors (most notably Eric Rohmer) as well as some of the most significant French experimental filmmakers of the decade, offers up an exemplary piece of montage.[34] Or, rather, she offers a subversion of montage. Film editing usually involves establishing narrative continuity, yet the opposite is the case in this film. There is no continuity between each shot, and each fragment of film seems disconnected from its preceding and succeeding sections. In an interview, Raynal drew attention to the importance of her past editing experience in her direction of *Deux fois*, the processes of which involve not only the image but also mixing "voice, music, sound."[35]

Deux fois, moreover, features a kind of politics that facilitates a new, different reading of Portabella's film. While both films are self-reflexive, they are equally texts brimming with extrafilmic cultural influence. There is in both a fugitive quality that is enigmatic certainly, but also more elusive. They convey a sense of the arbitrary and, indeed, of the slick and intangible movement of light.

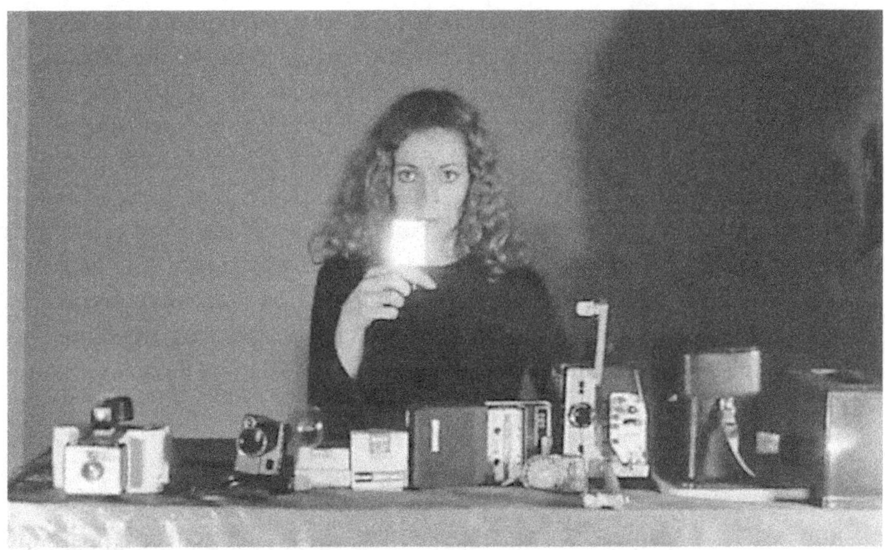

Fig. 2.4 Jackie Raynal, surrounded by photographic material, emits a flashing light from a mirror in *Deux fois*.

It is at this conjuncture of matter and methodology, media and materiality, and text and context that politics—feminism in Raynal's case and Francoist repression in Portabella's—might become relevant without recourse to allegory. *Deux fois*, however, also poses a feminist challenge to *Nocturno 29*, as we will see.

The image reproduced (see fig. 2.4) of the flash of light in the small mirror with Raynal standing in the shadows behind her own hand suggests the doubling of the subject that all mirrors produce. This doubling becomes, in time, a multiplicity that is contained in the tongue-in-cheek *deux* of the film's title. The flash of light, moreover, disperses that doubling and draws attention to the extra element of projection—another central material feature of film and light itself—beyond the screen. It suggests that there is both a connection among all these different elements contained in the photogram and, more significantly, a formal play with a blurring of the limits dividing on-screen and off-screen space. In this vein of doubling, Jonathan Rosenbaum, who has described the film as being about "coupling," extends that to other forms of "duplicity." He writes, "Faced by a team of feminist film theorists, Raynal admitted that the film is partially about 'the representation of the image of woman as a sign,' but apparently in the more footloose, less gender-conscious 60s she was more interested in exploring the sexy forms of duplicity between various sequences, their secret points of agreement and accord and strongest points of tension. It's a film about coupling (a man appears with Raynal in many of the sequences) but also about flirting with camera and spectator alike."[36]

This "sexy form of duplicity" recalls the erotic mode of *Nocturno 29*, but perhaps more interesting in this passage is the mention of "secret points of agreement and accord." A clandestine sense of complicity is at work, as Rosenbaum aptly proposes, between "camera and spectator." Amid the repetitions and editing tricks, the paranoiac relation to which Daney refers is to be found perhaps in the conduit between the interiority and the exteriority marked by the screen. If the title *Deux fois* has been translated as "Twice Upon a Time," its "two" unfolds to reveal multiple duplications that crowd in on Raynal's monopolizing individual presence on-screen. As Raynal films such emblematic Barcelona streets as the Rambla, members of the public open up to create a space and peer curiously as the camera cleaves its way before them.

The next image (see fig. 2.5) depicts the alluring and erotic yet disconcertingly mesmerizing image of Raynal in black stockings, topless, apparently vulnerable yet defiant—perhaps for this very reason—ambiguous to the spectatorial gaze as she urinates while staring directly at the camera. Directed toward the off-screen voyeuristic spectator while accompanied by two on-screen male actors, her look challenges the identificatory framing of classical narrative film that Laura Mulvey would write so cogently about a few years later.

Rosenbaum's "secret points of agreement and accord" here lie in the relation between the hermetic interiority of the film and exteriority as seepage, the secret as secretion or as a kind of distillation or extract to paraphrase Jean-Luc Nancy.[37] The overflow—quite literally—of both body and screen exceeds the limits of the body at a moment when the body exceeds the focus of the gaze, and it reveals the beyond of the outside. In this convergence of excesses (the body, the screen), the division between what Nancy calls "exteriority and interiority is dissolved."[38] The gauze-like border of the stockings is pressed tight to the skin as a kind of membrane, hymen-like. The textile-bodily infrathin is a breach of the dammed-up surface text—the skin—of the film, the pellicle/*película*, but it is also a loss of control to the point of rupture. This flow beyond the body and beyond the screen questions the off-screen space and not only breaks the division between Raynal's body and the exterior within the mise-en-scène but also breaches the boundaries of the frame itself. The excess streaming from the body turns the tables on the sadistic-voyeuristic masculine gaze and exceeds the filmic conventions of internal screen space and external spectatorship.

Such liquid excess extends to the porous epidermis of national boundaries. *Deux fois* is a French film shot in Barcelona, while the first public screening of

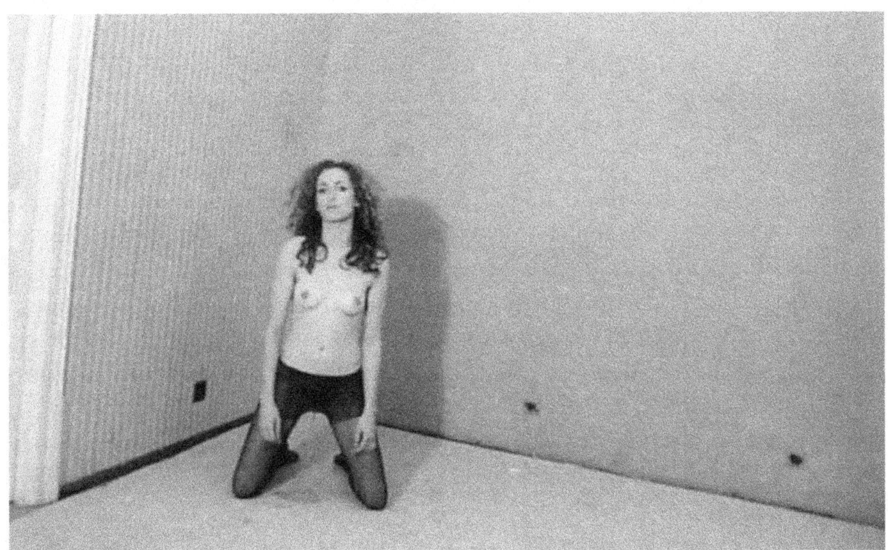

Fig. 2.5 In defiance of the male gaze.

Nocturno 29, whose director heralds from Barcelona, was in France. Nation is uncontainable within such boundaries, and the concept of national cinema is rendered redundant. In a sense, these films are contraband, smuggled across the frontiers of patrimonic classification, the inundation indifferent to illusionary national borders.

This spatial violation extends also to temporality. In a further conceptualization of infrathin, contraband becomes *contretemps*—a wildly unanticipated countertime that is unanchored to chronological order.[39] This notion of excess and overflow in the context of subjectivity resonates once more with Nancy's short book *Intoxication*. Nancy writes of "the sea swell where the abyss swirls around, man's *wine-dark sea* of a thousand turns, which ceaselessly returns to the self."[40] The idea here of the abyss, the void, the whirlpool, or the maelstrom that we have seen before is explicitly linked to the *propio*. The loosening of the manacles of identity and the flow that unbinds its confines facilitates in its spillover access to an exterior. This is one of the keys to understanding the significance of the previous chapter's discussion of trance cinema. For Nancy, writing in terms applicable to the films analyzed in this chapter, the untrammeled results of intoxication are "presences that are eclipsed in a trance, a dance, a rhythm."[41]

In a remarkable shot, Raynal films a Barcelona intersection on a gray, blustery day. The camera revolves 360 degrees, five and a half times around the crossroads. This flowing, looping circularity contra rigorous lineality—similar to that described in *Nocturno 29*, albeit in less excessive circumstances—is there in the sharp, formal lines of the crossroads marked out by the highways. The prolonged spinning pan produces an uncanny turbulence associated with filmic technology. This kind of swirling is what Martin Heidegger terms *Wirbel* in the context of the prepolitical polis as a kind of imperceptible marginal politics of the erotic. It suggests an intermediality at the very edge, at the supplementary point of encounter with excess, and with the kind of radical alterity that sees the loss of the subject, as in the trance film. In the spirit of Duchamp and Perec, this might be classified as infra: "Perhaps the πόλις is that realm and locale around which everything question-worthy and uncanny turns in an exceptional sense. The πόλις is πόλις, that is the pole, the swirl [*Wirbel*] in which and around which everything turns."[42] I will return briefly to this idea of the pole in chapter 7, but for now it bears consideration as a form of performative politics.

If the title *Deux fois* (Twice upon a time) proclaims the film's playful, storytelling nature, it also returns us to the paradoxical play on the individual female subject. Raynal dominates the screen throughout. It is a film that presents an authorial subject that is divided at all times. Raynal is a subject (both filmmaker and actor, character and autobiographical figure) whose signature—as editor, director, and actor—is stamped ambivalently throughout the film. Such a subversion of female authorship—in what might be described, with all its dreamlike quality as a trance film—recalls the precedent of Maya Deren. The visual fragmentation of the female subject is—as in Deren's trance films—the result of Raynal's skill as an editor. Cinematic technique and thematic content are inseparable. In a later chapter, I discuss the role of photographic performativity, but at issue here in both Deren's and Raynal's work is a combination of performance and performativity.

This splitting of the subject dovetails with the psychoanalytical and feminist approaches in film theory being pioneered at the time. It poses an interesting prefigurative supplement—an unwitting prologue and perhaps its counterpoint—to Mulvey's celebrated 1973 essay titled "Visual Pleasure and Narrative Cinema" in that it can be (and has been) read not only as a feminist critique of film spectatorship but as upending what the Camera Obscura collective in its 1976 analysis of the film (in an echo of Mulvey) describes as "the voyeuristic and sadistic nature of film viewing."[43] If *Nocturno 29* places Lucía Bosé as object of the gaze (of both the camera and her male counterparts), then Jackie Raynal's subversive authorship protagonism appropriates that gaze. This is the visual element that is central to both films discussed in this chapter and that Mulvey terms "looked-at-ness."

In this way, too, *Deux fois* inverts what we have already seen as the traditional power relation between spectator and screen presence. It is another instance of the dialogue between the on-screen protagonist and off-screen space. In response to Raynal's bold, unnerving monologue directed to the camera at the end of the film's first sequence, Louis Skorecki echoes Daney's comment cited earlier to insist that *Deux fois* is "one of the most precise films about paranoia." But, he goes on to say, "To see it is (also) a traumatic experience. The (invisible, of course) eyes that vigilate and pursue the young woman (without allowing her a moment's respite . . .) *our eyes and as such they look at us.*"[44] Paranoia here, as deployed by both Daney and Skorecki resonates not only with Dalí and the surrealist tradition but also, in the vein of the earlier discussion, with the idea of the infrathin, as the residue transmitted and secreted, a silent seepage through the porous film of the screen.

Mulvey's essay on the question of male subjectivity and female objectivization examines classical Hollywood narrative and male directors (particularly Hitchcock). Here, though, female directorship is at stake (and Mulvey herself directed films in the 1970s and early 1980s). As in Deren's work and some of Akerman's films, the female subject is foregrounded as splintered. The *I* of autobiography—that of Jackie Raynal—is fragmented, doubled, repeated, and ritualized in ceremony. There are echoes here of the Deren films and a foreshadow of a later film, Akerman's *Je, tu, il, elle* (1974). While this indicates perhaps something productively distinctive to the female voice, I am more interested in the question of subjectivity as grounded in the historical moment, particularly as these films critique essentialism in their fragmentation of identity. In the vein of Deren, the doubling alluded to in the film's title is reinforced by its incantatory repetitions. These are never real repetitions or exact copies of an original but are reshot, slightly different takes, reframings, or tricks of the camera.

A second *Camera Obscura* article in the same 1976 issue of the journal—a shot-by-shot analysis of the film—makes express reference to lighting early in its discussion of the first shot of *Deux fois*: "What appears as a natural image is a complex mediation of light, coming from behind Raynal, creating a halo, and from in front of her face, all set against an over-exposed or washed-out background."[45] Later in the film, in what *Camera Obscura* identifies as the seventeenth shot but is actually a series of shots, Raynal films a street billboard, a lit screen (or "computerized grid of lights") advertising the 1968 Spanish film *¡Dame un poco de amor!* (Bring a little lovin'!), directed by José María Forqué and Francisco Macián. Set to theme music performed by Los Bravos, we witness a violent struggle between a man and a woman (see fig. 2.6 a–d). The very substance of the representation, its material or medium, is fragmented as we

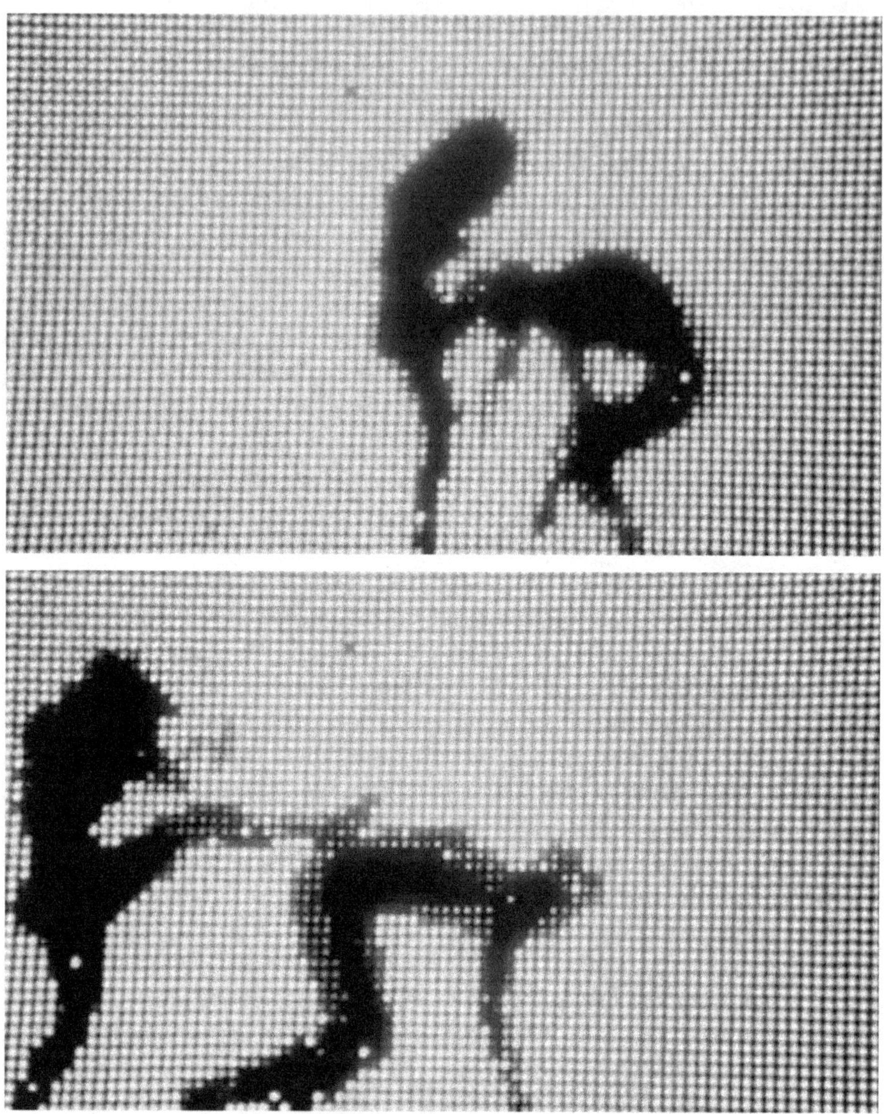

Fig. 2.6 a–d Sequence of electronic billboard images in Barcelona.

are privy to a pixilated couple in conflict. Furthermore, where the subject is doubled or splintered throughout the film, here it is pure light and shadow. It is a primitive artificial choreography in central Barcelona and a play on light whose illumination is a set of shards, diaphanous in the material composition of the form itself. Robotic, cartoonish, and dreamlike, composed and found (a fortuitous discovery on the high street), the sequence also makes use of a

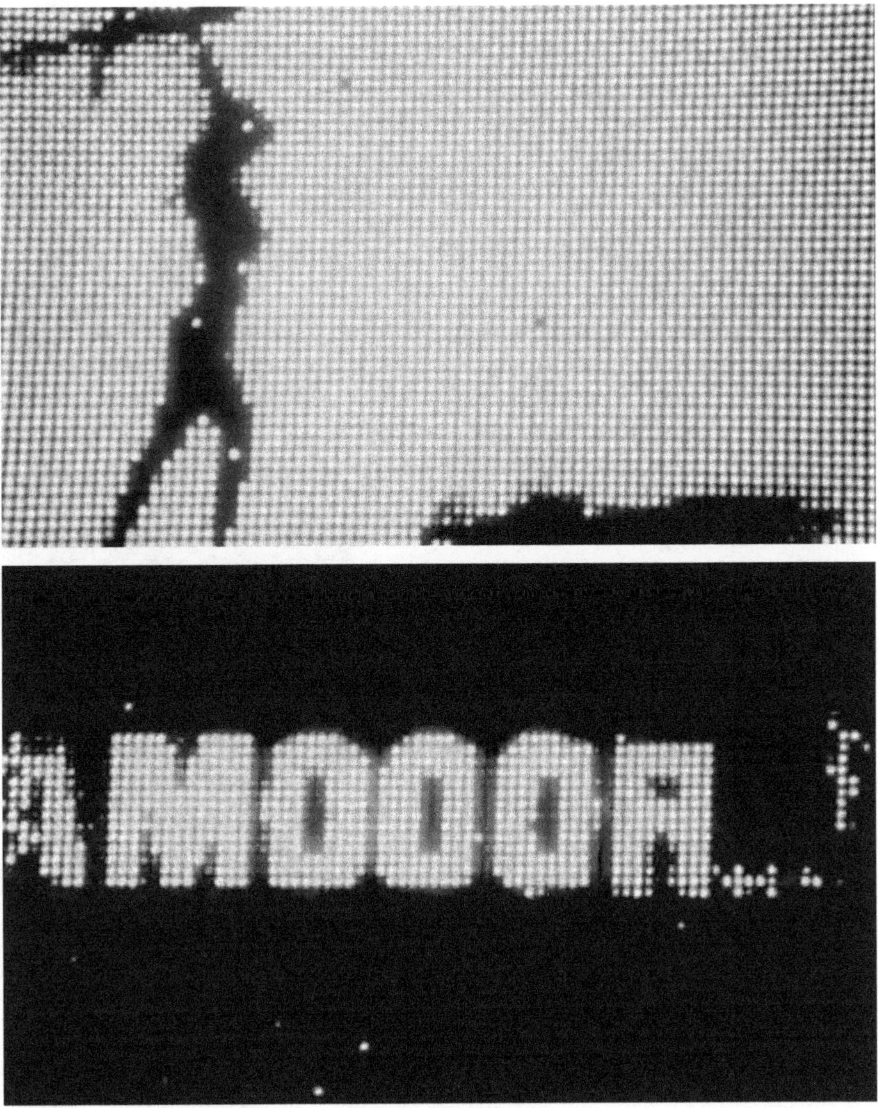

Fig. 2.6 a–d (*continued*)

medium distinct from the 16 mm footage that Raynal employs. It is only one of a series of instances in which other media intervene.

Maya Deren's work, conceptually similar to Raynal's (albeit in a very different register), suggests that the light of cinema is unmediated and that it possesses the kind of purity that would distinguish it from intermediality. In terms that seem apt to *Deux fois,* Massimiliano Mollona describes the characters of

Deren's trance films in the following terms: "Deren depersonalizes her characters by splitting them into double or triple personalities, reflections on mirrors or windows, living shadows, mirroring gestures, multiple camera angles. . . . They are fluid, multiple, and dismembered; they overflow the boundaries of the body and reveal themselves in body parts, landscapes, or objects. . . . Deren's actors have no individual agency or volition. What motivates them is the energy of the camera."[46]

Tellingly, Mollona also stresses the "overflow," the exceeding of boundaries and fluidity discussed earlier in *Deux fois*. Mollona identifies in Deren a link between this overflow and the specificity of filmic technology and (though he does not use the word) subjectivity. Raynal's deployment of such technology—both in the filming and the montage—while emphasizing fractured female agency also highlights a theatricality at work in her film that is absent from Deren's films. The *Camera Obscura* shot analysis observes that the sequence immediately prior to the billboard one is exceptionally theatrical: "Raynal and a man are standing in a doorway having a conversation. Toward the end of the shot, they look at the camera, and the lights which had illuminated them go out. The overwhelming theatricality of the shot is produced by the frontal position (both of the camera and of Raynal and the man), the obvious posing for an audience, the harshness of the lighting, the enclosed space and proscenium arch of the doorway."[47]

Adrian Martin aptly describes the same sequence as being like a "mummer's play." It is notable that *Nocturno 29* is almost entirely without dialogue, and its puppetry is a symptom of what is a kind of dumb show. As we will see shortly, Raynal is influenced by Rivette's interest in the theater. For now, though, we might observe that between the lighting and the theatricality and the natural and the artificial and in a set of variations on McLuhan's dictum on the pure, *Deux fois* poses a number of questions. In her book *Surface*, Giuliana Bruno writes of the relation between light and time in terms that evoke Duchamp's infrathin: "The space between darkness and light in which cinema theatrically dwells, is essentially a transitional space of unfolding temporal shifts. Such a space of projection can return us to the most fundamental passage of time, which is basically a passage of light."[48]

In his 2001 article on *Deux fois*, Martin notes the film's reference to *La vida es sueño*.[49] Sunlight and artificial light are motifs of Calderón's play, and, indeed, *Deux fois* arguably is a disquisition on dreaming and trance-like states. In an early sequence, Raynal wakes from sleep to note down her dreams (see fig. 2.7).

Severo Sarduy introduces his book on the baroque with a short text titled "La camera del eco" (The echo chamber), where he describes the *retombée*

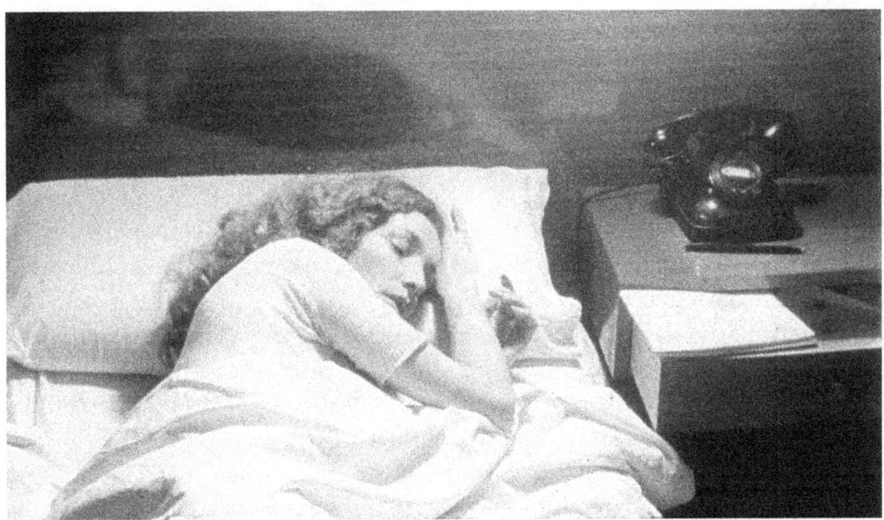

Fig. 2.7 Life is a dream.

(boomerang), or the reverberating effect of call and response already alluded to in *Nocturno 29* in the context of Eco and Narcissus. Toward the end of *Deux fois*, Raynal turns to Rivette-like theatricality with a pointedly specific reading of the most celebrated speech of *La vida es sueño*. Raynal delivers Segismundo's lines: "¿Qué es la vida? una ilusión/una sombra, una ficción, / y el mayor bien es pequeño: que toda la vida es sueño y los sueños son" (What is life? An illusion / a shadow, a fiction, and its greatest asset is small: life is but a dream and dreams are just that, dreams). An echo effect in the theatricality of the stage—and the staging—is one we have seen in the filmic technology (when Raynal reproduces herself in the same shot or in the two repeated sequences of the director/actor in the pharmacy) and the thematic coupling—or the "secret accords"—of the illumination/shadows, the ludic doubling of life and its representation. These elements reveal what André Bazin once described as the mixed or impure aspects of film. Bazin was discussing adaptation—the translation from page to screen—but we might similarly think of these extrafilmic intermedial elements as the contaminants, supplements, excess, and fragments that disturb claims to a univocal filmic homogeneity and that threaten to overflow from within outward.

The speech also has, though, a diegetic point. The celebrated Calderón quote spoken by Raynal in apparent ventriloquist female-to-male drag evokes (perhaps unintentionally) the first character to appear and speak onstage in the original play: the female Rosaura disguised as a man. This cross-dressing suggests a transfer of gender that disrupts—as in the original play—the relation between illusion and reality, dreamscapes and virtuality, metaphor and the original (the *propio*), filial relationships. One way this is done in the play is by intoxication: Segismundo is drugged with a sedative by his tutor-captor Clotaldo.

Theater features in many of Rivette's films but explicitly in films such as *Paris nous appartient* (1960), *L'Amour fou* (1969), *La bande des quatre* (1988), and, above all, the monumental *Out 1* (1971). Invariably Rivette posits the proximity of the theater to real life. He is preoccupied with the way theater expands, seeps beyond the stage, and overflows into life itself. The work of theater actors in Rivette's films spills over from their public performances to blur with their everyday existence. What permeates the boundaries confining the space of the stage in Rivette correlates in the work of Raynal with an exceeding of those of the screen and the spectator, in accessing the inaccessible. Both filmmakers dissolve the frontiers separating interiority from exteriority, and in doing so, they produce a kind of choreography, the sort of ritualized performance that Jean Rouch pioneered in his ethnographical films.

The central character of *La vida es sueño*, Segismundo, is imprisoned in a tower from birth and occupies an interstitial space between sleep and wakefulness. This in-betweenness is emphasized by frequent references to his hybrid condition as part man, part beast. Indeed, in an echo of *Nocturno 29*, Segismundo is referred to at times as a minotaur at the heart of a labyrinth.[50] The baroque motifs of light and darkness, day and night, and brightness and shadow permeate the play. To all intents and purposes, Segismundo is a character buried alive, chained to the walls of a tower. His knowledge of the world is limited exclusively to the teaching of Clotaldo.[51]

La vida es sueño returns us to the question of intermediality. Both *Nocturno 29* and *Deux fois* are charged with the cosmology of the baroque: darkness and light, circularity, doubling via mirrors and echoes, and allusiveness and unfolding artifice. The benightedness of *Nocturno 29* contrasts with the luminosity of Raynal's film, and the overexposure of the early shots in *Nocturno 29* contrast with the shadows in *Deux fois*. Both films also operate in the subterranean tradition of the historical avant-garde, from the early Buñuel-Dalí, to Deren, and to Raúl Ruiz (who directed his own film adaptation of *La vida es sueño* in the 1980s). This is a historically grounded genealogy that is filmically specific yet unanchored to the closure imposed by period or nation. The multiple texts here resound with and rebound off one another—like an echo—in what, following Philippe Lacoue-Labarthe, might be called the catacoustic. This idea is explored in chapter 6 in a discussion of the work of Andrés Duque, a contemporary filmmaker very much influenced by trance cinema.

Bazin—whose disagreements with Rivette were notable—observed that "the presence of the actor" onstage embodies the "essence" of theater and that this "presence" is one of the principle differences distinguishing the cinema from the theater. [52] But there is another feature concerning presence that separates the theater from cinema: the former is performed in the present, in real time. This proximity between presence, to which Bazin draws attention, and the present is an important part of this book that is analyzed in more detail in later chapters, but for now it is an issue that concerns and turns on questions of performativity, technology, production, and reproduction.

Notes

1. Lúcia Nagib, "The Politics of Impurity," in *Impure Cinema: Intermedial and Intercultural Approaches to Film*, ed. Lúcia Nagib and Anne Jerslev (London: I. B. Tauris, 2013), 22.

2. Marcel Duchamp and Paul Matisse, *Notes* (Paris: G. K. Hall, 1983), n11.

3. Ibid., n1.

4. Jens Schöter, "The Politics of Intermediality," *Acta Universitatis Sapientiae, Film and Media Studies* 2 (2010): 107–24.

5. Portabella has a particular interest in pictorial art. In chapter 3, I discuss his work on Miró (among others), and painting also features significantly in *Nocturno 29*.

6. Some of this material has been addressed by Eduardo Ledesma in his article "Intermediality and Spanish Experimental Cinema: Text and Image Interactions in the Lyrical Films of the Barcelona School," *Journal of Spanish Cultural Studies* 14, no. 3 (2013): 254–74.

7. Connected to "trance," and like Maya Deren, Jackie Raynal was influenced by dance (and, indeed, by many experimental filmmakers, among them Chantal Akerman, Shirley Clarke, Babette Mangolte, and Yvonne Rayner). Raynal's first film was a dance piece on Merce Cunningham.

8. The figure of the *propre* is key to this book. I will return to it later.

9. *La vida es sueño/Life Is a Dream*, Act 3, ed. and trans. Stanley Appelbaum (Mineola, NY: Dover, 2002), 166–67.

10. There is, of course, a long philosophical tradition around the question of light, from Plato to Descartes. My use of the word *photology*, however, refers more to the work of Merleau Ponty and Luce Irigaray.

11. Quoted by Patrick Deval, "More Light" in the pamphlet accompanying the DVD of *Ici et maintenant*, dir. Serge Bard, 1969 (Paris: Re:Voir 2015), 18.

12. Quoted by JeeHee Hong, "Material, Materiality," *Theories of Media Keywords Glossary*, Chicago School of Media Theory (Winter 2003), http://csmt.uchicago.edu/glossary2004/material.htm.

13. Quoted in Alexander R. Galloway, Eugene Thacker, and McKenzie Wark, *Excommunication: Three Inquiries into Media and Mediation* (Chicago: University of Chicago Press, 2013), 13.

14. *Nocturno 29* is not, strictly speaking, a film of the Barcelona School, because Portabella financed it independently of the group. As noted in chapter 1, Portabella maintained a discreet distance from the Barcelona School.

15. Portabella's interest in—and deployment of—the language of publicity has been noted by many commentators on his work.

16. Spanish film historian Luis Parés claims that Viadar was, in fact, the joint director of this film. He makes this claim in a note added to the official blog of the distributor and DVD production company, Intermedio (https://intermediodvd.wordpress.com/2012/06/27/). I have yet to find evidence that sustains this assertion. Parés did not reply to my inquiry about this.

17. I think here of a particular late 1950s and 1960s variation on modernism and use the term *late modernism* to distinguish it from such modernist manifestations as German expressionism or Soviet filmmaking of the revolutionary period.

18. Camera Obscura Collective, "An Interrogation of the Cinematic Sign: Woman as Sexual Signifier in Jackie Raynal's *Deux Fois*," *Camera Obscura, A Journal of Feminism and Film Theory* 1, no. 1 (Fall 1976): 12.

19. Jonathan Rosenbaum insightfully writes of *Deux Fois*: "On one level the movie is a kind of elementary editing puzzle that asks, 'How did I get from this long-take sequence to this one that follows it?' and/or 'What are the sexy forms of duplicity between these two sequences—their secret points of agreement and accord, as well as their strongest points of tension?' It's a film, in other words, about a couple, and about coupling—there is a man who appears with Raynal in many of the sequences—as well as repetition." Jonathan Rosenbaum, "Barcelona Boogie and Pittsburgh Punk," *The Soho News*, June 4, 1980, https://www.jonathanrosenbaum.net/1980/06/barcelona-boogie/.

20. Rosenbaum is Portabella's best-known supporter in the United States (a support cultivated by Portabella himself) and has consistently read Portabella's films as allegories of Spanish and European politics. While this is not irrelevant, I am more interested in other aspects of the films.

21. Poet, playwright, and cultural activist, Brossa (1919–1998) was a key member of avant-garde initiatives in Catalonia since the Spanish Civil War. One of the founders of the magazine *Dau al set* and the collective associated with it, he was also instrumental in a similar initiative, Club 49.

22. Josep Torrell, "La primera película política del estado español," in *Los "Nuevos Cines" en España: Ilusiones y desencantos de los años sesenta*, eds. Carlos F. Heredero and José Enrique Monterde (Valencia: Instituto de la Cinematografía y de las Artes Audiovisuales, 2004),449–53. Pere Portabella (March 2, 2010), http://www.pereportabella.com/es/textos/2010/03/la-primera-pelicula-poltica-del-estado-espanol-es.

23. Félix Fanés points out that the sequence recalls the "Cream Separator" sequence from Sergei Eisenstein's *Old and New* (1929). Félix Fanés, *Pere Portabella: Avantguarda, cinema i politica* (Barcelona: Filmoteca de Cataluña, 2000), 117.

24. Bosé is associated with the erotic given her collaborations with Antonioni, her marriage to the Spanish bullfighter Dominguín, and her role as a femme fatale in Juan Antonio Bardem's *Muerte de un ciclista* (1955). About Antonioni, Félix Fanés makes the cogent point that "no nos puede pasar por alto que en *Nocturno 29* hay ciertos contenidos compartidos con películas como *La aventura, La notte*, . . . o *L'eclisse* . . . : esto es, el retrato de la alta burguesia urbana a partir de la crisis de la pareja, con especial énfasis en el punto de vista feminine" (We should not overlook the fact that in *Nocturno 29* there is a certain content shared with films like *La aventura, La notte*, . . . or *L'eclisse* . . . : such as the portrayal of the urban high bourgeoisie seen from the perspective of a couple in crisis, with particular

emphasis on the feminine point of view). Ibid., 118. While this is unquestionably true, Fanés makes no mention of the formal aspect suggested by this comparison: that of light itself contained in the words *night* and *eclipse*.

25. The Collins online dictionary defines the Tardis from the *Doctor Who* television series as an "acronym of Time And Relative Dimensions In Space." It is distinguished (not unlike Derrida's concept of "invagination") as being larger on the inside than on the outside (https://www.collinsdictionary.com/dictionary/english/tardis-like).

26. Segismundo, who considers himself half man, half beast, also considers the tower he is held in a labyrinth.

27. Mario Cabré was also a star of sorts. A fairly unremarkable actor, he had previously been a bullfighter but is best remembered for his affair with Ava Gardner.

28. Eco, is of course, a mythological figure who finally only exists as the sound of her voice in a further connection with the sonic, reverberating effect of call and response.

29. I am grateful to my student Lucas Plazek for having reminded me of this effect.

30. *Gradiva* (1902) is a novella written by Wilhelm Jensen about which Freud wrote a key commentary. Derrida, in turn, comments on Freud's comments in *Archive Fever*. Mary Ann Doane also discusses *Gradiva* in *The Emergence of Cinematic Time*. The conceptual artist Victor Burgin describes his 1982 set of seven photographs titled *Gradiva* in terms similar to that of Derrida's view of the hieroglyph as discussed in chapter 1: "This form of visual art practice, to some extent, is analogous to pictograhic, hieroglyphic writing." Victor Burgin, *Between* (New York: Basil Blackwell, 1986), 124.

31. Serge Daney, "Portrait de Jackie Raynal," *Cahiers du cinéma* no. 334/335 (April 1982).

32. One might add to this list the early films of Marguerite Duras and *Daisies* directed by Věra Chytilová in 1966.

33. Nathalie Léger writes of *Wanda* (1970), the only film Barbara Loden directed and in which she starred: "A woman is pretending to be another, in a role she wrote herself, based on another . . . , playing something other than a straightforward role, playing not herself but a projection of herself onto another, played by her but based on another." Nathalie Léger, *Suite for Barbara Loden*, trans. Natasha Lehrer and Cécile Menon (St. Louis, MO: Dorothy, 2016), 66.

34. Raynal also worked on Barbet Schroeder's *Mediterranee* (1964).

35. In the context of feminism it is interesting to note Akerman's cinematographer Babette Mangolte contrasting comments in an interview with the *Village Voice* on the *Jeanne Dielman* collaboration: "At that time, ninety minutes was the norm for a film to be commercial, but Chantal did not want to excerpt things or do ellipses on the gesture. This was fundamental to the aesthetic of feminism. You don't do what men do. It's not an action picture. It's a picture that is about giving nobility to something that has never been represented: somebody cooking, somebody waiting." Eric Hynes, "'We Wanted to Invent': Babette Mangolte on Chantal Akerman," *Village Voice*, March 30, 2016, http://www.villagevoice.com/film/we-wanted-to-invent-babette-mangolte-on-chantal-akerman-8439030.

36. Jonathan Rosenbaum, *Film: The Front Line 1983* (Denver, CO: Arvon Press, 1983), 152–53.

37. Jean-Luc Nancy, *Intoxication* (New York: Fordham University Press, 2016), 16–17.

38. Ibid., 18.

39. In this context we might note that Rosenbaum's edited volume on Jacques Rivette includes a major interview with the filmmaker (conducted by Jacques Aumont, Jean-Louis

Comolli, Jean Narboni, and Silvie Pierre) titled significantly "Time Overflowing." *Rivette: Texts and Interviews*, ed. Jonathan Rosenbaum, trans. Amy Gateff and Tom Milne (London: British Film Institute, 1977), 9–38.

40. Nancy, *Intoxication*, 13.

41. Ibid., 18.

42. Martin Heidegger, *Holderlin's Hymn, "The Ister,"* trans. William McNeill and Julia Davis (Bloomington: Indiana University Press, 1996), 81.

43. "An Interrogation of the Cinematic Sign," 12.

44. Louis Skorecki, "Semaine des Cahiers: Deux Fois," *Cahiers du cinéma* no. 276 (May 1977), 51–52.

45. Camera Obscura Collective, "Interrogation of the Cinematic Sign." Camera Obscura Collective, *"Deux Fois:* Shot Commentary, Shot Chart, and Photogrammes," *Camera Obscura: A Journal of Feminism and Film Theory* 1, no. 1 (Fall 1976): 27–51.

46. Massimiliano Mollona, "Seeing the Invisible: Maya Deren's Experiments in Cinematic Trance," *October* 149 (Summer 2014): 171.

47. "Deux Fois," 33.

48. Guiliana Bruno, *Surface: Matters of Aesthetics, Materiality, and Media* (Chicago: University of Chicago Press, 2014), 116–17.

49. Adrian Martin, "The Experimental Night: Jackie Raynal's *Deux Fois,*" in *Jeune, dure et pure! Une histoire du cinéma d'avant-garde et expérimental en France*, eds. Nicole Brenez and Christian Lebrat (Milan: Mazotta/Cinémathèque Française, 2001), 306–8.

50. The motif of the labyrinth is also in Laura Mulvey and Peter Wollen's film *Riddles of the Sphynx* (1977) in the form of a children's game with liquid mercury.

51. On being released Segismundo returns to court only to demonstrate tyranny before finally returning for a second time as a kind of "philosopher king." It is likewise noteworthy that the play deals with not only the illusion of dreams but also the dissembling character of the image (the locket), the ideals (and illusion) of beauty, and the reflection of the sun (Estrella). As has been noted by others, Rosaura is an anagram of *aurora*, the dawn, the emergence of light.

52. André Bazin, "Theater and Cinema," in *What Is Cinema*, vol. 1, trans. Hugh Gray (Berkeley: University of California Press, 1967), 76.

3

THE DISCONTINUOUS LEGACIES OF PERE PORTABELLA

Between Heritage and Inheritance

I BEGIN THIS CHAPTER WITH A BRIEF DISCUSSION of sequences from two films that Spain's most influential independent and experimental filmmaker Pere Portabella directed in the early 1970s. The first is from the 1973 film *Acció Santos*. In this twelve-minute short, Portabella's longtime collaborator, composer, performance artist, and virtuoso pianist Carles Santos prepares to play Chopin's Prelude in C-sharp minor, Op. 45. The camera captures Santos surrounded by the lighting and sound technicians as he warms up his fingers before playing the piece. At what is almost exactly the midway point in the film, Santos stops playing and moves to an adjacent table. The musician then listens (with us, the spectators) to the recording. After a few moments, he places earphones over his head to listen alone and in silence (see fig. 3.1).

The camera moves slowly toward Santos, stopping in extreme close-up to focus on his facial expression, his eyebrows, and the movement of the reel of tape reflected in his spectacles. His eyes, fixed on the tape machine, fill the frame. The frame is marked, in turn, by the outline of his glasses in what might be described as a soundscape, the sight of sound. As the camera closes in even tighter, the only movement in the frame is that of the reel turning in Santos's iris. It is an ontologically filmic moment, a conceit of kinetic reproduction in which the cinematic eye meets the human eye to reproduce silence in visual form; it is both an acoustic image and an image of the acoustic.

The second example is the opening sequence of *Umbracle* (1972), which commences almost like a film from the silent era, with the grainy texture of the celluloid and a stark mise-en-scène. Actor Christopher Lee and a security guard of the zoological museum in Barcelona's Parc de la Ciutadella circle each other. Gliding between glass cabinets of stuffed birds, the two men mark out

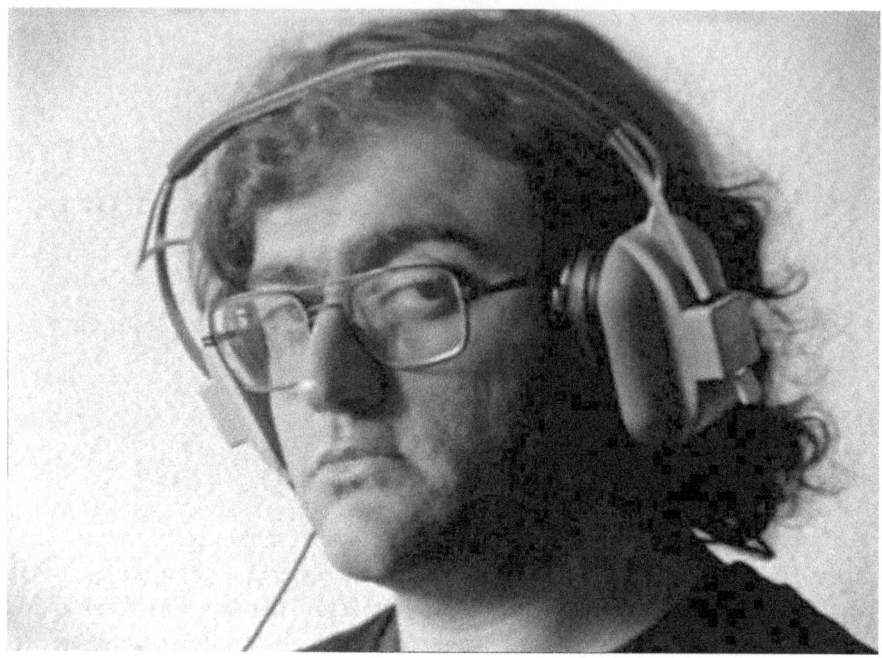

Fig. 3.1 The filmic image of the acoustic. Carles Santos recording.

a mysterious choreography of surveillance as they feign close examination of the taxidermic specimens while eyeing each other with suspicion through the blurred glass of the vitrines that shimmer beneath the translucent umbraculum that gives the film its title. Meanwhile, the audio track resounds with an increasingly intense, insistent choral humming, like the angry buzz of a fly (something to which I will return later). As is always the case in Portabella's work, the actors are not characters. They have no depth and no psychology. Rather, they are oblique signifiers that point us in particular directions. Lee, who is associated with the Dracula of Hammer Horror films, had appeared in Portabella's previous film *Vampir-cuadecuc* (1970), and is a figure synonymous with Nosferatu, the word Bram Stoker erroneously believed was Romanian for "not dead." Lee is thus a representation of the truly undead among the apparently undead, a Dracula among the stuffed, lifelike animals.

Furthermore, Lee is not an actor in this film. Rather, he plays a person named Christopher Lee, a shadow of his own character who, unsettlingly, by being himself is less real than the character he usually plays. He is what Jacques Derrida might call, in a different context, a "copy of a copy."[1] Lee is also a leftover from the earlier film, *Vampir-cuadecuc* (which itself was, as we will see, a reworking of previous filmic material). Both cypher and noncypher, Lee is, in a sense, very much a living dead character, a simulacrum of sorts. This sign with an ambiguous double meaning, this "shadow presence" of a Christopher Lee who is both only a vampire and not a vampire (nor even an actor), provides, together with the example of Santos, a way into reading Portabella's work in its entirety.

Supplement in *Vampir-cuadecuc*

Vampir-cuadecuc is, on one level, a vampirization of Jesús Franco's *Conde Drácula* (1970), whose set and actors were used by Portabella and his team simultaneously with the shoot of Franco's film. However, rather than being a film within a film, *Vampir-cuadecuc* is more akin to a photonegative of the original (something we have seen in previous chapters). While it is certainly a remarkable example of metacinema, it is also, on a theoretical level, coherent with *Umbracle* and *Acció Santos* in that it interrogates, in its avant-garde engagement with genre film, apparent oppositions and questions of discordant representation. *Vampir-cuadecuc* suggests a mobile, malleable, and fluid archive of filmic and historical material. Moreover—and this is the core of my argument—it highlights how Derrida's notion of the "supplement" is useful in an analysis of Portabella's work.

Derrida conceives the supplement as both a substitute and a surplus.[2] Aptly then, *cua de cuc* is Catalan for worm's tail—a resonant description of a projection, a prosthetic, or an excess—but it is also a term for the unexposed footage at the end of a roll of film. Clearly, that suggests a supplement or an addition that, like the photonegative, reflects the very materiality of film. The contradictory tension here is between vampirizing—a parasitic exploitation of Franco's film—and the leftover film footage or the excess that constitutes the worm's tail, as the word *supplement* means both to supplant and to complement. Later in this chapter, the figure of the parasite becomes important to the discussion.

Portabella's work, both in the individual films and throughout his lengthy career, is marked by discontinuity. His films are jagged, fractal collages of apparently disconnected sequences with jarring, atonal, and often incongruous soundtracks (which nonetheless invariably prove fundamental to the visual image). Within each scene or sequence, this discontinuity is marked by repeated violations of coherence, the match cuts that emphasize spatial and temporal continuity. These are films distinguished by their gaps, by the yawning spaces to be filled, by the dots to be joined. And while almost every piece of writing about this director (following Portabella's own cues in many interviews) has remarked on the rupture of Aristotelian narratological conventions—notably, linear narrative—few have questioned what this actually means.[3]

The origins of this methodology, particularly in Portabella's first films (as noted in the discussion in chap. 2 of *Nocturno 29*), can be found in the subversive aesthetic of Joan Brossa together with the joint work Portabella did with Carles Santos (who died in 2017). This aesthetic has, since the 1960s, greatly influenced the director's rejection of classical poetics. Santos had studied with John Cage prior to working with Portabella. Yet to add nuance to—though not to disavow—the previous chapter's argument in favor of formal innovation, to attribute Portabella's work exclusively to aesthetic experimentalism limits its scope and force. The ruptures that distinguish Portabella's work concern incompletion, of which discontinuity is a symptom. The thwarted narratives, the fissures, the function of the actors, the metacinematic techniques, the cultural ephemera, and the kaleidoscopic, rhizomatic structures can be explained in both poetic and political terms as the result of absences marked by supplements that complete the incomplete or refer to other absences or absent others.

Two Political Interventions: *Informe general sobre algunas cuestiones de interés para una proyección pública* and *El sopar*

Shot in the interregnum between the death of Francisco Franco in November 1975 and the initiation of the democratic process, *Informe general sobre algunas cuestiones de interés para una proyección pública* (General report on some questions of interest for a public projection, 1976) is both a film about discontinuity with the previous regime—that is, discontinuation by means of rupture or reform—and a film galvanized by a sense of urgency owing to the imponderable and unsettled conditions of its own production. One word, incidentally, that is conspicuous by its absence in this film is *transition* (the "official" name by which the period between the end of the dictatorship and the restoration of democracy has been retrospectively baptized by historians and other pundits) and it is an absence that can be appreciated only with the benefit of hindsight. In this sense, *Informe general* constitutes an undecidable. The protagonists of the film—leftists, nationalists, trade unionists, monarchists—as well as the filmmaker and his team quite literally did not know at the time of their participation in the shoot what the outcome would be of what is euphemistically referred to in the film as *el proceso constituyente* (the constitutive process). In this way, the film itself becomes a political intervention—and the sensation of immediacy is palpable—in that it seeks to generate the very conditions needed for a future politics: "Undecidability," writes Derrida in the afterword to *Limited*

Inc., "opens the field of decision or decidability. It calls for decision in the order of ethical-political responsibility."[4]

The political intervention constituted by *Informe general* suggests that it, too, is a supplement. It is both a forum for and a contribution to a debate concerning the immediate future in uncertain times and simultaneously, owing to its spectral character in the clandestine world of the illegal opposition (this is a genuinely underground film), a shadow presence that supplants the lack of legal democratic debate. Further, *Informe general* is a mosaic of filmic styles. Divided into thematic blocks, the interviews and group discussions among political figures are punctuated with newsreel footage of demonstrations in Barcelona and Madrid; fictionalized docudramas of arrests and torture of political dissidents; a report on the ghostly ruins of the Aragonese town of Belchite, which was destroyed during the Spanish Civil War; a guided tour of the Pardo Palace, the residence of the recently deceased dictator; an extract from the 1941 film *Raza*, the self-aggrandizing family romance and war epic scripted by Franco himself; and the ubiquitous presence of an actor grafted Zelig-like onto the historical events recorded on-screen.

Interestingly—particularly in the context of chapter 1's discussion of truth— *Informe general* is a film that, while clearly conscious of its own value as historical document, simultaneously raises questions about veracity precisely by violating the conventions of its own form. In this way, the undecidability of the transitional period has a corresponding undecidability in the materiality of the film itself. Moreover, the actor Francesc Lucchetti functions, in a manner not dissimilar to Christopher Lee in *Umbracle*, as a spectral supplement, a kind of prosthetic aid, who both complements and replaces filmic and historical reality, in a film about the undecidable prospects for political representation. And indeed, in an idea to which I will return in the final chapter of this book, this is a film that makes no real distinction between artistic and political representation, as is wryly suggested by a shot of the removal of the portrait of Franco and his wife, Carmen Polo, from the Catalan parliament, the Generalitat. Portabella himself, following the restoration of democracy, served as a senator and consequently was obliged to suspend (or to *sacrifice*) his filmmaking activity until 1989.

Without wishing to theorize the concept of sacrifice more than is necessary (though it is pertinent to my argument and is discussed later in this chapter in the case of Federico García Lorca), it is worth recalling that the concept of sacrifice has always been substitutional and representational—representation itself—the sign, a matter of something standing in for or on behalf of something else. It is interesting to note, in this context, that *Informe general* begins with a lengthy sequence of the mountainous Valle de los Caídos, where

Franco was buried until recently, and it ends with Monserrat Caballé singing an aria from Richard Strauss's *Salomé*, performed at the Palau de la Música in Barcelona. These two sequences that bookend the film serve as synecdoches, or supplementary signs, for the epic mode of the film itself and the grandiose monumentality of the transformations under way.[5]

If *Informe general* is epic in tone and wide-ranging in focus, *El sopar* (The dinner) made two years earlier, is contrastingly minimalist and intimate. This film is a conversation between five people at a dinner table. Significantly, though, both films are products of a situation—key moments in a historical conjuncture—and as such they generate situations in their own right. The five diners are recently released former political prisoners, and that experience is the topic of discussion, evidently established in advance. Because *El sopar* was even more underground than *Informe general*, and extreme security measures were taken during the shoot, there is a sense of crisis in the very process of filming. The imprecision of the location for the shoot is announced in the introductory voice-over. It took place in 1974 at an undisclosed location in Catalonia.

Not anticipated however were the particular external extradiegetical circumstances that coincided with the shoot. By pure happenstance, the dinner was convened on the same day as the execution of the anarchist militant Salvador Puig Antich in Barcelona. According to Portabella, the participants were informed of the execution on their arrival, and they were offered the opportunity to leave (given the level of police activity in the area in preparation for a possible popular outcry). Unanimously, the participants opted to continue with the film as an act of protest, to provide both a response and a media alternative to the official version of events. So, first, *El sopar* is a spectral, subterranean alternative to the state's narrative; it is a political action. Second, Puig Antich's physical absence, the fact of his death, while never referred to in the film, floats ghost-like above and around the discussion, rendered uncanny (it is mentioned in the introductory voice-over, thereby making the spectator aware of it). The film functions, thus, as a supplement, both by supplanting the regime's version and by serving as an act of mourning, marking bereavement, a response to the loss, and the absence or void created by Puig Antich's execution.

This is another kind of open space or gap that Portabella's fractured narratives seek to both represent and work within. There is here—as there is throughout Portabella's corpus—yet another play on the notion of representation. On one level, the participants in *El sopar* represent those who are absent (Puig Antich, the collective of political prisoners, and the voice of dissent). As individuals they represent their own differing political tendencies: anarchism, the Communist Party, trade unionism, feminism. They also represent sacrifice in their testimony and their experience. Meanwhile, the film represents them as a group.

The film's formal properties are worth considering. *El sopar*'s austerity is deceptive. Its unadorned mise-en-scène is like a Rembrandt canvas. Portabella employs a rich palette, the framing is somber, and the sweeping and rotating camera movements penetrate each individual as he or she speaks. There is a texture to Portabella's films that is almost tactile; there is a sensual plasticity similar to that of the sequence with Lucia Bosé in the previous chapter's discussion of *Nocturno 29*. At times, particularly in Portabella's earlier, more experimental films, as we have seen, this sensuality takes on an erotic form that resembles that of his surrealist antecedents, but this is almost never divorced from politics (both Portabella and Santos spent short periods of time in prison). The juxtapositions between the oneiric and crude historical reality, the erotic and the prosaic, and the consistent incongruities in Portabella's work form a kind of filmic discord, such as that described in the example from *Acció Santos*. This feature is something that goes beyond the Brechtian distance or Godardian unmasking of the cinematic apparatus with which it has been compared and to which I will return in a moment.

This filmic texture is as auditory as it is visual, and it is an expression of tension. *El sopar* ends in silence, but it is very much a material, audible silence, lasting almost two minutes. The silence follows a brusque outburst by the sole female participant in the conversation, Lola Ferreira, in response to Jordi Cunill's more lyrical recollection of his prison experience. The frame captures the awkwardness on the faces of the protagonists, and the soundtrack picks up the whir of the camera rolling, a segment of fruit being eaten, someone clearing his throat, a match being struck. It is a voluble silence that, in its very auditory materiality, expresses a sense of time lost in prison while also being an act of reflection on the death of Puig Antich.

The silence recalls the dissonance between the audio and visual tracks of the earlier films and the materiality of the filmic apparatus that is constantly present in Portabella's work. Josep Torrell has pointed out that the humming perceived (and mentioned earlier) in the second shot of *Umbracle* persists intermittently throughout the film up until the final sequence, when it comes to an abrupt halt when Christopher Lee suddenly claps his hands and kills a fly.[6] This is immediately followed by a sugary 1960s pop melody that has previously accompanied images of the mass slaughter of chickens in a factory assembly line. The contrast between the mechanized carnage and the lyrical harmony is ironic, shocking, and chimes discordantly with Santos's jarring soundtracks (voice compositions, everyday noises, scratched records that repeat Beethoven insistently). These are the atonal connections and confusions—synchronic departures and displacements between sight and sound, fiction and reality, the filmic and the profilmic, each supplanting rather than complementing the other—that form part of the ongoing interrogation of representation throughout Portabella's work.

The Miró Films

Portabella's metafilmic techniques—his own appearances like interruptions in his filmic texts and the unveiling of the cinematic apparatus—are more like those of an artisan than they are Godardian gesture. They concern acts of presence with political force. His manipulation of filmic materials is most exemplary in his three films about Joan Miró: *Miró l'altre* (1969), *Miró forja* (1973), and *Miró tapis* (1973). The latter two, made in the early 1970s, are about the teams of artisans (the iron smiths and laborers in the forge that produced Miró's sculptures and the weavers of his tapestries) who work behind the scenes of Miró's work. I want to reflect briefly here, though, on *Miró l'altre* (The other Miró), a film that predates the other two. The film is itself a supplement, as its title suggests, an alternative Miró, the "other Miró." Shot in 1969, it records the Colegio de Arquitectos' (Society of architects') homage to Miró organized as an alternative to the Barcelona city government's Miró celebration of the previous year (an official attempt to capitalize on Miró's international reputation). The film supplants, replaces, displaces, and supplements the official Miró by using the figure of Miró himself to undo his own work.

While *Miró l'altre* ostensibly interrogates artistic practice, it does so by focusing on disputed space: the neighborhood where Miró is working, the use of space in the work itself, and the filmic space. What at times purports to be profilmic proves to be manipulated by montage and palette (the alternate use of color and black and white, for example) as Miró is shot in the course of an afternoon painting a mural on the glass windows of the premises of the Colegio de Arquitectos before, with the help of his assistants and in defiance of customary notions of artistic corpus, he paints over and destroys his own work. It is a singular act of discontinuity, incompletion, a gap, a void, and a spectral presence, with the trace of the original lying below the suffocating blanket of paint.

Khôra, Mise en Abyme, and the Deferral of Origins

To follow the brief reading of space in *Miró l'altre* and move on from discussion of the politics of Portabella's aesthetics and the aesthetics of his politics, I turn to an analysis of space in his work that suggests a critique of identificatory affiliation—Miró's original work that he painted over and that is so often fetishized in the name of the nation or as uniquely artistic phenomena.

Whereas until now, I have highlighted the discrepancies between signifier and signified—the idea of representation—I now propose a theory of space in an effort to unveil that discrepancy.

As has been well documented, in 1972 the Francoist regime withdrew Portabella's passport to prevent his attendance at the US premiere of what is probably his best known film, *Vampir-cuadecuc,* screened in his absence at New York's Museum of Modern Art.[7] The biographical detail would be unimportant (Portabella eventually traveled to New York in 2007 for a retrospective of his entire oeuvre), a mere anecdote, were it not for what the passport and its absence signify. The passport enables, facilitates, and restricts movement, and perhaps more importantly, it interpellates its bearer as the subject of a nation-state, marking that bearer with an identity. The passport names its bearer into existence as a kind of qualified and authorized national representative, sealing affiliation.

Portabella has always questioned the bond between identitarian interpellation and the other figure with which it is customarily associated, heritage. The heritage film, of course, is the most self-aware—and self-proclaiming—of national genres. The next chapter examines the new historical film in Spain and its complex relation with heritage. But here I explore Portabella's later work—*Puente de Varsovia* (Warsaw Bridge) (1989) and *Die Stille vor Bach/El silencio antes de Bach* (2007)—in order to interrogate the kind of metonymy we usually call national cinema. I suggest here that Derrida's concept of *khôra* (inherited from Plato) provides a useful entry point.[8]

Khôra is a spatial term; it is, perhaps, space itself. Elizabeth Grosz describes it as "the space in which place is made possible, the chasm for the passage of spaceless Forms into a spatialized reality"[9] and as "the condition for the genesis of the material world."[10] A figure of the initial stirrings of life—a presignifying state—*khôra* is coded by Derrida and Plato significantly as feminine. Derrida recalls Plato's own definition in the *Timaeus* as the "triton genus," the third genre, "an oscillation between oscillations."[11] While Portabella has long been associated with political and cultural avant-gardes (his work in the Francoist opposition and his collaborations with Brossa and Santos), he has never been closely linked to Catalan nationalism, and, as noted, he has been disavowed at times by the Spanish state. It is perhaps significant that the two films I discuss here are, in their own recursive way, associated with a geography that extends beyond Spain's borders, and both question the discursive geography that conjures identities. I make the case for a mobile site that, while it eludes the discursive constraints of identity politics, a heritage, or what is claimed to be a shared inheritance, cleaves to what has fascinated Portabella from the very beginning of his directorial career: the material processes, the very materiality, the manual labor, the techne (such as that of the Miró films) involved in cultural production.

Eclectic and elliptical, *Puente de Varsovia* (1989) constitutes a spiraling mise en abyme. It is a film of a film within a novel; a looping, endlessly suggestive set of narrative departures and displacements. The film's linearity is thwarted by intertextual and intermedial interruptions (opera, television broadcasts, and home movies), and it is highly conscious of its own filming (indeed, as we will see, one of the film's motifs is the multiplicity of screens). The opening credits appear after twenty-five minutes, and when they do it is as if it were the filmic adaptation of the original novel, which, to frustrate another level of narration, it is not. Here, though, I am interested in the spatial play between levels of narrative inside and outside, within the diegeses and beyond, beyond the translucent membranes that delineate and divide them—divisions that, in a sense, reflect the fault lines of geographically determined identity itself. The formal structure of the film—its site, domicile, container, or receptacle—suggests an initial dislocation that is culturally specific but corrupt (in both senses of contaminated and illicit).

The romantic triangle at the film's center—the two male parts being the orchestra conductor and the prize-winning novelist, the third being the wife of the latter and lover of the former—gives the film its *khôric* nucleus. The two men are close, longtime friends. It transpires that the musician (an echo here of Portabella's scriptwriting collaborator Santos) has lived, like Portabella's other scriptwriting collaborator Octavi Pellissa, in Germany for many years and describes himself as "un adicto a la política" (a political junky), again like (in this instance) Pellissa, a long-standing member of the Communist Party, or perhaps even like Portabella himself.

And it is a film about disappointment and disenchantment. Released in 1989, the impending collapse of erstwhile socialist utopias and the degeneration of local and national politics in Spain are factors that bear on the film. The introductory twenty-five minutes are a searing indictment of the system of political, financial, and cultural patronage involved in awarding the perennially rigged Premio Planeta, Spain's most prestigious literary award. In hesitant, interrupted form, the two men maintain an argument throughout the film regarding fidelity to the creative process and their respective attitudes toward popular reception.

The woman who connects them is more than an intermediary. She is the "triton genus"—not only a third space but also, like *khôra*, a polymorphous one that seeps into all that is living. She is, moreover, also a biologist who we see giving a lecture on evolution at the university and who posits an origin to life, sexuality, and death. She gives *place* in situating the abundance of images of *organismos acuáticos* (aquatic organisms) (to cite her own lecture): the sword-fish in Mercabarna (the Barcelona wholesale food market) and the goldfish in the transparent plastic bag on the Berlin subway train, which the members of the Catalan theater company La Fura dels Baus destroy. She presages the fate of her lover, who, after the final acrimonious disagreement with his friend, will die while diving, plucked out of the water by a firefighting plane, scooped out like a fish from a primeval lagoon, before being deposited amid soaked ashes into the virginal landscape of the burning forest. In terms of the displacements of the film, it is significant that Puente de Varsovia (the name of a bridge in Berlin) should end in an unidentified location somewhere in Catalonia—a *masia* (farmhouse)—far from the city, bounded by water and accessible only by ferry.

This watery, originary, elemental imagery (which Derrida calls "the genera of being"[12]) is coupled with that of screens: the mechanical canvas on which artificially generated images are projected and unfolding virtualities material-ize (reminiscent—a reverberating echo—of what Heidegger memorably terms "the mirror-play of the worlding world").[13] Derrida says of *khôra* that it is beyond or prior to the notion of the sign as representation. It "is neither of the order of the *eidos* nor of the order of mimemes, that is, of images of the *eidos* which come to imprint themselves in it."[14] Thus, by being neither a cognitive formulation—an idea—nor a mimetic resemblance, it must be that enigmatic space, chasm, or abyss between the thing and its image, between signifier and signified—the unfolding place of mise en abyme. Like *khôra*, the screen is an emitting receptacle—it receives, produces, and transmits (sends out) images, as if it were a conduit or a passageway (we might recall that among the other names that Plato denotes for *khôra* are womb and mother, arguably both also "emitting receptacles").

In an early sequence of *Puente de Varsovia*, Carles Santos emerges onto a busy pedestrian precinct in central Barcelona, climbs onto a pedestal, and conducts an orchestra dispersed along the street on terraces and balconies. However, the members of the orchestra are only able to follow his direc-tions through television monitors. They are thus, in a sense, out of place, or removed. Irrespective—or perhaps because—of its public character (Santos's diegetic performance is unmediated in its direct confrontation with the public), it is a virtual concert, both live and mechanically recorded. It is also a con-cert whose filming stresses the midway point between interiors and exteriors. Santos conducts in the open air, after having previously been the subject of a long take that followed him at ground level from an interior passageway to his ascendance onto the pedestal. Contrastingly, however, the musicians are spatially distributed in intermediary, threshold positions, sheltering in the apertures of windows or in the shadows of pillars. Further, the transmission of information—both transmitted and mediated—through screens from conductor to musician is musically skewed in the filming. What we witness in the musicians' playing is not only physically displaced but also discordant, because it is not synchronized with Santos's direction.[15] Such discordance, however, is coherent with the notion of musical disharmony and with the discontinuities of Portabella's oeuvre. *Puente de Varsovia* was, after all, Portabella's first full-length film in eleven years.

Portabella's 2007 feature, *El silencio antes de Bach* is, like *Puente de Varsovia*, a mise en abyme, though paradoxically, this aspect is more oblique while the film itself is more accessible than the earlier one. Here the play of spaces disappearing toward infinity directly concerns a European heritage. Indeed, Portabella in an interview referred to this as a Europe "full of empty spaces."[16] Traversed by the meandering River Elbe and the autobahns, it is a film that maps out the fault lines of that legacy. Rather than acknowledging a common or shared European identity, such as that forged in the bureaucratic arenas of Strasbourg or Brussels, the film suggests a dis/articulated, dis/jointed Europe whose legacy is subterranean, with an inheritance of found objects, winding passages, passed-on messages, turns and returns, senders and addressees, performative send-offs, and envois and renvois.

As in the earlier discussion of Puig Antich, absence is a key element in *El silencio antes de Bach*. An envoy by implication suggests an absence: that of the receiver. In this film, the envoy is present in the truck driver who appears early on. Although culturally specific—he spent a thousand euros to have the Virgin of the Macarena painted on the door of his cabin—the truck driver is a German-speaking Spanish bassoon player. His peripatetic existence is played out across trans-European highways and in service stations and motels. Music is something he has inherited: "We have always played music at home," he says. But beyond being a practitioner of music, he also transports pianos in his trailer.

Elsewhere in the film, Portabella dramatizes the old apocryphal story about Mendelssohn's discovery of the sheet music of Bach's *Saint Matthew's Passion*, used by his butcher to wrap up meat. There is a lineage here that stretches to the present and loops to the film's envoy and beyond, when the owner of the piano shop, the receiver for whom the truck driver works, quotes from Pasolini's *Orgia*. Pasolini would in turn film the *Gospel According to Saint Matthew*. Meanwhile, the piano dealer's lover will shortly embark on a journey from Barcelona to Leipzig, her cello slung across her back, to meet with the current cantor of Saint Thomas Church, the position that Bach himself once held and to whom she will be introduced by a supposedly "real" descendent of Bach (the descendent is an actor, while the cantor is, indeed, real). Amid the very authentically professional and personal or genetic heirs of Bach, in a film whose discourse often revolves around questions of the sacred, there is a chain of profane, erotic connections that connect music to an alternative Europe, an *other* Europe whose repeatable, iterable genealogies—the traces, those faint presences that mark absences—link Bach to Santos and Pasolini to Portabella. The iterable and itinerant envoys of *El silencio antes de Bach*, rather than reinforcing Spain's European heritage, mark absences that imply a fracturing of the bureaucratic unity inherent in the term *European Union*, suggesting a fragmented Europe whose skewed, seismic heart is Leipzig, the site of the Allied carpet bombing of Germany and the Holocaust.

The virtuality in *Puente de Varsovia* is evident in this paradoxical mixture of fiction and documentary (similar to the presence of Christopher Lee in *Umbracle*). In the grafting of fiction onto historical reality (as occurs in *Informe general*), the film generates an alternative reality or place: a *para-site*. The relation is parasitic in both senses: a virtual or spectral place and something that feeds off something else. Indeed, *Vampir-cuadecuc* is overtly parasitic in the customary sense of the word, in that it makes use of the actors, set, and the mise-en-scène of Jesús Franco's *Conde Drácula*, but it is also supplementary and virtual in its meditation on the materiality of cinema itself, its quality as a photonegative of the original. In this sense, the parasite is also mise en abyme.

More than thirty years ago, J. Hillis Miller described the parasite in a celebrated essay in terms that recall the previous discussion as "the screen which is at once a permeable membrane connecting inside and outside, confusing them with one another, allowing the outside in, making the inside out, dividing them but also forming an ambiguous transition between one and the other."[17] The parasite is akin to what elsewhere in the same essay Miller describes as "the hymeneal bond."[18] This bond between signified and signifier—a screen, veil, or membrane—is most evidently intimate in music. I am not the first to observe that music is the cultural field where the gap between representation and the represented is most indiscernible, fused and thus the cause of a certain Derridean con-fusion, where "there is no longer any textual difference between the image and the thing."[19] Music, in its very intangibility, suggests the kind of unfolding and doubling on itself that is implicit in *khôra*, in the space (the absence) at its core. In this void, Jacques Attali identifies music's connection with the primordial.[20]

Para, moreover, conjures an image of spatial remove, or a complex absence in the virtual relationship between sender and receiver, as in the musicians of *Puente de Varsovia* that Santos conducts, or the musician–truck driver, both infinitely deferring their points of origin or arrival. But perhaps here the fields of music and film also bind other associations. The continuities and discontinuities that form the collaborative bond between Santos and Portabella recall Michel Foucault's brief essay titled "Pierre Boulez, Passing through the Screen," in which the French thinker discusses the meeting that would lead to the lifelong friendship between Foucault and Boulez as "not an ideal kinship but the necessity of the conjuncture."[21] By this he means the conjoining of two friends at a historical conjuncture of the political and artistic avant-garde as well as other conjunctions and conjoinings—between words, image, and music. It is also an essay about disjuncture, about Boulez's and Foucault's break with the past,[22] implicitly about the violence at the heart of (and inherent in) Europe in its sacrifices. As with the case of the truck-driving musician whose sacred representation (the emblematic—heraldic perhaps—representation of the Virgin of the Macarena) belies a legacy of violence, the figures of the parasite and the sacrifice (recall the absent presence of Puig Antich in *El sopar*) by means of audio and visual representation—that is, of form and content—come together in signifying practice to produce contradictory but complementary meanings with regard to individual conjunctures and historical/geopolitical configurations.[23]

Santos's own musical heritage is located in multiple, unfolding sites. As a pianist, performance artist, and experimental filmmaker in his own right, he is as influenced by his former teacher John Cage as he is by Bach. Silence, for example, which is so central to *El sopar*, recalls the title of Cage's most significant book of essays and constitutes—as noted in the discussion of *Acció Santos*—a key sonic element of Santos's work. Credited as having introduced minimalism into Spain, Santos's style is distinguished by its repetitive, insistent, iterative rhythm and composition. Derrida has identified (in a suggestive but highly questionable claim) a common etymological link between *iter* from the Sanscrit *itera* and *alter* from the Greek *allos*: both mean other.[24] Once again (and as discussed in previous chapters), the *allos* of allegory is subverted. Perhaps, then, it is not too far-fetched, in the same spirit of free translation, to suggest that *khôra* has an additional similar relevance, in the very music itself, to *El silencio antes de Bach*. Bach was, as is the present incumbent at Saint Thomas's, the musical director of a choir, of a chorus, and this is a film packed with choral moments.

It is clear that the mise en abyme in these films is different from the mirror imagery that traditional film studies often identifies in cine noir. Here, it concerns the chain of dislocated European legacies from Bach and beyond to Carles Santos, from Pellissa to Portabella, and to the material receptacles of recursive imagery piped through screens, reproduced endlessly, and generating disappointment, disenchantment, disquiet, and an uncanny sense of being out of place. If, however, the original notion of mise en abyme comes from

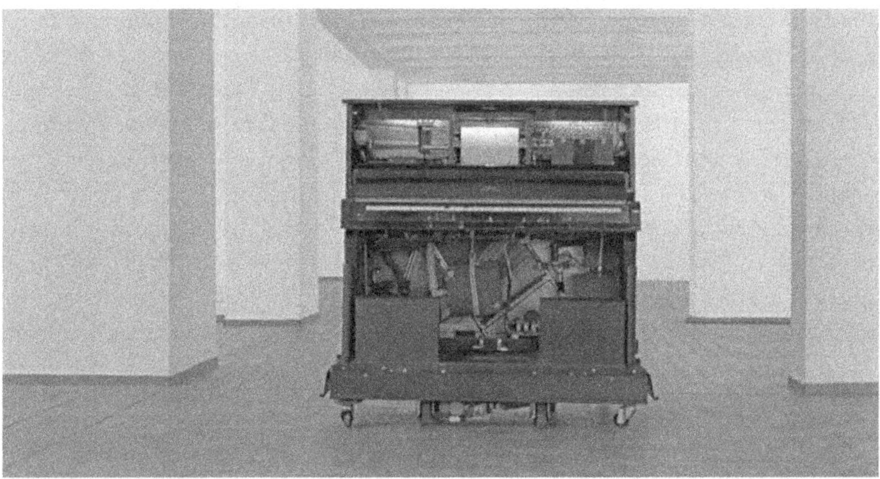

Fig. 3.2 The dancing piano in *El silencio antes de Bach*.

heraldry—the miniature reproduction of the shield within the shield (with a clear etymological connection to heritage)—and, therefore, an anachronism, then the legacies of Portabella are ana *choric*, para-sites, supplements of historical situations subject to infinite deferral. They also constitute a choreography (the origins of *khôra* refer to the Greek dancing ground called the *khoros*) of displacements within and beyond spatial confines and of discord among orders, whether they be national or conceptual, as suggested by the introductory eponymous Cagean sequence of *El silencio antes de Bach*: a silence, the empty white walls before the introductory chords of a dancing piano.

Coda: *Mudanza*

While the context of *El silencio antes de Bach* is that of a conflictive European legacy, that of Portabella's short film *Mudanza* (Removal) (2008) returns to the localized confines of Spain. Once again there is a piano—silent on this occasion—packed up, inert, and embalmed, its legs removed, shunted by machinery against the bare backdrop of textured walls. This twenty-minute film is coherent with its predecessors in that it involves a process of emptying out, vacating a space, creating an absence. It is also a film that intervenes in the current debate in Spain concerning national cultural memory, particularly regarding the losing side's most emblematic (and sacrificial) martyr, the poet and playwright Federico García Lorca. *Mudanza* was commissioned specifically for the "Everstill/Siempretodavía" exhibition at the García Lorca house museum in 2007 and received a limited public release in late 2009. This scriptless film records, in yet another meditation on techne, workers packing away the contents of the García Lorca family's summer residence in La Huerta de San Vicente in the province of Granada, so as to leave the building unencumbered for visitors to experience.

The process is elegiac. We are party to a work of mourning in the creation of a void to more fully appreciate the absent poet. The double absence, rather than reinforcing more absence, facilitates a presence. Formally, *Mudanza* is reminiscent of *Acció Santos*, the first film discussed in this chapter, in its play of visual and audio tracks. Indeed, *Mudanza* suggests a way in which, in hindsight, the earlier film might be interpreted politically. It is hesitant, almost tactile, in its focus on the texture of the vacated building, the whitewashed walls, the green window fittings, and the tiled floors that the imperceptibly slow-moving camera records. Likewise, the only noise we hear in the opening minutes of the film are the muffled sounds beyond the perimeters of the house, the rasping of sealing tape, and the workers' murmuring. The last third of *Mudanza*, however, as in *Acció Santos*, is recorded in silence as we tour the recently abandoned house and end up in a warehouse amid Lorca's evicted objects enshrouded in bubble wrap: the muted audibility of absence.

A key sequence in the film comes as we witness the process involved in the removal of a portrait of Lorca himself. Recalling the similar shot of the withdrawal of the portrait of Franco and Carmen Polo from the Generalitat described earlier in *Informe general* (shot thirty years previously), Lorca's own portrait is a representation, a sign, a substitute (a sacrifice). In this sequence, two workers embalm the painting in a plastic shroud before placing it in a wooden box, which is then nailed closed as if it were a coffin. I propose here, in conclusion, that *Mudanza* suggests that sacrifice is redeemable only by the removal of substitute objects, thus questioning the tendency of Spanish cultural memory to fetishize the figure of the victim.

The art historian Andrés Soria Olmedo, writing on Portabella's web page, has described *Mudanza* as a "still life" or, in its more apt Spanish translation, a *naturaleza muerta* (dead nature or a natural death).[25] Shot at the same time as efforts were under way (unsuccessfully) in Granada to exhume Lorca's body—to discover a previously hidden corporeal presence—the film confirms Soria's insight by making the poet's absence present, ghost-like and virtual. It is an evacuation of sorts amid the spaces generated by the film's representational play.

Notes

1. Jacques Derrida, *Dissemination*, trans. Barbara Johnson (Chicago: University of Chicago Press, 1981), 219.

2. Jacques Derrida, *Of Grammatology*, trans. Gayatri Chakravorty Spivak (Baltimore: Johns Hopkins University Press, 1976), 245.

3. See, for example, Augusto Martínez Torres and Vicente Molina-Foix's interview with Portabella originally published in *Nuestro Cine* 91 (November 1969) and reproduced in *Historias sin argumentos: El cine de Pere Portabella*, ed. Marcelo Expósito (Valencia, Spain: Museu d'Art Contemporani de Barcelona and Ediciones de la Mirada, 2001), 246.

4. Jacques Derrida, *Limited Inc.*, trans. Jeffrey Mehlman and Samuel Weber (Evanston, IL: Northwestern University Press, 1988), 116.

5. In 2016 Portabella released a documentary titled *Informe general II: El nuevo rapto de Europa*, a film that speculates on the possibilities of a new "constitutive process" in the aftermath of the 2008 crisis and the emergence of a new left-wing party in Spain called Podemos.

6. Josep Torrell, "Espejo de sí: Apuntes sobre *Umbracle*," in *Historias sin argumento: El cine de Pere Portabella*, ed. Marcelo Expósito (Valencia, Spain: Museu d'Art Contemporani de Barcelona and Ediciones de la Mirada, 2001), 323–24.

7. See, for example, Expósito, *Historias sin argumento*, 301.

8. Jacques Derrida, *On the Name*, ed. Thomas Dutoit (Stanford, CA: Stanford University Press, 1995).

9. Elizabeth Grosz, *Space, Time and Perversions: Essays on the Politics of Bodies* (London: Routledge, 1995), 116.

10. Ibid., 114.

11. Derrida, *On the Name*, 91.

12. Ibid., 95.

13. Quoted in J. Hillis Miller, "The Critic as Host," *Critical Inquiry* 3, no. 3 (Spring 1977): 445.

14. Derrida, *On the Name*, 95.

15. I am grateful to Susan Martin Márquez for drawing my attention to this point.

16. Pere Portabella, interview by Iris Martín-Peralta, "Entrevista a Pere Portabella," *LaHiguera*, July 8, 2007, http://www.lahiguera.net/cinemania/pelicula/3743/comentario.php.

17. Miller, "The Critic as Host," 441.

18. Ibid., 443.

19. Derrida, *Dissemination*, 209.

20. Jacques Attali, *Noise: The Political Economy of Music*, trans. Brian Massumi (Minneapolis: University of Minnesota Press, 1985), 27.

21. Mary Rorich, "Passing through the Screen: Pierre Boulez and Michel Foucault," *Journal of Literary Studies* 22, no. 3 (December 2006): 296–323.

22. Portabella has written of his friendship with Santos as forged in the political opposition to Francoism of the late 1960s and early 1970s. Expósito, *Historias sin argumento*, 113–20. Between 1970 and 1973, Santos stopped playing the piano as a form of political protest. Shortly after this period, Boulez and Foucault were politically allied in their opposition to the extradition of Red Army Faction lawyer Klaus Croissant from France to Germany. Michel Foucault, "Pierre Boulez, Passing through the Screen," in *Aesthetics, Method, and Epistemology*, ed. James D. Faubion (New York: The New Press, 1994), 241–44.

23. In this chain of associations, Derrida's use of the word *hymen* as that protective membrane or screen that both facilitates and impedes marriage marks both consummation and rupture. In *Dissemination*, Derrida draws attention to the musical element in this by reference to the hymeneal song of Greek and Roman mythology suggested in the

etymological proximity of hymn and hymen, in the closeness of the sacred and the profane: "First of all a sign of fusion, the consummation of a marriage, the identification of two beings, the confusion between two. Between the two, there is no longer difference but identity"—hence con-fusion. Derrida, *Dissemination*, 209.

24. Derrida, *Limited Inc.*, 7.

25. Andrés Soria Olmedo, "Naturaleza Muerta," on Pere Portabella's official website, January 22, 2010, http://www.pereportabella.com/es/textos/2010/01/naturaleza-muerta-es.

4

HISTORY, HAUNTOLOGY, REPRESENTATION

Spanish Cinema against Itself

THE HISTORICAL FILM TRADITIONALLY MAKES AUTHORITATIVE CLAIMS REGARDING cultural (or national) heritage. Indeed, the genre has been variously termed, at least in English, heritage film, period piece, or costume drama. This genre—for want of a better word—has since the early 1960s been of interest to not only film historians but also mainstream historians as a document of the past (and several books by professional historians draw on film). The historical film is a means by which the past can be represented, or rather the relation between past events and their filmic representation can be validated or staged in the name of historical authenticity, lending a *real* quality to the reenactment. Alternatively, such a relation can be considered symptomatic of a period, either as archival evidence or as allegory.[1]

The discipline of film history is an important institutional component of almost all university media and cinema studies departments. This is particularly true today, when digital conservation (and consequent expert verification) is not only possible but also vital. However, there are very few places in the world where film history is the dominant field in such departments. Spain is one of those places, and the dominance of film history there has little to do with film preservation. Nor does it share the doubts expressed by Fredric Jameson: "Above and beyond the problem of periodization and its categories, which are certainly in crisis today but which seem to be as indispensable as they are unsatisfactory for any kind of work in cultural study, the larger issue is that of *the representation of History itself*" (emphasis mine).[2] The importance of film history in Spain, does, however, have much to do with patrimony and the promotion, definition, and, above all, classification of a canon of national cinema. This leads to a near obsession with taxonomy and closure and the establishment of an order, or an official, immobile archive.[3] Evidence for this interest is provided by the number of dictionaries of Spanish cinema that are published on a seemingly annual basis. In Spain, film history is so dominant that, uniquely, anyone—myself included—who writes on film is interpellated as a film historian.

History has a particularly loaded resonance in Spain, and it is very much conditioned by the country's trajectory and the turbulent and difficult consolidation of modernity—the source, in part, of its claim to exceptionality—that culminated in the national trauma of the Spanish Civil War and the consequent dictatorship of Francisco Franco that lasted for nearly four decades. This conflictive history is, I suggest, the source for a particular kind of melancholia that still dominates film studies in Spain—an idea I will return to at the end of this chapter.[4] Vicente Sánchez Biosca—a Spanish film historian whose work I have great respect for—has observed that while the dictatorship sought to silence mention of the war and Francoism in film, the Transition and the restoration of democracy after 1978 also led to a cinema that initially went out of its way to avoid addressing the recent past. It was not until the 1990s when films about the war began to be made. Since then, there have been many, though they, too, might be termed on the whole as heritage films, turning either on anecdotes, hidden history, or biographical detail.[5]

"We see, here, how our present divides itself," writes Jacques Derrida, "the living present is itself divided. From now on, it bears death within itself and reinscribes in its own immediacy what ought as it were to survive it. It divides itself, in its life, between its life and its afterlife, without which there would be no image, no recording. There would be no archive without this dehiscence, without this divisibility of the living present which bears its spector within itself. Spector, which is to say *phantasma*, ghost (*revenant*) or possible image of the image."[6] While this chapter does not seek to engage with debates concerning the philosophy of history (other than incidentally), it turns on this concept of spectrality and the doubled image together with the notion of what Wendy Brown (who, as we will see, makes a cogent argument about melancholia) terms "contested historiography." It is an unsettled, unexhausted, and ongoing history that projects the traces of the past not only into the present but into the future as well. It proposes a fluid, mobile, unpredictable archive.

I offer an alternative historiographical operation that emerges from a structure of traces that, instead of justifying genealogical unity, seeks to generate uncertainty and discord. I will read four films, each distinguished by a historical charge but with very different registers, in order to present a fractal idea of the historical genre. (As an aside, I note that each of these films can only loosely be described as Spanish.) First, I discuss two Catalan films: Lluis Miñarro's *Stella cadente* and *Història de la meva mort* directed by Albert Serra, whose apparent subject matter has, contrary to the dominant teleology, little to do with the Civil War or the dictatorship. I then analyze works by two less-established directors: Óskar Alegría's documentary *La casa de Emak Bakia* (shot mainly in the Basque language Euskera) and *Crumbs*, a film directed by Miguel Llansó that was shot in Ethiopia and set in an imaginary and postapocalyptic future.

My proposition is that these—at times arguably—historical films destabilize the very genre of the historical film, and, in doing so, they not only call into question the way nation is represented on-screen and the constituent elements of national cinema but also interrogate the premises of the heritage film itself. Indeed, spectrality, the figure of which lurks behind historiography, poses a challenge to all forms of order, of which classification—the archive and genre— is exemplary and symptomatic of the melancholia to which I refer.[7] In the face of assuredly packaged historical narratives and the cultural nationalism of many Spanish film historians, I am interested in disharmony, precariousness, and fractured identities. I suggest, first, that pastness is staged performatively (albeit differently in each film) and, second, that the relation between past and present is not a straightforward movement ahead in time; rather, in the spirit of the previous chapter, it is represented, once again in undecidable terms, as an impossible bond.

To this end, I explore in the context of the historical film how a combination of two apparently contradictory terms as outlined in this book's introduction— an impossible bond—might contribute to my reading: *tele* from the Greek, meaning distance, or the space between communicating, relaying parties, and *telos* (also from Greek), meaning an end, culmination, goal, or purpose. I will return to this later, but here I suggest that what Derrida calls "teletechnologies" disturb temporality and thwart efforts (such as periodization) to bring about closure. I am interested in the encounter or opening, framed within an interval, between what Hannah Arendt once described as the "no longer" and "not yet."[8] At least one inescapable fact of the historical film is its relation to the event— that moment of significance in the past that changes the continual flow of time, alters popular feeling, or transforms political regimes.

The first two films discussed in this chapter have a singularity to them. They are singular within the generic as well as in their dealing with singular historical shifts. That is, they feature a "crisis of time" and temporality.[9] Each in its different way touches on the historical event from the sidelines, from the margins, and, significantly, from the periphery of the nation-state. History in these two films is both off-centered and decentered. While *Stella cadente* is located amid political crisis (and furthermore national crisis), in *Història de la meva mort*, the sense of crisis concerns the limit, the borderline that marks a historical change in European sensibility. Both films were made by Catalans and were shot in Catalan. The original DVD of Serra's film was released only with subtitles in English and French. And it is significant that all four films discussed in this chapter involve different permutations of arrival—unrealized, frustrated, and inconclusive. This, too, as we will see, concerns temporality and technology, telos and *tele*.

Stella cadente (Falling star) (2014)

Stella cadente is a tongue-in-cheek biopic of the brief reign of Amadeo de Saboya, who was invited from his native Turin to occupy the Spanish crown in 1870 by General Juan Prim (who was killed shortly after Amadeo's arrival). Running counter to the normative generic conventions of historical drama, *Stella cadente* is a luscious, louche artifice located in a time lapse; it is painterly, literary, full of strange sex and explicit depictions of bodily functions; it is dominated by still-life-like bowls of fruit that rots in sluggish, putrefying rhythm with the languid, stagnant, stilled movement of the film itself. Nothing much happens on-screen, just as little happened in historical reality (except for the stark choice facing Amadeo between what film journalist Neil Young calls "assassination or abdication," which we are periodically reminded of).[10]

Everything about the film suggests a historical interlude. It is, indeed, the story of an emergency, a monarchy as stop-gap measure. It is the story of a king who whiles away time, locked and isolated in his castle and removed from the people he is supposed to rule, subject to the machinations of fluctuating cliques of devious and capricious politicians. Meanwhile, in the distance, we hear the reports of bombs and the murmur of rioting mobs in the streets of Madrid. The monarchy of Amadeo de Saboya was brief. It lasted three years, from 1870 to 1873, before he abdicated and returned to Italy. The film—confined in its entirety, like the king himself, to the inner walls of the palace chambers and the surrounding gardens—captures the decadence and entropy of its epoch. It depicts the historical exhaustion of the period and the sense of an impending ending, poised at the brink (like the falling star of its title), at the twilight of an age on the verge of dissolution.

Stella cadente calls itself, in the introductory credits, an "entertainment" (a *divertimiento*—a diversion, a word that suggests both fun and a parting of the ways from convention). And it might otherwise be just that—a glossy and glib visual tour de force—were it not for the pure coincidence of the historical moment of its release. In an ironic twist of historical chance, but one that conjures the ghosts of the past into the present and the future, I first saw this film in Madrid the day after it premiered on June 2, 2014. That same morning, King Juan Carlos I of Spain announced he was abdicating the throne. Immediately after the screening, I caught the subway from the movie theater to the city's central square, La Puerta del Sol, squeezing through the turnstile to join the impromptu demonstration calling for the abolition of the monarchy, just as the police were trying to close the station to prevent further arrivals. This personal anecdote exemplifies the complexities of the relation between present-day reality and historical representation of the past. It calls attention to a certain ghostliness of parallel stories set apart by time, decadent regimes founded on archaic systems of order, popular upheaval, time out of joint, and the past impinging on the present and vice versa. There is a tellingly filmic overlaying of the past with the present in a spectral superimposition, which suggests a different relation between cultural representation and historical reality: of being and nonbeing and of ontology and hauntology.

Queer studies have pried the departures from heteronormativity away from questions of identity. Queer studies is emphatically not a new name for what was previously termed gay and lesbian studies. In this vein, we might say that all historical film is always already queered, because it is a question of re-creating the past by dressing up. In this way, historical film flies in the face of historicist approaches to film.[11] The queer is an apt mode for the off-centering of history. We might also say that historical film is always haunted in that its frame of reference is often (though not always) that of a period before the invention of film itself. This suggests an intimate connection between queer theory and hauntology. Formally, *Stella cadente* queers the conventions—the normativity and genre[12]—of the traditional heritage film in its comic depiction of a camp monarchy whose court is riven by sex and consumption. It is a genuine art film whose mise-en-scène is densely packed with references to an erotic pictorial tradition (Francisco Goya, Édouard Manet, Emil Nolde, Gustave Courbet—a Courbet masculinized, by the way), literature (Charles Baudelaire, Giacomo Leopardi, brothers Wilhelm and Jacob Grimm, Joris-Karl Huysmans), and a music wrenched from its time—ana-chronically—by the film's recourse to 1960s French pop melodies and outbreaks of dance (in the vein of films of the early 2000s such as *Marie Antoinette*, *L'Apollonide*, and *Moulin Rouge*).

The music, which is heterogeneous to both history and the genre, conjures an out-of-joint soundscape and a queered futurity; temporality is disturbed by incongruously kitsch departures. Amadeo at one point learns via a letter left behind by his wife, María Victoria, that she has abandoned him and returned to Italy (see fig. 4.1). In what might be described as a temporal mash-up, we see a curious example of representational crisis (at a moment of political crisis) in the combination of epistolary distance and filmic simultaneity portrayed by two people who are separate from each other. The sequence moves in rapid and

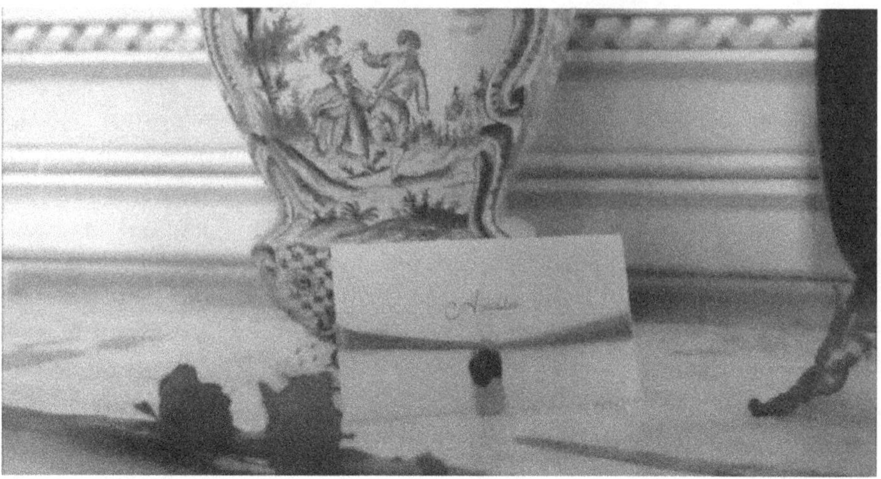

Fig. 4.1 María Victoria's letter to Amadeo.

fluid succession from the close-up of the letter and María Victoria's voice-over to the superimposed dance and pop music.

This perfunctory and startlingly comic sequence heralding the royal couple's separation posits a number of formal points that interrogate the complexity of temporality and spacing in terms of film style and technique in that they upturn notions of telos and *tele* in ways that are specific to the moving image itself. The superimposition of the second image (see fig. 4.2) immediately suggests a spectral simultaneity with an immaterial presence seemingly represented in material terms as artifice. In a film that deals with pause, or an apparent parenthesis in the historical continuum, here we have a distinctively filmic (or photographic) imprint in the form of an instantaneous image of an impossible unity (that of the couple) at the precise moment of their separation. But the paradox—the imprint or trace—is the product of a specific technology. Meanwhile, the postal motif points to *tele* in a serialized movement of juxtaposition generated by the physical distance between the two characters and the incongruent discrepancies between voice-over and personage, the written word and the voice, and the period and the soundtrack. Contrary to—and barely compatible with—the notion of juxtaposition, the envelope itself is an element that turns in on itself, suggestively binding the superimposed text/voice-over in its fold.

In a film in which alterity is primary, the division between Amadeo and María Victoria—hitherto a kernel of disturbance at the heart of the nation and the court—presented as unity confirms the queering already noted in the historical genre. The heterosexual couple here—in a state of being undone—is the

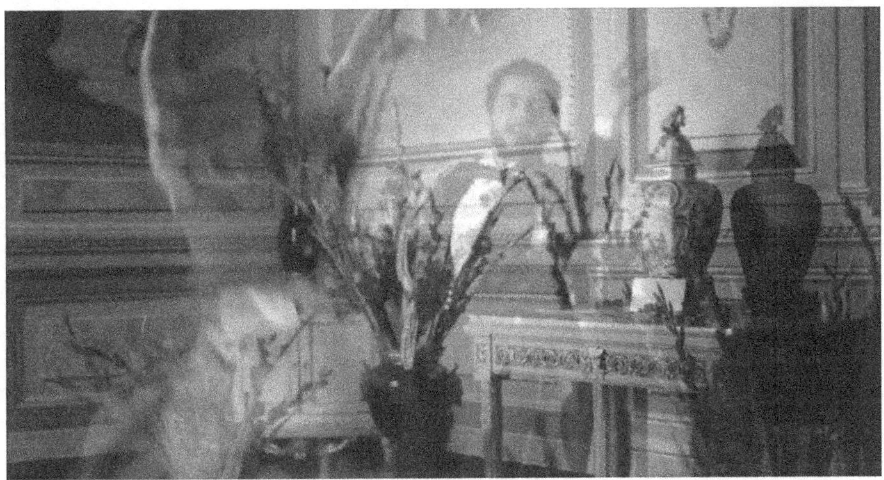

Fig. 4.2 Distance and proximity: the superimposed image of Amadeo and María Victoria dancing.

site of a queerness expressed in terms that are artificial. The impossibility of superimposition is clearly not what we customarily associate with realism. It is an example of the technologically uncanny, supplementary to nature, supernatural. The normal, the norms or rules of the real, are subject to constant questioning in a series of shifting ontologies that include those of monogamy, heterosexuality, and national identity. The encounter between these two apparently antagonistic movements—the immediacy, simultaneity, or nowness of superimposition and the progressive frame-by-frame displacements of juxtaposition—creates a distinctive tension, or aporia, between spatialization and temporalization.

In an essay on André Bazin's short text "The Life and Death of Superimposition," Daniel Morgan comments, "The topic of superimposition is, for Bazin, an occasion for one of his sustained attempts to criticize and undo the influence of the 'pure cinema' movement in 1920s France."[13] I have already addressed the question of impurity and intermediality in chapter 2, and later in this chapter I will return to the work of one of the exponents of "pure cinema," Man Ray. For the theorists of 1920s French film, superimposition was the uniquely cinematic means by which film could articulate thought: Morgan quotes Germaine Dulac: "'Superimposition is thinking, the inner life.'" In the same passage, Morgan continues: "Rather than a way to represent mental states on screen, Dulac suggests that superimposition itself constitutes cinematic thought: the act of bringing two layers of images together is in itself a way of thinking in and with cinema."[14] The idea contrasts with that of Sergei Eisenstein, who argued for a form of montage based on juxtaposition in a kind of filmic corollary to the Hegelian dialectic—on which Spain's film historians justify their own teleology. The combination here of layering and sequential progression disturbed by the letter, the envelope, and the superimposition characteristic of the cinematography indicates the spatialization of time and the temporalization of space that Derrida terms *différance*. *Différance* is also characterized by its insistence on a critical departure from all normativity, the kind of disturbance that is associated with the queer.

This disturbance is exacerbated by the anthropomorphic presence of animals in the film (other *beings*, or what Derrida once dubbed "biological *genres*"[15]): the rabbits that are chained to the dining table and then set free to roam the house and the palace kitchen, the bejeweled tortoise (a reference to Huysmans's late nineteenth-century novel of decadence, *A Rebours*[16]), and a dazzling blue-tailed peacock that hops onto the hapless monarch's bed. Also present are dream sequences that feverishly punctuate Amadeo's rarefied confinement; an exuberance of flowers and fruit; and an explicitly queer gaze in the abundance of waist-high shots of male groins, the masculine version of Courbet's *L'origine du monde* (labeled as such on-screen), the carnal, fleshy cook, and the presence and leading roles of well-known gay actors. The *cadente* of the film's title (and its cadence) is in the decadence, the de-cadence, de-falling (neither falling nor unfalling) as a synonym for the queer, the gentle swaying, unpredictable decadence of Amadeo's household under house arrest.

The overall effect is a kind of *détournement* of the heritage film, a queering of the already queered genre that directly addresses the ironies of the national question. While how to represent the nation is the key feature of institutional Spanish film studies, a feature that manifests itself in the claims that Spanish culture (and particularly film) possesses a unique capacity to assimilate and absorb difference (and thereby dilute it), *Stella cadente* presents in its mise-en-scène a filmic aesthetic in which history and historical circumstances are mobilized in ways that combine to undo the contradiction between form and content; between the film's visual image, its narrative, and its soundscape; and between on-screen action and off-screen reality. And in the undoing, it generates a bond between incompatibilities.

As if to condense the film's style with its screenplay, it is notable that Amadeo's diagnosis of Spain's malaise—ignored by government officials—is accurate and was ironically resolved in historical reality only by the Spanish Civil War nearly seventy years later. In this sense, *Stella cadente* is a film set in the future anterior haunted by ghosts that come back from its own future. The concept of parenthesis (the state that best describes Amadeo's interim monarchy) also functions or recurs in the formal structure of the film, which is bookended by two brief soliloquies delivered directly to the camera by Amadeo, the sidelined man of state. Both—from the outer boundaries of the film itself—address the national.

Història de la meva mort (2013)

Aside from being largely unconcerned with national trauma other than from the margins, *Stella cadente* and *Història de la meva mort* (The history of my death) have little in common thematically. They do, however, share a similar mise-en-scène. Both historical films are notable for their extraordinary lighting and photography (Jimmy Gimferrer was the cinematographer on both films),[17] and the films were released within a year of each other. Albert Serra's film, however, is not only *not* located within the Spanish state; it does not even mention Spain. This director (whose previous films, incidentally, were produced by Lluis Miñarro) turns his back on the national question altogether. Yet both films are, in a sense, equally parenthetical—that is, they both exist in parentheses.

Serra's cinema has long been seen as preoccupied with the temporal zone of dead time (Serra is very much associated with the so-called slow cinema movement). His films invariably focus on what the Harvard film archive gloss that accompanied the screenings there in 2009 termed as "overdetermined" figures from literature and legend (Don Quixote, the Magi, and, in this film, Casanova and Dracula). Serra's cinema is that of delay and deferral. His first full-length film, *Honor de cavalleria*, explores what Don Quixote and Sancho Panza do when they are not participating in heroic deeds, dramatic action, and tilting at windmills or engaging in courtship fantasy. Rather than interrupting time, Serra's films occupy the very space of the interruption; his films *are* pauses, the parenthesis itself. But in the same vein, they are also conjunctions. Like pauses, they are connective passages or transitions between moments in time. Yet, paradoxically, those times seem never to connect, and the transit is the place of an action—or inaction—that never reaches its destination. Time is the single most important element interrogated in Serra's films. His earlier work sought to pose filmic temporalities in dialogic tension with the claims to timelessness (fiction, myth, etc.), and his recent work has turned to history itself.

Història de la meva mort is a film perched on the precipice of a shift in historical sensibility that divides the age of Illustration from the Romantic period. This film occupies the space between the two, laying out, in a Benjaminian vein, a radiographic skein of the landscape of transition. Its title puns on the title of Casanova's memoirs, *The History of My Life*. What has been characterized as Casanova versus Dracula—reason versus the irrational, machines (erotic machines and writing machines, among them) versus animalistic impulses, intellect or science versus religion and superstition—transpires to be located in the void between those oppositions (the space, perhaps, of the historical event) rather than a staging or reenactment of such encounters. It is located in the gap between the life of Casanova's memoirs and death, the *mort* of Serra's film in a life span bracketed between different modes of representation. These function as heterogeneous elements held together and in place by a spectral bond.

The style of the film is marked by languor and length. Its rhythm lags (this is the source of much criticism of Serra in both this and his earlier films, but that this is precisely the point: his is a cinema of slack, of nondiscursive time). There is in this a spacing, an aperture (like the opening of a parenthesis) that marks a site of overlap between differences, the continuity of discontinuity, time discontinued and folded in on itself, in which the destination of its movement is questioned. Derrida once termed this "tele—without telos. Finality without end."[18]

Serra mobilizes the mode of historical film in order to discuss the material quality of temporality. History is not represented; nor is it a representation of period, say, in the vein of Jameson. Rather, it is an interrogation of the very premises that lead us to such classification; it is a film of temporal crisis. Like the pause itself, it simply *is* (at the aporetic brink of the transitional moment in historical time between the Enlightenment and Romanticism). It is, in a sense, performative cinema; that is, a kind of performative pastness (rather than a performance *of* pastness), which, in its reinterpretation of the past, transforms the same past in the interpretation.

Whereas *Stella cadente* disturbs time with its incongruous 1960s soundtrack that impossibly locates the film ninety years into the future, *Història de la meva mort* foregrounds the atavistic, the primitive, the ritualized, and particularly the sacrifice. The sacrifice is sacred and representational. As discussed in the previous chapter, it stands in for something else or acts on behalf of something or someone. In a spectacular sequence toward the end of the film, villagers sacrifice an ox. The village is near the farmhouse where Casanova and his manservant Pompeu are staying south of the Carpathian Mountains. Pompeu remarks that the ox resembles the Minotaur.

There is talk about young girls that have gone missing. The girls have, it is inferred, fallen into the clutches of a vampire. Though vampires are indexed by the motif of blood and the Romanian setting, the word *vampire* is never mentioned in the film. Incidentally, the name of Dracula is never mentioned either; he is portrayed as a peculiarly marginal, uncharismatic character closely associated with savage, primal nature, compared to the sophisticated Montaigne and Voltaire-reading Casanova. These characters are, notably, not the

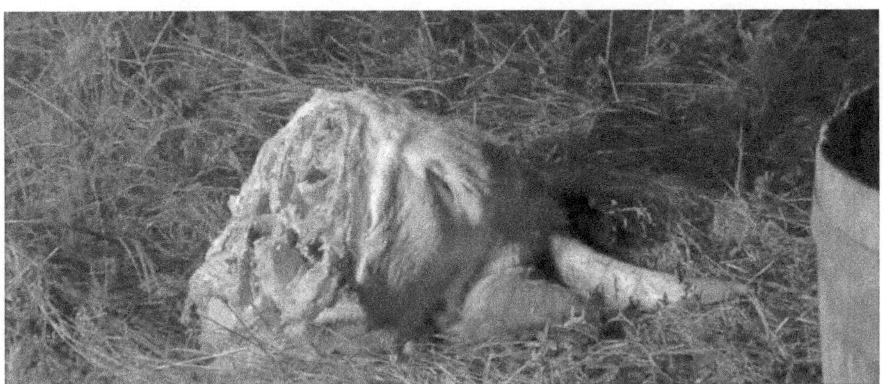

Fig. 4.3 The remains of the sacrificial ox in Serra's *Historia de la meva mort.*

personifications of their respective ages. Though located at the limit of epochal change, history here is defined and constituted by traces rather than by its horizon.

Casanova responds to Pompeu's mythological reference—as if to disavow representation in the historical charge of the transitional moment or, rather, to insist on its performative quality—with the words, "We are done with allegories." Sacrifice is a performative form of representation. It is something sent to appease or to placate the other as a substitute to maintain the order of things. The irony is that the film itself works against such order. The taciturn Pompeu and the loquacious Casanova offer a metacommentary on the action they observe (see fig. 4.3). Here the sacrifice is subtle, not expressed as such. Its atavistic quality suggests recursiveness, something sent back, as if *tele*-directed from its prior destination like an envoy returned from a previous time— ana-chronically—the *pre* of sent, here resuscitated, relayed, re-pre-sented. There is a sense in this sequence of the sacrifice, of myth, and of the originary out-of-history event. This sense is reinforced by the music that accompanies the images: a rhythmic, guttural rumbling; a vibrating tremor emerging from the bowels of the ground, from the very core of the earth. It is tremulous, primal, primordial, arcane, and, I would venture, pre-mimetic.

La casa de Emak Bakia (2012)

It is this crisis of representation—the pre-mimetic archaic, or the *arche*-trace, together with reference to Bazin's realist ontology—that I turn to now.[19] This discussion explores the idea of the spectral distance—the *tele*—that which separates and links but which is also already there—present before the present—in advance of being there (the *pre* of re-pre-sentation). Mark Fisher in his K-Punk blog describes the phenomenon in the following terms: "Hauntology," he writes, "isn't about the return of the past, but about the fact that the origin was already spectral."[20] Óskar Alegría's *La casa de Emak Bakia* (The house of Emak Bakia) is a film about luck, fortune, and making a film constituted by poetic chance—or what the director terms "accidental cinema." This film about the history of experimental film involves a search for and recovery of a lost name.

Names identify, of course; they are signs of identity. Names bring things into existence and give a kind of life to objects. The identificatory name becomes diffuse and dispersed across a singular geography marked by the division between life and death. And *La casa de Emak Bakia* blurs that line dividing life and death. This is a film about that hazy, indeterminate demarcation. The final sequences of the film tellingly play witness to the restoration of the original name of the historical house that features throughout the film. Workers are filmed installing stones carved with the words "Emak Bakia" above the entrance and at the gate, the threshold, of the house in question and its precinct. In a film in which gravestones figure significantly, the name here involves an act of engraving. As this finale—an epilogue of sorts—suggests, *La casa de Emak Bakia* is a film about all kinds of legacies and about film history as legacy, in which false closure and subsequent reopening loom large. In the last shot of the film, the lens cover closes the camera in a "finality without end," reminiscent of the "Sin fin" endings to Val del Omar's films discussed in chapter 1. In this film about a series of legacies, those legacies are shown to be discontinuous, disrupted, and disruptive in ways cultural, linguistic, national, and international. The filmic project here seeks to uncover those legacies, and this film unburies, or disinters, a turbulent inheritance.

Alegría's film is a cinephile's quest to find the source of his avant-garde antecedent, Man Ray's "cinepoeme" *Emak Bakia*. The earlier work was shot in 1926, reputedly in and around Biarritz, in a house located in the nearby town of Bidart in the French Basque Country. As suggested above, *La casa de Emak Bakía* is essentially about death and its prolongations, its multiple afterlives. A first version of the origins of the title of Man Ray's film proves apocryphal. *Emak bakia* (meaning "leave me in peace" in the Basque language, Euskera) was purportedly the epitaph on a local gravestone. The film discourses on many deaths: uncanny deaths, resurrections, cheating death, immortality, and finalities without ends. It is also a film about the trace of death, of which the tombstone on the grave and the stone bearing the carved name of the house are just two of many examples. These examples highlight the relation between trace and techne and thus the relation between the grave of engraving and the graphic sign of the written word grafted into the stone.

In the course of his peripatetic investigation, Alegría tracks down a retired clown whose tomb is in Biarritz. A photographic image of the man in a traditional clown suit imprinted in stone is one of the filmmaker's accidental discoveries during his visit to the municipal cemetery at the commencement of the project. This discovery, in turn, inspires a cinephilic disquisition on Fellini's theory on the immortality of clowns. As if to confirm Fellini, this clown, Raymond Hermann, is, it transpires, contrary to the evidence in the town cemetery, very much still alive. His past, a forty-year career as a clown, and his future, his tomb, are written, or engraved, on his grave. Or maybe, like the nameless Dracula-like figure in Albert Serra's film or Christopher Lee in *Umbracle*, Hermann belongs to the living dead. He thanks Alegría for having resuscitated him. In the site/cite of the resus *cita*tion, Hermann is disinterred, decrypted, as it were, in defiance of the ins *crypt*ion on his own tombstone.

Appropriate to the spirit of Man Ray's work, the swirling diffusion of the name Emak Bakia concentrates to form the mobile eye of a maelstrom in Alegría's film. The film notes that, in the 1980s, the most celebrated of contemporary Basque-language writers, Bernardo Atxaga (together with musician Ruper Ordorika, also interviewed in the film), founded the small press Emak Bakia Baita (The house of Emak Bakia) in homage to Man Ray, with the mission of publishing avant-garde works. Alegría accompanies Atxaga to an exhibition of Ray's photographs, which, at the insistence of Atxaga, they see in the dark, illuminated only by a flashlight. The eerie images emerge ghost-like from the pitch black of the gallery, stark and ghoulish against the wall.

This haunting is given an additional dimension by the film's soundtrack. In 1997, two experimental musicians, members of the Madrid-based group Migala, initiated a project they called Emak Bakia: "A perfect name with which to baptize a project concerning imperfect music," read Alegría's explanatory intertitles. Fifteen years later, the same musicians collaborated with Alegría. The music of the film consists of recordings of the traces of the house: wraiths of sound drifting in from the ocean; tapped-out rhythms on the wood-paneled columns; the creaking stairwell; the crash of the knocker on the main door; the spooks in the cupboards; the rattle of cutlery, plates, and keys; the haunting flow of running water; and the squeaks of secret nooks and crannies of the old house. These sounds were then mixed and put to music.

The articulations of the building, the very joints that hold the house in place, give new meaning to the notion of out-of-joint time; a signification that maps the history of the house itself. The sound of billiard balls scurrying across green velvet and the screech of rusty figures of table football remind us that today the house serves as a holiday home for French trade unionists. Such games have replaced the ballrooms of the Romanian aristocrats who built the house. One of the themes of the Emak Bakia project initiated by the musicians of Migala is called "Canción rumana" (Romanian song). The experimentalism at work here, the music pried from beneath the floorboards, is a variation of what Fisher, writing again under the moniker K-Punk, calls "sonic hauntology."[21] There is in this, moreover, a suggestion of the performative speech act: "The idea that the self-same house should compose its own soundtrack," in the words of the musicians.

Alegría follows a circuitous trace structure of references (not only footage from Man Ray's films or inscriptions on graves but also cemetery registers, archival photographs, letters, town records, and old postcards), each of which—together with the film's incidental musical accompaniment—leads richly to other oblique referrals and *renvois* that expand the meandering circuit. Abel Hernández, who made the recordings and is interviewed in the film, defines the concerns of the musical project as having more to do with working practices and incidental discoveries made than any kind of final result. This methodology reflects, in turn, Alegría's patchwork historiography, the series of displacements and contretemps he experiences as we accompany him on his journey through southern France, on a trajectory in which the convoluted, winding map traced out on the topography matters more than the ultimate destination. It is a voyage determined by fortune and luck and coincidence and happenstance and one that never achieves full closure.[22] Within this expansive referential structure, prewar Europe condenses in the Atlantic coastal border area, the southern corner that defines the outer limits of—and the liminal space between—Spain and France. Bidart is on the threshold of the concept of nation, at its margins both geographically and linguistically. Many of the interviewees in *La casa de Emak Bakia* speak Euskera and regard with bemusement the near obsolete and moribund phrase, *emak bakia*.

Alegría's engagement with Man Ray (who, like his French contemporaries, Geraldine Dulac among them, defined his film work as "pure cinema") pulls all these elements together in a filmic correspondence over the distance of time that is charged by this ghost-ridden location. Figures 4.4a and 4.4b highlight the complex differential interplay of traces between sameness and difference suggested by the filmic engagement's play on deferral and difference—*différance*. Among other things, we see the spectral reenactment of the ninety-two-year-old exiled Romanian princess, María Despina zu Sayn-Wittgenstein, who spent summers in the house as a child (before it was requisitioned by the Nazis during World War II) in parallel with the original footage of Man Ray's film. Once again, a carved stone—a cornerstone whose design is etched at the base of the column of the house terrace—provides evidence of similarity, of haunted place.

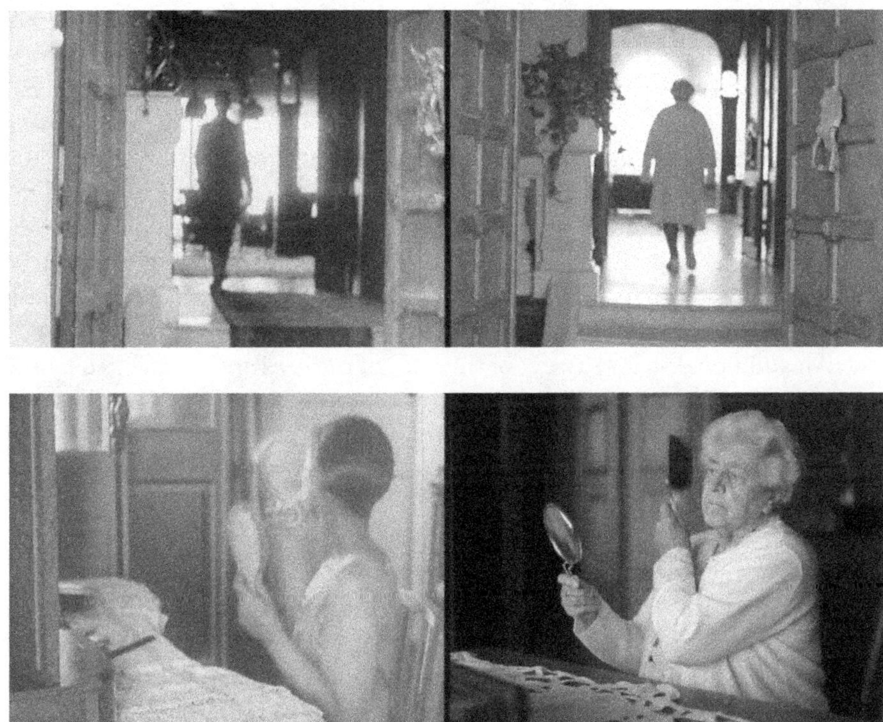

Fig. 4.4 a–b Man Ray's original stills in parallel with Óskar Alegría's in *La casa de Emak Bakia*.

The impossible newness, the simultaneity of superimposition of *Stella cadente* is here represented in the form of the split screen. It is noteworthy that the two techniques are specific to visual (as opposed to written) technology.[23] The earlier image from *Stella cadente* of the apparently simultaneous shot of Amadeo and his wife, María Victoria, in different places and at different times reveals the significance of teletechnology in this kind of representation. As I will discuss later in this book, Derrida insists that what we assume to be simultaneity or "liveness" is, in fact, always already deferred. The Derridean "living on"—with all the connotations of supplementarity contained in the word *survival*—might also be deferred liveness, an almost imperceptible supplanting of immediacy. Robert Trumbull puts this notion succinctly: "Since every moment passes away as soon as it arrives, any and every moment of experience, in order to 'be' at all, is necessarily defined by a repeating process of retention open to the next moment, to the future."[24] The fold in time that so interests Serra, the pop aesthetic of the superimposition in Miñarro's films, and the fortuitous bolt of lightning whose light lives on after it has struck in Alegría's work all point to the trace, or what Trumbull calls "the secondary retention of a past present." This is an afterimage or "imprint of something that is no longer, retained for a future to come." In other words, Derrida maintains (and this is a key element in Trumbull's paper), such retention, or the aftereffect of the immediate present—the instant—prompts its survival, the living on, via iteration, of the present into the future. This is the framework of Derrida's interest in teletechnologies as producing or generating this deferral of ending indefinitely, the deferral of any arrival. This is a future marked by irresolution rather than synthesis, by the not yet, by the process of becoming, by the perhaps.[25]

An additional spatial aspect of this idea of the *arrivant* is suggested by the first of the parallel screen photograms reproduced in figure 4.5. The stills show an entrance, a doorway. This shot, haunted by the predecessor that it imitates, is a gateway to both the past (the filmic legacy), European conflict, and an opening to the new world, the Atlantic horizon, the other side from whence Man Ray originated. Like the *sur* of survival, of living on, this supplementary space is a spectral geography of spatial history between past and future.

To clarify this notion, we might recall the parenthesis, the spacing, the *différance* discussed earlier. This is given form here in the frame of the two columns that mark the means by which the house is identified (through the original Man Ray film). There is, though, discordance in the staged similarity of these images, a rupturing disjoining of temporalities (historical and filmic) held together in the framing—that of the mise-en-scène marked by the mnemonic of the stone pillars and that of the borders of the photogram that open out to an unknown beyond. There is also perhaps a hint of Benjamin's celebrated revolutionary "blast" that opens the gates of the future for the messiah to pass through.

The Romanian princess recalls the night when she was a small child and the roof of the house was damaged during a storm, a fortuitous act of luck in the spirit of Alegría's accidental cinema. Her recollection presages a later storm in 1960, when a bolt of lightning destroyed the roof of the house.

"It isn't that the past casts its light on the present or the present casts its light on the past: rather, an image is that in which the *Then* and the *Now* come into a constellation like a flash of lightning," writes Walter Benjamin.[26] It is in this encounter between past and present that the aporia of time, the spacing, becomes evident, frozen and taut in dialectical tension.

Limitrophy and liminality, difference in the realm of the same, contamination of the pure—the fields that *La casa de Emak Bakia* explores—are, of course, also the terrains of the queer. The film features a lost house whose original name has faded into oblivion, set on a promontory facing the Atlantic

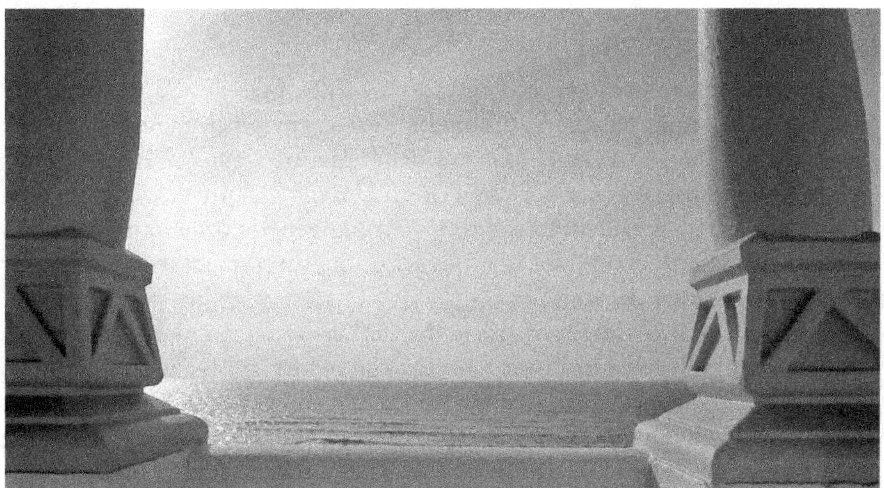

Fig. 4.5 The borders of the photogram and the gates to the future.

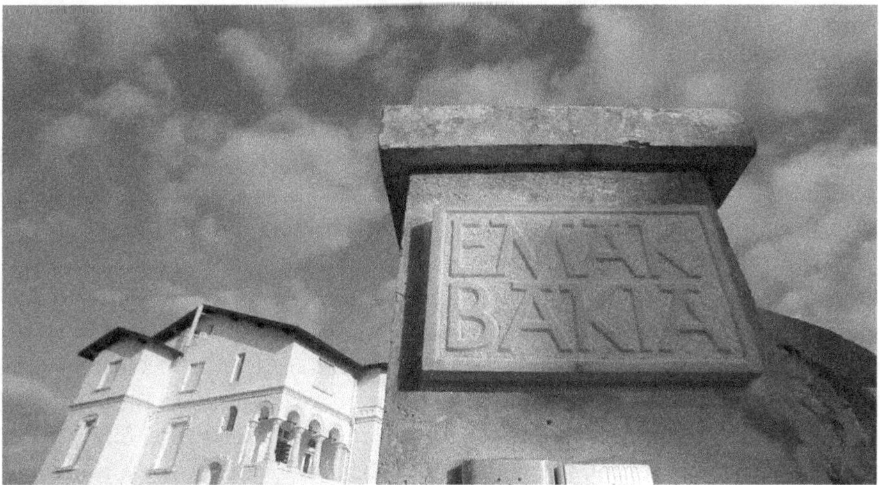

Fig. 4.6 The name en*grave*d.

on the far-flung fringes of Europe bracketed between two films from different discordant times, in a no-man's land of *différance*, within the parentheses of France and Spain, identifying with neither. The "impure," contaminated cinema of *La casa de Emak Bakia* directs our attention to the trace of history itself in the flecks, the debris of nondiscursive history, the mobile archive that eludes closure, and the differentiating arche-trace of hauntology.

Crumbs (2015)

The trace structure that connects the past with the present and the future to form a constellation of different temporalities at any given moment is never more evident than in Miguel Llansó's debut feature *Crumbs*. While almost universally dubbed a genre film by critics, *Crumbs* is, in fact, about impossible returns, incommensurable loss, unsettling generic order, and temporal disruption. *Crumbs*, moreover, is a film set in the supplement itself, in the *sur* of survival, life after the end.

Beyond the boundaries of either the nation-state or, indeed, of Europe, *Crumbs* is a film located in a time after the end of history, in a postapocalyptic world. A futurist tale, a science fiction film, a love story between outcast freaks, a road movie—it is all of these and more. Indeed, the promiscuous borrowing from filmic convention constitutes one of its key characteristics and presumably the reason why it has been classified as a genre film. Shot in Ethiopia with Ethiopian actors, the film follows the quest of Candy (Daniel Tadesse) to seek help from the godlike figure of "Santa Claus" to ascend to the spaceship that lingers omnipresent and shadowy in the haze of the sky, and which, it appears, has sparked to life once more after lying dormant for an indefinite length of time. This spaceship is the means by which Candy can return to the anonymous planet he and his companion Birdy (Selem Tesfaye) believe they come from. They are others in an alien world, extraterrestrials of mythical origins, of which they have no apparent memory.

The film is structured around Candy's trajectory through and across a series of otherworldly landscapes: lunar desert; lush and dense jungle greenery, the trees of which are populated by primates; and the urban wastelands of dereliction and dystopia, with abandoned buildings, machines, and vehicles. Nature is counterposed here to history. Candy and Birdy inhabit a lost bowling alley in the midst of the overgrowth of the encroaching forest in the shadow of a Ferris wheel, the trace of a forsaken fairground. In this strange, oxymoronic world of past and future, the natural and the artificial, and the melancholic hybrid of loss and the ludic, the easily spooked and physically deformed Candy ekes out a meager existence as a kind of Benjaminian ragpicker and accidental archeologist amid burnt-out wrecks of the detritus of war while dodging a menacing predator attired in Nazi garb and a gas mask.

The remains of the preapocalyptic world's material culture pepper the film (scattered like the film's eponymous crumbs), whether as trivial artifacts of a distant past—*our* tawdry present, with plastic trinkets, children's toys, and vinyl records—or a faux theology, with a popular religion that parodies Christianity as Candy and Birdy pray at the shrine of Michael Jordan, Birdy dreams of

Saint Pablo Picasso, one of the great creators of the distant past was the French supermarket chain Carrefour, and Candy carries a cheap amulet for protection. Popular twentieth- and twenty-first-century consumer icons have become "mythical." This combination of the archaic and the futuristic suggests a kind of dyschronia, a dyslexic kind of confusion of the dimensions of temporality, and a queering of time in which nostalgia and the elegiac cancel each other out. The present proves to be a slippery journey in constant movement and is never, in fact, present. Time is queered by Candy's crippled errancy.[27] This deviation or diverting of time is another variation on the anxious elusiveness of the now. *Crumbs* is not an allegory of our times, and neither is it a period piece. It defies the traditional historical mode by its otherness, with its imprecise futurity and the Ethiopian setting.

The present moment (of the film) is as fleeting and errant as Candy himself. Such deferral often turns on Candy's twisted body. Continually thwarted, having to negotiate and occasionally resort to futile (and self-defeating) violence, Candy's body is the site of the disjunction in the film's (half-serious) discourse on masculinity. He is a physical ruin wandering amid desolate wastelands and ruins, silhouetted beneath a merciless sun hunched against the sky, bearing a plastic Christmas tree in the crook of his arms, crossing volcanic lava fields spewing steamy malodorous pestilence. When he seeks to purloin a train and, on failing, is obliged to find his way by following the railroad tracks on foot, it transpires that the tracks are as warped and contorted as his spinal column.[28]

Candy's ungainly and misshapen body that undoes masculinity confirms the underlying queerness of the film, which is associated with the strange artifice of attributing value. In a wry parody (albeit an accurate one) of Marxist economics, the kitsch objects of the material past that are fetishized with a religious aura are given an arbitrary economic value by the subterranean pawnbroker to whom Candy sells his discoveries and whose iterative choral function in the film establishes him as a pivotal figure. The film's singular form of sampling bolsters the uncanniness of the pawnbroker's unscrupulous wielding of power through economics. As discussed in more detail later, the archive of pop culture at work in the film is a queer recourse. If Óskar Alegría's cinephilia draws on the historical avant-garde, Llansó looks, in this alternative archive, to that most unlikely of kitsch models of masculinity, the Turkish superman film *Supermen Dönüyor*, shot by Kunt Talgar in 1979. From the projection booth of a rundown movie theater Candy frequented as a child that endlessly screens the same film, Candy—his warped torso encased in the Superman T-shirt he believes gives him special powers—finds his foil and inspiration.

Candy's voyage involves trespassing on the property of others, crossing boundaries, and venturing into unknown, dangerous territory. Eve Sedgwick

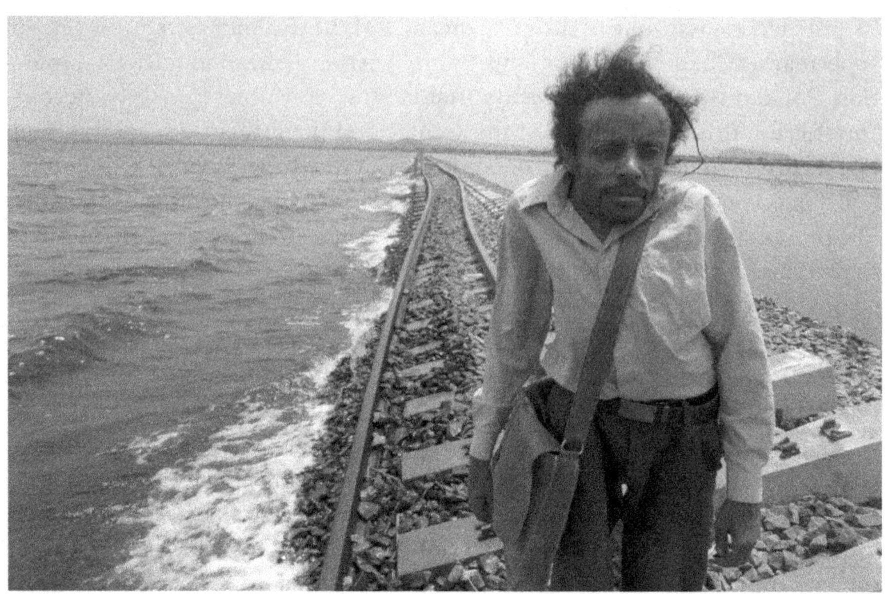

Fig. 4.7 Candy, whose spine is as twisted as the railroad tracks.

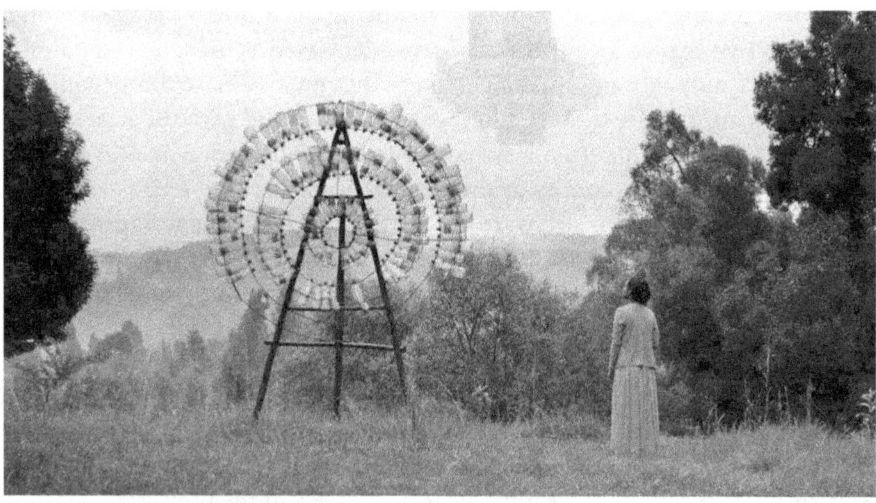

Fig. 4.8 The abandoned fairground in *Crumbs*.

reminds us that the word *queer* derives from *across* ("it comes from the Indo-European root *twerkw* which also yields the German *quer* [transverse], Latin *torquere* [to twist], English *athwart*").[29] There is a correspondence between the torsions of Candy's body and the noxious spaces he traverses. Just as the idea of a route to a destination, an arrival—so fundamental to teleological approaches to history—is complicated by the twisted railroad tracks, there is another suggestion of communicative fluctuation. From the shadows of the abandoned bowling alley where she awaits Candy, Birdy has a connection to Santa Claus via a tube, a black hole, the once-defunct mechanism that suddenly springs to life to deliver up bowling balls from its innards. This passage short-circuits distance and circumvents conventional telecommunication. Likewise, Birdy's restless slumber gives way to a form of telepathy, a sonic dreamscape that seeps from sleep to consciousness by which she converses with Santa Claus. These oneiric sequences add to the unsettled tone of the film and the voice of the other, disembodied, distorted, warbling, and phantasmal, in the mutedly hysterical murmurs of lost children and of other presences (from the past or the future) that linger and languish in the tunnel and are lost in the transmission—the screech of birds or bats and the hiss and crackle of electronic interference.

Amid the kaleidoscopic array of visual sampling at work in this film, the soundtrack is significant. Llansó deploys an insistent musical refrain, "Libet's Delay" from the concept album *An Empty Bliss Beyond This World*, produced by the ambient electronic musician The Caretaker (the artistic name of James Leyland Kirby), who specializes in sampling himself. Functioning as a mnemonic, the song's iteration is emblematic of the film as a whole in its haunting intonation, honeyed, sickly sweet, and aching with yearning. This melody returns each time trinkets are exchanged for money with the film's exploitative pawnbroker, only for the same trinkets to reappear orbiting the curvature of the planet Earth in a recurring shot overlaid by the pawnbroker's voice-over, in a clear low-grade allusion to Stanley Kubrick's *2001: A Space Odyssey*.

Leyland Kirby has made a career out of plumbing the ghostly effects of the musical archive, and the use in *Crumbs* of The Caretaker's work is particularly interesting in that—like Migala's Emak Bakia project—it complicates questions of cultural memory. Memory in this conceptualization is a field distinct from traditional historiography.[30] In the evocative soundtrack and in the film itself, memory conjures up nostalgia and longing. It is, though, a nostalgia of the future—what Jameson has called a "future anterior." Eclectic appropriations from a projected archive are drawn from the past and our contemporary present. However, unlike Jameson's claims that such work's operation of "estrangement and renewal" involves "the brutal transformation of a realistic representation of the present,"[31] here the register of supplementary futurity—life after the end—unsettles that past and present and challenges the realist basis for the historical genre.[32] By mobilizing such fragments, the archive disturbs rather than confirms temporal order, and it does so by distinguishing between history and memory and by complicating the mode of nostalgia. Musical sampling (and the same is applicable to film), John Doe says on *Dissensus*, is a form of "disinternment" (an echo here of the clown's story in *La casa de Emak Bakia*) "of styles, sounds, even techniques and modes of production now abandoned, forgotten or erased by history."[33]

Candy, who makes his living as a gleaner or scrap collector, embodies the fractured form of the film itself. Here, the ghostly melody released from the archive, from the crypt, is, while disinterred, simultaneously encrypted. The loss it expresses is intangible and discomforting. It evokes a false memory, homesickness for a past that has never been experienced by the film's protagonists, a fetishization of memory. In a world reduced to a wasteland and lost to nuclear catastrophe, a mysterious other planet about which we know nothing except for Birdy's and Candy's apparent desire to return to it, kitsch tack substitutes for value (the culmination of the commodity fetish), and a nostalgic charge runs throughout the film in the absence of the object of nostalgia.

The musical refrain alternates with the acoustics of the rain forest, rusty machinery, the stuttering start-up of the trains, and the mechanism of the bowling alley cranking hesitantly to life after years of disrepair and disuse. The sound is of dereliction, decay, and the disarticulation and disjoining of the masonry and structure of buildings and time itself. Disjuncture is the film's register; it is the crumbs that fall from the table as shreds, cast-offs, and leftovers. Sound, in this way, confirms the dyschronia mentioned earlier. Like time itself, its discord fragments and fractures around the rural and the urban and around the twenty-first century and the film's undated future, melodious and jarring, diegetic and off-screen, natural and synthetically produced. It is, as we have seen before, the technological uncanny.

The film's final shot shows the spaceship hurtling into the infinitesimal black space with Birdy and Candy aboard, only to explode, lighting up the sky in splintering sparks of fire—yet another destination, another arrival thwarted and eclipsed. *Crumbs* is, despite its comic tone, a mordant and dark film. Its historicity is queered. The sample of the sentimental croon "Libet's Delay," the ambient music haunted by the 1940s and 1950s, suggests "the period of classic science fiction films,"[34] often set in small-town America at the height of the Cold War, whose population was terrified of nuclear destruction. It was never located in Ethiopia. *Crumbs*'s otherness, its queerness, while historically grounded, defies the genre it embraces. The queer produces a cleavage with the film's claim to present a recognizable relation to contemporary reality (this is not a Jamesonian allegory of the present, and there is no discernible "collective unconscious" to be unveiled here[35]) while retaining the trace structure whose seepage delineates its historicity. Like Candy's spinal column, the contours of *Crumbs'* order swerve; nostalgia is denied its sepia filter. It is a film of misalignment and discordance, out of its time and out of place.

Coda: Against Closure: "Left Melancholia," Historical Discourse, and Spanish Film Studies

Much of this chapter concerns loss. I began with a critique of the historicism of the dominant trend in Spanish film studies: of film history as hegemonic within the academic field in Spain and how its dominance determines and distorts the shape of the discipline and has stunted its potential for intellectual development. In short, my complaint turns on the reasons that Spanish film theory has barely evolved since the latter days of the dictatorship (beyond the routine and untheorized deployment of such obligatory terms of contemporary discourse as *cultural studies* or *transnationalism*). The examples I cited stress the way that classification and categorization in the name of history have come to define a national canon and its limits. There is no doubt that the origins of this insistence on national film history commenced with the best of intentions: to rescue Spanish film from the distortions of Francoism and to introduce a theoretical analysis of the contemporaneous cultural situation precisely at a moment of crisis in the regime.[36] I suggest, nevertheless, in concluding this chapter that the enduring consequences of this are paradoxical. The failure to adapt to new times, new complexities, and, accordingly, new theoretical paradigms has produced a distinctive kind of melancholia, attributable to a singular generation of film scholarship in the Spanish state that has left a baleful legacy in its wake.

The modern history of Spain has unquestionably been defined by a series of defeats and losses (from the loss of Spain's last colonies in 1898 to the Civil War and the dictatorship). It is equally true that almost all the principle exponents of the historicist discourse in Spain have their origins in the anti-Francoist underground. Many of the leading figures in this discourse were militants in various clandestine leftist groups of the 1960s and 1970s.[37] It is no coincidence that the paralysis in their thought occurs around 1975, the year Franco died. By monopolizing the discussion ever since, such traditionalists (and I use the word in the sense of Benjamin's critique of progressive historiography) have come to stifle meaningful intellectual exchange both with the world outside the Spanish state and with their younger, more cosmopolitan counterparts within it. This is a different kind of anachronism from the productive one of the films discussed above. It is significant that the historicization of the dominant discourse is never itself historicized. In a scathing 1929 review of Erich Kästner's poetry, Walter Benjamin wrote of "left melancholia"—a term later taken up by Wendy Brown and, in a somewhat different way, by Enzo Traverso[38]—to describe the narcissism of certain leftists who cling to past heroics at all costs. In doing so, they risk losing sight of developments in the present, thereby failing to understand the full implications produced by the constellation of relations between past and present.

"Left melancholy," writes Brown, "is Benjamin's name for a mournful, conservative, backward-looking attachment to feelings, analyses, or relations that have become fetishized and frozen in the heart of the critic."[39] For Spanish film historians, it is not so much that time has not moved on, nor that they have no sense of the presence of the past in the present; it is more the case that the kind of disturbance that queer studies or hauntological approaches propose undermines the grounds on which the foundations of their perspective, their archive, is constructed. Against this melancholia, this chapter offers what might be called an "outlaw" reading of a diverse set of films that, in very different ways, offer a queer assault on the discursive foundations of the nation and its orders. The discussion focuses on incompletion, supplementarity, the parenthesis, the spatialization of time, and the temporalization of space. It looks toward an incalculable future that beckons, a becoming and a promise. The event in Benjamin is precisely that moment of potential transformation. In the words of Mark Fisher (again under the guise of K-Punk), "The 'spectre that haunted Europe' was not, after all, a returning revenant, but the avatar of the new."[40]

Notes

1. Fictional film also occasionally serves as historical documentation in its own right. I think here of Gilles Pontecorvo's *Operación ogro* (1979), based on the assassination in December 1973 of the then Spanish prime minister Carrero Blanco. The film's images of Carrero Blanco's car flying into the air have been used on many occasions but perhaps most significantly in Victoria Prego's televised series on the Transition that ran in the mid-1990s and that has come to establish the official historical narrative. Here the fictional or dramatized reenactment of real events has become a document testifying to those events themselves.

2. Fredric Jameson, *The Political Unconscious* (Ithaca, NY: Cornell University Press, 1981), 13.

3. One possible translation of the word *arche* is its reference to order. Part of my argument in this chapter is to complicate the word *archive* in the sense of ordering.

4. I want to make clear that my critique here is of neither film history as a discipline in its totality nor all Spanish film historians.

5. As noted in this book's introduction (in the discussion of *Vida en sombras*), such efforts to eradicate the war from film were not entirely successful. Víctor Erice's *El espíritu*

de la colmena (1973)—generally held to be one of the finest films in Spanish film history—is set in the immediate postwar period and concerns the overwhelming sense of fear and repression of that time.

6. Jacques Derrida and Bernard Stiegler, *Echographies of Television: Filmed Interviews* (Oxford: Polity Press, 2002), 51.

7. Wendy Brown, *Politics Out of History* (Princeton, NJ: Princeton University Press, 2001), 152.

8. Hannah Arendt, *Between Past and Future: Eight Exercises in Political Thought* (Harmondsworth, UK: Penguin, 1993), 9.

9. François Hartog, *Regimes of Historicity: Presentism and the Experience of Time* (New York: Columbia University Press, 2015), 16.

10. Neil Young, "Falling Star (Stella cadente): Rotterdam Review," *Hollywood Reporter*, February 6, 2014, http://www.hollywoodreporter.com/review/falling-star-stella-cadente -rotterdam-677765.

11. This observation owes much to conversations with my colleague Heidi Schlippackhe.

12. I doubt that I am the first person to observe that the Spanish word *género* means both genre and gender, a translation significant to this film.

13. Daniel Morgan, "The Afterlife of Superimposition," in *Opening Bazin: Postwar Film Theory and Its Afterlife*, ed. Dudley Andrew (Oxford: Oxford University Press, 2011), 128.

14. Ibid.

15. Jacques Derrida, "The Law of Genre," *Critical Inquiry* 7, no. 1 (Autumn 1980): 55–81.

16. I am grateful to my student Dag "Sasha" Lindskog for drawing this to my attention.

17. Gimferrer has a spectral role in *Stella cadente*, too. He not only is the film's cinematographer but also plays the corpse of General Prim (whose sole and logically silent role involves occupying a coffin for a few seconds).

18. Jacques Derrida, *The Post Card: From Socrates to Freud and Beyond*, trans. Alan Bass (Chicago: University of Chicago Press, 1987), 341.

19. In my view, Serra, like many of his contemporaries, is highly influenced by the filmmakers of the French New Wave. However, this influence takes a unique turn in Serra's work. Self-conscious acknowledgements of this legacy are found not only in his references (the most celebrated being the casting of Jean-Pierre Léaud in *La muerte de Louis XIV*, 2016) but also in his methodology, with the earlier films clearly influenced by the prescriptions of Bazin (the religious aspects, the influence of Rossellini, the use of nonprofessional actors, and the emphasis on the shoot). Indeed, in his essay on superimposition, Bazin writes, "The supernatural phenomena are essential to verisimilitude." André Bazin, "The Life and Death of Superimposition," trans. Bert Cardullo, *Film-Philosophy* 6, no. 1 (January 2002), http:// www.film-philosophy.com/vol6-2002/n1bazin.

20. Mark Fisher, "Phonograph Blues," *K-Punk* (blog), October 19, 2006, http://k-punk .abstractdynamics.org/archives/008535.html.

21. Ibid.

22. This emphasis on chance is, of course, a reference (sometimes explicitly so) to Man Ray's interest in his films to questions of luck. This is particularly the case of *Les Mystères du Chateau du Dé*.

23. Notwithstanding this fact, the written word is important in this film, both in terms of the intertitles that serve to explain the film's narrative and in the diegesis: the carved words, the names of houses, and the words of Man Ray's own intertitles.

24. Robert Trumbull, unpublished paper "Seeing and Believing: Derrida on Faith and the Moving Image," presented at the annual meeting of the American Comparative Literature

Association, Harvard University, March 2016. I am grateful to Dr. Trumbull for allowing me to read a draft copy of this paper.

25. I discuss the notion of the *hap* later in this book, especially in chapter 7.

26. Quoted in Brown, *Politics Out of History*, 166. The quote from Brown differs in some respects from Howard Eiland and Kevin McLaughlin's translation of *The Arcades Project*. For the purposes of filmic relevance, I have used Brown's source.

27. I have in mind here Eve Kovosky Sedgwick's comments in the foreword to *Tendencies*: "Queer is a continuing moment, movement, motive—recurrent, eddying, *troublant*." Eve Kovosky Sedgwick, *Tendencies* (Durham, NC: Duke University Press, 1993), xii.

28. I am grateful to Ronald Mendoza for pointing out to me that the figure of Benjamin's automaton in the first of the Theses on History is also, like Candy, a hunchback.

29. Sedgwick, *Tendencies*, xii.

30. Arguably, the term *historical memory*—much favored in Spain over that of *cultural memory*—is an oxymoron.

31. Fredric Jameson, *Postmodernism, or, The Cultural Logic of Late Capitalism* (Durham, NC: Duke University Press, 1992), 285.

32. There are many examples of this, but one in particular at which I was present was a panel at the Asociación Internacional de Literatura y Cine Espanoles Siglo XXI conference in Soria, Spain, July 2015, organized by Josetxo Cerdán and Miguel Fernández Labayen.

33. John Doe, "Sweet Virginia," *Dissensus*, October 10, 2006, http://www.dissensus.com /showthread.php?p=63263#post63263.

34. Jameson, *Postmodernism*, 283.

35. Ibid., 296.

36. It was very much in the spirit of the 1967 Sitges conference.

37. I am thinking particularly here of the Marta Hernández Collective (the members of which were Julio Pérez Perucha, Francisco Llinás, and Carlos y David Pérez Merinero, joined occasionally by Javier Maquia), and the later group constituted by some of the members of the collective around the journal *Contracampo*. Despite the obscure ideological origins of these groupings, their unquestionable minority status (they rarely number more than a handful of individuals), and the enormous changes in Spain over the last forty years, their influence persists. In recent years, younger scholars, often students of the former members of these groups, have published books and edited collections of articles from this period. In none of these is there so much as a hint of criticism. See Jenaro Talens and Santos Zunzunegui, eds, *Contracampo: Ensayos sobre teoría e historia del cine*, introduction by Asier Aranzubia Cob (Madrid: Cátedra, 2007) and Imanol Zumalde Arregi, *Camino de expiación: Travesías y derroteros de nuestra reflexión historiográfica* (Madrid: Liceus, 2007).

38. Enzo Traverso, *Left-Wing Melancholia: Marxism, History, and Memory* (New York: Columbia University Press, 2016).

39. Brown, *Politics Out of History*, 170.

40. Mark Fisher, "Hauntology in Dublin," *K-Punk* (blog), December 14, 2006, http:// k-punk.abstractdynamics.org/archives/008780.html.

5

THE *EX* OF EXPERIMENTATION
Against Periodization

THE TITLE OF THIS CHAPTER ECHOES THAT OF Akira Mizuta Lippit's insightful book *Ex-Cinema*, in which he draws attention to the double signification of the prefix *ex-* as outside and as former.[1] That is, it has both spatial and temporal connotations. The end of the 1960s and the first half of the 1970s saw the emergence in Spain of several young experimental cineastes—José Antonio Maenza, Adolfo Arrieta, Antonio Artero, Jesús Garay, and Antoni Padrós, among many others—whose work, even as experiment, has been largely overlooked by critical writing. I discuss some of these filmmakers elsewhere in this book, but here I focus particularly on work produced during the 1970s—often proclaimed to be *the* decade of experimental film in Spain and elsewhere. P. Adams Sitney devotes an entire chapter to the 1970s in his *Visionary Film: The American Avant-Garde, 1943–2000*, a book widely held to be the benchmark volume on independent cinema.

The apparent indifference demonstrated toward, or the ignorance regarding, the body of work in Spain that I analyze in this chapter owes much to (1) how difficult it is to access the films and (2) the fact that the films of these experimentalists stand at odds with the dominant (albeit invariably politically oppositional) avant-garde filmmaking of the time. The priorities of this period were focused on the imminent death of the dictator Francisco Franco and the country's uncertain future. In ways not dissimilar to the charges of dilettantism leveled at the members of the Barcelona School discussed in chapter 1, the filmmakers discussed here (Padrós, Gonzalo García Pelayo, and Arrieta) tend not to engage directly in political discourse. These cineastes are distinguished, in their own very different ways, by the marginal status that has led, until recently, to their near invisibility. With the express purpose of questioning such periodization, this chapter examines the work of three of these filmmakers from the 1970s as both exceptional and exemplary of the age.

Antoni Padrós, Accidental Experimentalist

Antoni Padrós is a discordant voice among discordancy. Contemporaneous with the filmmakers of the Barcelona School, Padrós found—or established—himself as a peripheral figure, both aesthetically and geographically. Born in Terrassa, a small town in the province of Barcelona where he continues to live, he spent his entire working life until retirement as a bank clerk despite his promising beginnings as a painter. His filmmaking took place on weekends, during vacations, and at night. Indeed, in his free time during the afternoons after work, he studied for two years at the Barcelona Aixalà school set up by Pere Portabella, where his teachers included Portabella, Román Gubern, and various members of the Barcelona School. In interviews, however, Padrós has insisted that he was never a fully integrated member of the group either socially or professionally and rarely participated in Aixelà's collective film projects because he always had to leave early to return to Terrassa to go to work at the bank the next day. Joan M. Minguet aptly describes Padrós as the Bartleby of Spanish and Catalan film: both a part and apart.[2]

Together with the notion of the experiment, the prefix *ex-* is applicable to Padrós's keen sense of exclusion, exterior, and exile (albeit self-imposed), his outsider status. The word *part*, meanwhile, captures a sense of metonymy, partialization, separation, residue, remains, and leftovers. These things are important in terms of both Padrós's filmmaking aesthetic and the material apparatus employed in the filmic process itself. *Ex* also suggests a Padrós in the corner, as it were, looking on from the sidelines, from the margins of the margins, as not only an eccentric figure but an *ex*-centric one. To quote Jacques Derrida in a different context, Padrós is a partialized figure who "centers . . . in a periphery." Interestingly, Derrida is referring to Paul de Man's definition of allegory as "the defective cornerstone of the entire system," which Derrida, in turn, redefines as "the most effective cornerstone. As a cornerstone, it supports it [the entire system] however rickety it may be, and brings together at a single point all its forces and tensions."[3]

Amid the few critical commentaries of Padrós's work, there has been a tendency to think of his films as allegorical of the Francoist regime. Padrós attributes to Vicente Molina Foix, for example, a text written to accompany a screening in London of *Shirley Temple Story* (1976) (a film that engages directly with the 1939 film version of the *Wizard of Oz*). Molina Foix makes the claim that the Emerald City of Padrós's film is Spain, and the Wizard of Oz represents Franco. It is perhaps understandable to read into these films in this way (and they do unquestionably engage in a form of political discourse, albeit from the sidelines); otherwise, they would be utterly incomprehensible. But in contrast to literal readings such as Molina Foix's, which seek to identify allegorical properties, this chapter offers, in the spirit of Derrida and de Man (and, indeed, of Padrós himself), a lateral reading of the two full-length features Padrós made in the 1970s.

There is, though, another aspect to this discussion. The codification of temporality—periodization—is itself, like allegory and clearly related to it, a form of representation. If the 1970s, as has been claimed, was the decade of Spanish experimental film, Padrós marks its most extreme limits. Like de Man's "defective cornerstone," Padrós's work destabilizes the order of the construction from within. I argue in my reading of the two films that their formal experimentation turns on the disruption of the relation between the ex- and the in-, the exterior and the interior. The entirety of Padros's body of work disturbs the coherence of periodized order. His films actively disavow the critical representation that has sought to locate them (even today) within a temporal period. Bookended by *Vampir-Cuadecuc* (1970) and Iván Zulueta's *Arrebato* (1979), the construction of the 1970s as the key period in Spanish underground filmmaking conceives of formal innovation as a correlate to political and social transformation. The ruptures signaled by experimentation have been interpreted as corresponding allegorically with the decline of the Francoist state, as noted in the earlier discussion of Portabella's *Nocturno 29*.

Irrespective of the interesting features of this pattern, I am concerned here with prolepsis, the foreshadowing of filmic representation of the first half of the decade—and in a sense the foreclosure—of the impending historical events. I prefer to think of this disturbance in temporality as a disturbance of the conceptualization of allegorical representation itself, as the same kind of closure contained in the impulse to categorize by period. Much highly influential writing within Spain on film (and other cultural production) has set about defining periods, decades, or, more commonly, generations (1898, 1927, etc.) in order to ground its critical reason. The example of Antoni Padrós's exceptionality challenges that kind of periodization, if only because it involves the kind of metonymic partialization, the classificatory slippage or seepage, and the excess associated with Padrós himself.

Finally, and connected again to periodization, before discussing the films, I highlight the experimental nature of Padrós's work and his filmic antecedents. Unlike many of his contemporaries (and this is what occupies most of Adams Sitney's chapter on the 1970s),[4] Padrós does not engage intellectually in formal cinematic experiment, in the sense of a concern with rhythm or illumination, as oblique paracinematic materialities bound up with myth, mathematics, or metaphysics, in the way of contemporaneous North American filmmakers, such as Hollis Frampton. By this I mean he does not reject narrative in favor of form. His films do tell stories, and their formal innovations are more consequences of circumstances. While Padrós's contemporaries, such as Antonio Arteta and Javier Aguirre, investigated structural questions of materiality, optical illusion, and screen space, Padrós's use of material makes him an experimentalist almost by accident. Previously, Portabella had experimented with the visual effects of sound negative when employed to produce visual film images. As noted in the discussion of *Nocturno 29*, the high-contrast results, together with the graininess of the celluloid, produced an effect aesthetically similar to that favored by the German expressionist filmmakers. Although very much substandard material, sound negative celluloid was by far the cheapest, and, unlike Portabella, who deployed it for aesthetic purposes, Padrós was obliged out of sheer economic necessity to use it. It gives his films their singular texture.

Padrós's influences, on the other hand, are found in German cinema, both of the expressionist period and among his contemporaries in the New German Cinema. Pop art, and particularly Andy Warhol, also left a mark on his work (a decade before Pedro Almodóvar). The jokey, erotic transgressions (the early short *Ice Cream* [1970] is clearly genealogically connected to Warhol's notorious 1964 *Blow Job*); the scatological; the tongue-in-cheek mocking of intellectuals, professional leftists, and committed "militant" filmmakers (Portabella himself, as we will see, is the occasional object of Padrós's barbs); the flippancy; and the delight in the superficial all owe something to Warhol. So, too, do Padrós's experiments with time in the form of repetitions, reversals, flashbacks, and insufferable length. Warhol is also found in Padrós's ironic use of icons of popular culture (such as James Dean, Che Guevara, and Marilyn Monroe)—homage as sabotage, to use Mery Cuesta's description—mobilized (and banalized) by the market of mass reproduction.[5] Padrós's background as a painter (also greatly influenced by pop art) informs the composition of his frames, the mise-en-scène, and the wry deployment of trompe l'oeil.

Lock-out *(1973)*

Padrós's first full-length feature is 1973's *Lock-out*. The word *out* in the film's title suggests exclusion, and the first sequence is a long interior take, a diegetic hint at the play on *in* and *out*, interior and exterior, that has a particular bearing on this film. This first sequence is one of only two interior sequences in the entire piece. The second one, which leads to the film's crescendo and denouement in the final section (shot in a series of long takes) dwells on the architectonics of a stairwell in a building that has fallen into dereliction and disrepair. The interiors, thus, function as parentheses that filmically delineate the borders of the film. Rather than following a coherent narrative of a written text, *Lock-out* follows a musical pattern, which is often bolstered by operatic accompaniment. The lengthy single take of the film's prologue moves through the luxurious surrounds of an empty palace. The shot recalls a Visconti film in its focus on the details of the lavish furniture, upholstery, and nineteenth-century material wealth. This scene of opulence is brought to a sharp halt by the sound of off-screen marching "outside" and the discharge of the rifles of a firing squad. This is followed by the film's title sequence.

Lock-out focuses on a group of people who have opted out of society and chosen to live in a garbage dump. Rita is a former prostitute, Rosa is a factory worker, María is pregnant and largely indifferent to the political-cultural debates ongoing around her, Paco is María's partner, and Walter is an Anarchist. Each of these main characters is bound by the confines of his or her own cypher-like definition. They are, in this sense, human metonyms—representatives of both the film's form and content—voices and bodies attached, ensnared, fraught, and awkwardly trapped in the roles that define them. This is a film that stresses limits and frontiers of all kinds—including those of the body—whose tensions arise from that repression and the excess that it provokes and produces.

Constituted by a set of episodic incidents, *Lock-out* zones in on these apparently sexually and politically dissatisfied individuals in their communal life and on how they interact or fail to do so. The group members spend their days foraging in the mountains of trash, eating beans directly from tins, and incoherently reciting texts (Fernando Alegría's *Instrucciones para desnudar a la raza humana*, Karl Marx's *Capital*, Søren Kierkegaard, fragments of poetry, and fashion magazines, to cite but a few).

Meanwhile, the film parodies advertising slogans (a billboard proclaims "Martini," and the group sings a jingle that publicizes lipstick) or imitates—mockingly—contemporary filmmakers (Godard, for example). There is at least one instance when both advertising and filmmaking are lampooned simultaneously. The slogan "Politícese con Danone" (Politicize yourself with Danone) is a direct and ironic reference to the apparent contradictions of Portabella's leftist militancy and his inherited wealth. (Portabella's family fortune derives from their ownership of Danone, the dairy products company, the contract for which was the result of his father's proximity to the regime.)

At the same time, a central feature of the film is its jarring counterpointed musical soundtrack. The variety of musical interludes (both diegetic and extradiegetic) prefigures Padrós's next film, the improbable musical *Shirley Temple Story*, and has an important effect within the folds of the diegesis itself. An interlude, moreover, is a pause that highlights the film's plays on temporality; indeed, the film is structured around time. This structure is revealed in the evident deterioration of the celluloid (to which we are alerted by the film's restorers before the film begins), the slow-motion photography used to represent oneiric or poetic moments; the flash-forwards and the flashbacks that punctuate, foreshadow, and/or reinforce with their iterations; and, finally, María's pregnancy, the period of gestation.

The network of citations—the written texts, the filmic references or quotes, and the music—points to virtual traces in a site of recycling. Appropriately, there is even a replacement actor who stands in for the Anarchist Walter midway through the film (in a Godardian moment), explaining directly to the camera that the libidinous Walter has not turned up for filming that day. Between the site of the garbage dump and the cite of citation is a primitive erotic charge chafing against the repressive structure of society that, like Freud's ex-citatory traces of *Beyond the Pleasure Principle*,[6] lurks beneath the surface of the film and the community itself and constantly threatens to derail order. This is indeed what happens at the end of the film in a climactic descent into chaos, death, and destruction that dynamites the project. There is a meeting here, in this network of citation of previous texts (their performative re-citing), between the two supplementary prefixes, the *ex-* of anteriority and the *re-* of return (of the repressed/the return to "civilization"), reworked within the confines of the landfill.

Shirley Temple Story *(1976)*

Padrós's most sustained piece of work is *Shirley Temple Story* (1976). Influenced by situationism, and particularly the work of Raoul Vaneignem, Padrós attempts in this film a *détournement* of the classical Hollywood musical. That, at least, is what has been suggested by the few commentators on Padrós's work, who frequently cite Vaneigem's *The Revolution of Everyday Life* as having a bearing on the filmmaker. While this is true, it is also a limiting interpretation. The most immediately striking feature of the film—a question of temporality—is its exorbitant duration of almost four hours. The film unmasks the magic of the childhood experience of the Hollywood fantasy—and particularly, in this instance, that of *The Wizard of Oz*. Symptomatic of this perhaps is the film's scatological structure in contrast to the "wholesomeness" of the original (in another prefiguration of Almodóvar). The film's initial premise is the selection of Judy Garland over Shirley Temple to play Dorothy (Temple had, of course, been the original choice, but because of her exclusive contract with Twentieth Century Fox, Metro-Goldwyn-Mayer turned to Garland). In Padrós's film, the radio announcement of Garland's new role prompts Temple—who delivers a monologue while sitting on the toilet—to embark on a quest to the Emerald City to demand an explanation from the Wizard himself.

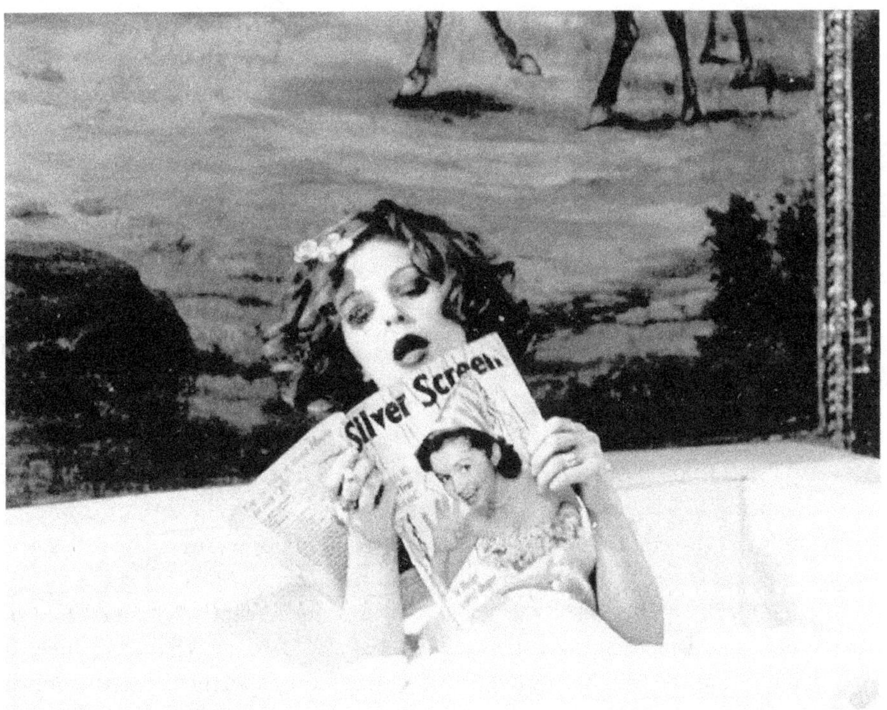

Fig. 5.1 Rosa Morata as Shirley Temple.

Throughout Temple's trip, she is accompanied by a chorus of three reactionary "daughters of Generals"—Pit, Pot, and Put—and is periodically ambushed, captured, plied with drugs, and sexually pursued by a trio of saboteurs who call themselves "anarcho-structuralists." The film is punctuated by a series of mini stories, film styles, incongruous interjections, and numerous obscure literary citations (Tuli Kupferberg's *1001 Ways to Make Love*, for example).

If Shirley Temple is Judy Garland's doppelgänger, her other, then Padrós's film as a whole is an outrageous and scatological alternative to the "original" antecedent. In contrast to *The Wizard of Oz*'s sugar-saturated Technicolor, Padrós offers stark black and white, a high-contrast negative of the original, a disembodied, ghoulish skeleton. *Shirley Temple Story* mobilizes a dazzling array of registers and filmic modes. While Temple (played by Rosa Morata; see fig. 5.1) is on-screen almost all the time, the film itself is a collage of filmic styles, including the hard-boiled detective story of cine-noir; German expressionism; *Gone With the Wind*; the vampire film; *Rebel Without a Cause*; and the most emblematically North American of genres, the musical. The overwhelming otherness of this film, its allography—or other-filming—prompts what Tom Cohen has described as "trace chains" routed and rerouted in time.[7] This is different from nostalgia or the deployment of childhood memories as psychodrama, dredged up and dwelled on by a contemporaneous filmmaker such as Stan Brakhage in his *Scenes from under Childhood*—a film that (though it is unlikely Padrós would have seen it) actually contains "a clip from a televised Shirley Temple movie."[8] In Padrós's work, one never perceives a sense of nostalgia. Instead we see what Cohen calls "mnemonic otherness,"[9] associations, contiguities, and citations. The film is a kind of spectral underbelly of the American musical, and musical forms abound. Among the more than fifty musical themes in the film are opera, ghostly echoes of Luis Buñuel (the same music that accompanies *Un chien andalou*), the piano of silent movies, boleros, *pasodobles*, and the songs associated with both *The Wizard of Oz* and Shirley Temple herself, artlessly mimed by Morata).

As is well known, the original 1939 film *The Wizard of Oz* (and before that, Frank Baum's novel) has been interpreted variously as an allegory of US monetary policy at the end of the nineteenth century, the populism of the 1890s, the New Deal, and the religious pilgrimage. If *Shirley Temple Story* is an allegory, it is an allegory of an allegory, a form that disturbs the "defective cornerstone" in the classificatory architecture, the very category of allegory. That said, there is no question that the film has moments that allude very specifically to the political reality of Spain. Rather than a straightforward allegory that corresponds to the figure of Francisco Franco, Padrós's Wizard of Oz is a carnivalesque reversal of the dictator, just as the date engraved on the frieze behind him shot at the Terrassa Casino—January 26, 1939—marks the occasion when Francoist troops entered the town at the end of the Spanish Civil War (according to Xose Prieto Souto). Dates are spectral (as we will see in chap. 9); they are the returning, repetitive code of the calendarium, singular precisely because of their iteration, the celebration of anniversaries. To engrave, to recall the previous chapter, is to leave a mark or a trace, to inscribe, and to entomb, suggesting an additional level of complexity to the film's allusions to its vampire precedents.

In concluding this section, I posit a preliminary theoretical point that may be apposite to the case of Padrós and that will reemerge in the course of this book. The torrential cascade of citations and references that pack and condense in Padrós's work—together with the parodies, inversions, and reversals—indicate a dense heterology, a tension or set of tensions produced of contradictions that sit ill with any attempt at enclosure, whether it be the direct correlation of conventional allegorical readings; the neat packaging into temporal periods, canons, or traditions; or the writing of national film history. All these fields, despite the efforts at closure, are marked by heterological tension, by the contraries, the counter within that constitutes an encounter or the otherness of exterior contagion that destabilizes. The multiple directions of Padrós's work (and life), the dissociation and the discordant doubling within the diegesis of his work and beyond it, between the filmmaker and his contemporaries of the Barcelona School, between the metropolis of Barcelona and the provincial Terrassa, between Spain and Catalonia, and between Shirley Temple and Judy Garland—all indicate internal conflict between the self and the other. What makes Padrós and his work singular is precisely its contamination by other work in its mosaic of citations. It is singular by virtue of exterior influence, its *différance*. Padros's apparent untainted isolation in Terrassa as a bank clerk—the paradox of his outsider status—depends on the external. The "proper," the *propio*, of the self—the possessive appropriation of interiority that draws inward simultaneously—extends outward to the ex of exteriority, the part and the apart in Padrós's work. It forms an impure biographical, material, textual-filmic bond forged of an encounter between impossible antonyms that Derrida, as we will see later, calls ex-appropriation.

Gonzalo García Pelayo at the Exit Point of Europe

A gnarled fisherman up to his waist in seawater thrusts his foraging spear beneath the stones in the pool left behind by the outgoing tide. Leering hungrily and with a triumphant yelp, he ensnares and penetrates an octopus trapped in the depths of its dark marine lair among the rocks. The octopus, impaled on the point of the lance, recoils and resists in the bright light of the open air. Its pink, fleshy tentacles—labia-like, curling, and coiling—react aggressively, opening and closing.[10] The ethnographic sequence moves as the observing camera shifts from above, articulating the fisherman as the object of study of the anthropological frame, to frame from below an assembled group of metropolitan visitors from the city of Seville. This sequence from Gonzalo García Pelayo's 1978 *Frente al mar* (Swinging) is a microcosmic representation of his work in its totality, a metonym of his fixation with the body and gender and with filmmaking itself.

This section explores how the form of the essay film, the theme of the erotic, and the question of subjectivity coalesce within the material frame of filmic structure, a historical-temporal frame, and the geographical frame of southern Spain. I focus on the significance of Andalusia in the work of this filmmaker as a spatial topos at a singular moment in modern Spanish history: during the country's transition from dictatorship to democracy, probably the most privileged period in national discourse today. Both Andalusia and the Transition have a singular force in the contemporary and historical Spanish imaginary. Between 1976 and 1982, García Pelayo produced a series of films in rapid succession, all of which are located in his native Andalusia, before reconvening his original career as a radio disc jockey and music producer. He returned to film in 2012, and since then he has been as prolific as he was during this earlier phase.

Part of what frames García Pelayo's relationship with Andalusia is his fascination with the region's popular culture. It is a gritty, hybrid culture that proves to be the spectral underbelly of the partialized representation of the Andalusia that the state has framed as a tourist paradise catering to foreigners. I focus my discussion here on two films that García Pelayo directed during this period: 1978's *Frente al mar* and *Vivir en Sevilla* (To live in Seville) (1979). The perspective taken is that of the doubled movement of generic and temporal disturbance that comes to subvert identitarian claims so prevalent in Spain by mobilizing them. Film historian Julio Pérez Perucha, in a clear allusion to the work of Christian Metz, has commented that García Pelayo deploys "a salad of syntagmas,"[11] and it is certainly the case that both of these films combine—incongruently and improbably—two apparently antagonistic modes of filmmaking: the essay and *destape* (meaning, literally, "uncovering"), the name given to the soft-core pornography that emerged in the latter days of the dictatorship and that took off spectacularly following the death of Franco with the subsequent lifting of censorship. In other work, García Pelayo has adopted the formats of the road movie, the Western, the juvenile delinquent film, and the rock musical, though none of his films could be described as conventional.

In the first of these films, *Frente al mar*, three couples gather in a house in Chipiona, a small coastal town in the province of Cádiz, to conduct a sexual experiment under the supervision of a "psychologist" (played, in an autobiographical twist that complicates the notion of the auteur, by García Pelayo's brother, Javier) who plays an active, participatory role. Over the course of a weekend, the couples exchange partners amid great confusion and consternation and with varying degrees of success. Each encounter is punctuated by seminar-like discussions among the entire group. Explicit in its sexual content, the film also dwells (see fig. 5.2) on the ethnography of the region and the local customs, characters, and practices. Indeed, the landscape and, more specifically, the topography is clearly relevant to the diegesis. If the edges of the frame mark the porous frontier between the screen and the real world, the action of *Frente al mar* seeks to breach borders (those of monogamy, for example); and yet borders are omnipresent. First, there is the presence of the coast itself, the physical border between land and sea (and the abundance of wetlands, marshes, and tidal formations in this part of the country). Although it goes unmentioned in the film, this particular area of Andalusia is both bound and destabliized by the contiguity and proximity of the national frame. Across the

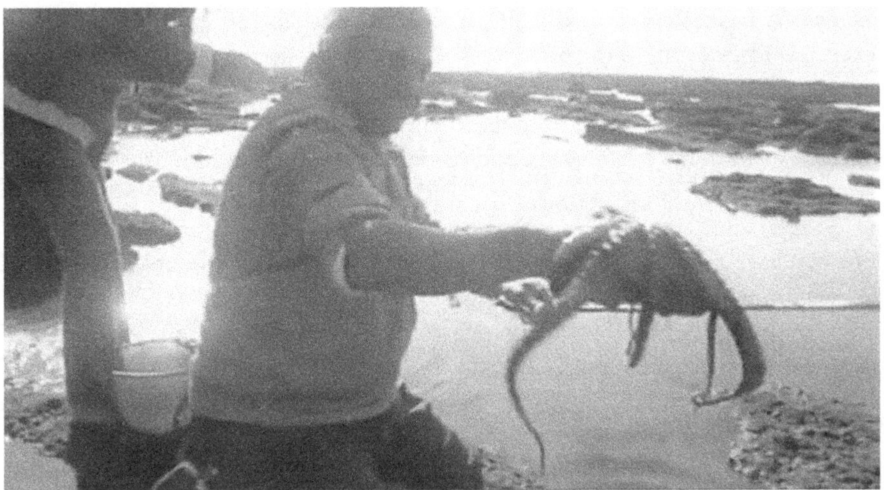

Fig. 5.2 Capturing the octopus in *Frente al mar*.

water directly south of Chipiona lies North Africa, and a short distance to the west, Portugal.

The physical piece of celluloid whose edges fold the diegesis of the film within the frame brings to mind an envelope-like structure, recalling the postal motif that Derrida holds to be so important. This structure evokes the disruption of the relation between origin and destination; it is similar to that which disturbs the constitutive elements—signifier and signified—of the linguistic sign, or representation itself. Like an envelope, "invagination," says Derrida, "is the inward refolding . . . , the inverted reapplication of the outer edge to the inside of a form where the outside then opens a pocket."[12] Like *sur*, the Spanish word meaning south (and associated with Andalusia) and the prefix of *surplus*, the Spanish word for envelope is—coincidently—*sobre* (a word that also suggests excess). The envelope also has an overflowing flap that exceeds its rectangular form—the same form, that is, as the frame.

The aporia here is in the obvious limits that mark the frame in contrast (but also as a shaping, productive complement) to the endless mise en abyme of invagination. The word *overflow*, as noted in chapter 2, suggests the ebbing sea of *Frente al mar* and is translated by the Spanish verb *desbordar*, literally meaning overflow but also the disruption of a border—des-bordar/un-border. *Invagination*, of course, in its rhyme with *imagination*, suggests that images produce their own overflowing echo amid the boundlessness of the erotic.

With this in mind, I examine this overflow, or watery seepage, in terms of excess (a fairly obvious trait of García Pelayo's cinema). The *ex-* of excess suggests an exceptionality also (in the context of space, its confines, and their excesses) to *ex*terior, to the outside. And the frame—the material frame of film itself—is, after all, notable for its *out*line. As framing defines the filmic image, its internal workings, the edges that demarcate the outside, off-screen world, and the relation between reality and its representation, it also marks other limits. In the age of celluloid, with which García Pelayo was working in the late 1970s, the *frame* is the term employed to define the photogram: the basic unit of filmmaking. The still, as others have observed, possesses the double meaning of stasis and pending temporality of pause and interlude as well as being the converse of movement. The frame (which we tend to conceive of in spatial terms) is also a temporal unit in the sense of the proverbial (and inexact) twenty-four frames per second of film. The frame also, however, marks a single point—an instant—in a sequence of a strip of film, as two of its sides define and denote a before and an after. Peter Brunette and David Wills have observed that the other sides of the frame, of the photogram, also mark contradictory, chafing elements that the frame folds within itself.[13] That is, each of the four sides of the frame marks a different heterological division within the space that the frame encloses: sound, image, past, and future. The outer borders of a piece of film apparently peripheral to the diegetic space come to define its narrative: the margins define the center. As an aside, one other heterological element chimes asymmetrically with the notion of periodization. If the frame takes the form or shape of a square, folded inward like an envelope, then it runs counter to the idea of a return and particularly the orbital movement of annual return and repetition— annual and annular—by which dates ring and encircle the calendar year.

Connected to this idea of an alternative calendar is García Pelayo's secular interest in ritual and formal practices of the sacred—mentioned earlier in terms of his fascination with Andalusian popular culture and festivities. *Vivir en Sevilla* uses music in two forms: as background, extradiegetic accompaniment to the film's action and as on-screen performance. In the latter use, the effect is that of a pause in the film's continuity, or a trance-like interlude, such as when the legendary *cantaor* (flamenco singer) Farruco sings with his troupe (see fig. 5.3) in an intermission that ostensibly has nothing to do with the diegetic action and yet divides the film almost exactly in two parts. As discussed in previous chapters, the trance film was a format pioneered by ethnographic filmmakers, and there is an element of anthropology running throughout García Pelayo's work. In all of his films of the Transition, the ritualized trance-like element exceeds time and renders it out of sync with conventional narrative or as discordantly ageless. Such an out-of-time effect contrasts radically with the invariable topicality of the film's experiment.

The framing of *Vivir en Sevilla* is marked by its own conflictual contemporaneity. An ancestral time frame (seemingly timeless) is at work within a very

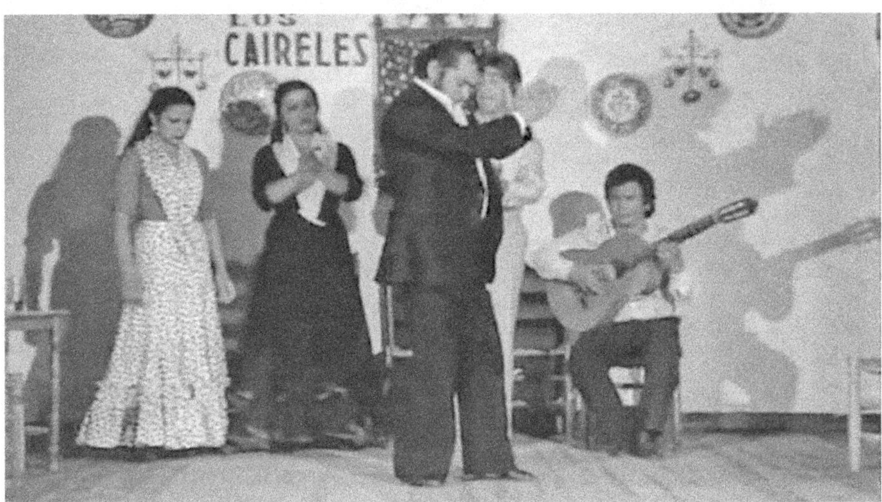

Fig. 5.3 Farruco in *Vivir en Sevilla*.

historically grounded and celebrated time frame, the Transition. A paean to the eponymous location of its title, *Vivir en Sevilla* is a city symphony. Miguel, the film's mercurial protagonist, is torn between two women and between two modes of love: erotic and spiritual. As with *Frente al mar*, the film combines contrasting generic registers—discursive and popular—but it also deploys different and incongruous on-screen codes. These include written script, voice-over, and direct address to the camera in specifically self-referential filmic moments, such as when the film's scriptwriter and the makeup artist intervene within the diegesis to discuss Miguel's dilemma. At the same time, the on-screen dates mark out a diary from April 2 to May 28, a period that contains the two major celebrations and signature festivals of the city of Seville: Semana Santa and the Feria de Abril. From the film's prologue, these two events are set against each other in competition. Amid the discourse on time and that of the contrast between text and popular spectacle, there is a similar tension between a linear time frame and what Derrida has called "the nonlinear duration of a process."[14] Further, even more than *Frente al mar* (which contains a passing reference to the absence of a divorce law in Spain, because such a law would not be passed until 1981), *Vivir en Sevilla* is littered with the traces of its time, stressing the discontinuity of the agelessness of the trance moments. The soundtrack features a rock-flamenco fusion that is distinctive of the Seville of the period; a strange, incoherent cameo by legendary blues singer Silvio; and a rendition of Victor Jara's "Comandante Che Guevara." Signs of the new political conjuncture include the painter Luis, who has returned from exile in London; protesting shipyard workers occupying the Giralda (the most emblematic building in Seville) (see fig. 5.4); and the film's

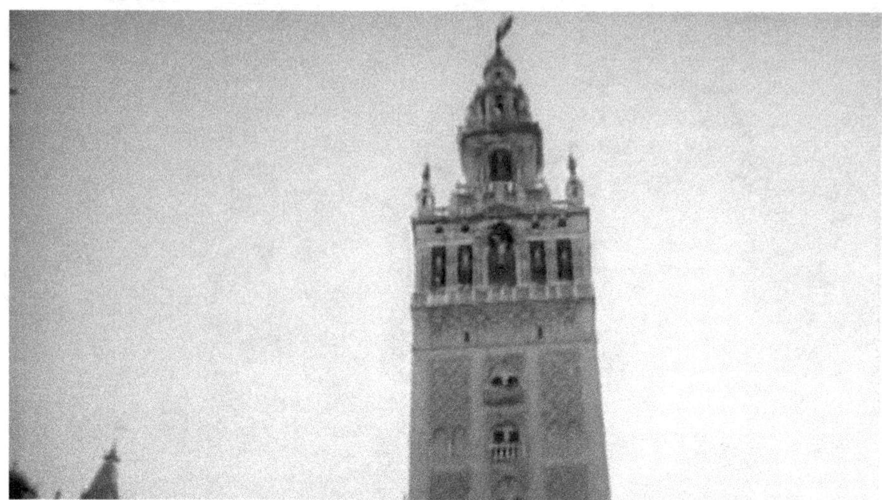

Fig. 5.4 The Giralda tower in *Vivir en Sevilla*.

final sequence, when Ana, lover to both Miguel and Luis, reads the text of the new constitution. In this constant to-and-fro and reframing through the streets of Seville's Jewish neighborhood, the camera and the city are charged with the juxtaposition of traces of the past and the present.

This culminating sequence not only frames Pérez Perucha's "salad of syntagmas" but does so in the context of the superimposition mentioned earlier. It is the key sequence in the Transition and in *transition* itself, a word that sonically contains the word trance. It is significant, furthermore, that the sequence highlights, in passing, the Callejón de la Inquisición (see fig. 5.5)—a passageway that, with all its historical connotations, is resonant with the passage of time. This shot, it might be noted, is also associated fleetingly with another period— that of the so-called golden age of Spanish literature—in its focus on the plaque dedicated to Miguel de Cervantes's short novel *Rinconete y Cortadillo*, a text located in Seville (fig. 5.6). The combination of the historical density with the visual image—the artless and amateurish swoop of the camera in a crane shot together with the written text on-screen and the torrential (and highly topical) voice-over of the radio broadcaster (Miguel)—functions to enfold its content, to overlay, superimpose, envelop from within and without, and to *invaginate*, ballooning within the frame and within the same shot not sequentially but hieroglyphically.

García Pelayo's career is also marked by a before and after, a temporal parenthesis. Always an outsider, before turning to film, he was a renowned music producer and radio presenter as well as a promoter and pioneer of what

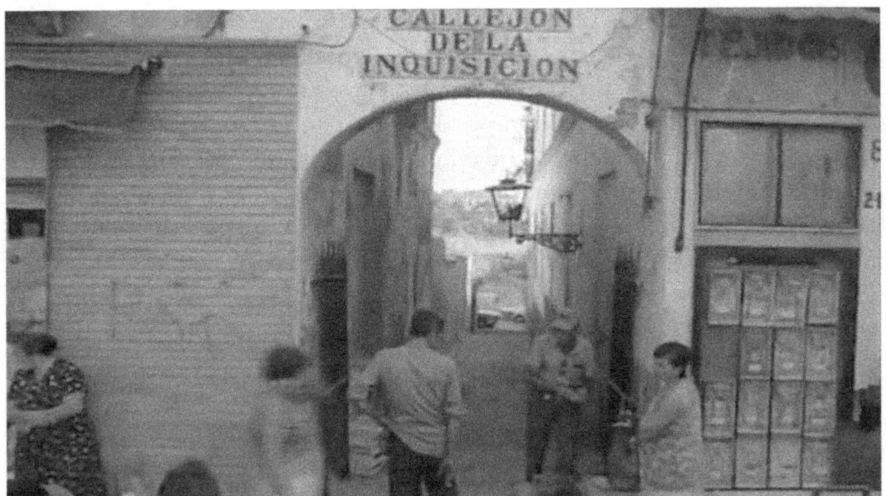

Fig. 5.5 The Callejón de la Inquisición in *Vivir en Sevilla.*

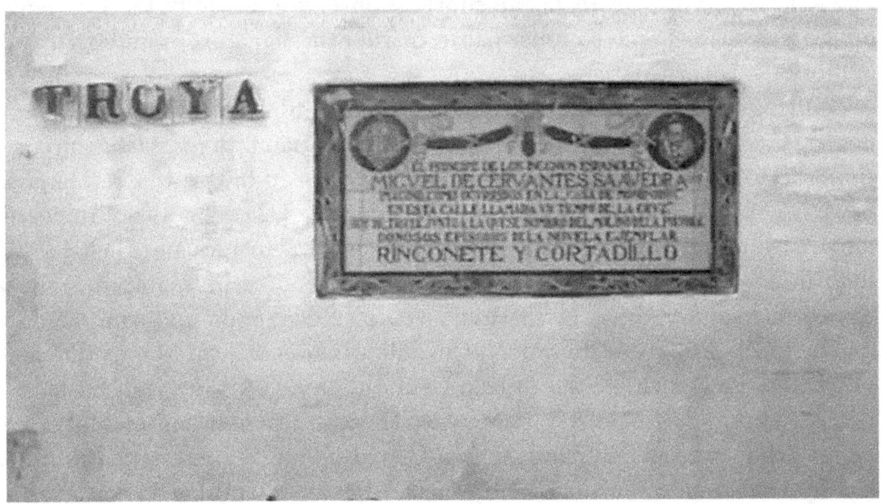

Fig. 5.6 The plaque commemorating Cervantes's novel *Rinconete y Cortadillo* in *Vivir en Sevilla.*

came to be known during the Transition as rock Andaluz as founder of the important Gong Records company. After 1982, he abandoned cinema and devoted his energies to professional gambling until 2012, when he returned to filmmaking with a prolific vengeance. Excess and the inappropriate, untimely, ill-fitting, and improper are what frame García Pelayo. He and his work disturb the proper of the appropriate, that of propriety, but also (as with Padrós) the proper of *propio*, the self, identity (the Spanish identification with the metonym of Andalusia), or that of the auteur's signature and the displacement of the proper name (as in the case of García Pelayo's brother, Javier). If the word *appropriate* suggests that pertaining to the proper, and *expropriate* that leading away from the self, then Derrida proposes *ex-appropriation* to describe the doubled simultaneous movement inward and outward in unresolved heterological tension, like the heraldic shield in Portabella's *El silencio de Bach*, the hieroglyph, the still, the photogram, or the frame itself.

Adolfo Arrieta, Unanchored *Expatria*

Identity as the proper has an even more pronounced disturbance in the work of Adolfo Arrieta. Alberte Pagán notes that this filmmaker's name appears in multiple improper forms in his films. He is credited on-screen as Adolfo González Arrieta, Adolfo G. Arrietta, V. González Arrieta, Adorfo Arrietta, Udolfo Arrieta, Vdolfo Arrieta, Adolpho Arrieta, Adelfo Arrietta, and Adelpho Arietta.[15] While clearly not an effort to conserve anonymity, these variants on Arrieta's name, on his proper name, disrupt the signature as authorial and authoritative confirmation.

Born and raised in Madrid, Arrieta made two films in Spain before abandoning the country in 1967 for Paris, where, more than fifty years later, he continues to work.[16] Like the other filmmakers discussed in this chapter, he was never an explicit political opponent of Francoism, and exile was not imposed on him by official persecution. Rather, his dissidence emerges more in his work than in any formal discursive sense. Pointedly ignored in Spain, in France, Arrieta helped found the Front Homosexuel de Liberation and continued to make films with the collaboration of such luminaries as Jean Marais (the former actor and erstwhile lover of Jean Cocteau), Severo Sarduy, Jean Eustache, Jonas Mekas, and Enrique Vila-Matas.[17] He was also a friend of Margarite Duras, who wrote an admiring review of his 1972 film *Le Château de Pointilly*.

It is striking, given that the filmmaker has done nothing to conceal his sexuality and his films are highly suggestive of homoeroticism, that the booklet accompanying the box set of Arrieta's reissued films in 2014 does not contain a single mention of homosexuality. It is a notable and telling erasure regarding both Arrieta's personal oeuvre and the cinematic genealogy with which he is associated. Arrieta's queer filmmaking is indebted to a certain poetic gay archive that includes, among others, figures such as Cocteau, Jean Genet, Kenneth Anger, and Jacques Demy. His films are theatrical, fantastical, and invariably set in the space of what has been dubbed mythic time, a zone of atemporality somewhat different from the trance time of García Pelayo and more akin to that of a children's fairy tale.[18] His debt to the cinema of Cocteau is undeniable. History is notably absent in these films. Not only is Arrieta biographically an outsider—a Spaniard working in France and a queer other whose nominal identity fluctuates wildly—his films are located beyond the boundaries of conventional time. They provoke a temporal disorientation. Because the queering of historicity—or the queer critique of historicism—is discussed in chapter 4, I focus here on queer temporality as it functions in Arrieta's cinema and reflect on how this, in turn, is connected to the heteronormative discomfort of his critics.

Chapter 4 draws on the parallels between queer studies and spectrality, and the work of Arrieta provides further evidence for such a proposition. He is a filmmaker whose work is located deceptively in a kind of perpetual present, and his films revolve around dreamlike ambiguities. Heteronormative narrative in film, and what Karl Schoonover and Rosalind Galt (invoking Elizabeth Freeman) call "chrono-normativity,"[19] tend to work in linear fashion toward closure, and the opposite proves the case in Arrieta's films. Schoonover and Galt identify a stylistics of dissident sexuality in film that is relevant to Arrieta (whom they do not discuss). Arrieta's films are notably oneiric, amateurishly atmospheric, and imbued with a suggestion of improvisation reminiscent of Jackie Raynal's *Deux fois*. They are also permeated by a set of repeated symbols and motifs. If the queer is a rejection of identitarian formulations, then, although difficult to classify, it is precisely its relation to time (and in this I am again indebted to Schoonover and Galt) by which some attempt at definition might be attempted. The aesthetic of queer cinema is often expressed through waiting, lingering, and loitering and the dilation or distention of time. In this there is a correspondence between the queer and the patience of the exile awaiting the possibility of a return with no guarantee of it ever happening—the sense that there is no home to return to. The often seemingly directionless movement of Arrieta's films provides perhaps the greatest evidence of their queer distinctiveness. Drifting has a dimension that undoes identity politics. To drift in French is *dériver*, a word that recalls the self-conscious practice of aimless wandering popularized by the Situationists (though initiated by the Surrealists, particularly André Breton and Jacques Vaché) but also the paradoxical idea of origin from which something (or someone) is derived. To be adrift, unmoored, undoes its own originary condition of derivation. The queer—at least in Arrieta's work—often has this sense of drift.

The figure of the angel is a recurrent presence in much of this work. An angel is a messenger, an intermediary, or an occupant of suspended time—the kind of temporal space within which these films are set. The angel figure is often played by Arrieta's favorite actor, Javier (or Xavier) Grandes,[20] who accompanied him from Madrid. I briefly discuss here three films that were made during Arrieta's exile. *Le Jouet criminal* (1969), *Flammes* (1978), and *Tam Tam* (1976) are works that, in a sense, delimit a disjointed time frame of only a partial body of work but one that undoes that time frame from within. They reveal a narrow aperture (a passage of time) and an internal *abyme*-like swirling expansion in ways similar to the invagination discussed in the previous section.

Le Jouet criminal *(1969)*

Le Jouet criminal, a forty-minute film, seems to be a set of interlocking dreams connected by a combination of sexual intrigue and angels. It begins with a shot of Jean Marais strolling with no great purpose along a path through a clearing in the woods. He lies down on the grass and appears to fall asleep. A younger man (Grandes) approaches and lies down beside him. Moments later, the younger man stands up and disappears into the undergrowth that borders the park. Marais contemplates the absence of the young man and meanders through the grass, watched by a woman. A man lingers in the background before standing up and entering the forest, followed by Marais. Bongo drums tap out a distant rhythm. There is an obvious suggestion here of a sexual encounter, a classic cottaging scenario. The sequence ends with a brief shot of Marais gagged and bound to a tree being released by yet another young man. What follows in the film's loose diegesis has been explained by Arrieta in interview, without which the film would remain largely incomprehensible. He says there is no logic to the film. Indeed, "It is the most surrealist film that I have made."[21] Fragments of dialogue are invariably expressed in enigmatic and elusive terms. In essence, the character of Grandes functions as a kind of supernatural gay intermediary between two sets of competing and overlapping straight couples, both of which Marais forms a part (in Arrieta's explanation, the two women in the film are his current and former wives). Of greater interest, though, than the psychodynamic of the film's narrative is the structure of desire at work that shapes the film's circularity, seemingly playing on heterosexual and homosexual monogamy with the figure of the angel not only as messenger but also a sexual contaminant that disrupts the configurations of convention and who simultaneously—and symbolically—maintains the taut suspension of time within which the charge of desire is played out. Grandes as angel is often quite literally suspended in the film, floating haplessly, a precarious pendulum hovering uneasily in the air. The first sign of his angelic condition takes metonymic form: A lost wing (a forlorn piece of paper, the like of which has appeared in previous films) is found abandoned on the paving stones of the street. Discovered by one of the women, it provides the motive for Marais's pursuit.

Marais is the focus of multiple desires, and his association with Cocteau gives the film an anachronistic twist as if to reinforce the particularity of its time and posit queer temporality as a pathology—or, in the words of Jean Ma, "a cinephilic clinging to a bygone age."[22] Marais's past, which merges with the present of the film, locates him in between time and place; it endows him with a ghostliness that is neither here nor there, oscillating like Grandes's floating angel in a midway position.[23] In this vein, the film's images function in an impressionistic fashion, allusive and elliptical. At one point, we fleetingly catch sight of a blue sky (in what is otherwise a black-and-white film), which also reminds us of the figure of the angel. Grandes's angel floats suspended between earth and sky. The first time Grandes appears, he lies down on the ground. Further, this is a film that—like much of this filmmaker's work—has been re-edited for release on DVD and makes visible elements only with the benefit of hindsight. The image of the blue sky was, in fact, there in 1969, but analog technology rendered it invisible until digital technology revealed it nearly fifty years later. The always already of queer futurity emerges only with techno-logical advancement.

Flammes *(1978)*

The sky of *Le Jouet criminal* returns in *Flammes*, but usually in this latter film it is a night sky. Shot in glorious color, Serge Bozon proclaims *Flammes* to be Arrieta's "best film," and it arguably is, at least aesthetically.[24] Several markers in *Flammes* feature the movement of time and help identify the work of queer temporality as a discordant shift in chrononormativity. As Barbara (Caroline Loeb),[25] the film's protagonist, grows up and progresses from child to young woman, she provides the clearest example of a conventional temporality at work. Nonetheless, everything around her remains the same. She is locked in a generalized state of melancholia that binds everyone in the household—her, her father (Dionys Mascolo[26]), and a succession of frustrated governesses hired to educate the recalcitrant Barbara—in affective paralysis. To borrow Ma's term, life in the chateau takes place in "suspended time."[27] Temporality is sluggish, and its current moves more as drift than direction. The pace is morbid. Set in a gothic-like chateau, enshrouded in the mystique of the night, this is a dream-scape of the standard eerie nocturnal soundtrack (owls hooting, thunder claps), and other similar horror movie effects (clouds racing across the moon). This is a haunted house.

Flammes focuses on Barbara's lifelong obsession with firefighters and her pursuit of the fulfillment of a childhood dream fantasy—the result of wak-ing during a storm one night and experiencing a vision of a firefighter (Xavier

Grandes) climbing through her bedroom window. Indeed, the entire film is structured around the dream fantasy. It is, to all intents and purposes, like *Le Jouet criminal*, a series of dreams. Dialogue in the film is pared down to a minimum (Arrieta insists that Grandes never really acted; he simply had "presence"), and communication is instinctual. The time lags of *Flammes* hold back and delay the progression of the film. While generating an often incongruous bathos, this diverts attention to the film's mise-en-scène and the richness of its composition. On one level, the film is visually luxuriant in its use of color, the shadows on the wall, the eponymous flames that punctuate the film, and the framing of the chateau's central staircase leading to the dining hall. On another level, the film is aural. To borrow once more from Bozon, the film is notable for its "nocturnal vibration that haunts films like a secret"[28] and that marks the rhythm of the night within the diegesis. This is also true of the shadows that distinguish the film's lighting. The framing of this film is pictorial, and its Rivette-like theatricality gives it an additional artificiality. There is a sense in *Flammes* of classical cinema in terms of its construction. It is, though, only a sense. *Flammes*'s formal elegance is like the *infrathin* of chapter 2 with regard to its relation to classical film; it is an imperceptible similarity, chameleon-like, a subtle hint marked by a difference that we might call queerness.

In an interview with Phillipe Azoury included in the *Flammes* press book and that foreshadows developments in film theory by two decades (the haptic, the affective, etc.) as well as the notion of *infrathin*, Arrieta reflects on an earlier piece of the film's dialogue when Barbara's father says to her, "A piece of your dream got stuck on the glass." Arrieta comments, "I love the idea that a dream is something that sticks. The first photographs were made on plates and the image was sort of glued to the surface. Celluloid is also a kind of skin or surface onto which we paste our dreams."[29]

Flammes's artifice belies even more. While this is a film marked by pauses, a festering stillness, and innuendo that concentrate its queer-spectral character, it is also distinguished intermittently by the flickering of flames, a subliminal life smoldering beneath the surface. Barbara locks herself away in her room with the Grandes character for an indeterminate time (though enough to arouse the suspicions and preoccupation of her father). Together with the firefighter, she orchestrates a suspended, sequestered, phantasmal eroticism that unfolds within the homogenous, moribund time of the household.

Amid these cloying atmospherics, the firefighter played by Grandes emerges as a kind of angel (although no actual angels appear in this film). He appears as if from nowhere, capable of ascending magically from the ground to the bedroom (see fig. 5.7). His speech is sparse and inflected by a foreignness. He is an untimely outsider and messenger who visits in a dream. His accent

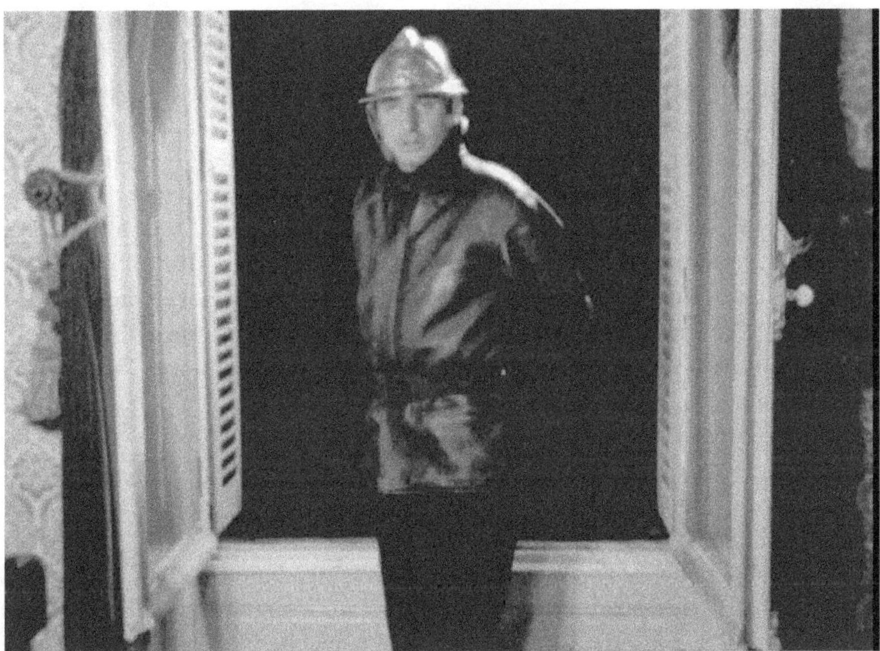

Fig. 5.7 Xavier Grandes as a firefighter in *Flammes*.

and uniform mark him as other; they are elements of difference that contribute to the queerness and enigma of the film. There is, moreover, a hint of incest in the relationship between father and daughter (Arrieta has described the film as "an immoral story," a "perverse story"). The story is limited to the cloistered interior of the chateau, within whose confines the firefighter—the guest from the exterior—has a disruptive function (in ways not dissimilar to that of the angel in *Le Jouet criminal*). An informal triangle emerges in a subdued, understated rivalry and a play on a toxic indoors and contamination from the outside.

Amid the stillness and stasis, Barbara is stifled, self-exiled to her bedroom, where she whiles away her time pasting collages or, when downstairs, creating houses of cards. This is the dead time of lethargy and inaction. Then she takes off to travel around the world in the company of Claire (Isabel García Lorca, the niece of Federico García Lorca), the one governess she has befriended. In the interview with Azoury, Arrieta speaks interestingly about how he conceived the relationship between Claire and Barbara: "Their rapport is based on the unspoken; it is very ambiguous. You feel there is something maybe lesbian, but also domination, masochism. I left it in the dark. Her harsh air combined with submissiveness and the way she runs after Barbara, bows before her should be sufficient to get an idea of what could happen how it could happen."[30]

Barbara returns home alone just in time to have missed a visit by her mother (a moment of desynchronization), but finds her gay half brother, Paul, who has been left there by their mother. Soon thereafter, Claire returns accompanied by Jim (Jeffrey Carey), who, it transpires, has been obliged to dress up as a firefighter to satisfy Barbara's fetish during their travels. As if to reinforce the haunted quality of the house, there is a constant, ritualized movement of entrances and exits, doors opening and closing, shadows into which people disappear or from where they inexplicably emerge. From the frame of the window, Paul and Jim are seen frolicking on the chateau grounds outside. The limits of the chateau, with its interiors and exteriors also mark the film's queerness and distort the contours of the outside world.

Tam Tam (1976)

If the ethereal figure of the angel evolves from winged intermediary in *Le Jouet criminal* to oneiric firefighter in *Flammes*, in *Tam Tam* (1976) and in the earlier *Las intrigas de Sylvia Couski* (1974), the angel takes the form of the transvestite in Arrieta's imaginary. *Tam Tam* is not only a self-consciously worldly film—its international references are multiple—but also otherworldly. Writer Enrique Vila-Matas, who appears in the film, recalls the film shoot in his novel *Paris no se acaba nunca* and comments that it is "the film with the most transvestites per square foot in the history of cinema."[31] Unlike the other two Arrieta films discussed here, *Tam Tam* is not so much a dream fantasy—though, in a projected sense, that is exactly what it is—as an experiment with realism. Vila-Matas quotes Severo Sarduy's (who has a major role in *Tam Tam*; see fig. 5.8) criticism of the film: "An excess of realism. In the transvestite there is an enhanced femininity (women imitate *them*) but Arrieta just directs them as actresses, without insisting on excessive cosmetics or the easily flamboyant aspects of the situation"(emphasis in the original).[32] I will return to Sarduy's comment shortly, but it is significant that what is translated here in the English-language version of Vila-Matas's book as "enhanced femininity" is in the original expressed as "suplemento de la femeneidad" (supplement of femininity).

The film commences with a black screen and the voice of Arrieta reading the list of cast members. This is followed by a brief single head shot of Javier Grandes, a shot of the bongos (the tam tam of the film's title) being played,[33] and a feminine character twirling a globe of the world hanging from a ceiling. Then there are a series of shots of Grandes in New York City. Jonas Mekas, who chaired the jury at the Toulon film festival, which had awarded a prize to

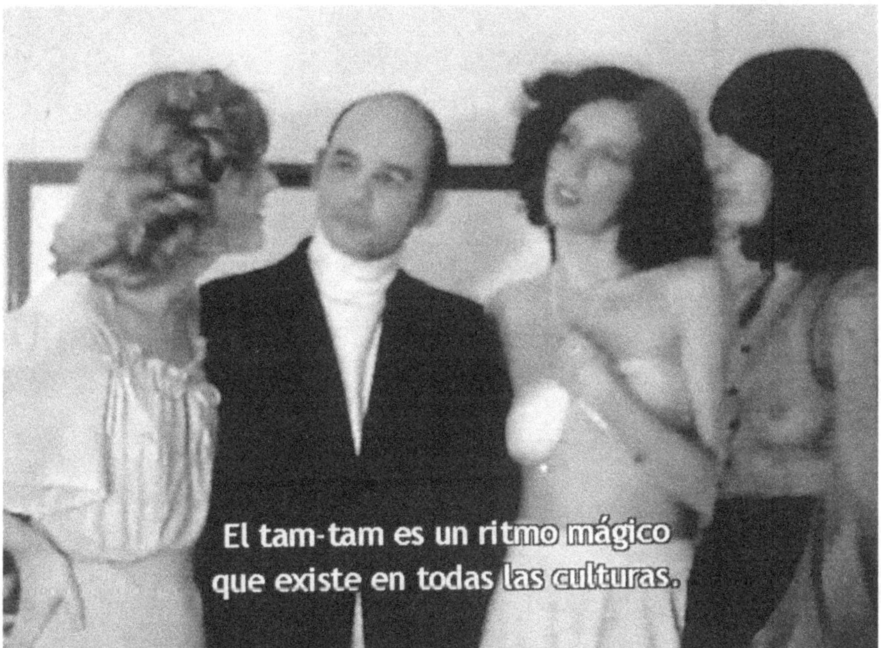

Fig. 5.8 Severo Sarduy in conversation with the transvestites in *Tam Tam*.

Las intrigas de Sylvia Couski a few years earlier, had invited Arrieta to screen his work at the Anthology Film Archives and lent him a camera during the visit. The result is a diary-type homage to Mekas's style of filmmaking. We see images of snowbound Manhattan streets and the Statue of Liberty shot offshore from a boat with Grandes at the helm. This brief section of the film feels like a home movie, yet it is a home movie that is not at home at all. It is a tourist film perhaps, but a singularly wintry one, and a film journal of sorts. There is a geographical displacement of the genre (and Mekas is also an exile) whose doubled quality is reinforced by shooting in Mekas's trademark style.

Central to this doubling is the element of waiting that Schoonover and Galt identify as one of the characteristics of the queering of time. The film proper takes place at a Paris apartment where a party is being held. Its only narrative thread is constructed around the nonarrival of Pedro Malmouth (Grandes), a famous writer who misses his plane and is stranded in New York. Instead, he sends his identical twin brother to attend the party. The twin mingles but goes largely unnoticed by the partygoers, who comment on the impending appearance of Pedro. A languid sense of uncertainty, a collective lingering, develops and permeates the entire film.

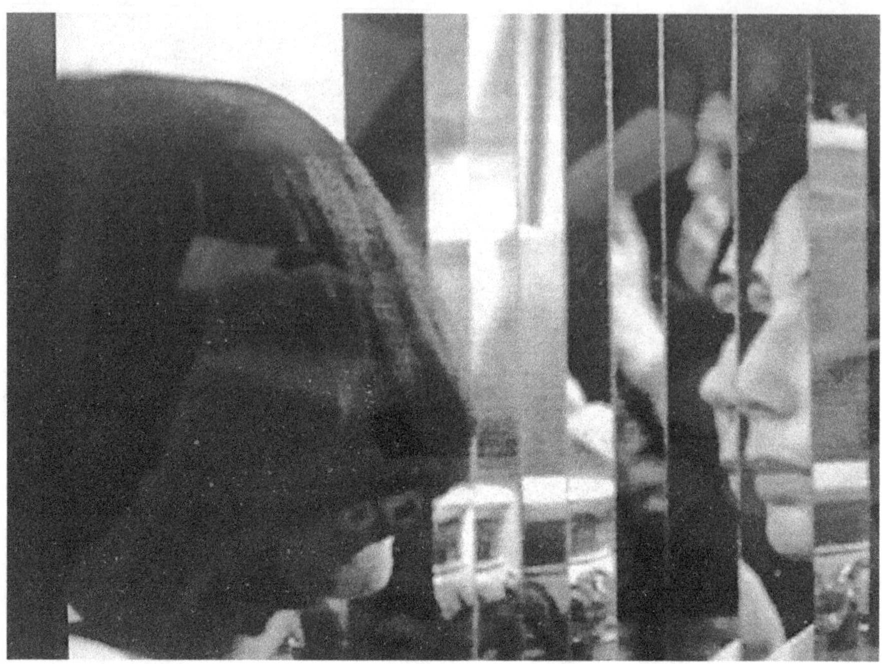

Fig. 5.9 The fragmentation of the faces in *Tam Tam*.

The continual return to the globe as a refrain, Sarduy's cosmopolitanism, the different languages spoken at the party (English, French, Spanish), the camp exoticism of an owl mask (and other masks), the rhythm of the bongo drums, and the multiple references to Andalusia all combine to create a sense of worldly out-of-place dispersion. The camera strays through the house, meandering among lackluster eavesdropped conversations, minor dramas, and images of faces fragmented and multiplied in a mirror.

While the party is located in a humdrum out-of-time, out-of-place, distended space of ennui—a kind of u-topia of transvestites and writers—in contrast to the early shots of New York City, a queer digression is inserted at the film's midway point. There is a sudden switch to southern Spain in what is possibly a dream sequence appended to the corporality of the film. This transportation to Spain is effected via a portrait shot of the face of one of the transvestites at the party, who—now in flamenco attire—emerges as the object of desire of swarthy, muscular cmen amid Latin archetypes: whitewashed houses, a single brightly colored flower, and stone water fountains. A second sequence portrays her seemingly as host, standing welcomingly at the entrance to a building bearing the incongruously hybrid name (and correspondingly orientalist kitsch architecture) La Pagoda Gitana (The gypsy pagoda).

The multiple doubling of the mirror and the presence of twins is distinct from the usual uncanniness that such images produce in cinema. And the same can be said of the masks and the drumming. The film's title contains a double (tam/tam), an iteration that punctuates the film insistently and whose ritualistic repetition invokes the trance. These elements reveal the supplement that Sarduy refers to when he considers the relation between transvestitism and femininity as not so much Arrieta's direction of the actors as the various inserts, the refrain of the music, and the interventions of Sarduy himself. These are all supplementary elements that coalesce in the dilation of time. Time is rendered discontinuous, unproductive, and incommensurable with the conventions of filmmaking, or the telos of heterosexual love, or the narratives of the nation, with their common demand for closure and the sealing of frontiers.

On "queer time," Schoonover and Galt write: "Slow cinema wastes our time, asking us to spend time in visible unproductive ways, outside efficient narrative economies of production and reproduction."[34] And, as we will see later, productivity and performativity will prove important features in this book.

Notes

1. Akira Mizuta Lippit, *Ex-Cinema: From a Theory of Experimental Film and Video* (Berkeley: University of California Press, 2012).

2. Joan M. Minguet, "Antoni Padrós Story," *Pensacions* (blog), May 6, 2014, http://pensacions.blogspot.com/2014/05/antoni-padros-story.html.

3. Jacques Derrida, *Memoirs for Paul De Man* (Chicago: University of Chicago Press, 1988), 73–74.

4. P. Adams Sitney, *Visionary Film: The American Avant-Garde, 1943–2000* (Oxford: Oxford University Press, 2002).

5. Mery Cuesta, *El terrorismo doméstico de Antoni Padrós* (Girona, Spain: Editorial Fundació Espais, 2002).

6. Sigmund Freud, *Beyond the Pleasure Principle and Other Writings* (Harmondsworth, UK: Penguin Classics, 2003), 28.

7. Tom Cohen, *Ideology and Inscription: "Cultural Studies" after Benjamin, de Man and Bakhtin* (Cambridge: Cambridge University Press 1998), 8.

8. Sitney, *Visionary Film*, 390.

9. Cohen, *Ideology and Inscription*, 8.

10. This reading of the sequence is greatly indebted to a comment made by my colleague Imke Meyer.

11. Julio Pérez Perucha, "*Vivir en Sevilla* de Gonzalo García Pelayo," *Contracampo*, no. 4 (July–August 1979): 60–61.

12. Jacques Derrida, "Living On—Border Lines," in *Deconstruction and Criticism*, edited by Harold Bloom (London: Continuum, 2004), 80.

13. Peter Brunette and David Wills, *Screen/Play: Derrida and Film* (Princeton, NJ: Princeton University Press, 1989), 104.

14. Jacques Derrida, *On Touching—Jean-Luc Nancy*, trans. Christine Irizarry (Stanford, CA: Stanford University Press, 2005), 96.

15. Alberte Pagán, "Sobre los ángeles: Entrevista a Adolpho Arrietta," http://albertepagan.eu/a-toupeira/adolfo-arrieta/.

16. At the time of writing, Arrieta has just released his latest feature, *Sleeping Beauty* (2016).

17. Vila-Matas, who had a small role (together with Severo Sarduy) in *Tam Tam*, writes about Arrieta in his novel *Paris no se acaba nunca*.

18. In the interview with Alberte Pagán, Arrieta mentions the influence on him (like Padrós) of *The Wizard of Oz*, which he claims to have seen fifty or sixty times.

19. Karl Schoonover and Rosalind Galt, *Queer Cinema in the World* (Durham, NC: Duke University Press, 2016), 266.

20. Grandes, who died in 2012, was, according to Vila-Matas, uncle to the novelist Almudena Grandes. Fernando del Val, "Enrique Vila-Matas," *Turia*, http://www.ieturolenses.org/revista_turia/index.php/actualidad_turia/cat/conversaciones/post/enrique-vila-matas-soy-el-que-se-desconoce.

21. Pagán, "Sobre los ángeles."

22. Jean Ma, *Marking Time in Chinese Cinema* (Hong Kong: Hong Kong University Press, 2010), 101.

23. Marais was also the actor in *Fantômes* (dir. André Hunebelle, 1964).

24. Serge Bozon, Edición de Intermedio DVD. Pack *Adolpho Arrieta. Obras*, 50–55. *Flammes* was released in 1978, a year that, as we have seen in the discussion of García Pelayo, has a particular significance in Spain as the inauguration of the new democratic period. Yet nothing of this is suggested by the film itself. It is as if it were located outside time and outside historical narrative, but in being so, it challenges precisely the idea of period itself.

25. Caroline Loeb began her acting career in *La Maman et la Putain* (1973, Jean Eustache).

26. Mascolo played the father in Arrieta's previous film, *Le Chateau de Pointilly* (1974), also about father-daughter relations. He had been married to Margarite Duras until 1956 and appeared in *India Song*.

27. Ma, *Marking Time*, 99.

28. Bozon, Edición de Intermedio, 55.

29. Philippe Azoury, "Interview with Adolfo Arrieta," in *Flammes* press kit (Paris: Capricci Films, 1978), 12.

30. Ibid., 12–13.

31. Enrique Vila-Matas, *Paris no se acaba nunca* (Barcelona: Editorial Anagrama, 2006), 80.

32. Ibid., 81.

33. The sound of bongo drums is one of Arrieta's signature motifs that appears in many of his films. *Tam Tam* is unusual in that the bongos are actually diegetically represented on-screen.

34. Schoonover and Galt, *Queer Cinema*, 277.

6

THE CATACOUSTIC AND THE COSMOPOLITAN

Rhythm and Timbre in the Films of Andrés Duque

I BEGIN THIS CHAPTER WITH A BRIEF CASE study as an entry point to the work of the Venezuela-born, Barcelona-based experimental filmmaker Andrés Duque. In one of his earliest shorts, the twenty-five-minute *Paralelo 10* (Parallel 10) (2005), Duque films the opaque routine of a Filipina woman at the intersection of Paralelo Avenue and Entença Street in central Barcelona. Each day, we are informed by an unidentified male voice-over (delivered in Tagalog) midway through the film, Rosemarie Cruz Obag[1] performs the same one-hour ritual at the same spot at the same time, 365 days a year. Resistant to hermeneutics, it is a public effectuation of the incommunicable.

The phrase "parallel 10" refers to both the major Barcelona thoroughfare—Avenida Paralelo—and the 10 of En *tenç*a. We are told also that parallel 10 constitutes the global horizontal coordinates of the latitude that traverses three continents and twenty-two countries, among them the Philippines. These are only the first of a series of disconcerting parallels and allusions that indicate an anagrammatical worldliness and an asymmetricality (one that plays on but also confounds translation) both in Rosemarie Cruz Obag's daily performance and in Duque's work as a global filmmaker.

With the aid of rulers and right-angle measuring triangles, Rosemarie delineates a baffling sequence of symbols, numeric calculations, and linguistic anagrams amid ritualized movements of her own (including sun salutes and a trajectory marked out with alarming fearlessness as she paces determinedly yet blindly across the intersection, ignoring the oncoming traffic). Faced with the normative regimentation of road signs and the grates and grills of gutters and sewers that order all kinds of flows in the busy street, she offers a disruptive act

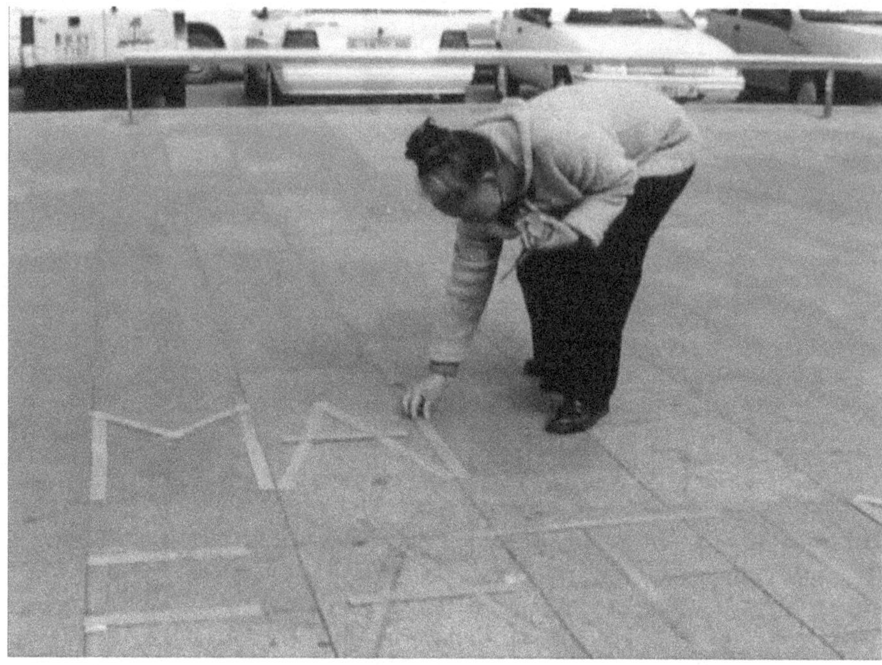

Fig. 6.1 Rosemarie's anagrams in *Paralelo 10*.

that breaks down, disorders, and mixes up the boundaries of the world with those of the street corner. Aligning the rulers to form the word *mapa* (map), she will later produce an actual folded map of the world and place it within a circle constituted by the plastic triangles before opening it and plotting global trajectories with a pencil (see fig. 6.1). She draws an outline on the map around the Iberian Peninsula and then selects apparently random letters from which she reveals anagrams and, by mixing up the letters, draws arbitrary associations in an elaborate exercise of connectivity: "Leonardo Da Vinci," "Song of Bernadette," "Son of Bernadette," "Tony Bennett," and, finally, "Frank Sinatra." The latter she retrieves and compiles from a selection of words that adorn the Barcelona manholes.

Although Duque does not fully appear in the film, he does partially. His camera-carrying shadow (captured within the frame) accompanies Rosemarie as she enacts her ritual. This elusive presence of the filmmaker is important, and it is a foretaste of Duque's many appearances in his later films (and particularly in two of his three full-length features). It also highlights an interesting correlation between the shadow and the echo (discussed below): both are pointers, indexes, references, and intangible hints of what purports to be original (the flesh and blood person, the sound of the voice). *Paralelo 10* ends with an abrupt change of register as the film switches to an epilogue provoked by Rosemarie's chain of associations, and on this occasion by the connections made by the filmmaker as if to continue the logic of shadowing.

In a brusque change of style, the scenario switches to a karaoke bar, where Marlon Manzano, the film's Tagalog narrator, is filmed singing an impassioned version of Sinatra's *My Way* in a kind of ventriloquism that survives in the filming, as a dying moment, quite literally as a supplement to life. The sound of the recorded music reverberates as Manzano's image gradually fades from the screen into translucent oblivion. It is a spectral moment uncannily connected to "haunting melodies" that involves a physical disappearance, a ghostly transparency, or the virtual product of a technological trick of the digital camera, but its combination of translucence and citation also indicates an inabsorbable visual and sonic residue, a trace, a literal resonance. This is the kind of echo and shadow that Jean-Luc Nancy has termed a "reflected structure," a redolent place of vibration or the space of a series of referrals or *renvois*.[2]

The disappearing figure and the music resounding within and seeping beyond a confined space recall the echo chamber of previous chapters, a to-and-fro, a call and response, an original emission and its delayed repetition. The internalized acoustic reverberation is akin to what Phillipe Lacoue-Labarthe has described, precisely in an essay on music and subjectivity, as "a 'catacoustic' phenomenon."[3] The celebrated song title, *My Way*, of course, implies subjectivity in terms of an imaginary selfhood. In this sense, *Paralelo 10*'s final sequence is coherent—as an acoustic correlation—with the earlier performance as Rosemarie's symbolic gestures are enacted beneath the glare and glint of the midday sun with the shadow of the filmmaker close by recording her action.

Lacoue-Labarthe observes that when Freud occasionally refers to music in psychoanalysis, it is only in the context of the lyrics of the music in question (opera, songs, musical theater, etc.), not the melody or the tune. The disjunction—the divergent opening—that emerges in the final sequence of *Paralelo 10* is between the style of the delivery (both of the musical rendition and the way it is filmed) and the literal meaning of the words spoken, their logical content, their sense. Here *sense* refers to both meaning and direction.[4] But it also refers to that associated with the sensorial, with hearing and listening: the conflation and the relation of—and between—these multiple uses of the word *sense* correspond to those of the sound and its echo, the catacoustic rebound, and an internal resounding—that is, re-sounding.

Lacoue-Labarthe focuses on rhythm, which, he says, indicates an "originary" prenatal state, the heartbeat of the fetus in the womb. And yet the phenomenon that we call rhythm is only rhythm by virtue of repetition. The rhythmic quality of a repeated beat requires duplication in order to be rhythmic. Life, then, is doubled from its beginning; even in its most embryonic of forms, the original subject is not unique (and rhythm as heartbeat is life-giving). Rhythm suggests it is born doubled.

Other features of rhythm are also significant to my argument here. First, rhythm is a contradictory marker of time; it measures time, but its beat and spacing breach time's flow. Second, in more specifically filmic terms, rhythm is the key element in montage. Finally, in Duque's work, rhythm garners a particular importance given the sparsity of dialogue and written text and given the function of music and various types of interludes. Perhaps of greatest significance is Duque's preoccupation with the human body. The interest is in not only the body's exterior movements, rituals, and dances—its performative aspect and trance-like condition—but also the sound of the body's unseen inner depths.

Paralelo 10 marks a key moment in Andrés Duque's professional trajectory. The film proposes an enigmatic disquisition on the world—a global intervention—from the perspective of a Barcelona street corner, performed by a cosmopolitan stranger; it is equally an exercise in cosmopolitan filmmaking practices, in film *as* cosmopolitics. It instantiates the relation of the subject with the world and between self and other.[5]

Duque's second full-length feature, 2012's *Ensayo final para utopía* (Dress rehearsal for utopia), commences with a visual self-portrait and an acoustic disturbance. Indeed, before we see any image during the title sequence, we hear a distant, unidentifiable sound, a rumor. Duque appears in the shadows of a closed room. Responding to the inquiry of a recent anonymous arrival obscured in the penumbra, the pensive filmmaker expresses sadness. The suggestion of dialogue here, though, dissipates and comes to nothing. It is a catacoustic moment with the voice in the shadows remaining unidentified and invisible, a mere voice. The camera then moves away from and behind Duque to reveal the figure of a dancing silhouette against the wall. An orange light pulsates steadily on the screen. The low-pitched rumble increases to a muffled crescendo, like the primal sound of a distant eruption.

In the sequences that follow this introduction, sound is as determining (and as apparently random) as the visual images. The shot described above fades momentarily to black, and the film's second sequence opens with an elderly man (Duque's father, Silvio) in a hospital bed connected to a tube and surrounded by machines. The sonorous rumble of the first sequence merges with melodramatic orchestration and the lurid delivery of a radio presenter. The metronomic pulsation of the light on the wall in the first sequence is repeated in miniature in the regular heartbeat illuminated on the life-support monitor.

Rhythm here is visual; the traditional contrast between aurality's intermittency and the instantaneity of the visual is collapsed. This rhythm both confirms the temporal linearity (the continuity of life) and interrupts it with the successive separations between beats. In what follows—a global visual backdrop to its sonic structure—the film takes us from Barcelona to Mozambique and to Venezuela, before, finally, the Duque family visits Italy.

As on other occasions in Duque's work, the opposition established between the natural and the technological—life span and its artificial prolongation—is questioned in these opening few minutes of the film. However, connected to the interrogation of that dichotomy is the way the soundtrack is distributed in measured doses amid the visual track. In a film in which sound and image predominate over dialogue and narration, the sonorous functions as a set of aural hyphens, as spacing with its phrasing assuming the quality of a grammatical conjunction. Musical phrases litter these filmic texts with no apparent coherence or uniformity, but their arbitrary distribution also punctuates the logic of their experimental nonnarrative texture and often does so in discordant correspondence with the visual track.

Complementing the temporal regularity of rhythm's beat, the ticktock of the clock, Jean-Luc Nancy turns to the notion of timbre, "which resounds in rhythmed space."[6] Timbre is the *original* release of sound, of sonic materiality, or the "archiglottal."[7] For Nancy, timbre is "a figure that is throbbed as well as stressed, 'broached by time,'"[8] whose reverberations are best opened up through the body in dance. Thus, the rhythmic beat previously associated with the womb, the prenatal matrix as originary echo chamber, and the confined space of reverberation, in Nancy's terms, indicates an element of sound that extends the ordering principle that Lacoue-Labarthe attributes to rhythm within a mimetic structure as measure or scansion. "Timbre," ventures Nancy, "is communication of the incommunicable."[9]

The borborygmic sound that forms the sonic bedrock of *Ensayo final para utopía* is intimately linked to its somatic theme, the correlation between sound and visuality, and the animate and the inanimate as expressed through technological representation of the body. The image of Silvio Duque's inert corpse first in a hospital bed and then in a coffin at the wake is followed by five freeze-frames of anonymous strangers in the street filmed as they are poised in midair (see fig. 6.2).

While these shots are frozen, they are not entirely immobile. On-screen these people vibrate. The shots are trembling with tension, throbbing, and quivering with the charge of stilled and palpable time in a temporal stasis that nonetheless seems to resist its paralysis. They are manifestly something other than still photography. Between animation and inanimation, between mobility

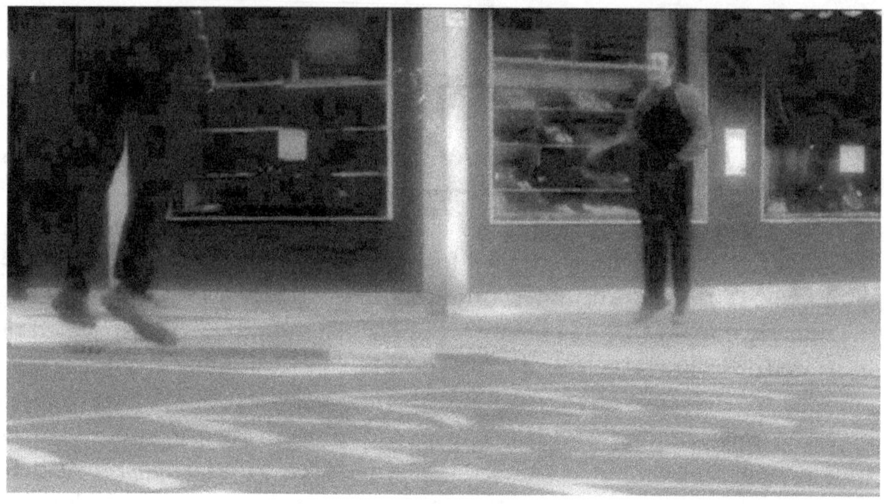

Fig. 6.2 The freeze-frame in the aftermath of Silvio Duque's death in *Ensayo final para utopía*.

and immobility, and in reactive proximity with death, like the catacoustic, their quiver hints visually at a reverberating space, the image of a pause in the continuum, an arrest in the flow of video technology. These shots recall Serge Daney's description of what he termed the "freeze image" as "petrified movement."[10] Both André Bazin and Walter Benjamin conceived of photography in terms of death and temporality, either as embalmment or an arrest of the inexorable forward movement of time.

These images, by virtue of their staggered, shuddering movement, seem specifically related to digital video, with its temporal ramifications, rhythmic alteration, and throbbing expanse. Likewise, if the musical term *interlude* (an important element in the work of Portabella, for example) is a sonic pause, an interruption in the melodic flow, then the visual equivalent in film might be the freeze-frame. Laura Mulvey, whose book *Death 24x a Second: Stillness and the Moving Image* turns on the theme of death, most notably the death of cinema itself, has identified in the freeze-frame an encounter between old and new media, between the still photograph and the fluid continuity of video, and, in pre- and postcinema, the creation of "an aesthetic of delay" that the freeze-frame exemplifies: "Throughout the history of cinema, the stilled image has been contained within the creative preserve of the film-maker, always accessible on the editing table and always transferable into a freeze-frame on the screen. It was video, arriving in the late 1970s and gaining ground during the 1980s, that first extended the power to manipulate the existing speed of cinema."[11]

Traditionally in film, the freeze-frame implies a point on the brink (of a new start, an uncertain future, a possibility beyond death). To this end, a sonic-visual parenthesis surrounds Silvio Duque's death. The final occasion in *Ensayo final para utopía* in which we see Duque's father alive is in a lengthy single sequence shot filmed in painstakingly real time as the ailing Silvio struggles to walk along a corridor. Barely able to maintain his balance, his frail figure taps out an irregular staccato on the wooden floor with his walking stick. It is the only sound heard for a considerable stretch of the film, and its rhythm continues as we watch him from behind as he maneuvers toward the dark aperture of the doorway at the end of the passageway and disappears. The convulsive rhythm marked out by his tremulous walking stick persists in his absence, outstays his presence, and, like the echoing reverberation of the voice of the fading karaoke singer in *Paralelo 10*, outlives him. While these two sequences frame Silvio Duque's death and what appears to be its pulsatingly gelled aftermath, they also enfold it and recall the act of enveloping as discussed in chapter 5. These sequences evoke, once more, questions of sound, rhythm and timbre, and interiority and exteriority as they coalesce within a catacoustic scenario, an echo chamber, a sonic folding, or invagination from whose redolence the subject is formed.

While this invaginating *abime*—the resounding, reverberating, enfolded hollow, or throbbing interiority—describes the interior-exterior relation, it also defines the *arche* space of Duque's cinematic legacies and brings us back to cosmopolitan authorship. If his familial lineage (the presence of his father) marks a logical passage of time, then his filmic antecedents provide temporal alteration.

"Rhythm," writes Nancy, "separates the succession of the linearity of the sequence or length of time: it bends time to give it to time itself, and it is in this way that it folds and unfolds a 'sense.'"[12] As outlined in the introduction to this book, cosmopolitan cinema differs from conventional transnational approaches in that it is defined by difference rather than similarity. Duque's cosmopolitanism is riven by discordance and incommunicable communication. The cosmopolitanism that interests me, moreover, emerges from the periphery. Duque's films constitute worldly encounters that take place over the course of his travels across three continents. The slightly awkward—albeit persistent—foregrounding of the autobiographical in Duque's cinema, his returns to an origin, and his sense of legacy (filmic and familial) recall *renvois*, the perpetual unsettled reverberation of an echo, the reflection of a reflection in a set of mirrors, a combination of rhythm and timbre, and untimeliness and difference. To return, once again, to Rosemarie Cruz Obag's performance in *Paralelo 10* as emblematic of this filmmaker's work, while the rhythm of Duque's cinema disturbs chronological temporality and sequentiality like the network of resounding and rebounding references we call cosmopolitanism, its "timbre," in Nancy's words, "is above all the unity of a diversity that its unity does not reabsorb."[13]

Josetxo Cerdán has described Duque's work as distinguished by an "overwhelming" subjectivity, by which he seems to refer to the autobiographical presence of the filmmaker in his own films and the personal content of the films.[14] I build on Cerdán's insight to reflect theoretically on what this might mean. Lacoue-Labarthe's notion of the catacoustic suggests an inner echo and an insistent coming back, like an iterative tune in one's head, or a kind of *renvois*. Self-address of this kind suggests a *s'envois*, a sending of something back to oneself so as to make sense. Nancy insists that this, in its echo-like structure, is the "sound of sense." These two effects—*s'envois* and *renvois*—in combination suggest that the echo, or the reverberating sound, is not enclosed or solipsistic. It is a means by which we can locate and explain the autobiographical and the biographical within the world. The autobiographical in Duque is autography, the writing of the self as other, an intimate self-portrait seen from the outside, or, as Akira Mizuta Lippit would express it, an "extimacy."[15]

A brief sequence in *Ensayo final para utopía* locates in cosmopolitan-sonic terms the autobiographical and the space of referral that I have been discussing. Commencing with an exterior shot in rural Mozambique, the camera tracks away from its abstract point of focus to reveal a hut under the branches of a tree. In the foreground, a hen waddles toward the camera traversing the red sand; in the background beyond and behind the hut are a cyclist and then a car on the highway. A cut switches from the hut's exterior to its interior. In the shadows of the hut—a kind of echo chamber purged of sound—Duque, identifiable in the penumbra only indexically by his distinctive spectacles, sits next to a guitarist. Played out in silence, the absence of sound leads us to focus on the mise-en-scène of the hut's interior. The play on light and shade indicates an exterior, the natural light from the window of the closed room and the reflected light in the mirror in one corner of the frame. Crudely drawn figures adorn the adobe walls. Obscured in the shadows, the features of the two men are barely discernible. We see the guitarist strumming and singing, mouthing, muted. The image is silent, and we make out little more than forms and moving shapes in the midst of an otherwise shaded image as the song is reduced to a soundless mime. "Sense," writes Nancy, "opens up in silence."[16] Meanwhile, the filmmaker sits at the guitarist's side, microphone in hand, recording the unheard music. This sequence highlights the complexities of the authorial or autobiographical presence of the director in his own film and the instability of the particular axis of the silent transit between subject and object or vice versa. Here, the idea of the subject, both that of the filmmaker and the guitarist (or indeed the sound of the guitar) is bound up with technology—a theatrical prop and an indexical contradiction (in that we are denied the sound the microphone promises).

Conceptually, the sequence warrants comparison with the final supplementary sequence of *Paralelo 10*. Whereas in the earlier film sound is mobilized in the destabilizing fading image, here, while music is eliminated amid the light and shadow of the image, sound is signified by its absence. The sequence is shot in such a way as to merge the exterior with the interior (in a similar convergence to that of the human subject and object in the filming). Listening here is represented both in silence and in an enclosed visual image. In musical terms, this is an interlude, a sonorous pause, and a sedentary one (in a film notable for its musicality and movement, particularly dance music, the two protagonists in this sequence sit almost completely still). Self-reflexive in its display of instruments of sound recording and mechanical reproduction, the sequence foregrounds the subjects of music and filmmaking. Both are present while refined, distilled to pure form, to technological metonym. They are refined to a shadow, an outline, the flash of white teeth in a face so obscured as to be rendered almost featureless, the hint of a hand movement as the guitarist strums, and a microphone. They are refined, that is, to a trace. Further, the sequence marks an interruption in the aural continuity of the film and recalls the film's first sequence, returning to the idea of rhythm as an insistent, emphatic marker, as beat, heartbeat, and life-giving.

The sequence discussed above comes at the end of a series of ethnographic-style shots filmed in a Mozambican village. The rural circumstances, far removed from the city and very different from the lengthy sequences of documentary (particularly that of the revolutionary period) and fiction film (notably the 1965 British feature *Mozambique*, directed by Robert Lynn), are plundered from the archive. The ethnographic shots of the village show barefoot children in ways that could have come from any Jean Rouch film. The complexity of the inclusions here return us to questions of naturalism and technology and, furthermore, to how they are represented. Among these silent sequences, a group of young boys playfully imitate the filmmaker, feigning imaginary cameras in their hands.

This suggestion of visual anthropology is also present in Duque's earlier feature *Color perro que huye* (Colored runaway dog) (2011). At one stage in the film, Duque shoots a religious ceremony in a Caracas street. In a scene of African, European, and indigenous syncretism, the primary initial focus is acoustic, in the rhythmic sound of drumming. The camera meanwhile homes in on a Bruce Lee T-shirt, before opening out to reveal crowds in the street, where a miniature Christ-like figurine bobbles above the mass of people, who chant *¡Hueso!* (bone!) and dance frenetically to the insistent drumbeat (see fig. 6.3).

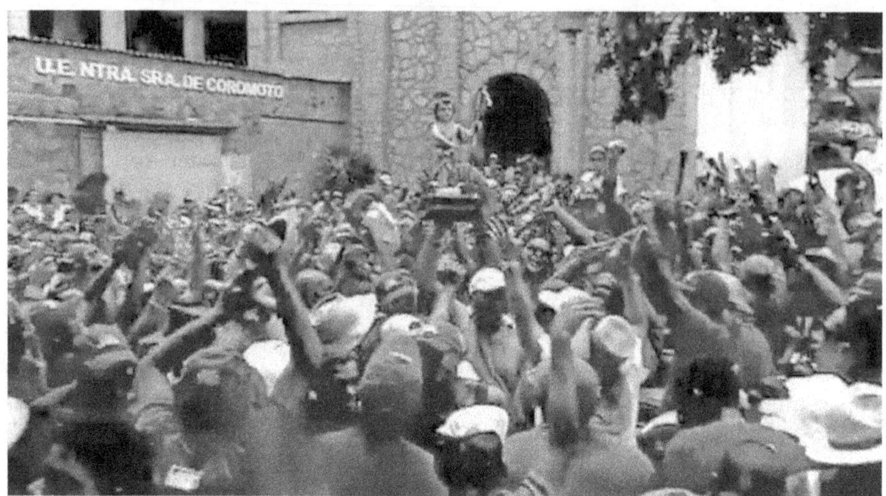

Fig. 6.3 Frenzied rhythm and trance in *Color perro que huye*.

The frenzy reaches a crescendo similar to the images in Esteva's *Lejos de los árboles*.

In one of the few academic articles on Duque's work, Elena Oroz and Miguel Fernández Labayen identify the centrality of the human body in this film and in Duque's wider corpus.[17] Further examples of this are provided later in this chapter in a discussion of a film that was made after the publication of Oroz and Fernández Labayen's article. For now, though, they note the contrast between the images of the dying (and finally dead) body of Silvio Duque in *Ensayo final para utopía* and the vibrant dance scenes that recall the trance films of Maya Deren, especially in the sequences shot in Africa. Drawing on personal correspondence with the filmmaker, Oroz and Fernández reveal the origins of the film's title as a direct quote taken from Robert Stam's book on Mikhail Bakhtin and carnival.[18] While this highlights a carnivalesque proximity of life and death, what interests me here is not so much the Bakhtinian bricolage—the merging and the morphing of disparate elements—that undoubtedly distinguishes the hybrid composition of this film and whose importance is rightly identified by Oroz and Fernández Labayen but the correlation between sound and visuality as expressed through representation of the body (which is indeed Bakhtinian), in the form of rhythm and movement, shape and silhouette. In a remarkable set of sequences that introduce the Mozambican section of *Ensayo final para utopía*, Duque films dancers and fashion models onstage in an empty auditorium (during a rehearsal, perhaps). The influence of trance film is marked by the horn-type samba-jazz-like music composed by Riz Ortolani[19] and the

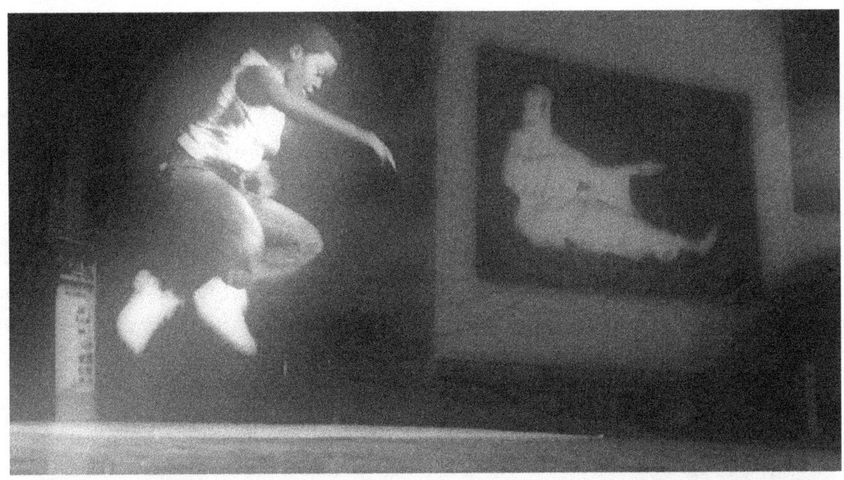

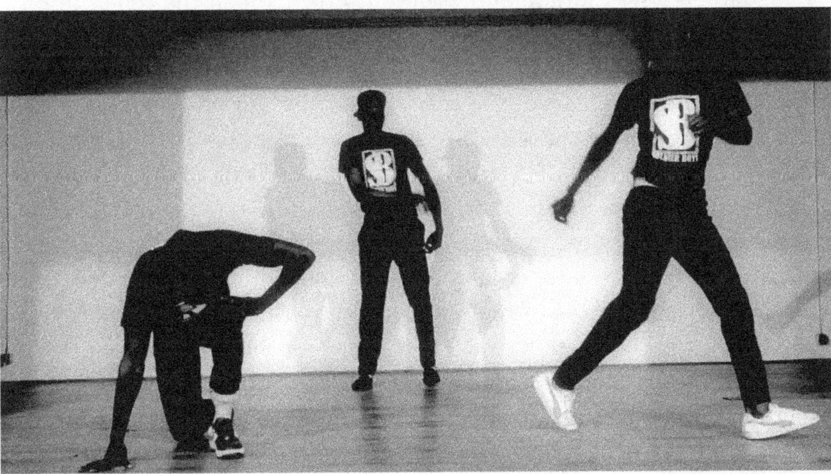

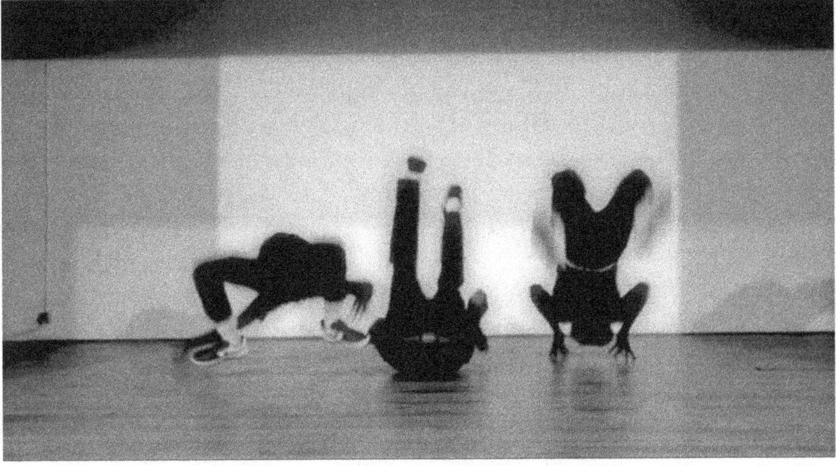

Fig. 6.4 a–c Trance sequences in *Ensayo final para utopía*.

slow-motion camera work shot from below that emphasizes the curves and contours of the human bodies. Another set of uncommented collage-type trance sequences—mainly in black and white—follows. These are charged with a homoeroticism sandwiched between images—some in color—taken from the archival footage of the revolutionary films and interspersed with occasional portraits. Almost all the images of the militant celebrations also involve dancing and chanting, together with inserts featuring revolutionary propaganda (see figs. 6.4a, 6.4b, and 6.4c).

Death and Writing

Duque's father, Silvio, although present on-screen and at the center of *Ensayo final para utopía* as the film's subject, is mute throughout. Recording the process of Silvio Duque's death, the film is also dedicated to him. Significantly, the written dedication appears at the very end of the film, in a looping temporal return. A filmic eulogy and a work of mourning, the final part of the film sees Duque senior resurrected. Seemingly healthy, there is no on-screen indication and no narrative commentary or edit to explain his apparent recovery and reappearance, his ghostly return from the dead.

The final lengthy and notably silent sojourn through Europe is composed of a series of shots of monumental Italy—the Leaning Tower of Pisa, the Sistine Chapel, Venetian canals—as Duque junior postmortem ransacks his own archive of material, the family travelogues that he has filmed in the past (and that include images of himself reflected in the mirror as well as his healthy father, the two of them together). This is flashback unsignaled as such, a recourse to the archive and to an autobiographical archive. Here the hereditary chain linking the son and the father, self and other, is reversed in the reordered temporality (thanks to the digital files stored on Andrés's computer, the past—the Duque family holiday—can be projected after the present marked by the fact of Silvio's death). Filmic experimentation with the archive facilitates an inversion in the filial-paternal legacy within a resonant silence; the experience is an alteration in time, an impossibly proleptical re-sounding recorded on film. There is also in this resonance an aural emergence from a primordial silence the listening, in which the *oto* of the ear and *auto* coincide in ways that extend beyond their homonymous status. This coincidence is something akin to an *archi-écriture* in the doubling of subjectivity and autobiography in the figures of the father and the son; they are both the subject of the film and, to paraphrase Nancy, "the individual subject who writes the text."[20]

Lacoue-Labarthe's essay reads, among other things, the eulogy delivered by Theodor Reik at the funeral of his friend and analyst Karl Abraham as recalled by Reik in his memoir *The Haunting Melody*. While this text does not deal in any way with film or with broader issues of sound, it is concerned with music and subjectivity. The text is prompted by death and by the figure of the other. Lacoue-Labarthe writes:

> Every autobiography is essentially an *allobiography*, the "novel" of an other (be it a double). The novel of a *dead* other. Just as Montaigne's essays are a tomb for Etienne de La Boétie and draw on the great exemplary dying figures of antiquity (beginning with the Socrates of the *Phaedo*), *The Haunting Melody* opens up with the death of Abraham and calls up the rival figures of Mahler and Freud. It too is a tomb: its initial form is that of a funeral eulogy. That Reik should "know" what is to be thought about the funeral eulogy in general, even that Freud should suggest it to him, changes nothing. On the contrary: autobiography, the biography of the *dead* other, is always inscribed in an agon—a struggle of pure prestige. Every autobiography is in its essence the narrative of an *agony*, literally. This is why (among other reasons) it is not incorrect to substitute "thanatographical" for "biographical": all autobiography, in its monumental form, is *allothanatography*.[21] (Emphasis in the original)

Epilogue: *Oleg y las raras artes* (Oleg and the rare arts) (2016)

The influence of filmmaker Iván Zulueta on Duque is unquestionable, but it is not necessarily a stylistic one. Duque's work at times is haunted by Zulueta's.[22] Duque borrows, often quite literally, from Zulueta's 1979 *Arrebato* in *Color perro que huye*, in which he revives the all-but-forgotten figure of Will More, one of the Zulueta film's lead actors.[23] As noted, Duque's cinema is highly autobiographical, at once intimate and worldly, a body of work that moves *dérive*-like across the globe while retaining its experimental form and format.[24] I conclude this chapter by placing Duque's corpus to date within the parentheses of his first major piece, *Iván Z* (2004), and his more recent feature, *Oleg y las raras artes* (Oleg and the rare arts) (2016), a portrait of eighty-eight-year-old Russian composer and pianist Oleg Karavaychuk.

Both *Iván Z* and *Oleg y las raras artes* are highly unconventional biopics, and both focus on personalities whose fame (or notoriety) belongs to a previous era. Zulueta's career as film director was over by the time Duque filmed *Iván Z*, and Karavaychuk was largely forgotten. Both men are, in their own different ways, anachronisms, throwbacks to a previous age. Indeed, large sections of these films involve the protagonists recalling the past, their now-distant moments of glory, and the people they knew. And, in the context of the Lacoue-Labarthe quote above, it is significant that both Zulueta and Karavaychuk died shortly after the release of their respective biographical films. Independently, these films function as elegies, as testaments to the work of their subjects and, more particularly, how that work has weighed heavily on Duque himself. Zulueta is both model and alter ego to Duque, his other. Duque's mobilization of his "overwhelming subjectivity" (to recall Cerdán's description), then, might be seen as the weaving of a complex path between the biographical and the autobiographical that involves an experimentation with different technologies and forms and in which death—or at least the proximity of death—prevails in ways similar to Lacoue-Labarthe's statement that "all autobiography, in its monumental form, is *allothanatography*." *Iván Z* is an idiosyncratic extended interview with a filmmaker *maudit* made decades after his final film. Shot at his family home in San Sebastián in northern Spain, the last sequence of the film shows Zulueta taking Duque's camera in his hands and marveling at it. It is a poignant and elegiac moment, far removed from the obsessive drug-fueled psychodrama of *Arrebato*.

Twelve years after *Iván Z*, Duque would film his conversations with a musician. Once again, to recall Nancy, the *oto* and the *auto* coincide. Androgynous and eccentric, like Rosemarie Cruz Obag in *Paralelo 10*, Oleg Karavaychuk is a bizarre, chaotic, unpredictable, and often irascible personality who occasionally displays hostility toward his interlocutor. A celebrated pianist and one-time student of Dmitri Shostakovich, he turned to writing (or improvising) film soundtracks after his work was banned by the Soviet authorities in the early 1950s. Karavaychuk composed scores for several Soviet filmmakers, including Kira Muratova, Sergei Parajanov, and Vasiliy Shukshin. In this little-over-an-hour essay, Duque films Karavaychuk at the Hermitage Museum, in the street and gardens close to his home in the Saint Petersburg suburb of Komarov, and, in a brief sequence, in a cafeteria. The composer expresses admiration for the czars, for Catherine the Great, and for Joseph Stalin ("It only goes to show the wisdom of the Great Leader," he says at one point), and disdain for Vladimir Putin.

Significant here—as in all of Duque's work—is the film's mise-en-scène, referring to not only the organization of the frame but also the camera work and the structure of sound. There is, furthermore, no profitable distinction to be made here between mise-en-scène and montage, in the traditional sense of the dichotomy established by film studies. The relation between space and sound that defines *Oleg y las raras artes*—in its focus on music—also informs retrospectively Duque's entire corpus.

This film begins with a remarkable sequence shot in a lengthy corridor of the antiquities section of the Hermitage adorned with wooden panels whose golden frames encase swirling baroque depictions of musical instruments, mythical animals, naked figures, paintings of landscapes within other paintings, and religious icons in a lavish display of excess. Duque's unmoving camera captures the sweep of the distance between it and the grand doors at the end of the passageway through which the diminutive figure of Karavaychuk emerges and makes his slow and shambling approach. When he is at medium distance before the camera, he speaks. Citing Gogol, he talks of the difficulties presented by the snow in the Saint Petersburg streets but notes that once a person is inside the Hermitage, the effects are transformative. "It is miraculous how the body inexplicably reacts when faced with the Arts," he says.[25] It is a foretaste of what he will later, at the end of the film, explain as the somatic relation between music and the body.

The film's structure, then, has a resonance, an echo; it is constructed around a repetition, a re-sounding of these sentiments. In a film that revolves around the idea of music, and often posits speech against music, it is interesting that, on one level, its diegetic thematic should be defined not by music but by speech and, on another level, sound should determine its structure. This point, however, is reinforced by the exceptionality of such sentiments. They contradict, in ways that are simultaneously coherent and incoherent with the film's dominant register, the prevailing irrationality and excessiveness, the unattenuated, unmediated lack of measure (or, as we have seen before, *demesura*) regarding the subject that permeates it.

The following sequence portrays Karavaychuk seated before the czar's piano at the Hermitage with its intricate painted decorations. His playing is incandescent, intense, and fleeting, again before an immobile, seemingly neutral camera. He plays the piano with a combination of violence and naturalness, in bursts that he himself interrupts to pronounce on matters current and historical. The result is an extraordinary, jangling, incoherent performance of verbosity, mired in past reminiscence and present-day bugbears, that contrasts with the clarity of the piano and its promise. While the pianist's playing is postponed again and again (on this occasion and at other points throughout the film), interrupted, paused, and abruptly broken off, once the music is finally played, it takes precedence over Karavaychuk's often senseless speech. It stresses the untimely. In a film haunted by the weight of the past, the piano is instantaneous, but its flow beckons toward the future; its sound is that of imminent deferral.

This idea of deferral and resonance is contained in the notion of the echo, in the lapse of time between the original sound and its repetition. What we see in this film is an idea of discontinuity, of thwarted Russian history and of a divergence between the subject of the biographical film—the *sense*—and the music. Nancy writes, "Music is the art of the hope for resonance: a sense that does not make sense except because of its resounding in itself. It calls to itself and recalls itself, reminding itself and by itself, each time of the birth of music,

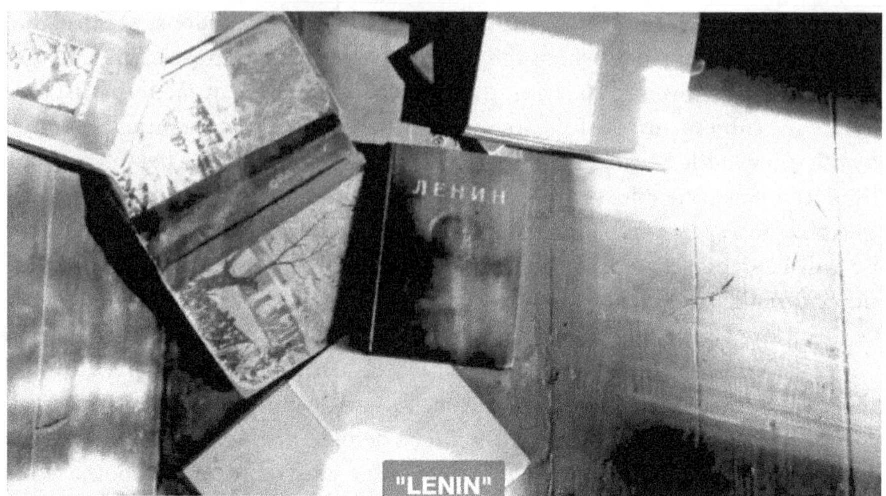

Fig. 6.5 The abandoned house in Oleg's neighborhood in *Oleg y las raras artes.*

that is to say the opening of a world in resonance, a world taken away from the arrangements of objects and subjects, brought back to its truth only in the affirmation that modulates this amplitude."[26]

As if to emphasize the anachronistic quality of his subject matter, Duque enters an abandoned house in the neighborhood where Karavaychuk lives. The sequence is shot in absolute silence. There is a sense, in the light that penetrates the dusty glass, of frozen time and of an absent sonic presence similar to that of the guitarist in the Mozambican hut discussed earlier. But that absence is increased by the emptiness. No one else is physically present; there are only objects: an atlas, a work by Lenin, and a book of astronomy on the windowsill (fig. 6.5). It is as if we are hearing the murmur of a past epoch, a return. "Music," writes Nancy, "is the art of making the outside of time return to every time."[27]

Shortly thereafter, Duque films Karavaychuk possessed by an internal musical reverie. His mouth emits verbal, muted sound, but it is musical all the same. It is given musical form through the torsions of Karavaychuk's body. In his displaced figure, out of place and out of time, we sense a haunting and haunted melody, writhing silently within the composer's slight frame (fig. 6.6).

Not only is this exemplary of Karavaychuk himself—in an interview with Manu Yañez, Duque remarks on Karavaychuk's "divina locura" (divine madness) and says, "He lives in a constant state of trance."[28] Though this is a consistent theme throughout the film, it makes explicit the trance-like relation between interiority and exteriority and the reconfiguring of sense through sound that pervades all of Duque's work. Karavaychuk's somatic relation to

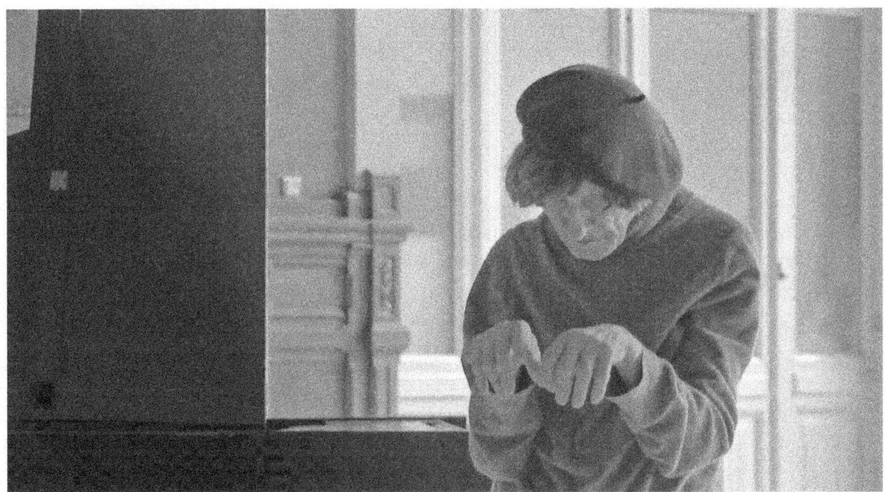

Fig. 6.6 Oleg Karavaychuk, a figure out of place and out of time.

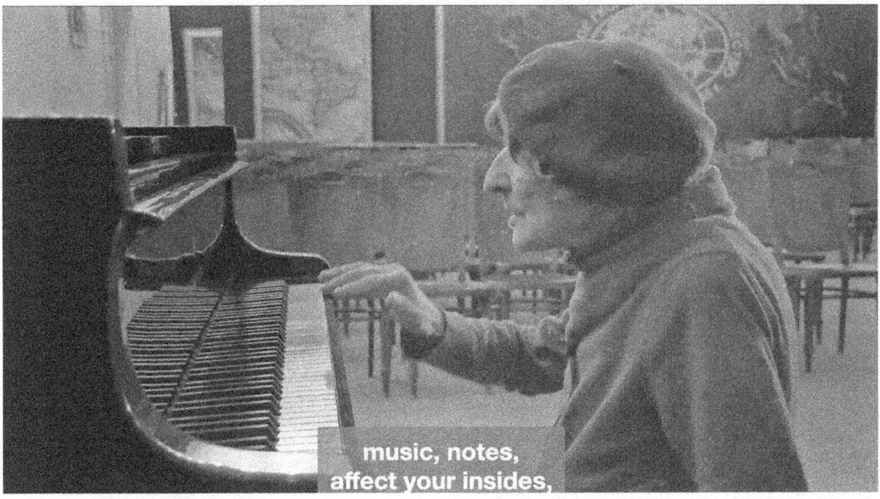

Fig. 6.7 "Music, notes, affect your insides."

music (at one stage, he refers to his "divine rhythm") recalls the initial sequence of *Ensayo final para utopía* with the dancing shadow and pulsating light, or that of Duque's father on his deathbed. It also recalls Duque's biographical portraits of Rosemarie and Zulueta and the creativity of their divine madness. Karavaychuk is at his most lucid when he says, "The inner self is associated with music and with dissonance" (fig. 6.7).

Notes

1. Although it is not mentioned in the film, Rosemarie Cruz Obag suffers from schizophrenia.

2. Jean-Luc Nancy, *Listening* (New York: Fordham University Press, 2007), 8.

3. Philippe Lacoue-Labarthe, "The Echo of the Subject," in *Typography*, 139–207 (Stanford, CA: Stanford University Press, 1989), 146. I am grateful to my colleague Ainsworth Clarke for suggesting I read Lacoue-Labarthe's essay.

4. The Spanish word *sentido* means both meaning and direction, as in the direction of traffic.

5. In an interview with Elena Oroz, Duque associates the very act of filming with otherness: "Cada vez que filmo soy otro" (Whenever I film I am (an) other). Elena Oroz, "Andrés Duque: A propósito de Color perro que huye," *Blogs&Docs*, July 4, 2011, http://www.blogsandocs.com/?p=1032.

6. Nancy, *Listening*, 39.

7. Ibid., 25.

8. Ibid., 39.

9. Ibid., 41.

10. Serge Daney, "Freeze-Image / Arrêt sur l'image," *Serge Daney in English*, June 18, 2009, http://sergedaney.blogspot.com/2009/06/freeze-image-arret-sur-limage.html.

11. Laura Mulvey, *Death 24x a Second: Stillness and the Moving Image* (London: Reaktion Books, 2006), 22.

12. Nancy, *Listening*, 17.

13. Ibid., 41.

14. Cerdán alludes to the relation between reflection and subject in Duque's work in a way that coincides with Nancy and that is central to my argument. Referring to *Ensayo final para utopía*, Cerdán states that the film "creates a fascinating game of mirrors with no connection other than his own subjectivity (which is overwhelming), between the personal loss of his father and a recent trip to Mozambique" (crea un fascinante juego de espejos, sin más conexión que su propia subjetividad (que es arrolladora) entre la pérdida personal de su padre y un reciente viaje a Mozambique). Josetxo Cerdán, "Apuntes de campo sobre el trabajo de Andrés Duque y Virgina García del Pino (o por qué los artistas son un coñazo)," in *Territorios y fronteras: Experiencias documentales contemporaneas*, ed. Vanesa Fernández and Miren Gabantxo (Bilbao, Spain: Universidad del País Vasco/Euskal Herriko Unibertsitatea, 2012), 149.

15. Akira Mizuta Lippit, *Ex-Cinema: From a Theory of Experimental Film and Video* (Berkeley: University of California Press, 2012), 38.

16. Nancy, *Listening*, 26.

17. Elena Oroz and Miguel Fernández Labayen, "Plug-ins del yo. Inscripciones autobiográficas en los documentales transnacionalesde Andrés Duque," in *El documental en el entorno digital*, ed. Miquel Francés, Josep Gavaldà, Germán Llorca, and Àlvar Peris (Barcelona: Editorial UOC, 2013).

18. Robert Stam, *Subversive Pleasures: Bakhtin, Cultural Criticism, and Film* (Baltimore: Johns Hopkins University Press, 1989).

19. Ortolani also composed the theme music for *Mondo Cane* (1962), a film often cited in comparison with *Lejos de los árboles*.

20. Nancy, *Listening*, 35.

21. Lacoue-Labarthe, "Echo of the Subject," 179.

22. Iván Zulueta (1943–2009) is best known for his extraordinary "underground" film from 1979, *Arrebato*, often considered exemplary of the dark underbelly of the exuberance of the post-Transition "Movida" in contrast to the celebratory films of his contemporary Pedro Almodóvar.

23. Will More, the artistic name of Joaquín Alonso-Colmenares y García-Loygorri, is the central character of Zulueta's 1979 *Arrebato*. He died in August 2017.

24. Duque has shot films at times on his cell phone.

25. In a private conversation, Duque told me that this sequence was shot mid-August. The weather was warm and there was no snow. Apparently Karavaychuk was quoting from a Gogol short story.

26. Nancy, *Listening*, 67.

27. Ibid., 67.

28. Manu Yañez, "Andrés Duque: 'Oleg Karavaychuk es alguien que me reconcilia con el mundo,'" *Otros Cines Europa*, October 7, 2016, http://www.otroscineseuropa.com/andres -duque-oleg-karavaychuk-es-alguien-que-me-reconcilia-con-el-mundo/.

7

TURNS AND RETURNS, *ENVOIS/RENVOIS*

The Postal Effect in Recent Spanish Film

*T*ODAS LAS CARTAS: *CORRESPONDENCIAS FÍLMICAS* (THE COMPLETE LETTERS: FILMED CORRESPONDENCE) is the title of an itinerant exhibition and subsequent DVD box set of five video dialogues between pairings of mainly Spanish filmmakers with their overseas colleagues. The project developed under the auspices of the Centre de Cultura Contemporània de Barcelona over three years between 2008 and 2011.[1] Capturing the directness of epistolary address, these engagements prove to be what filmmaker and critic Anna Petrus has felicitously referred to as a kind of "exquisite corpse": unfolding, incongruent, improvised, and juxtaposed composites.[2] Indeed, the term *exquisite corpse* evokes both a sense of a surreptitious relation or return to the surrealist legacy—closely linked to the history of the Catalan avant-garde—and the factor of chance, the unpredictable, or the untimely, with its rich implications for both film and philosophy. In this chapter I locate such questions in a context of iterability, citationality, and reversibility. I speculate on the complexities of filmic representation as well as on the consequences of technological change in the production of images.

Organized in the wake of the similar and highly successful Victor Erice and Abbas Kiarostami video installation experiment and exhibition (featuring the same curators, Jordi Balló and Alain Bergala), these filmed correspondences have an additional antecedent in Isaki Lacuesta's 2007 *Las variaciones Marker.* Though made without the direct or active participation of French filmmaker Chris Marker, Lacuesta's essay film begins in prologue—in the form of a written epigraph—with the text of an e-mail from Marker to Lacuesta's production company. This type of format is reproduced verbally, in the citation of other written missives, within the diegesis of the body of the film. Furthermore, Marker himself sets a telling precedent with his 1956 documentary *Letter from Siberia,* a wry, lucid epistle sent out into the world to anonymous receivers in the midst and mists of the Cold War.[3]

The *Correspondencias fílmicas* project—with all its Baudelairean resonance[4]—highlights one of the most interesting recent developments in Spanish cinema: the emergence of a group of young filmmakers whose work is marked by the widening gap between their production and their place of origin. I refer more specifically here to the opening up of the national to dissemination, to the disturbance within the national sign, its division or diversion, or what might be termed the nonarrival of the national letter. This is compounded by the fact that, as we have seen, Spain is a country whose cinema history, and writing on it, is distinguished by long-standing and tense debates over questions of national identity. This kind of collaborative, cosmopolitan venture provides the measure of the indifference shown by a new generation of filmmakers toward the concept of a national cinema. Their dispatches (*envois*) in this project are those of envoys of a sort, but not those of conventional ambassadors. The gap, or the distance inherent in the epistolary format (much played on in on-screen distantiation techniques, in the complexities of telecommunication, the necessary ellipses), opens up the spaces between origin and place; that is, the gap creates a turbulence surrounding the concept of location and disturbs the national as a discursive category.

Moreover, postal communication, Jacques Derrida suggests, implies not only a physical separation between two parties in different places connected by an unpredictable system of relay ("switching points," "the placing of posts," their stages and their staging, their positioning, and their poles) but also an inevitable temporal disequilibrium, a delay in communication, a necessary asynchronization.[5] It is worth noting that the postage seal—the thudding stamp reinforced by a thump on the soundtrack and the indelible impression that marks the design of the box set and each individual DVD menu—draws our attention to these staging posts in the transportation of mail and the fragility of the postal connection (fig. 7.1a). The seal is subject to the unpredictable violence of legal certification—its stamp of approval and its seal of authority—and to the unforeseen possibilities of being mislaid or subject to delay, division, or diversion.

Such discordance is not, however, contemplated in textual terms by Linda Ehrlich,[6] who accepts the classification first mooted by Alain Bergala, of correspondence as a synonym of correlation[7]—the notion that these filmic exchanges are based on compatibility; on similarities; on a communal sense of togetherness; on commonalities, parallel lives, and affinities; and on a definitive complicity between the different pairings. This kind of critical representation suggests a closed circuit in the untroubled and unbroken circulation of images following a smooth trajectory between signifier and signified, between sender and receiver. Iván Pintor Iranzo, discussing the Erice-Kiarostami correspondence (in a text included in the catalog that accompanies the set of DVDs and that Pintor Iranzo frames in the form of a letter), begins and ends his essay in circular fashion with the same sentence, which establishes a telos: "A letter always arrives at its destination."[8] I argue, however, that there is no guarantee of such completion. A letter's delivery, or arrival, is uncertain and constantly thwarted; its route is diverted; and it is subject to being mislaid. Invariably, fissures emerge in the circuit of communication. And I propose that this uncertainty of delivery is connected not only to the letter format but also to film.

As it happens, in a different text that appears in the same volume as Pintor Iranzo's, Bergala starts with the statement, "Every letter is motivated by an absence that it seeks to fill . . . that of the presence of the other."[9] Contrary to Pintor Iranzo's assertion, Bergala's introductory sentence suggests a skewed relation in the moment of the production or the writing of the letter, a presence conditioned by an absence and consequently marked in some way by its trace, the mark that makes present its absence. Added to the temporal delay or deferral inherent in the transmission of the filmed missives is that of geopolitical spatial difference. What transpires in this set of correspondences are dialogues marked not by reciprocation but by bifurcation and by the undermining of any claim to origins. At the same time, they are marked also by the destabilization of destinations and, in turn, that of the relation between addresser and addressee, signifier and signified. The letter is never expressed through indivisible simultaneity—there is always, and invariably, despite technological advances, an element of time lag, of being out of sync, and of the divided. The letter, therefore, is never a matter of correspondence in the sense of coinciding, but it is perhaps a question of coincidence in the sense of chance, the fortuitous event. As an aside that links to the question of chance, the Spanish word *destino* has two meanings: destination and destiny.[10] Moreover, *destino* is an anagram of another Spanish word, *sentido*, which (as we have seen in previous chapters) signifies meaning, sense, and direction.

Among the many and varied puns that Derrida cites with regard to the French word *cartes* (and applicable to the Spanish *cartas*) are not only letters but also playing cards and the cards of fortune tellers. The inspiration for Derrida's book *The Post Card*, Matthew Paris's erroneous illustration of Plato and Socrates in reversed positions, "comes from a fortune-telling book."[11] Chance, then, a question of fortune, is implicit in disturbing the possibilities of the letter's arrival at its destination. But more than just an error, this depiction is another reversal, one pointedly related to the hierarchical relations of dictation and writing as well as the Western heritage or tradition. Likewise, *carte/carta*

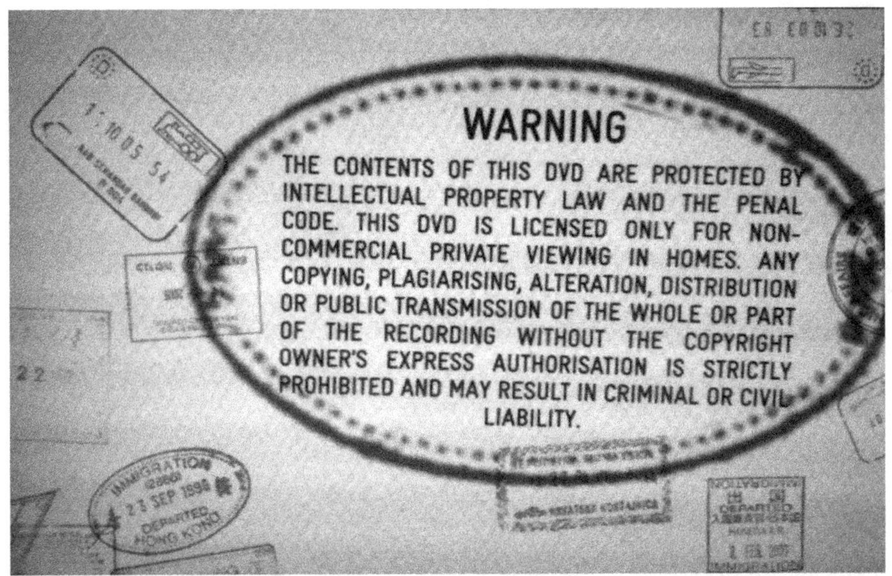

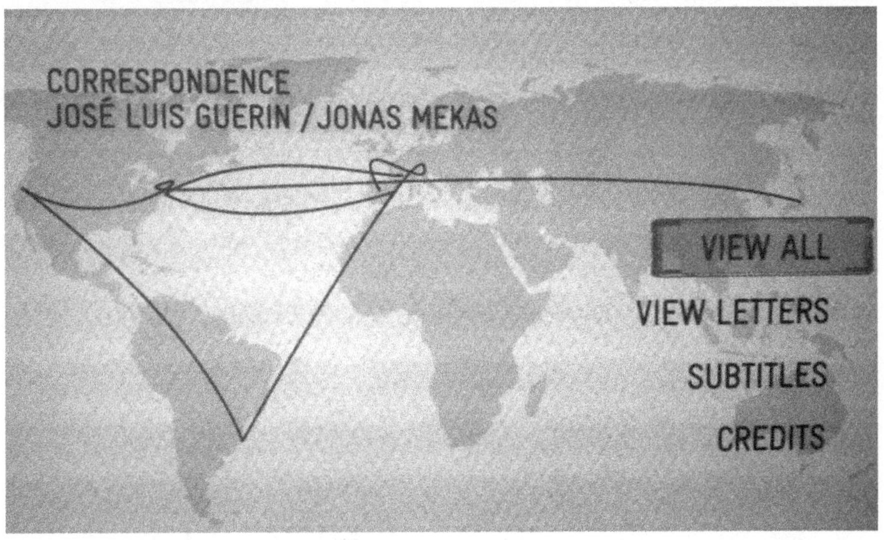

Fig. 7.1 a–b Images of worldly correspondence from the DVD cover of *Todas las cartas: Correspondencias fílmicas*.

is also a chart, a map, and a menu. The individual menus of the filmed correspondence DVDs are decorated—aptly—with an image of maps of the world with a crudely drawn line linking each pairing (fig. 7.1b).

The discussion in this chapter is limited to three of the five encounters: those between José Luis Guerín and Jonas Mekas, between Lacuesta and Naomi Kawase, and between Albert Serra and Lisandro Alonso.[12] In contrast to Ehrlich, my purpose is to suggest that these filmic letters are asymmetrical; that they indicate differences and ruptures; and that they are jagged and discordant engagements. I also suggest that what has been taken for compatibility can equally be taken for reversibility; indeed, that reversibility itself produces aporetic incompatibilities. The very word *encounter*, rather than signifying a meeting (as in the Spanish *encuentro*), in fact implies an internal dissonance, the counter within, or a disassociation.

*   *   *

Such discord is exemplified by the exchange between Guerín and Mekas. Couched in deeply affectionate terms, their respective correspondence could not be more different. Guerín travels the world with the briefest of—largely indifferent—occasional returns to his home in Barcelona (not only his place of residence but also the city of his birth) and only to nostalgically revisit his cinephilic memorabilia and offer an explicit recognition of Mekas's own example as a filmmaker. Theirs is an ongoing homage returned to again and again in each filmed letter, in the form of images and recollections. Each time, however, they are diverted (aptly for letters destined to never arrive at their destination) and deferred, taking, in Guerín's own words (in his final letter, as if to acknowledge that failure), "a different turn," a different direction.

Mekas, the old European and émigré, meanwhile remains firmly attached to his adopted home in Brooklyn and his offices in Manhattan (the trajectories between the two New York districts provide, in part, the rhythm to his contributions). There is a brief exception when Mekas (despite his express reluctance to leave New York) visits Poland and Slovakia. Faced with Guerín's enthusiasm for global travel, Mekas—the Holocaust survivor—gently proposes film as a bulwark against a fractured world. "José Luis, my friend in cinema," Mekas says mournfully on receipt of his interlocutor's celebratory missive detailing his sojourn in New England (and in particular a visit that he made to Thoreau's cabin at Walden Pond, a clear reference to Mekas's filmed diary of 1969). "You went to the New World," he says directly addressing the camera, "and I, *by mistake*, went to the old one. I went to Krakow."

Guerín's formal elegance, his respect for composition and for the confines of the frame, and his painterly mise-en-scène, contrasts with Mekas's wild, jazz-infused, feverish handheld camera that exceeds the boundaries of the frame while retaining the serial order of the filmed diary and the sequentiality for which he is best known, as he records friends, family, and things seen on the streets of New York, as he has done since 1950. Cinephilia is present at all moments in Guerín's films—indeed, it constitutes his central theme—whether as the humorous use of archive footage, his presence at film festivals (Venice, Japan, Lisbon, and Brazil, among many others), or his extraordinary homage to Japanese filmmaker Yasujirō Ozu in a series of sequences shot at Ozu's tomb at Kamakura. In Mekas, however, such cinephilia, while present, is muted, less pronounced, more ironic, and coyly expressed. It includes occasional clips from a personal archive, Peter Kubelka cooking, Ken Jacobs in London in the 1970s, a conversation with Jim Jarmusch late one November night in the street outside Anthology Films, and a Christmas card from John Waters.

Both filmmakers are identifiable by their distinctive, singular styles and their signature effects. In almost all his work, Guerín includes shots of drying clothes billowing in the wind on washing lines, while Mekas's rudimentary handwritten title credits mark, if not exactly beginnings and endings, then interruptions in the seemingly endless flow of his camera. This question of the signature puts into play, moreover, an array of questions related to subjectivity: biography, autobiography, and the on-screen presences of the filmmakers themselves.[13] Mekas's head and shoulders fill the frame at various moments in each letter, unlike Guerín, whose presence is rendered partial and reduced to his unseen disembodied voice. At one point, Mekas presents unsettling images of himself thirty years previously: the filmmaker present in the past.

Amid the complexities of the cosmopolitan and the domestic, the two fields that Guerín and Mekas occupy, alternate between, move within, and put into dialogue with each other to generate an intense engagement—albeit a skewed form of filmic connectivity—establish a productive confusion between the two filmmakers in which the subjectivities of the signature are disseminated within and beyond the frame in a kind of disturbed worldliness. It is a dialogue addressed on one level to filmic form itself, in that its ripples and echoes undo the very formal structures of filming. On another level, these films also confound the forward-moving strictures of conventional temporality; their address is at once to both the past and the future. In these pieces, both filmmakers recycle previously stored and private material while simultaneously providing a glimpse of the footage that would reemerge in future projects: Guerín's *Guest* (2010) and Mekas's *Outtakes from the Life of a Happy Man* (2012).

The filmic signature and particularly the use of writing—a graphism to which I will return in more detail later in this chapter—suggestively dovetail with what Peter Brunette and David Wills aptly term "the problematic of the frame and the signature."[14] The contrast of the photographic or filmed image and the spoken word is reinforced by the excessive qualities of the signature that, in turn, highlights the multiple implications of what Derrida calls the "divisibility of the letter" (between signifier and signified) that go beyond that of the sender and recipient and interrogate the indexical quality of the filmed image.[15] Within and between these texts, other cracks, filtrations, and leakages emerge—often concerning the divisions between writing, speech, and the visual image in their accumulation of references and citations—regarding cultural history and filmic legacies.

* * *

Lacuesta and Kawase's dialogue, significantly titled *In-between Days*, is initially mute—not wordless, but soundless. The division in the first letter sent by Lacuesta is between the image and the written word in the subtitles, an element that is supplementary to the filmic text yet was present from the early stages of cinema in the intertitles that accompanied silent films. Lacuesta, throughout his career (as we will see later), has manifested a particular fascination for the history of film (in ways very different from the academic discipline of film history).[16] Meanwhile, Kawase's letters are doubly subtitled—doubly supplementary—with Japanese calligraphy in one corner of the frame and Spanish subtitles lining the lower section.

Lacuesta begins with a reflection. A director notable for shooting on location far from his native Girona (he has made films in France, Peru, and Mali), he declares from the start that he will make an exception on this occasion. Early on he announces self-consciously that he will film at home in Girona and in the nearby town of Banyoles, where he was born. (In fact, like Guerín and Mekas, Lacuesta includes all kinds of other places—as if in a travelogue—from his and others' films). Lacuesta will also film—unusually—himself and his wife and collaborator, Isa Campo. This most cosmopolitan of filmmakers here creates a paradoxically itinerant home movie. As we will see later, though, it proves to be a haunted home movie.

As Derrida has pointed out in *Counterpath* (a word that, as Derrida himself indicates, is a homonym of the word *counterpart* and is particularly relevant to the discussion below), the French verb *arriver* means both to arrive and to happen.[17] To happen (and for this etymology I am indebted to David Wills) is linked to hap and thereby to chance[18]—to the surprise of the play of exquisite corpses—to the undecidable, the perhaps, the fortuitous accident, the unforeseen consequences of happenstance, or the mishap (recall that Mekas describes his visit to Eastern Europe as a "mistake"). A pivotal moment in the Lacuesta-Kawase correspondence comes when the two filmmakers decide to meet in person in Banyoles, Spain, with a view to filming—exceptionally—together and in 16 mm celluloid, as opposed to the digital video employed to shoot the other letters. A technological mishap during the haphazard processes of the camera and the laboratory results in irreparable damage to the footage. The film that they shoot together is badly exposed, and Lacuesta uses what is left, a set of pixilated images, to speculate on who might have filmed what.[19]

This fifth letter also draws attention to the vestiges of a bilingual and multidisciplinary avant-garde legacy obliquely represented by a palimpsest of visual and verbal images, whose very abstraction suggests a conceptual encounter between distance and representation itself. And it is this dialogue between abstraction and representation that casts doubt on the question of authorship, the absence of a specific signature. Despite the correlations professed by its curators, the *Correspondencias fílmicas* project depends from the outset on the clearly defined division between the two cineastes, whose identifying signature is, in this letter, apparently collapsed—or if not exactly collapsed, then countersigned. That is, an initial reversibility is at work, and it is the first of many in which subjects and objects are confused. The pixilated images of indistinguishable figures (not just of the objects filmed but also of the subjects filming) with which the letter commences are constituted by a set of stills that end with a perfectly clear and discernible photogram (or photograph) of Kawase, camera in hand, her young son at her side, on the shores of the Banyoles lake: the cineaste photographed filming. This is followed by a chiaroscuro, fluttering, curtain-like sheen of seemingly aquatic movement (an image whose impression is reinforced by the sound of flowing water), behind which lies something concealed, enshrouded, and veiled, both beneath the surface of the lake and behind the drapery of the screen.

These sequences, first, suggest a potential reversibility of the concepts of abstraction and representation in film. They are images that evoke a screen to the material surface of cinematic projection or perhaps to celluloid itself, the "elemental" material—an exceptional materiality in this instance—of the 16 mm footage or the paradoxical transparency (here made opaque) of both the material called film and the filmic representation. Second, the unspoken word that appears as text on the screen (in the Spanish subtitles that for this letter appear, significantly, not in the lower section of the screen but in the center of the frame) is *velado*, a Spanish word that in specialized photographic terms means badly exposed (and the opposite of *revelado*, meaning revealed), but it can also be translated as veiled.

While Lacuesta's words are themselves freighted and fraught scriptural images, visual representations that overlay and overburden the abstraction of color and movement, they are followed seconds later by another layer, as yet another track—the musical soundtrack—is laid on the image. The arrangement by avant-garde performers Enric Casassas and Pascal Comelade is pointedly titled "Sense el ressó del dring" (Without the echo of ringing) and is an adaptation of a poem of the same name by the early twentieth-century Catalan futurist Joan Salvat-Papasseit. Meanwhile, Lacuesta's own unspoken, written script—while disconnected in terms of signification from the Salvat-Papasseit/Casassas-Comelade text—appears on-screen, simultaneous to the musical recitation, line by line, as if constituting a set of verses, each describing an instantaneous visual snapshot in a speculative commentary combining what might be occurring behind the oblique images with the themes that have emerged reiteratively throughout the entire Lacuesta-Kawase encounter and whose motifs resound like a surrealist poem: "A lake. / Your son / running around the lake / or a striped tiger. / You and me, dancing flamenco / or trying to. / The tomb of my best friend / And my grandparents' grave / A downpour. / A cloud shaped like a hippopotamus. / Clouds like flaming giraffes. / A cloud like a normal boring cloud / A deep kiss."[20]

An additional linguistic division emerges here. While Salvat-Pappaseit's poetic text is recited to music in the original Catalan, Lacuesta, who is bilingual but has to date made all his features in Castilian, writes in Spanish only for his text to be translated into English to facilitate Kawase's understanding of them.

More significantly, this fifth letter provides another link to the surrealist tradition, to the surrealists' fondness for depth and for the unconscious. The unconscious lurks below the surface in the very reversibility discussed earlier as well as in the surreptitious form of the political unconscious via the unspoken presence (purportedly disavowed yet whose trace—in locational and auditory terms—is present) of Catalonia and the Catalan language in Lacuesta's work.[21] The surrealist imagery of surface and depth prompted by the indistinguishable—and thus displaced—presence of the Banyoles lake connects again to Lacuesta's long-standing interest in the history of film and, in particular, the history of film in Catalonia.[22] As if to return us from the abstract image to a specific sense of place, Lacuesta resorts to the archive with images shot in 1912 by the Spanish pioneer of silent film, Segundo Chomón, of the same lake as part of the film *Gerone, un Venise espagnole*. This use of citation is ghostly in at least two distinct ways. While the subject matter of Lacuesta's own narration alludes to death—that of his grandparents and the enigmatic, never-explained death of his best friend—Chomón's film haunts Lacuesta's and lurks behind it and beneath its surface film, veiled like the abstract imagery of the earlier damaged footage as an uncanny legacy and iteration that hints at an absent presence.

Lacuesta's final letter is written as an addendum in the form of a postscript and contradicts the filmmaker's earlier assertion that, exceptionally, he would dispatch his missives from home. Titled "P.S. From Very Far Away," the post-script plays on the very notions of distance and proximity that have pervaded the correspondence with Kawase. The supplementary letter, this appendage, commences with a series of sequences of everyday life and the landscape in northern Mali, where Lacuesta at the time was shooting his full-length film *Los pasos dobles* (2010).[23] Lacuesta then offers Kawase a gift in the form of yet another film directed by Chomón, the 1907 *Acrobates Japonais*, set to music and created or mixed entirely artificially by Lacuesta himself in the editing room.

Once again, the music is composed and performed by Pascal Comelade.[24] The composition, titled *Skatalan Logofobism*, is a weightily ironic consideration of the national question, as the wordplay of the title poses a stark counterpoint to the immediately preceding images of Mali. However, these juxtapositions, while indeed ironic, are much more than that. The dialogues both establish a bond, sealed by signatures and countersignatures, between the two filmmakers (counterparts) and simultaneously create secret passageways (counterpaths) between the frontiers that divide techne and poiesis, home and abroad, the national and the transnational, filmmaking on location and in the studio, nature and artifice, and the borders between different—seemingly irreconcilable—cultures. This set of aporias emerges from an open network of quotations. Such citationality is of the same order of citation as that employed by Lacuesta in his earlier work on Marker. (Lacuesta's 2007 essay, moreover, makes a point of commenting at length on the international dissemination of Marker's signature, its worldly character.)

What Lacuesta reflects on here correlates to that which he produces: a layered archive of precedents and an unsettling iterative inheritance. Passageways, however, contain an additional paradox. They not only are breaches in the barriers of artificial construction but also constitute the telos between sender and receiver, the very route by which the sign is maintained. They are the (filmic) route or conduit through which light—that specifically filmic materiality—shines. Light, precisely that which is cast into doubt by digital technology, is thwarted in this fifth letter by the multiple layers of abstraction, sound, and script in addition to the delays and lapses between the projection of the image and its reception.

Writing and speech, image and music, the filmic and the profilmic, abstraction and representation, depth and surface, distance and proximity, past and future—these divisions are at the heart of the filmed correspondence project, each pairing being potentially reversible and thereby threatening to destabilize the entire project. In the same vein with respect to their capacity for such reversibility, Derrida describes postcards in the following passage: "One does not know what is in front or what is in back, here or there, near or far, the Plato or the Socrates, recto or verso. Nor what is more important, the picture or the text, and in the text, the message or the caption, or the address. Here, in my post card apocalypse, there are proper names, S. and p., above the picture, and reversibility unleashes itself."[25]

*   *   *

Just as Lacuesta's films delve into a film heritage founded on a material relation, Mekas raised questions concerning cinema and the avant-garde. Mekas, who died in 2019, was widely considered a key figure in North American avant-garde filmmaking, and his style is (seemingly) based on chance, the spontaneous and the serendipitous, the objets trouvés of everyday life, and his own found or rediscovered footage and outtakes.[26] Just as there is an engagement with sequentiality in the diary form that vies with the wild improvisation of Mekas's camera through its untimely yet reiterative quality—a rejection of narrative cinema in favor of fluidity while also being suggestive of formal instability—one equally notes an apparently conscious play with the symbols of order and seriality in the content, the mise-en-scène, of the footage itself. In sequences packed with oblique and symbolic self-reference, Mekas, one of the great archivists of underground cinema, the founder of Anthology Films, and a filmmaker clearly conscious of his own legacy—that which he has inherited and that which he will leave behind—matches his raw material with formal practice in a correspondence with himself regarding the avant-garde. But Mekas, a cineaste whose work is largely made up of outtakes, is also a literal outlaw; he works outside the law.

At one stage in his fourth letter, he pans his camera over the table in his office, with its half-unpacked boxes containing volumes of the *Oxford English Dictionary*. He turns to his bookcase—zooming in and away—to pause before the stern binders of the dictionary, as authoritative a text as any and one that functions as law, its defining quality insistent on closure. And yet the line of volumes is pockmarked by the absence—the gaps in the alphabetical and numerical order—of those tomes still in their postal packaging, yet to be positioned in their place.[27] As if to further (and teasingly) continue the reflection on this disruption, Mekas's camera returns to an exemplary volume of the dictionary that lies open on the table to the "A" pages. Drawing close (another proximity), he dwells momentarily on the word *aleph*.[28] The shot immediately following this one—in juxtaposition with the *Oxford English Dictionary*—presents another text that also commences with the letter A, the open page of an unidentified book whose epigraph, and the object of the camera's detailed focus, is a direct quote—a citation—from that most unruly of surrealist writers, Antonin Artaud (among whose many contributions to surrealist film was the screenplay for Germaine Dulac's 1928 *La Coquille et le clergyman*). Despite the apparently indiscriminate sweep of the camera movement, the selected citation seems not to be an arbitrary choice, both for its alphabetical irony (AA) in contrast with dictionary order and for the content of the reference itself. Artaud's text comes from a discussion of documentary film, in which—controlled by the capricious and elliptical movement of the camera—we can fleetingly decipher such phrases as "the last refuge of partisans of cinema," "poetic," and "spontaneous and direct aspects of reality," in what constitutes an elusive and indirect declaration of intentions, a manifesto of sorts, a signature.

At an early stage in this fourth and final letter, Mekas proclaims off-screen, in the vein of surrealism and with direct reference to the unconscious, that "Dreams will save us, reality is not saving us." Moments later in the same letter, Mekas films himself sniffing a sprig of lavender plucked from a bush on the street. The shot is taken from below, the camera held awkwardly by the filmmaker at waist height so as to film his own face upturned, in a sense inverted or reversed. In another sequence from an earlier letter (discussed in more detail below), he returns to his own personal archive of footage, which he shot three decades previously. As expected, the word *NEGATIVE* appears stamped above the monitor—the outdated cutting-room screen—but it is inverted, upside down, and reversed; it is a negative in both senses of the word, as the substance that constitutes photographic material and negation as the opposite of positive.[29] Furthermore, the written word as both diegetic material—as in the Artaud citation—and as either rudimentary typescript or hand-inscribed mark grafted by the traditional film artisan onto the celluloid, is important to Mekas in this and in all his previous work.[30]

Just as dreams are a symptomatic trace of the unconscious, the surrealist heritage makes itself equally felt in Mekas's fascination with the everyday, his primary material. In another letter, Mekas films at close quarters a bedraggled and moribund pigeon sharing a stoop with a couple consuming a pizza. It is an incongruous and surreal moment captured in the New York everyday that chimes with the painstaking sequence of worker ants shot by Guerín at Ozu's graveyard in startling detail as they labor to haul a twig up a wall, failing, falling, and starting over again. Clearly inspired by Ozu, these sequences are suggestive of perseverance in the face of an elusive existential adversity, a veiled Beckettian futility. In both cases, the nonhuman subject, contiguous with death, provides an anagrammatical paradigm of human behavior that is clearly related to the earlier discussion of Kawase's use of the photogram (and in its obliqueness, that which is concealed beneath the surface). It is one in which the contemplative and the dramatic registers are rendered indistinguishable by the filmic context and also in which time is stilled in a pause or quietude that points symbolically to the delicately balanced and porous frontier between life and death, as if the heart had experienced a momentary tremor.[31]

While death is intrinsic to the form of these letters, it also permeates them thematically. Mekas's contribution—like its previous iteration, *Walden*—to these divergent encounters contains the motif of the cycle of the seasons, both another impression of regulatory order (the seemingly inexorable passage of time) and a poetic legacy of the pastoral elegy. This, too, however, suggests a law in tension with the improvisation that marks Mekas's work. Like Pintor Iranzo's circular letter that insists on the letter's arrival, natural cycles are clearly not reversible. However, the idea of untimely improvisation engaged in a work of disruption within the framed image of Earth, structured on its axis and supported in orbit by its poles, whose temporality is governed by the natural order of seasons,[32] points—in a key aporia—once more to the diverted, misdirected light of film. It conveys both the notion of the passage of something that has passed—the past, something that is not present—and the porous filmic conduit between projection and reception whose sending is subject to being mislaid and delayed. It is a suggestive inheritance that gestures, in similar fashion, toward film's intimate relation to death to draw out the spectral traces that film retains.

Guerín relates the tragic story of Slovenian critic Nika Bohinc, who was murdered in the Philippines after conducting a television interview with the Catalan filmmaker in Lisbon. In Guerín's narration, we experience a sense of uncanniness produced of the experience of seeing their meeting reproduced—in a sense, resurrected—from beyond the grave in Guerín's own tribute to Bohinc as Guerín lightheartedly subverts the same interview ("I tried to invert the relation between interviewer and interviewee," he says). In another instance of the reversible, Guerín uses his portable camera to film the interviewer (in an echo of Lacuesta's shot of Kawase filming) and subjects her to a biographical interrogation.[33] As we have already seen, Lacuesta's return to his origins in Banyoles is haunted both by the memory of the deaths of those close to him and by his cinematic ancestry.

In the same vein, the term *exquisite corpse* also suggests a link between death and film preservation with the project of the archive itself, and, of course, it makes explicit the citationality to which I have referred previously. Mekas, the film archivist, in his own words, "rescues" his "fading, fading footage" from the 1960s and 1970s. "My footage is fading," he says. "It is very old, very old. But it is still holding." We see the screen on the primitive domestic Moviola bouncing around as Mekas struggles to control his handheld video camera while flipping through the footage. The two technologies—each pertaining to a different time—sit awkwardly together, their compatibility questioned by the jerky movements that mark the hiccups and discordance in temporalities.

Another apparent paradox thus emerges: that between the temporalities of technology and the time of nature, the cycle of seasons implicit in Mekas's poetics. What I referred to earlier as a fractured world becomes relevant here in a disruption of the two poles of the Earth that disturbs purportedly natural temporalities. Like the screeching, discordant wheels in need of oil of Mekas's editing machinery or the imbalance marked on-screen by the conflicting analog and digital technologies, Mekas posits a world that is off-kilter. Meanwhile, the same filmmaker is also a memorialist, whose mission—in filmed diaries, notebooks, and archives—is to record the passage of time and loss, to still time, to hold it in abeyance. Lacuesta visits the Darder Museum with its taxidermist specimens (among them the controversial "Negro de Banyoles," a nineteenth-century effigy of an African bushman who, following protests, was returned to Botswana in the 1990s)—another type of archive of holding time—reminiscent of the embalming that Bazin cites as evidence for his ontology of the photographic image (a reference to which both Nicole Brenez [on Guerín] and Petrus [on Lacuesta] make). Lacuesta himself, in the filmed public discussion that accompanies the DVD, makes the claim that filmmakers are "the taxidermists of the 21st century."

* * *

The most enigmatic of the set of video letters is the exchange between Catalan Albert Serra (whose work is discussed in chap. 4) and his Argentine counterpart, Lisandro Alonso. Friends and born the same year, 1975, both filmmakers have been labeled as minimalists by critics, and both are associated with the so-called slow filmmaking movement in contemporary cinema.[34] Unlike Guerín and Mekas or Lacuesta and Kawase, however, Serra and Alonso make no attempt to address each another directly. Here, the nonarrival of the filmed letter is represented quite literally. In the Serra-Alonso exchange, there is no reply, no response, no returned mail. Unlike their colleagues, who produce a series of short missives, Serra and Alonso only manage one film each, and in neither do they acknowledge the other or, indeed, the *Correspondencias fílmicas* project itself. Initially skeptical of the entire idea, Serra and Alonso have produced films that seem to have deliberately turned their backs toward each other.

The disproportion, or asymmetry, between the two films is most evident in their respective lengths (among the many plays on temporality in both the filmmakers' works): Serra, uniquely among the participants in the project, rejects the short form, preferring the lengthy and looping epistle over the succinct postcard. His film lasts for more than two and a half hours, while the duration of Alonso's film is a mere twenty-two minutes. Serra, while combining the banal with the aesthetic (and the theological) in the vein of his previous features, has made a film about the interstices of filmmaking located within those very interstices: the "making of" a film that was never, in fact, made (or else it is the film itself filming its own making). Serra's film is aptly labeled by Olivier Père a "road movie"—another route or pathway or passage—and its central contradiction lies in its stasis.[35]

For all its length and its peripatetic quality, not one single shot uses a moving camera during the first two hours of the film. Connected to this contradiction is the fact that the film is shot on quite literal physical and temporal margins: roadsides, riverbanks, anonymous hotel corridors, and during lunch breaks. The concept of shooting on location is turned on its head. Place, however—or, rather, displacement and emplacement—is important in the apparent absence of address.

Of equal importance and connected to place is the film's framing in terms of both its framework and the frame that delimits the content of each shot and photogram. The film's internal rhythm is generated in the dialogue between verbal improvisation and formal filmic practices in ways that link the notion of envoy as unrepresentative representative to representation itself. Serra, his crew, his entourage, and his usual group of technicians and actors, all of whom herald from Banyoles (Serra's hometown) and are loquacious Catalan speakers, are displaced to the hills of Toledo in La Mancha (one of the early sequences of the film is shot against the backdrop of an archetypal whitewashed windmill). In a culmination of reversals, of the reversibility of cultural legacies and citations, this unofficial delegation of representatives has decamped from Catalonia to Castile via a filmed passageway that both connects and divides, to whence it has been summoned or cited, to comment exhaustively on the otherness of Spain, its foreignness, its legacy,[36] and its heritage. Spain—or its synecdoche, Castile—is the subject of the postal residue, the source of constant discussion, and the object, or address, of the film's dialogue: bullfighting, Francoism, the Spanish Civil War, Cervantes. The nation here emerges as the reversible passageway.

Alonso's film, meanwhile, is equally self-reflexive. Its unspoken enigma—the film, as is habitual in Alonso's work, has practically no dialogue—ends with the plot of a future prospective film script read out prosaically from a piece of paper, itself a sort of letter whose origin and destination are unclear. The film is shot in the same wooded location as Alonso's first full-length feature, *La libertad* (2001), and implies the presence of Misael Saavedra, the woodcutter of the earlier film. In fact, the two films serve as distorting reflections of each other.

Alonso's film is untitled, while Serra's film expansively proclaims itself *El Senyor ha fet en mi meravelles* (The Lord has made marvels in me). Serra's film is baroque in its verbal ingenuity and filmic artifice; Alonso's film is muted and understated but shares Serra's naturalism in its use of nonprofessional actors. Serra's actors are physically imposing, while Alonso's are anonymous, taciturn, silent, and slight amid the menace of nature. They are silhouettes flitting among the trees. The characters of the dogs in the film are as developed as the humans they accompany. Finally, as in *renvois*—to return and to repeat, a remittance of sorts—the two films return us to a temporal paradox; they refer us back. Serra's actors, like a retinue of revenants returning to the scene of unfinished business, constantly cite their previous errant iterations as Sancho and Don Quixote in Serra's *Honor de cavalleria* (2006) as well as an undetermined film in the making. Alonso reintroduces us to Misael Saavedra and a familiar location—and to a screenplay of a potential film in the making. Serra's and Alonso's films return us to their previous work and the implicit promise of future work to come.

Notes

1. The echoes of this project continued to resound for several years. In December 2012, a version of the Guerín-Mekas dialogue was exhibited at the Pompidou Centre in Paris. It was followed in April and May 2013 by an exhibition of the work of Albert Serra, featuring his 101-hour film *Los tres cerditos*. The original exhibition was shown at the Centre de Cultura Contemporània de Barcelona, La Casa Encendida in Madrid, and the Centro Cultural Universitario Tlatelolco in Mexico City.

2. Anna Petrus, "In Between Days: Pequeñas revelaciones de lo íntimo, lo efímero y lo invisible," in *Todas las cartas: Correspondencias fílmicas* (exhibition catalog) (Barcelona: Centre de Cultura Contemporània de Barcelona and Intermedio, 2011), 176.

3. Other antecedents in the body of work associated with Spanish national cinema include Basilio Marín Patino's *Nueve cartas a Berta* (1965), a film that relays into the present in the work of Virginia García del Pino as discussed in this book's afterword.

4. I refer to Charles Baudelaire's sonnet "Correspondences," which forms part of *Fleurs du Mal*. By happy coincidence, however, the young (unrelated) French filmmaker Eric Baudelaire also provides a highly apt example of the postal motif, focusing on its unreliability, in his 2014 film *Letters to Max*.

5. Relevant to this idea is the aporia (referred to throughout this book) proposed by Derrida in one of his discussions of Martin Heidegger of the temporal disturbances within the concept of representation. Although representation has often been considered (with the emphasis on the *re*) as the repeat of a presentation—that is, the repeat of a prior sending—it could be deconstructed (in thinking of "the possibility of impossibility") with attention paid to the *pre*, to mean the repeat of a sending prior to its being sent: re-pre-sent. See Jacques Derrida, *Aporias*, trans. Thomas Dutoit (Stanford, CA: Stanford University Press, 1993), 13. Derrida is thinking here of *Vorstellen*. This kind of temporal disturbance, that something that has already been sent cannot be repeated prior to its sending—"the already not yet"—is what undergirds Derrida's claim that arrival cannot be guaranteed. Jacques Derrida, "Envoi," in *Psyche: Inventions of the Other*, vol. 1 (Stanford, CA: Stanford University Press, 2007), 110.

6. Linda Ehrlich, "Letters to the World: Erice-Kiarostami: Correspondences Curated by Alain Bergala and Jordi Balló," *Senses of Cinema*, November 2006, http://sensesofcinema .com/2006/feature-articles/erice-kiarostami-correspondences/.

7. Alain Bergala, "Erice-Kiarostami: The Pathways of Creation," *Rouge*, 2006, www .rouge.com.au/9/erice_kiarostami.html.

8. Iván Pintor Iranzo, "Queridos Víctor y Abbas," in *Todas las cartas* (exhibition catalog), 49.

9. Alain Bergala, "Te escribo estas imágenes," in *Todas las cartas* (exhibition catalog), 21.

10. Derrida himself links the two words (though not their Spanish translation) in his essay "Le facteure de la vérité," in *The Post Card: From Socrates to Freud and Beyond*, trans. Alan Bass (Chicago: University of Chicago Press, 1987), 436.

11. David Wills, "Post/Card/Match/Book/*Envois*/Derrida," *SubStance* 43 (1984): 28.

12. The reasons for this are mainly to do with length, but it is worth considering that each of the so-called Spanish representatives of the three is also Catalan (they herald from Catalonia), and this book seeks to raise questions regarding national identities within the confines of the Spanish state.

13. The signature, in its most literal sense, is also relevant to the postal motif. I think here of registered mail, which has to be signed for in order to be delivered.

14. Peter Brunette and David Wills, *Screen/Play: Derrida and Film Theory* (Princeton, NJ: Princeton University Press, 1989), 13.

15. Derrida, *The Post Card*, 489.

16. Lacuesta's interest is in a filmic legacy (something that reemerges throughout his work) rather than the ordering principles and rigid laws of the academy.

17. Jacques Derrida and Catherine Malabou, *Counterpath: Traveling with Jacques Derrida*, trans. David Wills (Stanford, CA: Stanford University Press, 2001), 2.

18. We often speak of chance encounters or, as Guerín remarks in response to Mekas's comment that he went to the old world "by mistake," in terms of unforeseen things captured by the camera, produced by the imperatives of technology: mis-*takes*. The methods and procedures of filmmaking and its grammar, law, and ordering principles—the take, the shot, the sequence, and so on—produce their excesses, in which Mekas specializes. *Mistake* contains, of course, an echo or variation of the outtake (see the later discussion on Mekas's fourth letter).

19. The sequence is available for viewing at "Isaki Lacuesta Naomi Kawase: Correspondencia(s)," YouTube, December 2, 2001, www.youtube.com/watch?v= uelECpZEWGc.

20. This is an edited selection of the lines that appear on-screen, not their totality.

21. At a public colloquium with the two filmmakers conducted in Catalan at the Centre de Cultura Contemporània de Barcelona (filmed and included under the rubric "Additional Material" in the DVD), Lacuesta at one point expresses an observation in Castilian only to rectify, tongue in cheek, with the words (spoken in Catalan), "Whoops, sorry, in Catalan, no? After all, this is being financed by the Generalitat [the Catalan regional government]." This additional material and the accompanying book in the DVD box set are not only supplements to the filmed epistles but also other underlying tracks, spectral irritants that haunt, condition, and often contradict the letters themselves.

22. Lacuesta's first feature, *Cravan versus Cravan* (2002), involves recourse to archive material and witnesses of early film spectacles in Barcelona.

23. *Los pasos dobles* is a fiction film, but Lacuesta simultaneously shot a documentary on Spanish painter Miquel Barceló, who, at the time, resided for part of the year in Mali, titled *Los cuadernos de barro.*

24. Kawase's final letter immediately prior to Lacuesta's is titled "What He Remembers," a set of stills that record her young son's experience of the trip to Catalonia. Shot exclusively in Catalonia (in Barcelona and Banyoles), the letter is also set—in an act of reciprocation constitutive of a countersignature—to a musical composition ("Sampo") performed by the Japanese group the Pascals, which, according to the text that accompanies the DVD, is inspired by Comelade. As part of the dialogue, this combination of styles, tastes, cultures, and mutual influence suggests, once again, a countersignature rather than correspondence. Furthermore, the montage that Kawase employs here—in its use of still photography—recalls the practice pioneered by Chris Marker in his most celebrated film, *Le Jetée* (1962). Guerín also employs this technique in his *Unas fotos en la ciudad de Silvia* (2007). In these ways, the paradox of the signature lies in its dissemination rather than in its association with artistic integrity, autonomy, and the individual. Important to my argument, the still—the photogram—is connected to the filmic frame and, in turn, etymologically, to representation. As noted earlier, the word *still* derives from the German *stellen*, the same word whose significance for Heidegger lies in his key concept of *Gestell* (enframing) and in the different meanings regarding representation that Derrida discusses concerning the words *Darstellung* and *Verstellung.* There is, of course, a further postal link to *still* in its similarity to the Greek word *stello*, meaning to send.

25. Derrida, *The Post Card*, 13.

26. In this sense, Mekas puts into practice one of Artaud's observations on the value of documentary film briefly glimpsed in the line of text captured in his fourth filmic postcard that reads "the poetry of objects."

27. Relevant here to the previous discussion of the hap—fortune, fortuitousness, and error—is Mekas's declaration of intentions in *As I Was Moving Ahead, Occasionally I Saw Brief Glimpses of Beauty* (2001): "When I began . . . to put all these rolls of film together . . . the first idea was to keep them chronologic. . . . But then I gave up and I began splicing them together by chance, the way I found them on the shelf, by pure chance."

28. Without wishing to read excessively into Mekas's intentions here, this brief sequence recalls not only Borges's book of stories *El Aleph* but also the introductory sentences of what is probably Derrida's most celebrated essay, "Différance":

> I will speak therefore of a letter.
>
> Of the first letter, if the alphabet, and most of the speculations which have ventured into it are to be believed.
>
> I will speak, therefore of the letter *a*.
>
> Jacques Derrida, *Margins of Philosophy*, trans. Alan Bass (Chicago: University of Chicago Press, 1982), 3.

29. Early in the "Envois" section of *The Post Card*, Derrida writes: "Socrates writing, writing in front of Plato, I always knew it, it had remained like the negative of a photograph to be developed for twenty-five centuries—in me, of course" (9–10). Another sense of the negative here connects to the earlier discussion of passage. Derrida himself has played on the French word *pas* as meaning both not and step. The latter is also true of the Spanish word *paso*, which links phonetically to passage and perhaps also to Lacuesta's film *Los pasos dobles.*

30. It is important to note, as a measure of the technological evolution in filmmaking, that Mekas's practice of writing literally on the celluloid is not, in fact, what happens in these letters, which are shot in video. (He comments on this at one point toward the end of his third letter: "I am not even filming. I'm taping, videotaping.") Here the notion of grafting is questionable, given that what Mekas does is film his writing. Much of his work—and particularly his second letter—reflects indirectly on the differences between the two technologies and the distance between the materials and the materialities in which writing itself intervenes. In this vein, during his visit to the Jewish cemetery, Mekas focuses his camera on the broken stones engraved with fragments of inscriptions in Hebrew.

31. For further discussion of the concept of the still, see note 24. This also has a relevance to the discussions in previous chapters on the recourse of the freeze-frame.

32. I have in mind here Derrida's encounter with saxophonist and free jazz composer Ornette Coleman. See "The Other's Language: Jacques Derrida Interviews Ornette Coleman, 23 June 1997," trans. Thomas S. Murphy, www.ubu.com/papers/Derrida-Interviews-Coleman _1997.pdf.

33. This, of course, is reminiscent of Derrida's experience of seeing himself with Pascale Ogier, in *Ghost Dance*, as mentioned in the introduction to this book.

34. *Slow cinema* is an indiscriminate term employed to describe an international tendency over the last decade or so in the work of certain influential but widely differing filmmakers, from Pedro Costa to Bela Tarr, Apichatpong Weerasethakul, and, at times, Abbas Kiarostami.

35. Olivier Père, "LA/AS, Pensamiento salvaje y minimalismo grandioso," in *Todas las cartas* (exhibition catalog), 151.

36. The pun here—much employed by Derrida himself—is on the common etymological root of the terms *delegation* and *legacy* to, on the one hand, link them with the terms *representative* and *representation* and, on the other hand, extend that to the dual meaning of the word *citation*, both quotation and legal summons. A summons is, of course, mailed or delivered by courier.

8

RETROSPECTIVE FUTURE PERFECT

History, Black Holes, and Time Warps in the Films of Los Hijos and Luis López Carrasco

BY ADOPTING THE NAME LOS HIJOS (THE CHILDREN), the members of this Madrid-based filmmaking collective appear to deliberately draw attention to the concept of inheritance and to their condition as heirs. Indeed, Los Hijos's creative nonfiction cinema is distinguished by an acknowledgment of its generation's uncomfortable relationship with its predecessors, one predicated by the archive.[1] These films are also—in part owing to the collective nature of their project—distinguished by a variegated subjectivity whose singularities are difficult to reconcile and marked by the morphing and expansion of concepts such as authorship and autobiography. Their diffused signature challenges conventional notions of the film auteur in ways that might be termed—to paraphrase Jacques Derrida—autography, such as that in the work of Andrés Duque.[2] In both instances—the generational and the autographic—the filial link looks forward and backward in time, and temporalities become charged with oblique and seemingly impossible political commentary. This "bond," to cite Elizabeth Rottenberg in her definition of the spectral, "links what will not be linked."[3] In the same knowing way, exemplary of the ambiguous and highly conditioned paradigm of their legacy, Los Hijos's films are often dedicated to the members' parents or to their families.

In this chapter I argue that lineage and genealogy in the work of Los Hijos disturb claims to historical lineality and that this is the result of a critical discourse concerning representation. This might be expressed, in filmic terms and in the spirit of luminosity as materiality that pervades this book, as a beam of light projected from one generation to another, variously condensed, refracted, and diverted by the obstacles of temporality that thwart its continuous flow. J. Hillis Miller reminds us that the word *aporia* derives from Greek, meaning "no passageway." "An aporia," he writes, "is a blind alley in a logical sequence, an impasse that forbids going any further."[4] This exploration of the films of Los Hijos discusses the aporias of legacy and the interruptions produced by technologies of vision and sound that exemplify them. The immediacy of film, the particular instantaneity of its form of representation—as noted earlier—while suggesting presence and a present time, in fact always points to a present that is always already past, whose nowness is always other.

Formed by three members—Luis López Carrasco, Natalia Marín Sáncho, and Javier Fernández Vázquez (all born between 1981 and 1982)—Los Hijos is among the most distinctive and interesting of the cohort of young filmmakers that has emerged in the aftermath of the 2008 economic crash in Spain.[5] Almost all the members of this new generation of cineastes shoot with digital technology, a medium the integrity of whose signifying components or indexicality—as has been exhaustively documented throughout this book—has been cast into doubt.[6] Although this observation is not new, in the case of Los Hijos, it is of particular importance; at the heart of its members' work is an engagement with the encounter between nature and technology. There is, further, a direct correlation between the political aspects—the content—of their films and the material form of the production in terms of the technology, apparatus, and materials the group employs.

I will return to the question of digitality later, but first I reiterate that the key argument of this chapter turns on how form and content historicized through Los Hijos's preoccupation with nonlineal temporalities might be read as political critique.[7] Further, I suggest that these films not only complicate but also negotiate a passageway between the traditional oppositional division of physis and techne. Film's technology not only modifies and adds prosthetically to nature, as all technology does by definition, but its specific mode of disclosure also brings concepts of the natural into question. I argue that the tenuous but suggestive connections between contraries apparent in Los Hijos constitute what Miller terms "an encounter with otherness,"[8] a dialogue suggested by black holes that, in different ways in the texts of these films, connect, absorb, and dilate distinct temporalities. To this end, I offer a reading of two of the three features that Los Hijos has made to date and conclude with a discussion of López Carrasco's individual debut, the 2013 *El futuro*.

As children of the generation that brought "representative democracy," free market economics, and neoliberalism to Spain, the complex national, historical, and sentimental legacy of Los Hijos has provided the primary sources for the group's films. But an additional inheritance is filmic, both in national and in international terms.[9] Highly literate cinematographically, Los Hijos draws deeply (critically, ironically, and, at times, irreverently) from its antecedents.

The combination of archive material and citation gives the group's work its particular resonance. The films of Los Hijos are charged with a particular tension produced of the recursive combination of national historiography and filmic materiality that, at the same time, eludes facile allegorical readings.

In spectral terms, these films express a critical spirit of the age and their generation, but it is a spirit that, while harking backward, simultaneously leaps forward in time. Their critique is of the tradition (the national, the filmic, and the national-filmic) with which they are associated. The results are jarring, dissymmetrical encounters between generations and between modes of representation. Representation here is constituted by forms, genres, or modes (in this instance, the modes of nonfiction or documentary film) and by the technologies of sight, visuality, and teletechnology. Derrida, referring to such technology, alludes to this "irreducible difference of generation" and adds that, as if to complicate Miller's "encounter with otherness":[10]

> From the moment that I cannot exchange or meet a glance, I am dealing with the other, who comes before me; an absolute autonomy is already no longer possible. And I cannot settle my debt, I can neither give back nor exchange because of the absence of the other, which I can't look in the eye. Even if I do it or think I do it, viewer and visible can only succeed in one another, alternate, not be confused in the other's eye. I can't see the eye of the other as viewing and visible at the same time.[11]

This heteronomy, a spectral gaze both inseparable from and critical of the national-political heritage to which it is bound and belongs and yet whose eye it cannot meet, is the principle characteristic of Los Hijos. Exemplary of this are its early experimental shorts that engage with the group's immediate forebears from the archive of Spanish film to which the members clearly, though critically, consider themselves indebted. Films such as *El sol en el sol del membrillo* (2008), a lighthearted but lucid dialogue with Víctor Erice's 1992 documentary on painter Antonio López, and *Ya viene, aguanta, riégueme, mátame* (2009) highlight this critical inheritance. The latter of these two shorts returns to the locations of four emblematic scenes in the recent history of Spanish film (Erice's *El espíritu de la colmena*, Montxo Armendáriz's *Historias del Kronen*, Pedro Almodóvar's *La ley del deseo*, and Vicente Aranda's *Amantes*), and it recreates, in the form of subtitles, the disembodied dialogue of the iconic originals (a technique, as described below, also deployed in *Los materiales*).

By revisiting, in these pieces, the precise places and reproducing with absolute exactitude the original sequences in the physical absence of their original protagonists, both the places and the original films become haunted. The displacements produced in the time that has lapsed form a ghostly asymmetry in a disjoining of place, person, and time. Originality itself—that of the work of art or of the national sign—becomes a matter of uncertainty as these antecedents are conjured up from the past as both homage and disavowal, whose debt cannot be settled "because of the absence of the other which I can't look in the eye."

In a sense, Los Hijos constitutes the unconscious of the national tradition to which it ambivalently subscribes in ways that might be described as chiasmatic, a Derridean spacing or *mise à l'écarte*, that disturbs unitary or unproblematic ancestral affiliation. Los Hijos's relation to the national canon is—to appropriate the words of Miller—that of being "other to itself."[12] Such spacing has formal filmic implications: it simultaneously holds together, complicates, and disturbs questions of surface and depth, horizons and vertices. Further, the iterative quality of filmic time (and the tradition seeks to codify such time) functions spatially as a vortex or an abyss, a gap whose spiraling, apparent groundlessness is framed and delimited by and within this spacing.

Los materiales (2009)

The menu of the DVD of *Los materiales* (The materials) displays a shot of mist descending over distant mountains, a veil of cloud behind which we can just discern the outline of the landscape.[13] It is a shot that appears periodically throughout the film. Los Hijos's next feature, *Circo* (Circus) (2010),[14] has a similar shot, and its third, *Árboles* (Trees), also uses the shot as its starting point following a prologue. In a second recurring technique in *Los materiales*, the camera films from the interior of a car outward through the windscreen. Reminiscent of the cinema of Iranian filmmaker Abbas Kiarostami, the shot captures slanted sunlight and filters and befogs it; it is both a barrier and a bond. The car's glass windscreen draws attention to the horizon of its own technology as it provides an additional frame within the filmic frame, an extra limit that demarcates the border between reality and representation.[15] The Spanish word for windscreen, *parabrisas*, moreover, recalls Miller's analysis of the prefix *para-* in "The Critic as Host" discussed in chapter 3. "Para," he says, "is a double antithetical prefix signifying at once proximity and distance, similarity and difference, interiority and exteriority, something inside a domestic economy and at the same time outside it."[16]

A third reiterated shot in *Los materiales* is of the dirt track of the film's initial sequence. And, as if to emphasize its significance, the image is reproduced on the box cover of the DVD. The unpaved road leads nowhere; or, rather, it comes to an abrupt stop at the edge of a reservoir. A variation of the shot occurs toward the end of the film when the filmmakers (who are shooting once again from the interior of the car through the windscreen, this time on the highway and at night) are obliged to pull over and turn back because of the wildfires that

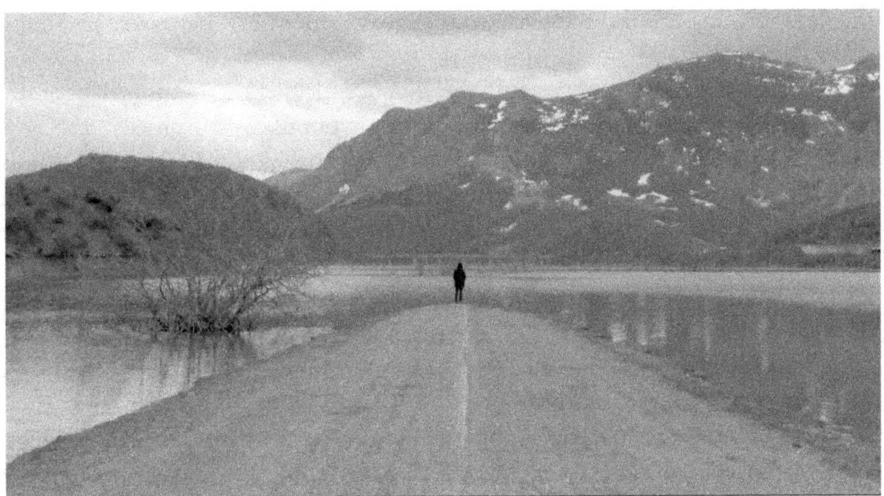

Fig. 8.1 "Disquieting impasses"—aporias in *Los materiales.*

light up the sky, illuminating and silhouetting the dark mass of the surrounding hills. These shots of the fires are "disquieting impasse[s]."[17] And they are, to recall the earlier definition, literal aporias. However, they are also examples of a film technique in the combination of artisan-like (and artless) tracking shots with the very real tracks of the road. Tracks—like documents or documentary film—are traces, and the traces here are imprinted—manmade or scorched— on the landscape, constitutive of the filmmaking process itself (see fig. 8.1).[18] Such traces of human incursions and shaping of the landscape are also thematically important to *Los materiales.* In this play between lightness and darkness, it is significant that this film is shot in black and white.

Deliberately flooded in 1987 to build the reservoir that dominates this film, Riaño, in the province of León in northern Spain, is also the hometown and birthplace of one of the members of Los Hijos, Javier Fernández. The historical fact of the construction of the reservoir—and the resistance to it (at one stage, the filmmakers discuss a rumor that the local residents had considered approaching the Basque separatist organization ETA [Euskadi Ta Askatasuna] to bomb the dam)—leads to an ironic and understated historicization. It is history as underlying suggestion, temporal parallels, subterranean allusion, and spectrality. Despite the Franco regime's common association with modernizing construction projects such as this state-funded intervention in rural life and landscape, and particularly the dictatorship's visual telematic representation of the inauguration of reservoirs as emblematic of state propaganda newsreel broadcasts, the Riaño dam was, in fact, constructed in the democratic period during a Socialist government presided over by Felipe González.[19]

But the analogy is pertinent; the democratic period is indeed haunted by its authoritarian predecessor. And Riaño is populated by ghosts. The new town (Nuevo Riaño), built high on the banks of the artificial lake, is filmed as if stricken by urban blight, neglect, and abandonment. Newness is rendered tawdry, dilapidated, decayed, and haunted by absences. In a couple of lengthy sequences, the camera dwells on the geometry—the angled windows that parallel the frame of the screen in Mondrian-like compositions—of the seemingly uninhabited apartment buildings' flaking paint, empty flowerpots, and crumbling masonry. Throughout the film, such sober images are accompanied by a silent written commentary of subtitles whose text—independently of the visual track—functions as a spectral supplement in counterpoint to the visual images. We hear no voices, only the hollow echo of the wind ricocheting through the streets, the sound of emptiness.

The ghostly effect of the written text is reinforced by its disturbance of chronological temporality, the means by which it disjoins time. Two comments in the written text illustrate this. The first is the realization by the filmmakers that their presence at the site of the ancestral family home of one of their members is anomalous, and the generations are reversed: "We are older than the town itself," proclaims one subtitle. The second comment explicates the sense of loss: "There is little left of traditions and things like that. They have been lost." The unattributed, anonymous nature of these flecks of written conversation—we can only guess which of the three filmmakers' voices is contained in each fragment of text—contributes to the tenor of incompleteness and the lingering, latent, unspoken meaning of unfinished business.

The collective and individual parties—authorship itself is slippery—vie with one another throughout the film. The filmmaking processes—the disputes and alliances between the three filmmakers—form part of the diegesis of the film. This, too, marks a kind of spacing, the *différance* that holds the filmmakers together as a unit while retaining what separates them individually. Even the phrases most evidently and identifiably attributable to autobiography—for example, those we assume to be Javier Fernández's, whose grandfather, we have been informed, died in Riaño, as did his father, having opted to stay in the town after the family moved to Bilbao after the flooding ("My father stayed. And he died here")—posit, by virtue of their anonymity, an element of uncertainty, of missing links in a sequence and a ruptured chain that uncomfortably binds family to location.

This sense of unresolved trauma is returned to again and again. Its iterative quality condenses—formally, technologically, and thematically—in the film's central sequences (central both in terms of their importance and because they occur midway through the film). In one of the film's rare moments of audible diegetic speech, Pedro, one of the locals, agrees to guide the filmmakers into the woods of the surrounding hills, where Republican guerrilla fighters sought refuge in the aftermath of the Spanish Civil War. Off-screen Pedro promises to lead them to where the *maquis* (the fighters who waged guerrilla attacks after the end of the war) were summarily executed by Francoist forces in the 1940s and take them to a well where the bodies were reportedly dumped. Communication among the filmmakers, meanwhile, is transmitted telegraphically by means of subtitling.

In a strikingly lyrical sequence, while Javier Fernández and Natalia Marín accompany Pedro, López Carrasco remains behind with the camera in a copse.[20] The footage that follows has the feel of an experiment, shot and preserved as if unedited and forming the raw materials that evoke the film's title. The sequence begins in silence. Pedro's outstretched arm emerges from the right-hand side of the frame. He walks across the screen. The light catches the lower left-hand corner of the frame, revealing not only its translucent but also artificial condition (like the reflected beam of the sun filtered through the car windscreen earlier). In a sudden eruption of sound, we hear the whir of the camera, the wind, and the rustle of leaves. The camera focuses on the branches and the shimmering light filtered through the cover of leaves. The mottled, porous light is tellingly reminiscent of the ripples of the manmade lake beneath which the historical Riaño lies. Then a violent pan leftward captures Marín and Fernández, laden with recording equipment disappearing beyond the trees. The lyrical naturalism of the leafy bower, filmed by the unmoving camera, is rudely punctuated by zooms, by the sudden jerk of the same static camera, the consequent loss of focus, the clanking noise of the equipment, and the mismatched illumination.

What seemed unedited material is, it transpires, highly edited—or at least the artifice and the apparatus clash violently with what purports to be the placid depiction of nature. López Carrasco then changes lenses to produce not only a distancing effect but also, in the hole of light with its black surround, a visually telescopic effect, or that of a microscope. Although we are, in fact, watching the same leaves as before, we seem simultaneously to be witnesses to both a cosmological, galactic effect—as if viewing through a telescope—and that of the microcosm, the detail. In the circle of light at the heart of the black screen, distance and proximity conflate. Such a contradictory technique foreshadows the black dot that breaches the celluloid of López Carrasco's film *El futuro* discussed below.

This prolonged sequence serves as a kind of interlude to supplement a film whose rhythm is marked by lulls and tensions. The tensions are frequently those that arise among the three filmmakers. Significantly, this particular meditation—López Carrasco's work alone—suggests an individual crease in the fabric of authorial collectivity. His personal style contrasts with yet complements Fernández's autobiographical influence on the film and what appears to be Marín's mediating role. These formal features, moreover, while giving the film its very particular tempo—this sequence functions like an adagio—have a curious thematic correspondence. Just as the naturalism of the initial shots is disturbed by the jarring deployment of technology (camera movement, sound of the motor, loss of focus, etc.), so, too, the subject matter of the set of sequences that constitute this central passage of the film deals with the disturbance of nature.

The untimely deaths of the Civil War and postwar periods that lurk undiscovered under the ground and the traumatic legacy of the old town beneath the surface of the reservoir indicate a disturbance of nature by technological intervention, the physis-techne dichotomy. Unnatural death lines the substrate of the landscape and of the film. It is significant that in a film about frustrated pathways—Miller's "blind alleys"—and "impasses," Pedro fails in his endeavor to find the well where the *maquis* corpses were concealed, and the filmmakers experience an array of technical difficulties while filming him.

Early in *Archive Fever*, Derrida links documents (and *Los materiales* is a "documentary") and topology to the notion of the archive, which is subject to dispute and necessarily guarded by an authority, the archons. "The archons," Derrida writes, "are first of all the documents' guardians. They do not only ensure the physical security of what is deposited and of the substrate. They are also accorded the hermeneutic right and competence."[21] A significant element of Los Hijos's project in this and other films is to dispute that "hermeneutic right." Here the substrate—topological and cultural, physis and techne—is open to multiple interpretations. It is palimpsestic in the unburied corpses and the elusive signs of the unresolved national trauma that lie beneath the surface, making its absence present. Of equal and related significance aboveground is the film's preoccupation with the altered landscape, the human/technological assault on and shaping of nature and natural form.

Finally, for Los Hijos, the filmic legacy connects the impossible aporia of the physis-techne binary. In the film's introductory sequence—of which the shot discussed earlier figures—the shadowy figure of a woman (Natalia Marín) is set against the bleak image of an imposing snow-flecked mountain landscape. We hear the zip of an equipment case and see the dirt road leading toward the mass of water. Marín ambles to the water's edge at the end of the road and pauses before finally turning back and walking toward the camera. The first words expressed on-screen, once more in the form of unattributed subtitles, are, "Isn't this just the most Angelopoulos shot I've done in my life?" The screen then fades to black to reveal the title of the film. However, the rhetorical question posed seems, like an echo, to demand a response. The prefix *eco-* derives from the Latin *oeko* and, in turn, from the Greek *oikos*—importantly, the institution that houses the archive. The word *eco*, though, is most commonly associated with the natural environment, as in ecology. Its homonym *echo*, meanwhile (again, to recall the archive) conjures notions of resonance, repetition, and citation. The citation in this case is to Greek filmmaker Theo Angelopoulos, followed moments later by references to Alfred Hitchcock and Italian filmmaker Michelangelo Antonioni, forming a cinephilic archive. Also conjured are notions of reverberation, reflecting waves, and outwardly spreading ripples, like those of the reservoir or of the wildfires in the hills around Riaño that spread like viruses (and whose light against the darkness sets the landscape in relief—in *contre-jour*—and simultaneously impedes forward movement). Finally, the ideas of echographies, hyperlinks, and black holes are summoned. The homonyms *eco* and *echo* suggest an intangible aporetic connectivity and coexistence between nature and the archive of filmic citations. I will return to the notion of eco in the following discussion of *Árboles*, but for now I note that both *Los materiales* and *Árboles* are structured, divided, and linked, chapter-like, by black screens.

Árboles (2013)

Árboles (Trees) begins with a black screen that opens to reveal not an image of a tree but a human portrait: a black-and-white silent medium shot of a young woman (Diana Tijerín). Eduardo Cadava, writing about photography, has detailed the connections between trees and human faces and the marks of the passage of time inscribed on their respective surfaces. Faces, like trees, contain the imprint of their past in the present, their distinctive signature. This suggestive parallel is extended in Los Hijos's feature, from the trees of its title and the portrait of its prologue to Spain's colonial past in West Africa and the effects of the contemporary crisis on the residents of the outskirts of Madrid. Both faces and trees—impossible correlates—are, like archives, depositories of the past. The paradox is, as Cadava has pointed out, that they "are both singular and never simply themselves."[22] The portrait, the face, is singular-plural, and its paradoxical surface-substrate is charged with archival force, like the individual trees in a forest.

The young woman of this first sequence is clearly engaged in a silent dialogue with someone else. We do not know with whom, but the encounter could be with the off-screen filmmaker(s) or the camera itself. The self-consciousness of the woman's demeanor—nervous, with an embarrassed smile, and pensive—draws out this sense of the presence of an other, reminiscent of Derrida's description in *Echographies* of the dissymmetrical experience of being watched. Even the glint of the light on the glass of her spectacles (like the interior car shots from behind the windscreen of *Los materiales* or the reflection that marks the camera lens of López Carrasco's sequence in the wooded clearing) indexes another elusive translucent presence. Again, like the muted subtitling of *Los materiales*, the invisible, inaudible presence of otherness, (off-screen, elsewhere, otherwise) is emphasized through formal composition and highlights what is absent, what lies beyond the frame, and the discomfort of meeting the gaze of someone off-screen watching unseen.

After nearly two minutes, the shot shifts to another portrait: a man's bald head bowed, denying an immediate view of his face. A flicker of the woman's hand on the far left side of the frame reminds us of her partial presence. The man (José Alberto Vallés) lifts his head for the portrait shot; his eyes stray from the camera into midair, displaying an awkwardness before the camera similar to that of the woman's moments before and with the same avoidance of eye contact. The screen dissolves to white, and the word *Árboles* in stark black type appears. The film proper commences thenceforth in color.

The porous nature of the word *portrait* in relation to temporality illustrates its internal aporia. Its *por* looks forward to a future that is yet to arrive (the Spanish word is *porvenir*), while the *trait* harks back to a past, a residue, and a trace. Behind these portraits that bookend *Árboles* (the silent images of this prologue set the stage for the final images accompanied by sound and an audible explanatory dialogue), a domestic homescape and a family lineage unfold (the talk of a small child and of grandparents). And the metonymic political trait of the portrait—like the expanding ripples of the Riaño lake—reverberate beyond it. The surface—sur-face, a supplement to and of the face—of the portrait points to a paradox and to an underlying depth that will emerge, as if from the mist, to mark the bare outlines of Spain's current economic disaster, record unemployment, and, most notably, the country's housing crisis. The surface-depth parallel of the portrait that opens and closes this film acts as a cypher for the ghostly contemporaneity of national history—particularly as concerns contemporary urban space, the superficies of new construction projects, the surface of the city, and the gruesome colonial past that haunts it. Furthermore, the fade to white gives way to the previously mentioned signature sequence of the descending cloud veiling the landscape. On this occasion, the landscape is not the bleak, mountainous terrain of León shot in black and white that dominates *Los materiales* but the lush greenery and vegetation of the dense Equatorial Guinean forest.

A related archival substrate supplements the aporetic images of *Árboles's* visual surface by deploying a number of discursive registers in written and oral form: storytelling, legal documents, and historical testimony. These texts emerge from the darkness of the screen, from behind the steamy mist draping the mise-en-scène.

In the central block of *Árboles*, shot in Equatorial Guinea, two young women (Antonia Silebo and Pilar Loheto) travel around the country before arriving in the capital, Malabo. These shots of everyday life have all the characteristics of ethnographic film. A static observational camera films children playing, rain-drenched streets, a marketplace, a religious procession, the vibrant colors of clothing, and shots of the thick forest. Meanwhile, the two women tell stories to each other. These stories—recounted in a mixture of Spanish and an indigenous language—relate anecdotes regarding the history of Spanish colonial domination of Equatorial Guinea and the intimacy that the indigenous people have had with the forest. One story, told by Pilar in the doorway of an abandoned prison building, describes how people lured to the city as it was being constructed—*la ciudad nueva* (the new city)—would simply slip away into the trees at night and disappear. The attempted urban conquest of the forest was undone, the constructions capitulated in the face of encroaching vegetation, and the new city became a ghost town.

As in *Los materiales*, nature and urban development—physis and techne— combine spectrally in the oral narratives. And they do so in startling juxtaposition to the spoken-word narratives in ways that recall questions of film technique, the technology, the archive, and the texts that appear in black letters against a white background or, vice versa, in white letters against a black background. The eerie whiteness of this montage—whose texts derive from archival documents, logbooks, and legal treatises from 1778 and 1953 (which refer explicitly to the original condition of Equatorial Guinea as penal colony) suggest a ghostliness and a sinister bond between discordant temporalities (the eighteenth and twentieth centuries) held together by the discourses of legality, corrective punishment, racism, and urban development.

La ciudad nueva—as in the doomed, corrupt urbanism of colonial Guinea—returns in the final third of *Árboles*. Switching back to the black and white of the film's commencement, these sequences are shot in the Ensanche de Vallecas, a utopian urban extension—another spectral supplement—of Madrid that was constructed in the early 2000s to extend the traditional working-class district of Vallecas further toward the east.[23] The portrait shots of *Árboles's* first and final sequences are integrated within an urban landscape (we assume that this is where the couple lives). If, though, Equatorial Guinea was a penal colony hacked out from the forest, then the trees and architecture of the Ensanche de

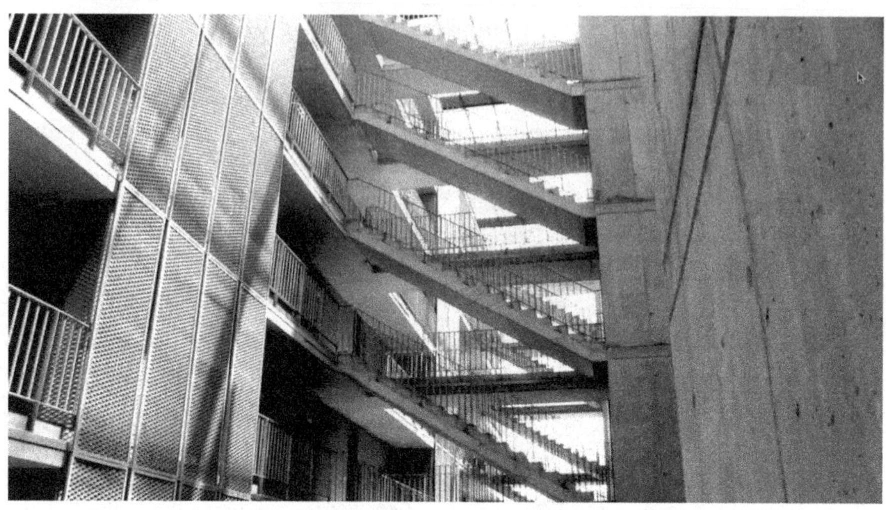

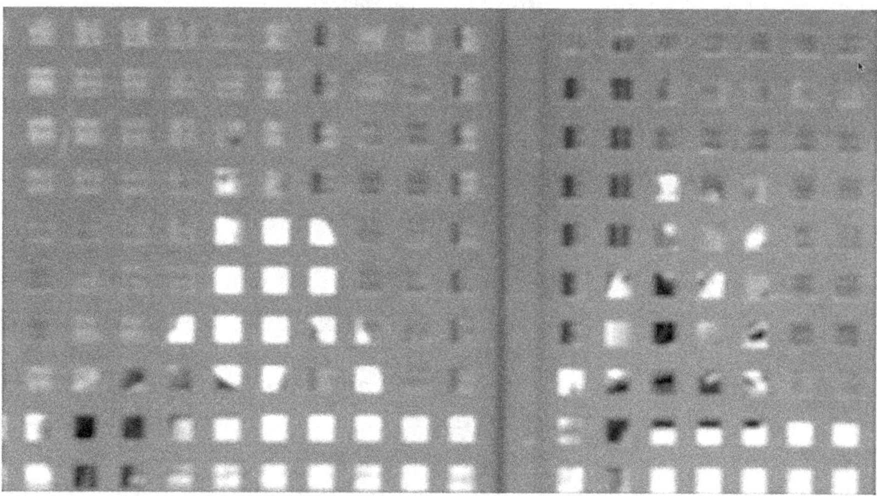

Fig. 8.2 a–b The carceral architecture of El Ensanche de Vallecas in *Árboles*.

Vallecas—the bare metallic lines of electricity pylons, streetlights, stairwells, and networks of grates, wires, frames, and steel bars—also possess all the characteristics of incarceration (see figs. 8.2a and 8.2b).

Further, while the buildings of the new colonial city (and the prison) in Guinea were abandoned by the local workforce—shipped in, press-ganged, and conditioned to European temporality for construction purposes—this new appendage to the metropolis, its extension into what was until recently

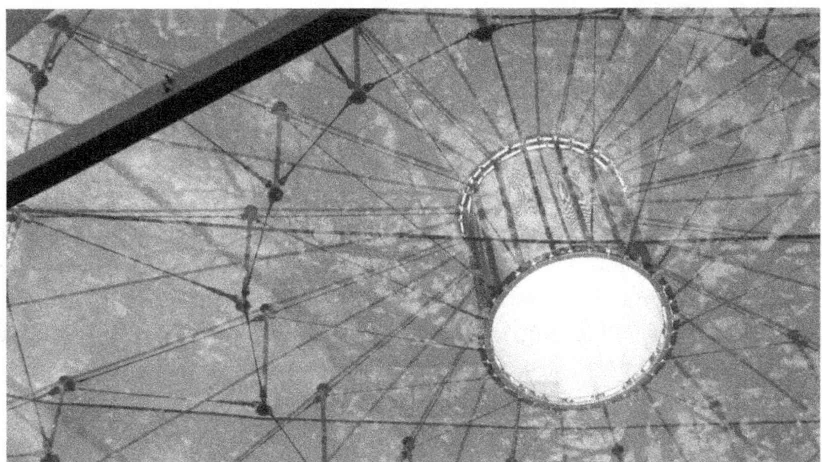

Fig. 8.3 The *eco-bulevar* of El Ensanche de Vallecas in *Árboles*.

farmland, is also (like Nuevo Riaño) underpopulated. Here, though, it has been reduced to a ghostly imitation of its original conception as a direct consequence of the collapse of the Spanish housing market in 2008.[24]

The utopianism of the Ensanche de Vallecas is signaled by an architectural experimentalism concerned (in an echo of the earlier discussion of *Los materiales*) with ecology. The encroachment of the city into nature is the focus of the first shots of *Árboles*'s final section. The cage-like structures captured in these black-and-white shots are, in fact, attempts to create giant patches of greenery amid the sparse and spartan desolation of the *meseta* (plateau) landscape of central Spain.

Variously called *eco-bulevar* or *bulevar bioclimático*, these artificial trees line the officially named street, the Bulevar de la Naturaleza (see fig. 8.3). The use of human technology to conquer nature is charged with irony as the metallic images demonstrate the manifest absence of humans: the catastrophic results of the bursting of Spain's *burbuja inmobiliaria* (housing bubble). Between these two ghostly locations, the tropical African rain forest and the artifice of a Madridian arboretum, a third geographical locality is inserted within the diegesis of *Árboles* as a different kind of bond, a hinge in the body of the film, exemplary of the spacing, the chiasmus, to which I earlier referred. Titled "La Casa de la abuela" (The grandmother's house) and shot in Águilas, Murcia, this intermediary section is distinguished—between the steam-drenched oppressiveness of Equatorial Guinea and the monochrome of Vallecas—by luminosity and by the sunlight of the Mediterranean coast. It also contains in condensed form all the elements of the film in its entirety, albeit elliptically.

This section begins in bright color with a close-up of leaves imprinted on the sleeve of an elderly woman's housecoat. While the camera of the other two lengthier parts of the film barely moves, objective in its register of what occurs before its lens, the first minutes of this fragment are marked by rapid-fire subjective filming. Moving in and out of focus, the camera lingers on the various members of López Carrasco's family, among them the eponymous grandmother of this section's title. The camera homes in on mottled skin, feet, a profile, a mane of hair, and the dappled light cast by the shade of the slatted blinds.

In its claustrophobic interiority, in the nonverbal sonic effects of the disjunctive acoustics (while human conversation is elided, we hear the sounds of the street and the chirp of birdsong; we catch a glimpse of López Carrasco's brother close in age and appearance to Luis mouthing inaudibly), a skewed self-portrait emerges that is marked by difference and deferral and that again complicates and diffuses the autobiographical while retaining the signature as autography. Here the off-screen other is the filmmaker himself, invisible on-screen but technologically intrusive with his probing camera, as in the sequence of *Los materiales* when he is left alone in the forest to experiment.[25] More significantly, the presence of the filmmaker's close relatives reminds us not only of the natural but also the genealogical associations of trees: family trees.[26]

Slowly and intermittently, the camera switches to an exterior, to a woman (López Carrasco's mother) sitting on the apartment terrace framed by fertile green leaves under a canvas awning speckled with petals that have dried in the sun. A low-angled shot reveals the apartment block and a palm tree in the foreground. The section ends with a return to the objective camera with shots of housing blocks that open to the cityscape of Águilas at dusk.

The sequences of López Carrasco's family foreshadow the final passage of *Árboles* in Madrid. Here we return to Diana and José Alberto, now shot in dialogue. Their discussion is represented—like the forking limbs of a tree—as a double portrait. The couple talk about the future and their unseen, absent daughter. In a double iteration (an echo of the stories told in Equatorial Guinea and a future hereditary repetition), Diana recalls a book of tales she had read as a child at her own grandmother's house (a recursive story that unravels in its own telling, whose plot is to be found—performatively—in the very act of its recounting) that she, in turn, wants her daughter to read. If the silent images of the film's opening indicated an off-screen other beyond the frame, its audibility upon closure—its references to the future to come and the return of the past—discloses the other as now. Like the aporetic "blind alley" from out of the film's disjoining technology and the sense of socioeconomic crisis, the uncertain promise that emerges from the portrait's background gestures toward a *porvenir*.

El futuro (2013)

As a coda and conclusion to this chapter, I read *El futuro* (The future) the first feature that Luis López Carrasco directed alone. Derrida, in *Archive Fever*, glosses Freud's archivistic method as "the retrospective logic of a future perfect."[27] The phrase resonates well with *El futuro*, a film that engages directly and critically with the archive. Made in 2013, *El futuro* is explicitly located in historical discourse. And in juxtaposition with its title, it is clearly and unmistakably—and unnervingly—located in the past. The film is set in 1982. We know this for a number of reasons, but first and foremost because of how it begins. The film commences with the then future prime minister Felipe González's victory speech resonating out of a black screen, in confirmation of the success of the *Partido Socialista Obrero Español* (Spanish Socialist Workers' Party, or PSOE) in the 1982 general elections. The words of the speech are significant, haunting not only the film but also present-day Spain: "Not one single citizen should feel distant from the beautiful labor of modernization, progress and solidarity that we should bring about between all of us," says González in one of the rare sequences of the film in which voice is audible. We might recall at this point that the three members of Los Hijos were all born between 1981 and 1982, and López Carrasco himself was less than a year old when González made his victory speech.

It is in this context, as much as that of the 1982 Socialist electoral success, that *El futuro* was made and might be read. In many ways, the film's critique of representation lies in its performativity in that it conforms to Miller's succinct definition: a "performative statement brings into existence the condition it names."[28] What, then, to return to this chapter's initial proposition, lies at the heart of *El futuro*—and what it addresses both directly and by allusion—is once more a generational legacy (as already observed, Los Hijos collective does not call itself Los Hijos for nothing). This legacy is drawn from an archive (radiophonic and filmic) whose inheritance lingers on as a sense of afterness—or belatedness—accompanying the successes and the failings that one generation has passed on to another. They are not so much part of the present, as constitutive of that bifurcating element of otherness that disjoins the present from the contemporary and facilitates political critique, the other, that is once again, of now.

It is no coincidence that the film, following the recording of González's speech, commences with what seems to be a house party host's hangover, a dulled and disagreeable aftermath. The party itself comprises almost the entire sixty-eight-minute film. It is significant that at the end of the film, the camera moves outside (for the only time in the film) to an urban exterior and focuses on the streets and buildings of a Madrid neighborhood clearly set in the present (as signaled by the presence of air-conditioning units, which were not available in 1982, and apartment blocks that were constructed in the late 1980s and early 1990s).[29]

El futuro is a film that is neither historical document nor, apparently, a fiction film. Like the other films made by Los Hijos, it disavows such classification. In many ways, it takes on the appearance of an amateur production, like an artisanal home movie. Shot over a weekend using (unusually) a 16 mm camera employed to provide an anachronistic, material authenticity, *El futuro* captures—either in a neutral fly-on-the-wall style or intrusively close to the participants—a party that takes place (we assume) in 1982, because it coincides with the Socialist election victory and perhaps celebrates it. We are privy to members of the young Madrid bourgeoisie who have descended on an apartment to drink, dance, flirt, take drugs, and exchange inane and inconsequential conversation.

The decor of the apartment, the fashion of the clothes, the makeup worn, and, above all, the musical soundtrack, re-create the atmosphere of the period of the *movida madrileña*, the exuberant cultural explosion of the late 1970s and early 1980s that spread throughout Spain but was particularly associated with the city of Madrid. There is no plot, no narrative beyond the improvised on-screen action. And though the film could be confused with the period piece genre, it is not a costume drama. *El futuro* shares none of the commodification of pastness that Mark Fisher, in his critique of contemporary pastiche, has dubbed (following Simon Reynolds) "retromania." It contains none of the nostalgia that inundated Spanish screens, and particularly the country's television screens, throughout the 1990s and 2000s, in which re-creation of the past was reduced to temporal disjuncture deprived of its uncanniness or "taken for granted," heralding, to cite Fisher again (this time quoting Franco "Bifo" Berardi), "the slow cancellation of the future."[30]

The experiment and, in large part, the interest of López Carrasco's film, lie in its concern with filmic materiality and in its preoccupation with time, not only in *El futuro*'s re-creation of the historical period but also in its administration of filmic time and chronological time. If *Los materiales* plays on space delimited by frames, this film tests the limits of time and operates at its liminal edges, squeezing, compressing, and syncopating temporality. In addition to using celluloid, as opposed to the more common and much cheaper digital video that López Carrasco and the other members of Los Hijos have previously worked with, the director and his technical crew deployed lighting and sound equipment of the early 1980s. The roughness of the editing, the abrupt cuts, and the blemishes of the film itself add to the impression of a film made in 1982 (except we know, and are periodically reminded, that it was not).

López Carrasco mixed professional and nonprofessional actors (many of whom were simply friends of the director and did not know one another prior to the shoot) and asked them to behave as if they were at a real party. Though there was an original script at the start of shooting, it was abandoned (with one exception, discussed below) as the party progressed. As an experiment, *El futuro* is clearly influenced by the work of John Cassavetes in the clustered, seemingly improvised action and the probing intensity of the camerawork with its dense and urgent quality and its prying and eavesdropping proximity. Likewise, there are overtones of Andy Warhol's experiments with time and human behavior in the simple filming of what emerges before the camera lens, with little or no direction, and within which drama develops at the limits of the shoot, from the concept—another experiment—rather than a script. Indeed, dialogue in *El futuro* is practically impossible to discern because of the music and the poor sound recording (both the consequence of the technology of the time and the natural cacophony resulting from the party). Cassavetes and Warhol are, of course, among those filmmakers who influenced the generation of Spanish cineastes that emerged around the time of the *movida madrileña*, and notably the work of Pedro Almodóvar and Iván Zulueta.

Indeed, Zulueta lends an important influence to *El futuro* that connects filmic materiality and cinephilia. Returning to the initial moments of the film, having located its historical moment in the politics of the period—namely, Felipe González's speech—*El futuro* proves equally indebted to cinephilic antecedents as to that moment. In interviews, López Carrasco has said that *El futuro* was inspired—he describes it as the film's genesis—by a fleeting few shots culled from a sequence of Zulueta's cult 1979 film *Arrebato* in which Olvido Gara (better known as Alaska)—one of Almodóvar's early muses and a central figure of the *movida madrileña*—enters a room full of partygoers with a birthday cake.

One of the key films of the *movida madrileña, Arrebato*—in its darkness and pessimism—stands in stark contrast to Almodóvar's films of the same period. The sequence from *Arrebato* is interesting because it is an extract from a film within a film. It is part of the Super 8 footage that the character of Pedro P. (Will More) sends to filmmaker José Sirgado (Eusebio Poncela). The footage was shot by Zulueta himself as personal memorabilia and incorporated into the montage of Arrebato later.[31] *El futuro*, then, which purports to be a representation in the form of an impression, a re-creation of the period (I will return to this point later), is, rather, mise en abyme: a chain of hypertexts that form a tumbling mass of citations of films inside other films generated by a network of references and generating more in turn. Zulueta's home movie within *Arrebato* returns thirty years into the future, reincarnated or reimagined as a film called *El futuro*.

Again, this suggests a visual spacing as mise en abyme conditioned or colored by *mise à l'écart*. Such an interpretation permits a furtively political reading suggested by Walter Benjamin's fourteenth and fifteenth theses on the "Concept of History," which contain his most cited critique of progressive historicism. Benjamin posits *Jetztzeit* "now time"—the charged revolutionary moment of the instant—that draws on the past—"the tiger's leap into that which has gone before"—to interrupt "explosively . . . the continuum of history."[32] It is precisely this continuum of history, in its appeal to national citizenship, modernization, and solidarity, to which González appeals in his victory speech.

There is an additional pointed reference to another film of the period—the only part of the original screenplay of *El futuro* to survive the actual shoot—when two of the guests at the party engage in an animated but amicable argument over political militancy (interestingly, they are shot slouched beneath a table as if in a void, a vortex, a separate *abîme* of their very own that sets them apart from the rest of the party) (see fig. 8.4).[33] The dialogue here (which refers to the armed Basque separatist group ETA) is a direct, albeit unattributed, quote from an Andalusian worker resident in the Basque Country interviewed in the 1983 *Atado y bien atado*, the second part of Cecilia and José Juan Bartolomé's suppressed documentary on the Transition, *Después de. . . .*[34] Afterness here is once more out of sync with the time of its address, mobilized paradoxically through the *abîme* structure as a political-filmic reference in ways that again highlight a discordant untimeliness, to both the *pre* and the *re* of representation. A film shot in 2013 and set in 1982 quotes (implausibly) another film released in 1983.[35]

I present here two speculations that are prompted by the idea of *abîme*. First, the word *abîme* derives from *abyss*, which, as Martin Heidegger reminds us, means the absence of ground (*Abgrund*). There is a tension in *El futuro* between recognizable historical specificity as provided by the archive and the unsettling feeling produced by representation born of the infinite quality of *abîme*. A sense of groundlessness—the gap or *écarte* that spacing opens up—is felt in the future anteriority of the film's material historicity in terms of both its cinephilia and its unspoken allusion to legacy.

Second, like a surreptitious link in the chain of mise en abyme, just as Pedro P.'s Super 8 film is a supplement to *Arrebato*'s diegesis, a foreign body grafted onto the main body of Zulueta's text (an artisanal production of the director's other, his alter ego), so, too, its appropriation by López Carrasco is parasitical—to return to the earlier discussion of Miller's *para*. *El futuro* feeds

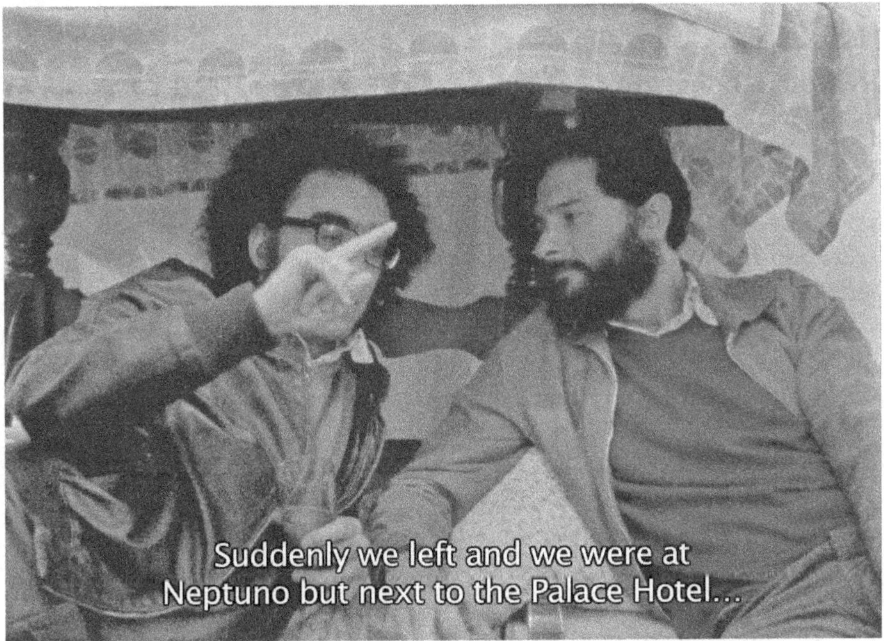

Fig. 8.4 Discussing militant politics under the table in *El futuro*.

off its filmic ancestor, which in turn haunts its descendant. The spectral bond between the past and the future is maintained—aptly for the paranormal—in a place, an apartment that is itself an artifice, a film location—a site and a para-site, a virtual space haunted by the paranormal. Haunted by the ghosts of the *movida madrileña* and Felipe González (whose presence, still felt today in contemporary discourse, provides a spectral connection between the public sphere and private life), this private party, like all parties, has a host—the main body—and guests—parasitical strangers or outsiders whose arrival and whose entrance through the doorway—the threshold between the exterior and the interior, between the public and the private—is experienced as an interruption.

Interruption, to recall Benjamin's thesis on history as temporal disturbance, rupture, or disjuncture, the sudden and unexpected appearance of ghosts, undergirds *El futuro*. Significantly, the film begins with an interruption, that of the voice of a radio broadcaster. At 2:30 a.m. on the morning of October 29, 1982, the radio announcer breaks into Juan Pardo's rendition of *Suspiros de amor* to announce that the transmission will switch urgently to the Socialist Party headquarters. The next voice is that of Alfonso Guerra, the PSOE's erstwhile deputy general secretary, who, in turn, introduces Felipe González.[36]

The interruption is important for a number of reasons: Historically, the PSOE victory marked a political breakthrough as the first leftist government elected in Spain since 1936. It interrupts the continuum of center-conservative rule of the post-Franco era, breaching its consensus inheritance. The interruption also came roughly eighteen months after another televised and much-repeated interruption in the democratic process (an interruption marked by another interruption, the forced cessation of the live TV broadcast and its reduction to a black screen) when members of the Guardia Civil led by Lieutenant Colonel Antonio Tejero burst into the Spanish parliament on February 23, 1981. That interruption signaled the end to future right-wing plans to topple democracy and arguably marked the end of the Transition.

Furthermore, the insistent motif of interruption in *El futuro* paradoxically approximates form and content and renders them indistinguishable: filmic diegesis and materiality, mise-en-scène and montage. Aside from the arrival of guests as interruption, at one point toward the end of the party, the frivolity and the free-flowing movement of the montage are interrupted by a return to the past in the form of still photographs from a family album. These photographs, shot against the ironic acoustic backdrop of Aviador Dro's song "Nuclear, sí," indicate the Francoist family past—the childhood—of (we assume) the hosts and guests present at the party.[37] These photographs haunt the future of their own time, or the future as not what it was. Like the earlier conversation between the two men under the table whose references to the situation in the Basque Country of 1982 echo the current situation of resistance to the state, these still photos suggest a return to the future in a ghostly form. A Francoist childhood visually traces a disjointed link between the dictatorial past, the youthful democracy of the *movida*, and the present period distinguished by economic crisis, popular disenchantment, and social fracture.

Interruption in the continuum of history of different times is produced as a result of the different technologies, each of which is marked in some way by temporalities: fading family photographs from the 1960s, the 16 mm film, the archive recordings, and the soundtrack's emphasis on minor and long-forgotten songs of the *movida* (none of the enduring musical classics of the period are heard in this film). One could read this as a comment on the digital technology that López Carrasco and Los Hijos have used previously. While their work consistently revolves around temporalities and is notable for its distinct historical charge and preoccupation with the past, digital technology (as opposed to analog or celluloid) arguably exists in a kind of permanent present. Unlike the dated family photos or the overexposed shots and other flaws that I will discuss in a moment, digital video does not deteriorate with age. It is, in a sense, impervious to the passage of time.[38]

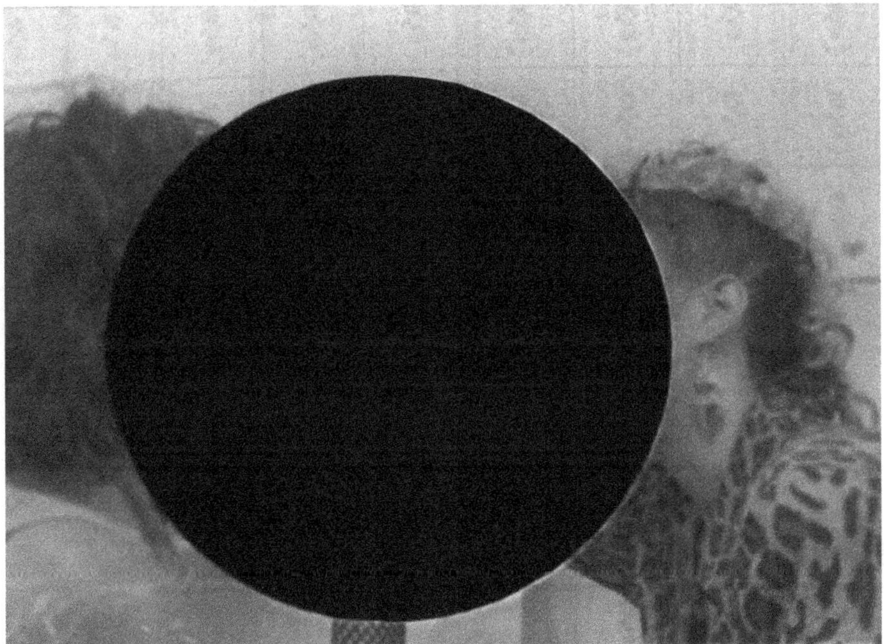

Fig. 8.5 A black hole in *El futuro*.

Finally, the instantaneity of the historical moment—the interruption—is shot against a black screen shielding and veiling the future that González addresses. The black screen of the film's commencement returns partially, in fragmentary mode, toward the end of the film in the form of interruptions, editorial breaches (referred to earlier as blemishes or flaws and signs of antiquated montage), intermittent marks on the texture of the celluloid, distorted acoustics suddenly silenced, and the very historically specific cinematic material that marks this film's pastness.

The black dot shown in figure 8.5 reveals—in self-conscious fashion—the materiality of the film's imperfect montage, and it also has, I suggest, a diegetic component. The black circle suggests a hole, a vortex, and a void—a material correlation to the *abîme* of the film's textuality, references, and cinephilic citations. It suggests a quite literal black hole, like that mentioned earlier in this chapter. It is a time tunnel, a conduit connecting the past with the future, and a sign of the spectral bond that haunts and binds the elusive present. It thereby links—by means of disruptive interruption—not only the representation of different coexisting temporalities but also other apparently irreconcilable oppositions, the discordant materialities of sound, light, and image and the modes of fiction and nonfiction and analog and digital technologies. These impure elements that bind and seal representation—by which I mean one thing standing in for another—also produce a contradictory implosion at the center of representation itself. This is most evident in *El futuro*, but it is equally applicable to the collective work of Los Hijos as a whole. My argument here is that the same elements that constitute Los Hijos's imperfect cinema, shot through with critical cinephilia, extend beyond photographic materiality and politics—representation itself, as we will see in the final chapter—to haunt and destabilize claims to national allegory.

Notes

1. Although cultural memory is not central to this chapter, clearly the relationship between the generations of the democratic period is often complicated by questions of memory and by its commodification or packaging for official purposes.

2. The conception here is of an authorial signature that is simultaneously identificatory while also disavowing the national legacy or the filial bond or seal (an ambiguity that is central, I argue, to the work of Los Hijos). This, of course, is not only important in modern film theory but, rather differently, also imbues Derrida's philosophical project, and does so beyond *Specters of Marx*. We might also recall that Hamlet deploys his father's seal by using his inherited signet ring to change his stepfather's orders that he (Hamlet) should be killed on arrival in England, thereby *sealing* the fate of Guildenstern and Rosencrantz (act 5, scene 2).

3. The full quote, highly relevant to this chapter and to the book as a whole, is as follows:

> Derrida calls the bond between singularities—the bond that links what will not be linked *spectral*. To be spectral is to be neither present nor absent; it is neither to be nor not to be. Indeed, the spectral, says Derrida, is what exceeds all ontological oppositions between absence and presence, visible and invisible, living and dead. . . . A bond that is spectral is, therefore, something that cannot be contained within any traditional concept of community. It is a protest against citizenship, a form of political solidarity that is opposed to the border politics of the nation-states: it is what Derrida calls *the democracy to come*. In other words the spectrality of the bond affects the very essence of the possible. It makes possible the impossible, the coming of the other, the invention of the future.

Elizabeth Rottenberg, "Introduction," in *Negotiations: Interventions and Interviews 1971–2001* (Stanford, CA: Stanford University Press, 2002), 5.

4. J. Hillis Miller and Manuel Asensi, *Black Holes / J. Hillis Miller; Or, Boustrophedonic Reading* (Stanford, CA: Stanford University Press, 1999), 303.

5. Notable among contemporaries of Los Hijos are Andrés Duque, Virginia García del Pino, Óscar Alegría, Lois Patiño, Xurxo Chirro, Elías León Siminiani, and many others, some of whose work is discussed elsewhere in this book. Though not the primary concern of this chapter, I note that the noncommercial nature of the work of these filmmakers and its underground quality has generated a certain spectrality in the exhibition and distribution of their films. In the last few years (coinciding with the crisis), a shadow network of film

exhibition at the margins of commercial outlets has sprung up in Spain, consisting of Internet platforms such as plat.tv. and margenes.org and festivals specializing in the promotion of new filmmakers such as Punto de Vista in Navarra. Likewise, the Madrid Cineteca provides a new venue for documentary films unlikely to be screened elsewhere.

6. This is particularly relevant given that Luis López Carrasco's *El futuro*, discussed later in this chapter, was shot in 16 mm film for self-reflexive, or metafilmic, reasons.

7. By political discourse I refer to the allusions, often expressed with great subtlety, in the work of Los Hijos both to the history of Spain (the Francoist dictatorship, the Transition, the country's colonial past) and to its conflictive present on which that past weighs. I refer here particularly to López Carrasco's film *El futuro*, which was made in the aftermath (and is highly informed by) the 15-M or Indignados movement that commenced in 2011. However, while connected to this in terms of my critique of conventional historicism, it is not the primary interest of this chapter. Chapter 9 deals extensively with the films of the 15-M.

8. Miller and Asensi, *Black Holes*, 309.

9. Exemplary of the transnational cinephile culture within which Los Hijos participates are its members recent dialogues with Lucien Castaing-Taylor and Véréna Paravel of the Sensory Ethnography Lab in the 3 × DOC events in Madrid (March 14, 2014) and with US-Belgian artist Vincent Meesen (June 25, 2014), whose own work lends itself to hauntological interpretation. Los Hijos has acknowledged the influence of experimental filmmakers such as James Benning (Benning's 2004 *13 Lakes*, for example, haunts *Los materiales*). Los Hijos also has been at the forefront of efforts to promote largely unrecognized Spanish filmmakers from previous generations (see note 10).

10. Los Hijos has recognized the legacy of political cinema of the 1970s and in 2013 curated a cycle of films on militant politics of the Transition. To this end, the group has worked closely with filmmakers Cecilia and Juan José Bartolomé, among others.

11. Jacques Derrida and Bernard Stiegler, *Echographies of Television: Filmed Interviews* (Oxford: Polity Press, 2002), 122.

12. Miller and Asensi, *Black Holes*, xi.

13. The presence of a similar shot in Erice's *El espíritu de la colmena* (1973) may be coincidental, but the interest of Los Hijos in its illustrious predecessor would suggest otherwise.

14. Time is also an important element in Los Hijos's second feature, *Circo* (particularly the time of labor and that of the working day). I do not write about *Circo* here.

15. Tom Conley reminds us of the French homonym between *limitar* and *l'imitar*. Tom Conley, "Site and Sound," *Modern Language Notes* 121, no. 4 (September 2006): 852.

16. Miller and Asensi, *Black Holes*, 186.

17. Ibid., 435.

18. *Los materiales*, while concerned with the raw material of film itself—with illumination, acoustics, and the physical apparatus of filmmaking—also has no narrative as such. The film is improvised with much of its footage seemingly consisting of outtakes that in a more conventional film would have been discarded in the editing process. There are overtones and hints at various points in *Los materiales* of a parodic use of the conventions of the use of found footage in recent horror films (for example, Daniel Myrick and Eduardo Sánchez's 1999 *The Blair Witch Project*).

19. Such was the degree of local opposition to the reservoir that during the protest campaign there were many arrests (including of Riaño's mayor). One resident committed suicide, among the deaths that haunt this film. "Violentos incidentes en Riaño tras el suicidio

de un vecino," *El País*, July 12, 1987, http://elpais.com/diario/1987/07/12/portada/553039201
_850215.html.

20. Although not mentioned in *Los materiales*—and the absence itself is striking—Julio
Llamazares's 1985 novel *Luna de lobos*, which centers on the guerrilla warfare waged by
fugitive Republican soldiers following the official end of the conflict, is set in this region.
The filmed adaptation of 1987, directed by Julio Sánchez Valdés, was shot in Riaño. It is an
interesting example—from filmmakers known for their filmic literacy—of a noncitation or
citation by means of omission or ellipsis.

21. Jacques Derrida, *Archive Fever: A Freudian Impression*, trans. Eric Prenowitz
(Chicago: University of Chicago Press, 1998), 2.

22. Eduardo Cadava, "Trees, Hands, Stars and Veils: The Portrait in Ruins," in *Portraits*,
ed. Fazal Sheikh (Göttingen, Germany: Steidl, 2011), 12. Cadava is not writing here
axiomatically but referring to the specific portraits taken by photographer Fazal Sheikh. My
point, though, is similar to and inspired by Cadava's correlation of portraits and trees.

23. These sequences point to the long-standing filmic tradition of the city symphony,
which is indexed and subverted in this film.

24. In his blog, Paul Nadal draws attention to the relation between techne and the city:
"Plato understood politics as fundamentally belonging to the domain of *techné*, politics as
first and foremost a political skill to be learned, an art or, better yet, a kind of technology of
the *polis* (city)." Paul Nadal, "Heidegger's Critique of Modern Technology: On 'The Question
Concerning Technology,'" *Be Late* (blog), July 12, 2010, http://belate.wordpress.com/2010/07
/12/heidegger-modern-technology.

25. The diffused autobiographical references conditioned by technology also recall the
silent, subtitled sequences featuring Javier Fernández in *Los materiales*.

26. Noteworthy here is the rhizomatic quality of the genealogical tree. In a private
conversation, López Carrasco informed me that his mother is not the daughter of his
grandmother and the feet seen in close-up are those of his aunts (who otherwise do not appear).

27. Derrida, *Archive Fever*, 9.

28. Miller and Asensi, *Black Holes*, 309.

29. The substrate of *El futuro* is lined by a series of references and materials (buildings,
photographs, and archives) that combine and confuse different time periods: the Francoist
dictatorship, the 1980s, and the contemporary period (including the indignation provoked by
the current economic crisis and the failings of the political class). I suggest that form (both
filmic form and the media support employed) disjoins content but that, in turn, it is itself
disjoined within the diegesis of the film. This, I would argue, is what lies at the center of the
critique of representation.

30. Mark Fisher, *Ghosts of My Life* (London: Zero Books, 2014), 9.

31. There is an additional echo of *Arrebato* in *El futuro*: both films are primarily (with
significant interruptions) located indoors. This both generates a sense of suffocating
claustrophobia and gives significant weight to the occasional exterior sequences of both
films. The overall effect is to create another link between impossible and irreconcilable
opposites (inside and outside).

32. Walter Benjamin, "On the Concept of History," in *Selected Writings*, vol. 4, *1938–1940*,
ed. Howard Eiland and Michael W. Jennings (Cambridge, MA: Harvard University Press,
2006), 395.

33. The dialogue is muffled and practically inaudible. We hear snippets of conversation,
but it is virtually impossible to follow the gist of it. In this instance, for example, it is

impossible to know the substance of what is being said without the English subtitles or the explanation in interviews that López Carrasco has given. It is interesting that this happens precisely at the point in the film where the original script is retained. This is similar to the dissonance produced in *Los materiales* when we hear the crunch of gravel underfoot but large parts of the dialogue between the filmmakers goes unheard and yet is represented on-screen by subtitling.

34. Divided into two parts (*¿No se os puede dejar solos?* and *Atado y bien atado*) and shot in 1979 and 1980, this film was subjected to a series of bureaucratic impediments designed to prevent its release. It was finally screened legally in 1983. Ángel Fernández-Santos, "Después de . . ." obra 'maldita' del cine de la transición, se estrena con tres años de retraso," *El País*, November 3, 1983, http://elpais.com/diario/1983/11/03/cultura/436662004_850215.html.

35. In an additional instance of temporal disturbance in the context of political mobilization, Elena Oroz points out that the dialogue also describes—in terms of location and activity—the encircling of the Spanish parliament building on September 25, 2012. The action formed part of the popular reaction to the current financial and political crisis and is firmly and freshly located in the memory of many Madrileños. This, together with the shots of the anomalous 1990s housing, creates another instance of not only temporal discontinuity but also its inverse: the persisting, insistent, interruptive continuities in the form of ghostly returns. Such ghostliness is further emphasized in the still photographs of the Francoist childhoods that visually trace a discordant link between the dictatorial past, the recently restored democracy of the *movida madrileña*, and the present conjuncture of popular disenchantment with the country's institutions.

36. The figure of Alfonso Guerra himself is charged with spectrality. A former deputy prime minister and a key figure of both the Transition and Felipe González governments, he remains uniquely present to this day as the until recently only surviving and continuing congressman of those who entered parliament in 1977 (he retired from parliament at the end of 2014). Guerra's parliamentary longevity points to another black hole or time warp in Spanish history in that he has been vocal in defending the unity of Spain in the face of the possible secession of Catalonia from the Spanish state. A skewed temporal correlation (disjointed time) exists between Guerra's ghostly, uninterrupted, almost-forty-year tenure in congress and the interruption of the announcement, of which, on this occasion he is a disembodied protagonist.

37. The title of this song—pertinent only with the benefit of hindsight—recalls, in the form of an echo that reverberates in counterpoint through recent history, both the campaigns against nuclear power and the presence of US air bases on Spanish territory of the 1980s and 1990s and the PSOE's ambiguous slogan during the 1986 referendum on Spain's entry into NATO ("OTAN, de Entrada, No"), an ambiguity clarified (and dispensed with) by Felipe González's decisive intervention shortly before the referendum.

38. This assertion is, of course, open to debate. Other commentators have argued that digital reproduction does, in fact, deteriorate. My point (and the source of my doubt) is that what ages is the technological support rather than the substance (the digital code), which can indeed be preserved intact, seemingly unaffected by the passage of time, by updating both the software and the hardware that permits its reproduction.

9

¡NO NOS REPRESENTAN!

Performativity as Militant Film, the 15-M Archive

AS NIGHT FELL ON FRIDAY, APRIL 10, 2015, a demonstration was held in front of Las Cortes, the Spanish parliament. A few days earlier and in the same building, an initial vote had taken place that would have made this protest illegal were it not for the fact that the protesters, rather than being flesh-and-blood people, were, in fact, holograms. This virtual demonstration was organized to protest the vote the week before to initially approve the Ley de Seguridad Ciudadana, or, as it has been dubbed, la Ley Mordaza (the gagging law). Among other restrictions, the law banned protests in the vicinity of the parliament. The virtual protest was, to all intents and purposes, a visual and visible riposte to a law that pledged to decree, and thereby render, opposition invisible.[1] No crime, though, would be committed—or at least not one that was prosecutable. Projecting these images of approximately twenty thousand people chanting slogans in the square and street in front of the bronze statues of the lions at the doors of parliament would be, for the foreseeable future, the only way to conduct dissent. It was a protest in which the participants were clearly and eerily not present.[2]

Technology (a projector and a set of microphones) conjures up in mutated form glowing transparent figures bearing placards. It does so by unsettling and exceeding —placing in crisis—not only the laws of legislation but also those that frame the traditional limits and limitations of the screen, in its move outside the frame itself and beyond the laws of the filmic image. Technology extends and expands the filmic-political practice of resistance to the ongoing repression in unstable contemporary capitalism and executed by its nominal representatives in parliament. It performs the social-technological turbulence of our times.

Significantly, the ghostly protesters traverse the walls that the image has long established between representation and represented, between the sign and its referent. The holograms posit a series of ontological questions concerning presence and being. Likewise, the metaphorical function of the lions—symbolic protectors of the seat of Spanish politics and the nation's capital—that allegorically guard the gates of parliament, solidly constative in their metallic materiality, is undone (in a very unmetaphoric way) by the radiographic images that expose the inner workings of the regime. It is this relation between the outside and the inside produced by technology that is the subject of this final chapter.[3]

I address the question of how the visual image represents real historical events at the very moment that those events take place before the camera lens rather than in the form of either reenactment or as journalism synthetically reproduced in editing rooms and packaged for public consumption. How does the image refract, rather than reflect, historicity in such a way as to produce it? The evolution of the filmic apparatus today has a technology capable of bringing about the changes that it has, to date, only been able to record. What is interesting about the hologram protest is that it is not a representation at all. It is the protest itself rather than a symbolic substitute; its X ray translucence is both cause and effect, substance and image. Can similar technology thus deployed—given the apparent simultaneity of the signifying process suggested by digital film's lack of a material negative—be termed representation of any kind? What are the implications for political film in the digital era? And what, finally, is the relation of today's political filmmakers with their historical forebears, and how might the historical antecedents of militant cinema be mobilized?

To explore these questions, I examine the evolving and residual relation between the photographic image and actuality in light of digital technology as an instrument of contemporary activism with a view to locating this latter field of filmmaking genealogically in relation to the precedents of the "classical" period of militant cinema. I do this by analyzing a group of films that have emerged out of one of the most dramatic and potentially transformative moments in Spain since the Transition: the 15-M movement, whose most repeated and emblematic slogan was, "¡Que no, que no, que no nos representan!" (No, no, no. They don't represent us!). What distinguishes these filmic texts and their context, I claim, is a particular notion of performativity that goes beyond and exceeds its reference; its very exorbitance disturbs temporal frameworks, whether in terms of the instant of the filming or with regard to the broad sweep of history or to the tradition of filmmaking itself. Haunted by the past of the archive that prompts them, these films stretch out to acknowledge and interrogate the unknown, incongruent future. To appropriate a phrase of J. Hillis Miller, I ask what constitutes "the destiny of . . . legacy."[4]

This chapter complicates not only the question of how to represent history (both the filmic genre and the academic discipline) but also the importance of time in the film process itself. The chapter is inspired, in part, by the brief description offered by Víctor Moreno of his admirable documentary *Edificio España* (2012) at the introduction to a public screening of the film on June 6, 2014, as "a small allegory of our recent history," which echoes the title of a filmed conversation between Moreno and Samuel Alarcón (*Edificio Alegoría España*).

Allegory is, of course, as discussed previously, a means by which history is traditionally represented. While throughout this book I have questioned the figure of allegory as commonly associated with Fredric Jameson's influential concept, what is true of allegory, to cite Tom Cohen's neat description, is that it "invoke[s] parallel logics." The same could be said, again paraphrasing Cohen on Walter Benjamin, of cinema itself, "translation," "materialistic historiography," or, indeed, and pertinent to the virtual protest described earlier, the hologram.[5] Rather than thinking of allegory as a kind of extended metaphor that—at the level of discourse—occupies the place of actuality, I view it as metonymy, a displacement, or a horizontal shift marked by slippage toward the margins where the past inhabits or infuses the present by association or evocation. This process happens by means of "material elements of the past as they exist in the present—objects, images, narratives, documents, detritus"[6] rather than through vertically imposed metaphor. Following other commentators (Cohen and Paul de Man among them), I think of allegory as what I have previously termed "other" discourse—a form of representation that accompanies rather than substitutes for or supplants the actual events to which it refers. Allegory, to employ Jacques Derrida's suggestively apt term (particularly in relation to the events of Madrid's main square, La Puerta del Sol), is metonymic in that its representation of the whole "centers it . . . in a periphery, shapes it, stands for it."[7] Extending the idea of a cultural correlate to political representation, I configure allegory as a ghostly or countergenealogy, an othered history of militant filmmaking, in which the relationship of present filmmaking to the past is that of residue. It is citationally linked to what Cohen calls "anteriority as *virtual*"[8] (emphasis mine) and is inscribed in its successors by means of what Cohen terms "the teletechnological routing and force of trace-chains" that create "an *allographic* practice to come."[9]

Clearly, the 2015 hologram protest is relevant here. That is, the correlation is contiguous and heterogeneous rather than synthesized or consensual or illustrative and didactic, as in a parable. I argue for an allegory as heterology, at odds with the components of its own internal correlation, whose "parallel logics" are discordant with one another. To this end, I suggest that the past produces effects in the future. A correlation is marked by difference with the potential for a rupture in the future "to come." Although I will return to this point at the end of this chapter, for now I insist that this engagement with the mobilization of filmic antecedents alters—indeed, provokes a break within the concept of allegory itself—that which associates it with national discourse.

As the critique of representation lies at the heart of this book, in this last chapter I propose the concept of performativity as a means to productively refigure this notion of a metonymic allegory to conceptualize this rupture within the consensus—in this instance, as determined by the 1978 Spanish constitution and the discourses of the Transition. I do this in light of the extraordinary emergence of political films within the Spanish state in the wake of the events of May 15, 2011—the 15-M. This dated context conforms to what Derrida has described as telegraphic metonymy, a term that captures both the shorthand of the telegram and a sense of relay.[10] The alteration that theoretically addresses the question of allegory that haunts this book constitutes a fundamental part of the regime of representation that it critiques.

I echo Derrida's observation (deployed in his work on the archive[11] and repeated in the posthumously published book-length interviews on the subject of photography[12]) that the digital image is productive rather than representative of the event it purports to record. In its productivity, performativity becomes political as it brings about and produces the change it "represents." Its constitutive properties enact a discordant irruption into the consensus (one, in the case of Spain, imposed under the threat of violence and negotiated under duress and coercion[13]) that is not only unauthorized and unprecedented but, in its transformative gesture to the future, also laden with promise. This "originary performativity that does not conform to preexisting conventions, unlike all the performatives analyzed by the theoreticians of speech acts, but whose force of *rupture* produces the institution or the constitution, the law itself, which is to say also the meaning that appears to, that ought to or that appears to guarantee it in return"[14] (emphasis in the original).

This performativity (which I define more explicitly below) provides—particularly with respect to its technological support—a way to theorize, in the context of film, what Amador Fernández Savater, in reference to the 15-M, has posited as "a change of sensibility" in Spanish society. I am sympathetic with Savater's view but theorize beyond what he has proposed.[15] I hypothesize that the particularly proleptic notion of performativity, like the 15-M itself (as we will see), disarticulates the ill-fitting temporalities of the post-1978 social contract. Following Derrida, I propose that interpretation—including, or particularly, filmic representation—is performative when its representation, rather than reflecting or reproducing the thing it represents, changes what it interprets.[16]

Above all, the 15-M poses a democratic objection to the institutions and systemized institutional practices that have been erected and sustained precisely in the name of democracy.

I suggest, in the vein of Derrida's critique of institutionalization—and particularly the appropriation, naming, and authorization that it involves—that the productive work of the performative is disadjustment, a metonymical shift in the institutional criteria of naming. Such disarticulation has political ramifications (among them those concerning popular sensibility), but it is also at work within the constitutive elements of film itself, in film's archival substrate and material support. I suggest that the performativity of film lies in its capacity to intervene in a context and change it in the way of a speech act.[17] However, it goes beyond that.

This chapter surveys a selection taken from the archive of the many films to have emerged out of the events of the spring and early summer of 2011. The chapter concludes with a detailed analysis of the work of Ramiro Ledo Cordeiro (one of the most interesting of the cohort of young contemporary political filmmakers in Spain), whose work stands consciously within a tradition of militant filmmaking; whose references stretch back variously to the 1930s, the 1960s, and the 1970s; and whose films move away from the centralized location of La Puerta del Sol in Madrid to the fringes of the nation-state.

I first saw a sample of the films discussed here, appropriately enough, on an anniversary, a precise and significant date: May 15, 2013. The screening occurred two years to the day—its revenant—since the events that initiated the occupation of Madrid's central square. The event was held in the city's Cineteca under the interrogative rubric (in English) of "¿Spanish Revolution?" Of the seven short films screened that evening, at least three of them (Los Hijos's *Enero 2012, o la apoteosis de Isabel la Católica*, David Varela's *Historia monumental de la España contemporánea*, and *Las variaciones Guernica*, directed by Guillermo Peydró) refer to Spain's historical, monumental, or artistic heritage to comment on the political actuality of the country. There is an allegorical element to each of them, but it is an allegory riven by disjointed temporality. Rather than allegorical films themselves, they are comments on the traditional allegorical nature of representation, and particularly the representation of the nation. Allegory in each of these films, instead of correspondence, is distinguished by disrupted time, by an inappropriate or forced correlation. The past is discordant with and disruptive of the present; it is incongruous and ironic. In each of these cases, a self-conscious positing differentiates the allegory from the traditional use of the term or the way in which Jameson seeks to conceptualize allegory politically. This self-consciousness is performative, meaning that the present is insistent in making its presence felt but in such a way that its self-reflexivity, rather than being an aim in itself, eludes its own temporality. The present is divided in the instant of its own production. Instantaneity, formal structures, and the topicality or political relevance of the thematic content prove elusive. Time is disjoined.

A fourth film, directed by Isaki Lacuesta, actualizes the virtual past with images of the present (all of which contain, as we will see, an unbeknownst proposition for the future) by using the Super 8 footage shot by amateur filmmaker (and real estate agent) Pep Armengol of the first democratic election campaign in 1978 and earlier images, shot by Armengol in 1967, of a *matanza*, the family tradition of killing a pig, carving it up, and making sausages. The images of the pig being slaughtered are inserted—punctuation like—within the sequences of the 15-M assemblies in Barcelona. The soundtrack, narrated by Armengol, concerns the noxious effects of the current economic crisis and contrasts with the lighthearted ironic intertitles imposed by Lacuesta of the "Indignados."[18] The result is an interesting comic juxtaposition of audio and visual/textual tracks. The element of a yet-to-be-determined future in this ten-minute film lies in Armengol's proposal (a critique of the passivity of the 15-M) that a minor act of terrorism should be adopted against those responsible for the economic crisis, and in doing so he clarifies the analogy between the *matanza* and the resistance with a popular Catalan refrain: "Sense sang no fan (o no poden fer) botifarrons" (Without spilling blood, you can't make blood pudding).

Two years later, Lacuesta would take up Armengol's suggestion in his fulllength film *Murieron por encima de sus posibilidades* (They died beyond their possibilities) (2014), a comedy about a group of patients who escape from a psychiatric hospital and assault the subaquatic headquarters of the chairman of the Central Bank. This film posits a curious *ana-chronic* generic hiccup, in that, on one level its title contains an echo of Raoul Walsh's *They Died with Their Boots On* (1941), but it also stands in the tradition of 1950s Spanish comedy associated with filmmakers such as Luis García Berlanga and Marco Ferreri. Anachronism—"time out of joint"—is also in the custom of the *matanza* and in the material support of the now archaic, aged, and dated Super 8 format whose graininess contrasts uncannily with the pristine digital video.[19] This encounter, articulated in Lacuesta's film, between two temporalities, two modes of filmmaking, and different generations of popular culture marks a meeting point, a conjuncture sealed—signed and countersigned—around an event that takes the name of a particular date, May 15, the 15-M.

Among the various denominations associated with the ongoing mobilizations (Indignados, etc.), the 15-M predominates. This date is made singular by virtue of its commemorative iteration, here encased tentatively, inquiringly, and dubitatively in the word *revolution*—"¿Spanish Revolution?"—with its revolving connotations of *volver*, the volte-face, the turn, the turnabout, the re-turn, the re-*volte*. The revolution referred to here is linked to a date whose identifying mark acts as signature, suggestive of temporal disturbance whose gesture to the future contains a charge. More than a critique of the past, it is an inaugurating rupture, a division in the instant of its own time. It is a rupture with the previous performative injunction of the 1978 constitution, whose words and articles enjoined, conjoined/conjured, and bound Spanish civil society in the "national contract," or, more importantly, provided the ground instituted in and by its text—its speech act (as we will see below)—of what has come to be known as "democratic Spain."

If, as is my contention, the 15-M marks a sea change in the national sensibility and that its rupturing quality is that of an event at odds with the chronological continuum of history, it is because, arguably for the first time, the discourse enshrouding this contract has been called into question by a substantial sector of the population in the name of democracy. The political class or caste responsible for the national contract has sustained it by recourse to a particular rhetoric—again a performativity—that is equally resolutely sustained, popularly and intellectually, by the mass media and the academy.

The 15-M and its repercussions, which over the following weeks and months rippled outward from the center of Madrid to the city's neighborhoods, were distinguished in their day by a sense of urgency, immediacy, and instantaneity that was almost televisual in its directness. It was, moreover, filmed—transmitted live—recorded in the kind of extensive and saturated way that only the technology of the current historical period can permit.[20]

Located not only in a particular space, a locality, La Puerta del Sol, the 15-M was—as is hinted at by the widespread perception that it was filmed in real time—also situated within a clearly defined frame of temporality. The encounter of the 15-M was inspired by, provoked by, and directly addresses the ongoing economic crisis. Crisis indicates fragmentation, uncertainty, precariousness, and groundlessness. The singularity of critical time—the fracturing time of crisis—is compounded by the name, the very specific appellation of the 15-M, the fifteenth of May 2011. As a calendar date, it resounds in the here and now, and its singularity requires repetition through memorialization or, paradoxically, by means of a putative live recording, its reproduction in handheld video cameras and cell phones, and its materialization in seemingly intangible immaterial form and archived online.

The singularity of the 15-M is reinforced by reproduction, repetition, and the persistence of its trace, its iteration—and by what remains, what is left in its wake. The time of crisis is also one of urgency, emergency, an emergence, a turning point, and a becoming. Indeed, the document of documentary film is not a matter of historical record but rather an archival imprint of disjointed time. Such singularity points to a disarticulation with both that which went before and its present now. Derrida might term such an event as marked by *différance*—that is, difference and deferral (not May 14, not May 16)—a disturbance not only in the relation between past and present but within the present itself. The performative act or action in actuality opens up a spacing (interestingly conducted within real disputed urban space), constitutive of and constituted by its legacy and its promise of the future to come. For Derrida, later in the same passage on performativity quoted earlier, "In the incoercible *différance* the here-now unfurls."[21]

The disjoining singularity of the 15-M—its date not the present now but its other—is also a generational one. It is less a youthful uprising (as it was lazily characterized by the media) than a break with the generation that defends the discourse of the Transition, which Guillem Martínez has dubbed the *CT*, or *la Cultura de la Transición* (The Culture of the Transition).[22] What Martínez describes is the discourse of representation: on the one hand, historiography as representation—the archival institutionalization of the Transition—and, on the other, with the emphasis on the significance of the word *representation* within that discourse, the weight lent to, and the aura surrounding, the concept of representative democracy as inaugurated by the Transition and the 1978 constitution. Such is the force with which that discourse has been consolidated that, prior to the 15-M, discrepancy was not tolerated or admitted. It became a performative (in the sense that the word is employed by speech act theorists), an axiom—as prevalent in the official Left, the political parties of the Left, and the trade unions as on the Right—that whoever questioned the legitimacy of the discourse of the Transition was, perforce, antidemocratic. The 1978 constitution brought about exactly what it describes and cannot, as such, brook any contradiction that might cast its grounding principles in doubt. My proposal in this chapter is that the performative irruption called the 15-M does exactly this. And it does so by its trace of pastness that conserves in the metonym of its named date a promise of futurity that seeks to identify not only the break with the political inheritance but also the material changes in filmic technology that are marked particularly by questions of temporality.

Labeled disparagingly by those hostile to the 15-M as utopian—and thus, impossible, unthinkable, out-of-time, timeless—the uprising did at times seem to aspire to be a utopia, though one very much located in time and dated, as it were, performatively speaking. It is a gesture that heralds the arrival of change in the form of the other, an attempt to create the conditions for another emerging alternative world. In fact, "Otro mundo es posible" (Another world is possible) was one of the slogans of first the antiglobalization movement of the late 1990s and early 2000s[23] and later of the 2003 campaign against Spain's participation in the invasion of Iraq. The slogan reemerged in 2011 as a functioning otherly exemplar of alternative possibilities put into practice at the heart of Madrid's business district and a symptom of critical cosmopolitanism. The 15-M marks a performative incision, a cut in the relation between past and present; like all dates, it marks a caesura in time. It brings forth. The word *perform* contains its futurity in the *per* (or the *por* of *porvenir* discussed in the previous chapter) that points to the change that, in its disarticulating articulation, it enacts and brings about. It is the *form* or de *form*ation of *form*al practice—the rupture with that which con *form*s—that produces the alteration.

In this vein, I emphasize—following Miller—the difference between this notion of performativity and the more frequently referenced deployment of the term associated with Judith Butler. Butler's work on performativity is a theory of subjectivity that, in its rejection of essentialism or an inner self, is based on repetition and the performance of identity.[24] Likewise, this chapter's idea of performativity has little to do with theater or live dramatic performance. Nor does it adopt—except incidentally—Bill Nichols's taxonomy of the performative documentary.[25] That said, it is clear that in the context of popular protest—in the occupation of public space, the subjective use of filmmaking, a certain staging, and particularly the purported filmic representation—these various definitions of the performative overlap to a certain (albeit limited) extent with Derrida's particular use of the word. For Miller, as it is for Derrida, a performative statement not only is what it describes; it produces it.[26] A "performative statement," Miller writes, "brings into existence the condition it names."[27]

The Films of the 15-M: A Brief Survey

Although I will not analyze it in great detail, I briefly mention Basilio Martín Patino's *Libre te quiero* (I love you free), is probably (in part owing to the prestige of its director) the most celebrated film to come out of the 15-M. Patino's focus on the festive aspects of the days and weeks he spent shooting the various 15-M protests in the square and beyond provides the kind of coincidence between performance and performativity to which I have just referred. *Libre te quiero* records and celebrates performance in sounds, rhythms, musical and theatrical events, and the movement of the body (particularly the youthful body). This veteran filmmaker mobilizes all his filmic experience and resources in a gesture toward a future of future generations. Pertinent to my argument, though, are the film's formal properties and, above all, its montage.

Patino is best known for his early feature, the 1971 *Canciones para después de una guerra*, which is an extraordinary composition of found footage and sonic archive material deployed to evoke the postwar period in Spain. Playing on sentiment and nostalgia and using images of Francoist propaganda, Patino invented his own form of political cinema in the editing room. Forty years later, although shot by Patino himself with a handheld digital camera, *Libre te quiero* is also a film whose effect is largely created through its montage. Both films, *Canciones para después de una guerra* and *Libre te quiero*, have no commentary; they simply are. The images—visual and acoustic—stand for themselves performatively. But they are also performative films in that they are not what Nichols has defined as observational documentaries; they do not simply record what is before them. There is a clear political intervention that is produced by and in their composition—that is, in their montage. Each film is, in its own very different way, a montage film, but importantly, both films are located in, bound up with, and products of specific historical time, critical moments, and moments of crisis. They both dissent from that time and are antonymic with the time of their production.[28] And in their gaze—one film looks backward in time, the other forward—the moment of their production is elusive. The discordance of Patino's work, like the event of the 15-M itself, while highly actual, is dissonant with its own contemporaneity—whether in 1971 and 2012—exemplary of the kind of performative gesture to which I have been referring.

Where Patino's film stresses the ludic and the light, Sylvain George's *Vers Madrid: The Burning Bright* is lyrical, as its title suggests (the ambiguity of the French *vers*, verse/toward Madrid and the reference to William Blake's poem *The Tyger*). It is also much darker and forms a lurking, potentially explosive alternative to Patino's sun-splashed festivity. More explicitly militant in its expressed partisan stance, *Vers Madrid* is shot almost entirely in black and white, and the film possesses an extraordinary beauty. Yet—and therein lies its performative strength—its aesthetic quality never undermines its political commitment, nor is it a decorative correlate. Rather, the film's expressionism is found in its aesthetics and politics being indistinguishable. Such political performativity as aesthetic practice echoes a lengthy tradition of militant filmmaking (such as that of Joris Ivens, Italian neorealism, Alain Renais, Pier Paolo Pasolini, and others).[29] Further, its politics are often the product of its aesthetic choices, exemplified by the juxtaposition of the live discussions of the assemblies in Sol (which were continuous and interminable) with the leaden symbols of national unity that pepper the city of Madrid and that, in the film, serve as metonyms of the crisis itself. These politics condition the rhythm of the film marked, in turn, by its displacement from the high energy of the activities in Sol to the lulls, the interludes beyond the square, and its muted violence.

In these *lapsus*, the creases in the folds of the film's texture—its errant other beyond the groundedness of the central square—the film elliptically follows the precarious life of an illegal Moroccan immigrant who functions as the choral, spectral underbelly to the celebratory atmosphere of Sol. This unnamed, anonymous figure of alterity ekes out a shadow existence in the submerged economy of the city. His ghostliness contrasts with the subject matter of many of the discussions in Sol on immigration, racism, and discrimination. While the space of Sol is under occupation, the Moroccan wanders across the avant-garde footbridge of former city mayor Alberto Ruiz-Gallardón's emblematic urban showcase Madrid Rio and describes himself as "lost in space."

The spectral element of *Vers Madrid: The Burning Bright* is enhanced by the presence of Agustín García Calvo, the author of the poem "Libre te quiero," appropriated by Martín Patino as the title of his film. García Calvo made regular appearances in Sol in the early summer of 2011 and became a symbolic historical link with the past (he was dismissed from his position as professor of Latin at the Complutense University of Madrid in 1965 for his opposition to the Francoist regime). His appearance in the film, however, takes on an additional, poignant, and performative aspect. García Calvo died a few months after the events in Sol had quieted down, thereby giving his presence in the film a ghostly quality, something beyond, in excess of his life. We note his appearance in the film, three years after his death, as uncannily alive and whose function is both diegetically and biographically a vestige of the past. This, together with the fact that he is the author of the poem whose adaptation to music by Amancio Prada and deployment in Martín Patino's film, allude to an iterative series of afterlives in an example of the singular-plural. Moreover, if García Calvo's past—his personal, political, and literary history—colors the present, then part of the subject matter of this intervention is the future. García Calvo poses the future as negative for change in the face of the packaged and programmed future of clocks and calendars that serves only capital and the state and that, in García Calvo's view, means death, the organization of death.[30]

There is, though, another way that García Calvo's afterlife is felt. In our present-day knowledge of García Calvo's impending death, a posthumous presence, subject and susceptible to those others—the others of altering, of Benjaminian allegory, in teletechnologically produced virtuality—who have survived him and whose prolongation marks the lurch from past to future (recall the subject matter of García Calvo's speech) depends on that virtual trace or spirit (fig. 9.1). The image of García Calvo at the 15-M assemblies in George's film is an example of Cohen's "trace-chains" which I referred to earlier: "To ask where allegory in its prehistory . . . prefigures an *allographic* practice to come, is also to note where the latter suggests not only that mnemonic otherness evinced by

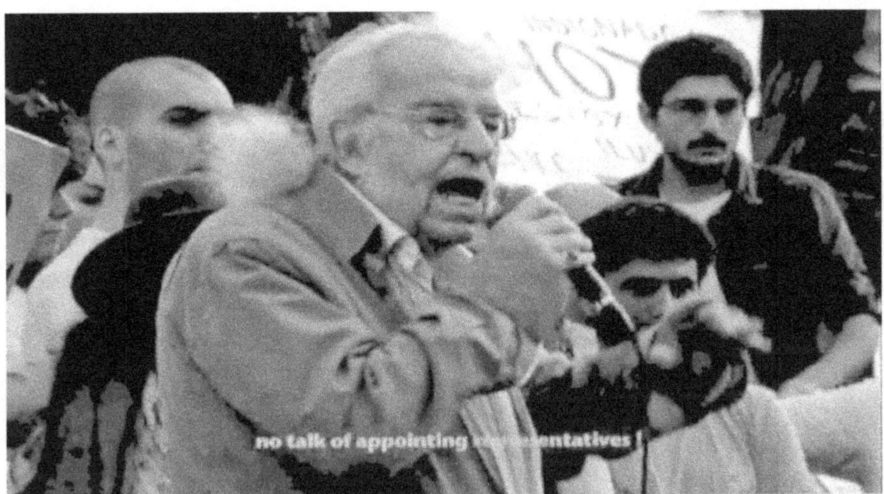

Fig. 9.1 Agustín García Calvo addresses the crowds in La Puerta del Sol.

the facticity of prefigural inscription but the *altering* impact of material signs on (and against) anterior traces, altering or engineering the teletechnological routing and force of trance-chains, the recasting of anteriority and the production of reference."[31] (emphases in the original).

Flavio G. García's project *Video-Derives*, which forms part of the "¿Spanish Revolution?" screening and DVD, consists of two short abstract pieces shot in and around La Puerta del Sol during the encampment. García, an activist and a participant in the 15-M from the beginning of the protest, does not produce reportage. This is not a journalistic enterprise in that the objective of his films is not to garner visual evidence to counter misrepresentation by the mainstream media or to expose police brutality (there were commissions, groups, and individuals doing precisely that). Nor is it, despite García's sympathies, propaganda. García's abstract work is nonetheless political in the performative sense that I outlined earlier. That is, in its very abstraction, by exceeding formal boundaries, it is, in its own right, a political intervention. In the two shorts, *Sol* (just over five minutes long) and *Air Vigilance* (a little over twelve minutes), García experiments with the sonic texture and the patterns of illumination thrown up by the swirl of the protest.

These suggestive filmic performances—which form part of the collective enterprise of the 15-M rather than representing it, substituting for it, or advocating on its behalf—run the gamut of sensorial registers. They include the menace of the police surveillance helicopter with its insect-like hover and the rhythmic whir and throb of its propellers (a motif present in many films of the 15-M,

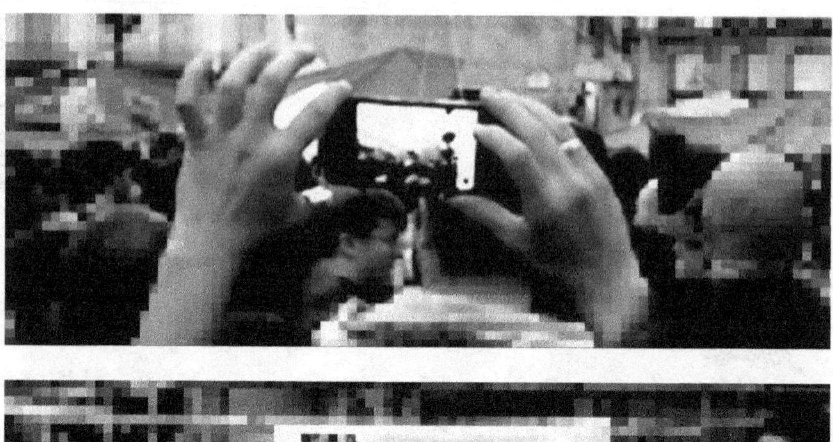

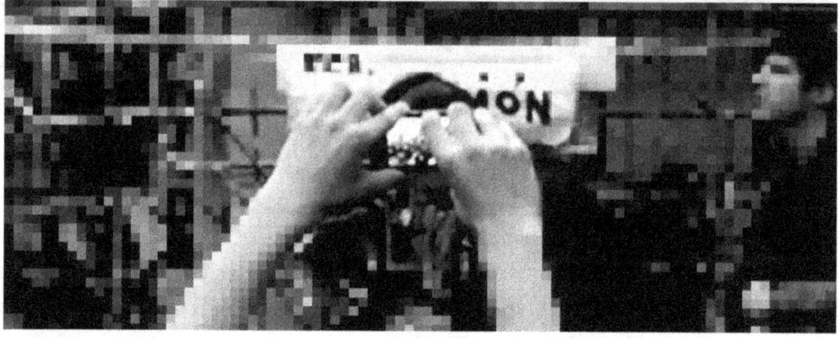

Fig. 9.2 a–b Two photograms from Flavio G. Garcia's *Video-Derives.*

among them Sylvain George's[32]), the confusion of noises, the clashes with the police, the celebrations, and the claustrophobia of the close-up, which predominates in *Sol.* There is, as some commentators have observed, an excess of sound and images in García's work; the screen collapses into pixilation, suggesting that such excess impedes vision and prevents interpretation. Such an observation suggests that this surplus is disruptive. The immediate effect, though, is one of fragmenting representation that calls attention to its own technology. *Sol* consists of a series of shots of people filming in the square with their cell phones. While the crowd bustles around the limits of the frames within frames, the sensorial, affective appeal is produced by an awareness of the materiality of the cell phone camera itself (see figs. 9.2a and 9.2b).

What we see here is a fragmentation of space characteristic of all photography but with the additional fractal framing distinctive of the digital in that there is no material negative on which to imprint the image, just the repeated image of the image on-screen. In a sense, this secondhand imagery comes to define its own production (shot on a cell phone, the focus of the short film is on the proliferation—the singular-plurality—of cell phone cameras each producing its own film, of the same, different images). Likewise, it is noticeable that amid the plurality of apparatus that facilitates the mise en abyme, the metonym or synecdoche returns once more in the pixilation. Pixilation is the fragmenting of a totality or a component of a larger entity rather than a photographic blur. In this instance, the synecdoche overlaps the temporal with the spatial. The images—the mise-en-scène—in the sequence of García's shot are marked by a spacing, by the division of space within the screen frame and between frames. The spacing of the images defines their making. The combination of the pixilation on the surface of the photogram and the mise en abyme of the camera filming another cell phone filming while pointing to a series of tensions between part and whole, interior and exterior, surface and depth, form the spacing and spatialization distinctive of the digital image.

The mise-en-scène of these shots—the organization of materials within the frame, their staging—marked by the iterating mise en abyme is, in turn, in the chiasmatic effect of the pixilation a *mise a l'écart*. This effect is produced within the frame, within the shot in a spatialization contiguous with the focal point of the cell phone image itself that runs counter to the forward movement of narrative. This visual spacing, vertiginous in its excess, prompts yet another division of space beyond the clustered frame, that of the square under occupation. La Puerta del Sol is the site of the city's groundedness. It is *kilometro zero*, Madrid's very own ground zero.[33]

In addition to the spatial division, the filming suggests a temporal deferral. There is a clear break produced in the shot, a disjoining of the present not only from the future and the past but from itself, the putting into practice of what Derrida has called "a division of the instant." Real live time or simultaneity, Derrida argues, does not exist. Rather, we occupy the space between the no longer and the not yet, and in the directly recorded event there is always some kind of imperceptible lag, or "an extremely reduced 'différance,'"[34] here made visually apparent in the image recording apparatus capturing the profilmic event. Arguably, the combination of technology that permits the production of an image without material support—what Derrida calls "photographic performativity"—the filmic texts themselves, and the location function to collapse (like the pixilation of the image) the distinction between profilmic, the filmic, and the postfilmic, in which the filming becomes a form of archiving.

Supplement and Archive in the Films of Ramiro Ledo Cordeiro

The very title of Ramiro Ledo Cordeiro's *VidaExtra* (Extralife) (2013) evokes (and maybe invokes, performatively) an image of supplementarity. The supplement, the addendum to something larger, is also metonymic. In *VidaExtra*,

Ledo offers a militant film whose subject matter is militancy itself. The performativity of the piece is more than just a reflection on political commitment; it is also evident in the film's militant intervention. The film enacts what it describes. But as a commentary on the subject of militancy itself, it has a metapolitical-filmic quality in its own right. Its references, moreover, are multiple, both formal and thematic. *VidaExtra* is the culmination of several years of filmic experimentation carried out by Ledo, which, unusually, combines formal experiment to incorporate a political legacy and establish an archive of resistance.

In one of Ledo's earliest films, *Cine clube Carlos Varela* (2005), the young director digitalizes and edits the original Super 8 footage shot by revolutionary socialist and Galician nationalist Carlos Varela. Between 1971 and 1980 (he was killed in an accident in 1980), Varela used his domestic camera to record the emergence and evolution of the largely unacknowledged national-popular movement in Galicia of late Francoism and the Transition. Varela was also responsible for organizing a network of cine clubs, which distributed and screened the classics of militant film (Santiago Álvarez, Joris Ivens, Sergei Eisenstein, Jorge Sanjines, etc.) throughout the region. *Cine clube Carlos Varela* is also commemorative in a way, as a work of mourning both for Varela and for a movement that saw itself, despite (or perhaps because of) its national aspirations, in the tradition of the international anticolonial struggle, and especially that being contemporaneously waged in Latin America. The Varela film focuses on two aspects that have distinguished Ledo's work ever since: political militancy and a notable cinephilic interest in the materiality of film in reworked footage and montage.[35]

In the hitherto unwritten history of Spanish political cinema, Carlos Velo figures as a precedent, a militant filmmaker avant la lettre.[36] His 1930s work foreshadows much of the committed films of later decades, with its focus on ethnography, working practices, and the unjust distribution of wealth in Spain. Notable among the films he made at this time are the documentary *Almadrabas* (1934), which depicts in detail the processes behind the tuna industry, from the capture of the fish to the tinning production, and *Galicia* (1936), of which only a fragment remains.[37] *Romancero marroquí* (1939), which Velo directed during the Spanish Civil War, was itself distorted by misappropriative montage. What was originally conceived of as a Robert Flaherty–type ethnographic film of a family in the tribal population of the mountainous Rif region in northern Morocco was transformed and deformed into Francoist propaganda that celebrated the colonial relation with Spain. The result is an interesting disjunction between the supple plasticity of Velo's camera style (despite the re-editing) and the hectoring propaganda-imbued narration added after Velo's exile.

The manipulative potential of montage is perhaps the subject of Ledo's work on Velo more than six decades later. While, as we have seen, many contemporary filmmakers hark back to their predecessors in spectral ways, in Ledo's references, the "parallel logic" at work in his film on Velo (as with Varela) is ethnographic and filmic. In *Galicia 1936–2011*, Ledo, together with his aunt, Margarita Ledo Andión, revisits Velo's 1936 lost film by resorting to three separate sources: the remaining eight-minute version screened at the 1937 Paris International Exposition; the sequences that were used, incorporated, or recycled by Esfir Shub in the Russian film *Ispanija* (1939), whose images in Ledo's film are taken from Italian television; and the two reels of Velo's original footage discovered in the archives of the former Soviet Union by Russian film scholar and specialist in visual anthropology, Vladimir Magidov.[38] In these examples, Velo's legacy has clearly been much abused and distorted by both the Right and the Left. Ledo's essayistic experiment with Velo, composed in the editing room, is conscious of this. His composition is made of remains, like Benjaminian ruins that, amassed and juxtaposed in the montage, provide a commentary on their own history. The archeological performativity of this essay creates—as does the Varela film—a critical counterhistory of a Galician filmmaking of fragments, exemplary of performative interpretation as transformative.

The pertinence of the montage essay to the questions that I address in this chapter is more formally expressed in the twelve-minute short *El proceso de Artaud* (The trial of Artaud) that Ledo made in 2010. An exercise in cinephilia in its appropriation of Carl Theodor Dreyer's *The Trial of Joan of Arc* (1927) and an example of the "recasting of anteriority" that Cohen discusses, the short also has a political-cultural discourse: the expulsion of Antonin Artaud by the Surrealists for criticizing the decision of the group to affiliate with the French Communist Party in 1926. It is a form of unauthorized critical cinematic interpretation which, to use Derrida's words that define performativity, "transforms the thing it interprets."[39] The film begins with an explanatory on-screen script, which, given its relevance to this chapter's focus, I quote in full:

> En 1927 al filmar las actas de un proceso acontecido 500 años antes, lo que en verdad registraba Carl Theodor Dreyer eran los rastros de otra exclusión, ocurrida algunos meses antes. La de Antonin Artaud del grupo surrealista. La maquinaría procesal medieval irrumpía en las reuniones de amigos. Lo invariable de las maneras del tribunal hace surgir de la película una nueva puesta en escena en que la ficción origina un nuevo documento.

> [In 1927, on filming the proceedings of a trial that occurred 500 years previously, what Carl Theodor Dreyer really registered were the traces of another exclusion that happened some months earlier. That of Antonin Artaud from

the Surrealist group. The medieval judicial machinery intervened in the meetings of friends. Invariably the ways of the tribunal give rise in the film to a new mise-en-scène in which fiction originates a new document.]

We are confronted here by a filmic analogy (the respective trials of Joan of Arc and Artaud) represented by two separate but intertwined films (the appropriation of Dreyer's text by Ledo), different regimes of writing, the script of Dreyer's text, and the script of the interrogation to which Artaud was subject. The insertion via montage of Artaud in the place of María Falconetti (in a film in which Artaud was an actor) in the 1927 film is a grafting that is also *graphting*, in the sense of a textual, scriptural interjection of an other, an *allos*, as in *allography*. There is also a contemporary insertion (by Ledo himself, seen only partially from the side and from behind) of the photograph of Falconetti within the written text of the book *Adhérer au Parti comuniste?* (a volume of the documents of the archives of the Paris Surrealists published by Gallimard).

An introduction is provided by Ledo's explanatory text, whose operative word is the deployment of the verb *originar* (in an echo of Derrida's "originary performativity"), which, in the reworking of Dreyer's film, resuscitates—postmortem in a virtual afterlife—the figure of Artaud, in a prosthetic addition to the life and work of both men. The shadowy fragmented presence of Ledo gives the film a hint of autobiography (the autobiographical in Ledo's film, albeit diffuse with the presence of family members and the importance of Galicia, is often there) of the self or, to use the Spanish word once more, the *propio*. All these aspects of the film suggest an exercise of exappropriation (the richly creative doubling produced of the unauthorized interpretive movement of the performativity that I have established throughout this chapter, the heterologic that differs radically from and contrasts with the ideological appropriation of *Romancero marroquí*).

With this Derridean neologism (*exappropiation*), I seek to describe the doubled play of the *propio*: that regarding authorial property in the appropriations from Dreyer's film and the written text from the Surrealist archive and, in these introductory sequences, the additional, extra framings whose contemporaneity is evident and exterior to the film proper. (Some of these are within the mise-en-scène in the lectern, the book, and the photograph.) These features create an aporia that mobilizes both incorporation and dispossession, the in and the out, the self and the other. And, in the other meaning of *ex* as former or anterior (as in Cohen), the aporia turns on questions of temporality. Appropriation, of course, contains another meaning: propriety, the appropriate, the authorized, the authentic, and the author. All these meanings contrast with the inappropriate, the improper, and unauthorized author or reader whose free interpretation alters the thing it interprets.[40]

While we have already seen the way exappropriation figures as both introjection and projection, the tension that holds together internal contradictions, what is explicitly put into play here is the aporetic encounter between paradoxes—that is, the encounter between different texts and between interiorities and exteriorities, which, in turn, produces or originates the new. Rather than the analogy of an allegorical reading by which the present corresponds to a historical or mythical past, such an encounter draws on the precedent to rework, or re-*cite*. In a way, the encounter undoes and dispossesses the original citation (*ex-citation*, Freud's "excitatory traces" of the central nervous system discussed earlier) to posit something new, an excess that supplements and stimulates from the outside. The *in, im,* or *intro* meets and merges with rather than opposes the *ex.* Artaud is *ins*erted in the body of Dreyer's text by Ledo, for example. Or there is the hint, the suggestion, or the *in-sinuation,* as if the sinews of the body (that is, the content) of the film were the form and the format itself.[41]

The cinephilic quote in this way proves performative. Instead of the coy knowingness by which filmic literacy is often referenced, this performativity advances the relation between text and context into territories (political and filmic) that are yet unexplored. Ledo's films invariably invoke the dead—forebears and others such as Dreyer, Velo, Varela, Artaud—and the fragments of previous eras of filmmaking belonging to distant but discrete periods of the 1930s, 1960s, and 1970s. They prompt posthumous life; life beyond life (a *survival* of sorts), supplementary to life, the *extra* of *vida.* Central to my analysis here is the idea of the filmic legacy as partial, as a remnant (as noted in the earlier discussion of Ledo's investigation into the Velo film), or an exergue of the main body of the work referred to. This relates to the idea of what is left or left over at the margins of the corpus of film history, the remains, *restos,* the dead bodies, the corpses on the fringes of history of Benjamin's theory of allegory. This supplementary logic—the part that disturbs the whole, both outside and essential to it—is the metonymic allegory to which I refer throughout this chapter and, indeed, throughout this book.[42]

Inspired by Peter Weiss's *The Aesthetics of Resistance* (a book whose most recent English translation is introduced at length by Fredric Jameson),[43] *Vida-Extra* has many of the apparent connotations of political allegory.[44] From Weiss, Ledo borrows (and, given his own presence in the film, though always with his back toward the camera—inhabits) a means of not identifying the novel's narrator. The novel (and the film) commences on a specific date (September 22, 1937, in the case of the novel), two days before the unnamed narrator leaves for Spain to join the International Brigades. Weiss's exhaustive detailing of the condition and the crisis of the European revolutionary Left between 1937 and

1945 combines allegorical monumentality with the techniques of documentary film seemingly expressed in real time.

Meanwhile, *VidaExtra*'s discourse on militant action—bolstered by its echoes of the novel's sequences of Barcelona during the Spanish Civil War and its various palimpsests (historical and filmic)—departs significantly from Weiss's novel.[45] In their early sequences, both the novel and the film commence with what are apparently allegorical scenarios. *The Aesthetics of Resistance* begins with the protagonists standing before the frieze of Pergamon in Berlin, described in painstaking detail and at length by the novel's narrator. This moment, with which the novel and the historical moment it seeks to record, is itself dated, and its solemn tone spells out (almost literally) the significance of the date: "And thus, on the twenty-second of September, nineteen thirty-seven, a few days before my departure [to Spain], we stood in front of the altar frieze, which had been brought here from the castle mountain to be reconstructed, and which, painted colorfully and lined with forged metals, had once reflected the light of the Aegean sky."[46] The frieze tells a story, a myth that corresponds to the dramatic historical conjuncture within which the youthful protagonists of Weiss's novel find themselves as revolutionary socialists in Nazi Germany.[47] Indeed, the characters of *The Aesthetics of Resistance* function throughout the novel as cyphers, historical representatives through whom debates and ideas are voiced; they are themselves allegorical of a generation. They never act independently, and their anonymity forms part of their militancy.

VidaExtra, on the other hand, also includes images of Greek figures in its early sequences: mythological statues guard the main entrance to the neoclassical building in central Barcelona defaced by graffiti and are acted on (textually) by contemporaneous sources exterior to the allegory itself (see fig. 9.3). Their representative category has been challenged. Ledo has been keen to stress his debt to Weiss's novel, and yet the spectral logic of *VidaExtra* lies precisely in the performative mobilization of that legacy rather than in its reproduction or adaptation.[48]

The focus of the early sequences of *VidaExtra* is on a haunted place. The first shots consist of a set of archive stills, photographs of the interior of the Hotel Colón in Barcelona's Plaza de Cataluña, which, we learn, was demolished and rebuilt in 1941 as the Banco Español de Crédito. This is the same bank that was occupied on September 28, 2010, on the eve of the following day's general strike, otherwise known, in the common use of metonyms to describe significant dates, as the 29-S. As the sequence proceeds, what we assumed were photographic images of the historical building are revealed—as the camera draws away—to have been taken directly from a tourist website; that is, they are digital reproductions stored online. Punctuating these introductory sequences are

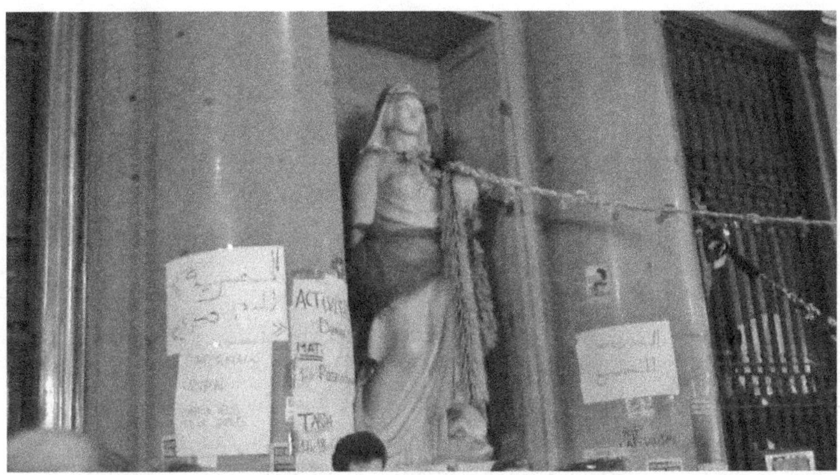

Fig. 9.3 The entrance to the Banco Español de Crédito in *VidaExtra*.

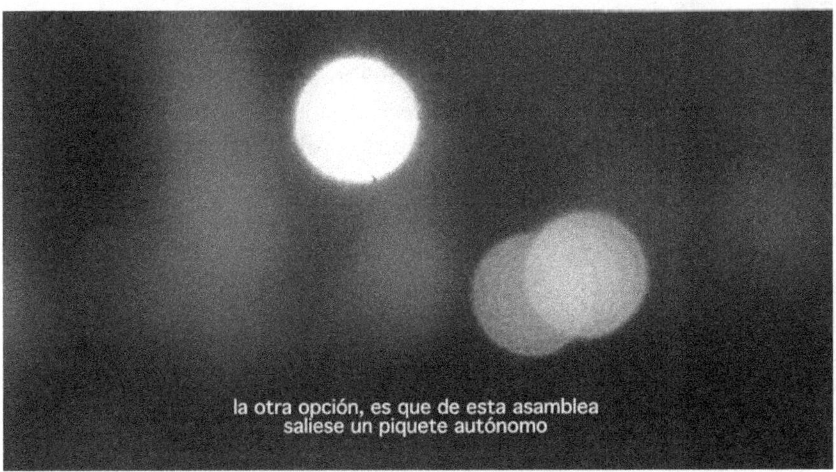

Fig. 9.4 Planetary spheres orbiting in the darkness in *VidaExtra*.

a series of abstruse visual images of disconcerting illumination, the unfocused lights like planetary spheres orbiting in the darkness (see fig. 9.4), and the distorted soundtrack recorded *en directo* of the popular assembly called to plan the next day's action.

We see no faces here amid the shadows and unfocused lighting. We hear only the voices of those intervening in the mass meeting (the filmmaker is sternly instructed not to identify the participants in the assembly). This is interrupted by a lengthy insert—another introjection, as in the Artaud short—of the original German text of Weiss's description of revolutionary Barcelona in late 1937 whose action takes place in the same location (the Hotel Colón, which, at the time, was commandeered as the headquarters of the Catalan Communist Party) as that occupied in September 2010.[49] The building opposite the bank on the far side of the Plaza Cataluña and now the site of the department store El Corte Inglés was previously the site of the Hotel Victoria, where the protagonist of *The Aesthetics of Resistance* signs up to work for the anarchist Federación Anarquista Ibérica/Confederación Nacional del Trabajo (Iberian Anarchist Federation)/National Confederation of Labor, or CNT/FAI). Added to this underlying ghostliness is a projection onto the building's facade of the words "Ja és vaga a El Corte Inglés" (Now it's strike time in El Corte Inglés)—a mischievous, poltergeist-like *détournement* and pun on the retailer's marketing slogan at the time: "Now it's springtime in El Corte Inglés." The projection also recalls the hologram protest discussed at the beginning of this chapter. The performative-spectral force of image projection is mobilized as the medium of resistance itself.

This introductory series of images emphasizes not only a palimpsestic genealogy of political resistance but also the complexity of its representation in terms of the different material support employed. The fading photographs and yellowing paper of the pages of Weiss's novel (in another sense of datedness) are contained and reproduced here as computer code rather than as light-sensitive photographic images. They are captured in the data that constitute the digital format, which does not age.[50] It is notable that if palimpsest is, generally speaking, represented spatially, then the reproduction of Weiss's text is sequential, and it functions metonymically. A fragment of graying paper, mildewed with age, the German text unreels like a strip of celluloid, as if its technology were analog, in a single continuous line across the center of the black screen over several minutes.[51]

The remaining section of *VidaExtra*, of about an hour, is a conversation among five people sitting at a table discussing the events of the 29-S and the nature of political commitment. This section appears to engage directly with Pere Portabella's 1974 *El sopar*, a film in which (as we have seen in chap. 3) five former political prisoners gather in secret to discuss the experience of the militant in Franco's jails. Indeed, toward the end of Ledo's film, there is an explicit (and erroneous) reference to *El sopar*.[52] Portabella's film, like Ledo's, was performative: Five militants discuss militancy, as both a clandestine film and filmic act of resistance, militancy itself. Shot the same day—another commemorative date—as Salvador Puig Antich's execution, *El sopar* takes on an additional defiance. Its performativity constitutes an act of mourning. Both *El sopar* and

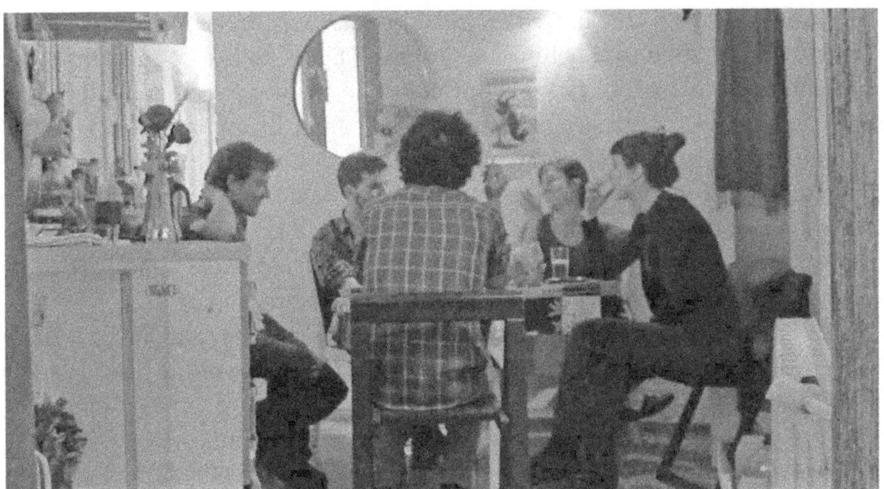

Fig. 9.5 The conversation on political militancy.

VidaExtra have a projected element to them in the sense of a future unknown at the moment of filming but highly significant at the time of screening. The conversations in both films, though clearly edited, take place in real time. The conversations are framed by their subject matter, but they are spontaneous, unprompted, and unscripted; their historical present is charged with a shared sense of impending crisis.

VidaExtra's other major intertext (with Weiss's novel) is Jean-Luc Godard's 1968 *Un film comme les autres*. As in the Godard film, Ledo's protagonists are anonymous. In *VidaExtra*, the participants in the conversation are not only enshrouded in shadows (and the film's play on illumination is important) but the film's soundtrack, the recording of the conversation, is also deliberately out of sync with the images of the speakers so as to impede identification between what is said and who is saying it. In *Un film comme les autres* (which also consists of a conversation about militant strategy, on this occasion between a group of Nanterre University students and workers from the Renault factory in the wake of the Paris events of May 1968), the speaking subjects are shot from behind or below so as not to reveal their faces and with the dialogue disconnected from the speakers. Ledo has acknowledged the influence of *The Aesthetics of Resistance* in this anonymity. Within the dense series of conversations that abound in Weiss's novel, and while the individual members of the group of young German revolutionaries are named, it is impossible to distinguish who says what in the course of the many discussions and debates that take place throughout the novel. Likewise, *VidaExtra*'s oblique homage to Robert

Bresson—a poster of the latter's *Lancelot du Lac* constitutes the solitary decor on the whitewashed wall behind the group—alludes to Bresson's claim (cited by Ledo in a press interview) that one comes to know a person more by his or her voice than by their face.[53] As in Godard's film, Ledo's is also punctuated by shots of the street confrontations and picket-line activity filmed during the September 29 general strike. One sequence of *VidaExtra*—commented on in the course of the discussion—in which we see a car set on fire during the disturbances in Barcelona, mirrors the French newsreel images appropriated by Godard's film of a similar incident during the 1968 riots in Paris.

While Godard divides his film in two and replays the same (largely inaudible) soundtrack twice over, Ledo manipulates the time of his film, possibly even more self-consciously. Almost imperceptibly, the action of the film unravels in reverse in an interesting variation on the discussion of reversibility in chapter 7. We see the tail end of the conversation first, and the film then works its way backward in time. The effect—together with the disjunction of sound and image—is disconcerting. Each time the individuals stand up to go to the bathroom or to replace their beers from the kitchen, we only see them from behind (the way the film is shot means they often appear to walk backward). In this way the characters' anonymity is not only preserved in the filming but also is a key part of it. The theatricality of the movement is the product of the processes of shooting film rather than of acting by the participants. Performativity lies in the fact that formal filmic practice *is* the thematic content. Meanwhile, the naturalism of the scenario is disrupted by the filming in ways that are more Godardian than Godard. We only become aware of what has happened (despite the subtle disjunctive movements on-screen) because of a linear trajectory indexed by the progressive illumination throughout the discussion from darkness to light.

This unsettling phenomenon highlights another important factor concerning temporality (to which I have alluded earlier): that of the date. Undergirding *VidaExtra*'s discourse on militancy, which is notably despondent and pessimistic, is a series of dates whose significance vies with the quite literal shadows, citations, and ghostly anonymity of the film's subjects. The date is singular, yet only by virtue of its repetition, whose iteration convokes and is convoked by commemorations and anniversaries. The date, that is (like García Calvo's intervention in the assembly in La Puerta del Sol as recorded in Sylvain George's film), depends on its singular-plural condition.

We have already seen in *VidaExtra* one date—September 29, the day of the general strike—telegrammatically signaled by the synecdoche of the 29-S and the main topic of the film's conversation. However, midway through the discussion, it transpires that the film was shot on May 1, 2011. May Day is a significant date in militant working-class history and an anniversary that the participants in the film recognize as important.[54] Indeed, part of the conversation revolves around which of the rival demonstrations each person attended earlier that day.

Of even greater weight—again importantly unbeknownst to the on-screen participants, whose disenchantment and sense of defeat is notable—is the fact that a mere two weeks later, Spain would witness what was arguably the most important explosion of popular unrest in recent memory, the 15-M. That is, the entirety of the film's postproduction process took place with knowledge of the 15-M, but the film does not acknowledge it.[55] The date here is not the past. For the purposes of the film, the 15-M belongs to the uncertain future; it is a pending date of significance only in retrospect. Directed by a filmmaker who has made a point of resorting to the datum, the archive, to conduct various forms of filmic archeology, *VidaExtra* is a film haunted by its own future.[56] Historical discourse is subverted by the date. History—conventional history as a set of dates and data—is at odds with this date, the 15-M. I earlier referred to the emblematic date, following Derrida, as a performative incision, a cut in time, a demarcation in temporality. The date is enigmatic, and it is the signature of exceptionality and of a slippage in *Jetztzeit*, in the here-now, and in the haecceitic instant. It is discordant with, dissociative rather than representative of, the period. The date marks an encounter between the now and its other.[57]

The final sequences of *VidaExtra* constitute appendixes or supplements affixed to the film. The conversation concerning militancy, which has been conducted entirely in Castilian, is interrupted by an abrupt return to the assembly of September 28, 2010, of the early sequences of *VidaExtra*. Against a black screen and for six uninterrupted minutes, we hear a reading in Catalan of the manifesto of the occupiers of the Banco Español de Crédito ("el movimiento 25-S"). This is followed by the rap of the hip-hop group Malandrómeda delivered in Gallego that gives the film its title and whose insistent refrain is "Unha vida extra / fóra deste lugar / extraterrestre" (An extra life / out of this place / extraterrestrial). Here both content and form converge in a cosmopolitan performativity: the *other* languages of the Spanish state come to the fore in a text that stresses not only the *extra* of supplementarity but also that of the extraterrestrial, of an *other* world. The final shots of the film—in contrast to the ponderous deliberation of the earlier discussion—overlaying the latter section of the rap are the speeded-up, rewound images of the events of September 29 and 28, rapidly projected in reverse. There is in all this—and in concluding I will attempt to connect this—a notable change in tone, a performative interpretation that jars inappropriately, and perhaps exorbitantly.

The 15-M, an Exorbitant Reading

On September 6, 2014, in Madrid I participated in a roundtable discussion sandwiched between screenings of *VidaExtra* and *El sopar* at the inaugural session of a cycle of films devoted to mapping the tradition of militant film in Spain under the rubric of *40 años no es nada* (40 years is nothing).[58] The event and the cycle brought together different generations of militant filmmakers from within the Spanish state, and the encounter was not without its moments of controversy.[59] These tensions, though, on that evening and throughout the following days' discussions—concentrated in specific dates—proved productive in that they point to a historicized relation (and a turbulent one) between the past and the future, an alliance between singularities of different specific times.

These debates brought to the fore Cohen's "virtual anteriorities" and complicated the concept of "the teletechnological routing and force of trace-chains" by exemplifying a generational encounter in physical and material form, of which the April 10, 2015, hologram protest is symptomatic—an encounter that might be termed *performative*. Such a legacy, though disputed in this case, had been foretold. In 1969, Fernando Solanas and Octavio Getino envisaged arming the people with cameras as a revolutionary act. ("The camera is the inexhaustible *expropriator of image-weapons*," they wrote in their famous manifesto "Towards a Third Cinema,"[60] emphasis in the original.) Today's digital technology has made such a seemingly utopian aspiration a reality. As Flavio García (among many others) has demonstrated, one can make a film with a cell phone and exhibit or route it not only to a mass audience but also beyond the frontiers of the nation-state. Nonetheless, the encounter between the militant legacy, the cinephilic subtlety of essay films like Ramiro Ledo's, and the global space of contemporary teletechnology proves discordant as the discussion the evening of September 6, 2014, suggests. This date connected generations of political filmmakers and simultaneously staged their division, forming both a continuum and a discontinuum. "A date is a specter," writes Derrida. "But," he continues, "the spectral return of this impossible recurrence is marked *in* the date, it seals or specifies itself in the sort of anniversary ring secured by the code. For example by the calendar. The anniversary ring inscribes the possibility of repetition, but also the circuit of return to the city whose name a date bears."[61]

The connection that Derrida's makes between the date and the city calls to mind another tradition—another *return*—of militant filmmaking in Spain. Mateo Santos's CNT/FAI newsreel *Reportaje del movimiento revolucionario en Barcelona* (Report of the revolutionary movement in Barcelona) is a film that focuses on a particular city and is tied to a specific date: July 19, 1936. An early shot in Santos's film also shows the Hotel Colón. Barcelona is not only the city of Ledo's film, but its early sequences and especially its references to Weiss's novel are haunted by the Spanish Civil War. The war also inaugurated a new phase in international political filmmaking (by André Malraux and Ivens, among others).

The ring to which Derrida refers (and it is noteworthy that he locates it within a "code"), moreover, is the marriage ring. Significantly, in Spanish this is called the *alianza*, the sign of circumcision that marks a birth and identity as a heterology, the seal of an encounter with the other. The continuum of the circle is paradoxically marked by the cut of the date the ring commemorates. The ring is also an orb (as Derrida has discussed on other occasions), a sign of the *orbis* that encircles the world.

Just as the 15-M is a metonym for an ongoing shift in sensibility in how political resistance is conducted within the Spanish state, its commemorative, iterative singularity whose circularity and continual return contains within it its beginning and its end—the annular ring is annual—is also a metonym for an entire year of global struggle. Events associated with specific locations—Tahir Square, Wall Street, La Puerta del Sol—refer to a different rotating, reverberating calendar whose action was relayed around the world via a teletransmission indistinct from the political activity itself. The lights of the assembly in *Vida-Extra* also suggest an alignment of planetary spheres in orbit. Furthermore, such a sequence holds together an expressiveness with an echo of impressionist film in a tension that might be described as performative.

It is notable that while the events of 2011 commenced in Tunisia and extended throughout the globe, several Madrid-based filmmakers have drawn on the international character of the revolt in their work. Cecilia Barriga's *Tres instantes, un grito* focuses on the assembly as a form of democratic practice in La Puerta del Sol, Occupy Wall Street, and the seven-month-long high school occupations in Santiago de Chile of 2011. María Ruido, in light of the overthrow of the Ben Ali regime, revisits the legacy of Frantz Fanon in Tunisia, linking the contemporary situation to the historical struggle against colonialism. Meanwhile, Carlos Serrano Azcona, whose films often dwell on the ritual-performative quality of street protests in terms of both their visual and sonic force, draws parallels between Spain and Mexico in *Banderas falsas* to question the disputed site of the street itself. All three directors have personal, autobiographical links to these three countries.

The *extra* of *VidaExtra*—the excess or surplus that spills over at the identitarian fringes of the nation-state (and of Catalonia or Galicia)—extends to the world. This *ex*orbitant, *ex*iled cinema of return is global in its range and marked by temporality, beyond and before, the anterior *ex-* that comes back to haunt from the *other*world (again *allography*)—the alternative of the "Otro mundo es posible" slogan—of film and politics signaled by the 15-M.

Finally, this supplementary prefix *ex-* also complicates the concept of representation itself. In a variation of the graph/graft relation to writing, in Spanish the verb *exprimir* means "to squeeze"—that is, to gather together, clutched in firm concentrated intensity so as to extract. Its antonym is the verb *imprimir*, meaning "to print." There is here a relation to the reproduction of a form of writing. Connected to this is the idea of *press*—the *primir* of *exprimir* and *imprimir*—a word that links squeeze with printing. Furthermore, if *imprimir* could conceivably be translated as "to impress," then *exprimir* might also be translated as "to express." To express an idea, a concept, a form of expression, is, of course, a representation. It is a form of projection that contains within it a sense of the performative.[62] The *ex* of expression posits a performative break within constative and constitutional forms in a pivotal move in which the accumulated past is mobilized in a gesture toward a future.

The rupture by which Derrida defines the performative is that with the conventions of form. But another factor makes performativity political. In an article in the *London Review of Books* that echoes Derrida, Tom McCarthy writes, "What the real represents is an event . . . a violent rupture of the form and procedure of the work itself."[63] The rupturing event at the heart of the 15-M is in its promise, in its performative interpretation of the regime of 1978. The performativity of the 15-M changes the constatation of another date: December 6, 1978. This date of the constitution is commemorated each year as a national holiday and as a celebration of representative democracy. It is a date that not only defines democracy but produces it. Its commemoration renews annually an old newness that, in its day, claimed to signal a break with Francoism (while surreptitiously retaining many of its structures), and its expiration date is foretold in the expectancy promised by the 15-M.

To return to the earlier question of allegory, if analog film works by analogy—the sequentiality of celluloid—the code of digital film is, like all codes, metonymic in a different way, in its very signifying structure. This *is* the performativity of digital photography. The films' digitality in their formal practices and technological formats not only challenge representation but also change the very thing they are filming. In this crux—of which Ramiro Ledo's films are paradigmatic—political and filmic practices meet in the divided and dividing instant of the present to enact in performativity—to *ex*ecute—the move from the now to the new. This is the very transformation that Amador Savater points to with regard to a change in sensibility in Spanish society. The films' conjuring of the repressed political-filmic ghosts of the past and their circular orbital return institute—beyond questions of national or any other identitarian affiliation—changes in the present moment. And they produce, in turn, a new politics of return that carries within it an uncertain future without guarantees, whose presence is inscribed and grafted into the trace-chains in the *ex-* of cinephilic citation and supplementarity—*exappropriation*—and whose heterogeneous force contained within "the originary performativity" itself breaks with its context, constatation, convention, or constitution.

Notes

1. The law went into force on July 1, 2015. At the time of writing, although moves are afoot in the Spanish parliament to repeal it, it remains in force.

2. "Cómo Fue la de Hologramas contra las Leyes Mordaza," *No Somos Delito*, April 14, 2015, http://nosomosdelito.net/article/2015/04/14/como-fue-la-manifestacion-de-hologramas-contra-las-leyes-mordaza.

3. There is a suggestion here in the *ley mordaza* of a certain tradition of monstrous production; of a legal rationale that, in turn, gives rise to an opposing monster (reminiscent of Goya's etching "El sueño de la razón produce monstruos," part of the *Caprichos* series). I am not the first person to observe that the Spanish word for monster, *monstruo*, shares an etymology with the verb *mostrar*, meaning "to show" or "to demonstrate."

4. J. Hillis Miller, "Derrida's Remains," in *For Derrida* (New York: Fordham University Press, 2009), 73.

5. Tom Cohen, *Ideology and Inscription: "Cultural Studies" after Benjamin, de Man and Bakhtin* (Cambridge: Cambridge University Press, 1998), 4.

6. Jeffrey Skoller, *Shadows, Specters, Shards: Making History in Avant-Garde Film* (Minneapolis: University of Minnesota Press, 2005), xviii.

7. Jacques Derrida, *Mémoires: For Paul de Man* (New York: Columbia University Press, 1986), 74.

8. There is an echo here of Benjamin's celebrated phrase quoted in chapter 1: "In allegory the observer is confronted with the *facies hippocratica* of history as a petrified, primordial landscape." Walter Benjamin, *The Origin of German Tragic Drama*, trans. John Osborne (London: Verso, 1977), 166.

9. Cohen, *Ideology and Inscription*, 8.

10. Derrida notes the iconic date September 11, 2001, which he describes as "the telegram of this metonymy." Jacques Derrida, *Philosophy in a Time of Terror: Dialogues with Jürgen Habermas and Jacques Derrida*, ed. Giovanna Borradori (Chicago: University of Chicago Press, 2003), 86.

11. Jacques Derrida, *Archive Fever: A Freudian Impression*, trans. Eric Prenowitz (Chicago: University of Chicago Press, 1998), 17.

12. Jacques Derrida, *Copy, Signature, Archive: A Conversation on Photography* (Stanford, CA: Stanford University Press, 2010), 5.

13. Contract theory makes the claim that it eludes the "naturally" violent impulses that lie behind the pursuit of power and "peacefully" facilitates a negotiated solution of minimum pacts. In the case of Spain, the prospect of a continuation of the military dictatorship under

a different (and potentially worse) administration focused the minds of the parties involved and left them with very little choice.

14. Jacques Derrida, *Specters of Marx: The State of the Debt, the Work of Mourning and the New International*, trans. Peggy Kamuf (London: Routledge, 1994), 30.

15. Savater is probably the best-known intellectual of the 15-M. His comment, which he has repeated on several occasions before and since, was made in the form of a question he asked me at a symposium on the 15-M held at the University of California, Berkeley, March 5, 2014, in response to the first (and, at the time, very different) version of this chapter.

16. The reference here is to Derrida's fascination and engagement with Marx's celebrated phrase from the eleventh thesis on Feurbach that "philosophers have only *interpreted* the world, in various ways; the point is to *change* it." Karl Marx and Frederick Engels, *The German Ideology* (Amherst, NY: Prometheus Books, 1998), 123; Derrida, *Specters of Marx*, 51.

17. Miller defines the "performative enunciation" as "a way of using words to make something happen." Miller, *For Derrida*, 94.

18. This is, of course, similar to what Lacuesta does in his video correspondence with Naomi Kawase (see chap. 7).

19. I want to make clear that by "ana-chronic" I am not suggesting that it is an anachronism in the sense of being old-fashioned, nor that this is an exclusively Spanish tradition of comedy. It is, in my view, clearly not (contrary to what other thinkers, including Lacuesta himself, have posited). I am thinking of Italian and English comedies of the 1950s.

20. Most of the initial filming was done by video activists and professional filmmakers. The mainstream media outlets in Spain by and large ignored the events in Sol until the international press coverage prompted them to address it.

21. Derrida, *Specters of Marx*, 30.

22. Guillem Martínez, *CT o la Cultura de la Transición* (Barcelona: Mondadori, 2012).

23. "Another world is possible" and "The world is not for sale" were the themes of the second World Social Forum in Porto Alegre in 2002.

24. Judith Butler, *Gender Trouble: Feminism and the Subversion of Identity* (London: Routledge, 1990).

25. Bill Nichols, *Introduction to Documentary* (Bloomington: Indiana University Press, 2001), 34.

26. Elsewhere Derrida has said, "Everywhere a given ethical, juridical, political space is given to performative acts, which is to say languages which produce events, and which insofar as they produce events also give rise to institutions—a vast field." "Performative Powerlessness: A Response to Simon Critchley," *Constellations* 7, no. 4 (2000): 467.

27. J. Hillis Miller and Manuel Asensi, *Black Holes / J. Hillis Miller; Or, Boustrophedonic Reading* (Stanford, CA: Stanford University Press, 1999), 305.

28. *Canciones para después de una guerra* is a much more obvious montage film in that it was created entirely in the editing room from archive material without the use of a camera. What I suggest here, though, is that *Libre te quiero* is equally well a montage film but one whose archive is constituted by the ongoing, shifting events before the camera. Here the distinction between the two key discrete moments in film production—the shoot and the edit—is blurred, as is, too, that traditionally associated with the interpretation of film: mise-en-scène and montage.

29. The Spanish Civil War, of course, was an early scenario for pioneering partisan filmmaking, Ivens among them.

30. García Calvo's exact words are: "No hay que tener futuro. El futuro es cosa de ellos, es un invento que viene de arriba, el tiempo de los relojes y los calendarios por lo que interesa en su computo al capital en primer lugar, y también el estando en cuanto al número de almas. Todos los días os dicen que tenéis mucho futuro y mientras os dicen que tenéis mucho futuro os ocultan que con futuro lo que quieren decir es muerte." (We shouldn't have a future. The future is their thing, it's a thing that comes from above, the time of clocks and calendars which serves the calculations of capital in the first place, and then the number of souls. Every day they tell you that you have a great future while they tell us that they conceal from us that what they really mean by future is death.)

31. Cohen, *Ideology and Inscription*, 8.

32. Jorge Tur Moltó's *Ja arriba el temps de remenar les cireres* is another of the "¿Spanish Revolution?" films.

33. La Puerta del Sol is also the headquarters of the regional government, whose building—formerly the site of the feared secret police, the Brigada Social—is adorned with plaques commemorating another date: 11-M, March 11, 2004, the date of the Al Qaeda commuter train bombings.

34. Jacques Derrida and Bernard Stiegler, *Echographies of Television: Filmed Interviews* (Oxford: Polity Press, 2002), 129.

35. Ledo's interest in ancestry and heritage extends beyond film to his own family. He has collaborated with his aunt, the film historian and cineaste Margarita Ledo Andión, in various films. Meanwhile, his uncle, Xose Lois Ledo Andión, is one of the agrarian union leaders of the 1970s who feature in *Cine clube Carlos Varela*. Ledo is currently involved in an arts and screening center in Santiago de Compostela called Numax after the occupied factory and consequent workers cooperative in Barcelona filmed by Joaquim Jordà in 1978.

36. Although sympathetic to the Republican cause and a cultural activist (as a student in Madrid, he was a figure in the organization of cine clubs), Velo was not affiliated with any political party (despite claims that he was a member of the Communist Party). That said, his work is clearly leftist; *Galicia* was envisaged as a project for the "misiones pedagógicos," and Velo went into exile in Mexico after the Spanish Civil War. Later in life, he became close to Galician nationalism.

37. Velo's work of the 1930s is, of course, contemporaneous with that of the British documentary filmmaker John Grierson. Perhaps, though, of greater significance in the context of this essay is the militant continuum in Velo's transatlantic career. In 1972, he shot a remarkable speech delivered by the soon-to-be-deposed Chilean president Salvador Allende at the University of Guadalajara, Mexico, which can be viewed at http://www.youtube.com /watch?v=K1dUBDWoyes.

38. Ágatha de Santos, "La 'Galicia' de Velo amplía horizontes," *Faro de Vigo*, December 26, 2010, http://www.farodevigo.es/sociedad-cultura/2010/12/26/galicia-velo-amplia -horizontes/503598.html. Significant in this article are the observations on the missing soundtrack, believed, according to Fernando Redondo Neira, to be a distortion by the Communist Party.

39. Derrida, *Specters of Marx*, 51.

40. In the same vein, the concept of *exappropriation* also complicates the notion of a subjective cinema often associated with the essay film.

41. The prefix *ex-* can mean "out" (as in external) as well as "former." Perhaps, though, it can also mean outdated, whose double meaning might be encapsulated by the words *expired* and the untimely *out of date*.

42. I am, of course, greatly indebted in this paragraph to Miller's essay "Derrida's Remains."

43. Peter Weiss, *The Aesthetics of Resistance*, trans. Joachim Neugroschel (Durham, NC: Duke University Press, 2005).

44. Weiss was also a filmmaker and counted among his collaborators the Polish-French proponent of militant cinema Edouard de Laurot. In an article published in 1955, Laurot points to something avant la lettre that coincides with my own argument (and that of Derrida's and Miller's) concerning performativity. According to Nicole Brenez in an article on militant cinema, Laurot argued that "the task of the artist is 'proleptic' in the sense that an artist possesses 'the power to perceive futurity within the present,' and this power opens up a moral creation of the world." Nicole Brenez, "Édouard de Laurot: Engagement as Prolepsis," *Third Text* 25, no. 1 (January 2011):64.

45. Ledo himself would probably disagree with me about this. I refer to his 2011 master's thesis "Filmar la historia a partir de Peter Weiss."

46. Weiss, *Aesthetics of Resistance*, 7–8.

47. This introductory passage contains many examples, one of which is the following: "The gods, confronted with the spirits of the earth, kept the notion of power relationships alive. A frieze filled with anonymous soldiers, who, as tools of the higher-ups, fought for years, attacking other anonymous soldiers, would have altered the attitude toward those who served, boosting their position, the kings, not the warriors, won the victories, and the victors could be like the gods, while the losers were despised by the gods." Ibid., 4.

48. In 1979, Harun Farocki traveled to Stockholm to interview Weiss. In another example of the Galician director's filmic-political legacy, thirty years later Ledo himself interviewed Farocki. Ramiro Ledo, "Harun Farocki: Trátase de volver a mirar as imaxes e facer que sexa posíbel empezar de novo," *Xornal de Galicia*, June 13, 2009, http://www.ramiroledo.com.

49. At the time of writing, the same building has been purchased by Spain's richest man, Amancio Ortega, and leased to Apple.

50. In this book's critique of representation and its conceptualization of the temporal disruption contained within the word *represent* (see *envois*), we might note (with Derrida in "Shibboleth: For Paul Celan") that the postscript of a letter, the supplement that exceeds the body of the text, in Spanish is *post data*, in *Sovereignties in Question: The Poetics of Paul Celan*, trans. Thomas Dutoit (New York: Fordham University Press, 2005).

51. This also reproduces in filmic terms the effect of the technique employed by Weiss himself of experimenting with time. The action of the novel appears to take place in real time, in the here and now.

52. In conversation with the filmmaker, Ramiro Ledo told me that, in fact, he had not seen *El sopar* prior to shooting *VidaExtra* (September 6, 2014).

53. Comments from Ledo extracted from a published interview with Montse Dopico in Praza Pública, May 2, 2013, reproduced at http://ramiroledo.com. Bresson's film plays on the close-up, on the detail without revealing faces. The first few sequences are notable for not identifying the characters by filming them behind the visors of their helmets.

54. Again, like all dates, May 1—May Day—is a metonym whose historical, political, and social connotations extend far beyond the temporal limits it demarcates.

55. This point was raised during the colloquium with Ramiro Ledo by both David Varela and, notably, Alfonso Amador, director of the film *50 días de mayo*, a documentary about the 15-M in Valencia. As I emphasize later, I participated in this discussion.

56. Something of this future uncertainty also exists in *El sopar*, a film shot prior to Franco's death and only released following the restoration of democracy. The participants in the film were, like everyone else, aware of the impending death of the dictator. In this sense, it, too, is haunted by the future. What is at stake in both *El sopar* and *VidaExtra* is the uncertain future of political militancy itself.

57. In "Shibboleth," Derrida, discussing Celan, comments, "It is necessary that the mark which one calls a date be *marked off*, in a singular manner, detached from the very thing it dates; and in that this de-marcation, this deportation, it become readable, precisely, as a date in wresting or exempting itself from itself, from its immediate adherence from the here and now; in freeing itself from what it nonetheless remains, a date." Jacques Derrida, "Shibboleth: For Paul Celan," in *Sovereignties in Question: The Poetics of Paul Celan*, trans. Thomas Dutoit (New York: Fordham University Press, 2005), 389.

58. The other participants in the discussion were David Varela and Samuel Alarcón (the organizers of the film series) and Ramiro Ledo himself. Varela is one of the filmmakers whose work featured in the "¿Spanish Revolution?" screening and DVD.

59. Two of the people who criticized Ledo's film from among the public were Amador Savater, who compared it unfavorably with *Un film comme les autres*, and Tino Calabuig, one of the founding members of the Colectivo de Cine de Madrid, a pioneering group of political Spanish filmmakers of the 1970s. The latter criticized *VidaExtra*'s form as "film" and suggested that it should have been drastically reduced in length and would have been better as a video clip. It is notable that both doubted the film's militant force—and pointed to a purported lack of vigor—compared with the classical period of militant film.

60. Fernando Solanas and Octavio Getino, "Towards a Third Cinema," in *Film Theory: An Anthology*, ed. Robert Stam and Toby Miller (Oxford: Blackwell, 2000), 279.

61. Derrida, "Shibboleth," 18.

62. I am indebted here to Tom McCarthy's article in the *London Review of Books* in which he discusses Francis Ponge's stunning prose poem "The Orange." Tom McCarthy, "Writing Machines," *London Review of Books* 36, no. 24 (2014): 21–22.

63. Ibid.

AFTERWORD

Unruly Archives: La décima carta *and* Buenas noches, España

Spanish Cinema against Itself: Cosmopolitanism, Experimentation, Militancy is a book about deferred arrivals and the impromptu, improbable, and incongruent encounters that defy the statutes and status of representation and its forms. At the time of writing, Spain is experiencing its most serious political and institutional crisis since the restoration of democracy in 1978. Torn asunder by internal tensions and riven by corruption scandals and demands for regional self-determination, the country (and primarily its population) is also still recovering from the severe austerity measures adopted by the government. The long-held aspirations of Spain's rulers to be treated as equals by the international community have been thwarted, in another deferred arrival. With a political class apparently indifferent to the needs of its people, it is little wonder that the filmmakers discussed in chapter 9 regard themselves as disenfranchised by the nation, its rulers, and its institutions. Such a historical conjuncture focuses the debate concerning political and cultural representation that this book seeks to provoke.

Given the circumstances of the more than a decade-old crisis, it is perhaps not surprising that a new generation of Spanish filmmakers and scholars has developed in the shadows, at the sidelines, and, to a large degree, despite national institutions. The filmmakers who have emerged since the mid-1990s are distinguished by a freshness of vision, their embrace of and experimentation with new technologies and digital and analog materialities, and their unprejudiced worldliness (this is, after all, a generation that has had the opportunity to travel, learn languages, and discover different cultures). Genuinely cosmopolitan, these cineastes (and the critics of the same generation) are also remarkable for their filmic literacy in both international cinema and their dissident forebears at home. I finish this book, then, with a brief discussion of two films that exemplify these two elements.

Virgina García del Pino's affectionate portrait of and engagement with the work of Basilio Martín Patino (whose final film is discussed briefly in chap. 9) highlights the kind of spectral linkage to which I have referred repeatedly here.

Titled *La décima carta* (The tenth letter) (2014), García del Pino's film echoes the postal motif highlighted throughout this book. Indeed, early in the film, García del Pino says to Martín Patino that she conceives of the film as a collaboration, as his "tenth letter" following on from the title of his first feature, the 1965 epistolary film *Nueve cartas a Berta* (Nine letters to Berta). *Nueve cartas a Berta* was one of the emblematic films of the New Spanish Cinema, the peculiar and short-lived collaboration between the more liberal elements of the Francoist state and the opposition filmmakers (mentioned briefly in chap. 1).

Punctuated by a succession of clips from the films Martín Patino made during the latter period of the dictatorship (after *Nueve cartas a Berta*, his work was conducted clandestinely and only screened publicly after the death of Franco), García del Pino's *La décima carta* films Martín Patino at his family residence in Salamanca and then as he revises his archive at his home in Madrid. The film is structured around a series of dates over a nine-month period (from September 2013 to June 2014) when García del Pino visits and films Martín Patino and tries to piece together his recollections. In a sense, the film functions as a diary and as a mnemonic. Indeed, it raises all kinds of questions concerning history and memory itself. Ravaged by the passing of time, the fact of age, Martín Patino's memory is failing, and he complains persistently about it. His lament is moving. He does not recognize the photograms and newspaper articles his interlocutor presents him. He has no desire to attend a public screening of his own extraordinary 1973 film about three state executioners, *Queridísimos verdugos* (Dearest executioners), which he shot in secret and was not exhibited publicly until 1977. Martín Patino has mislaid the book that inspired the film, and García del Pino helps him find it in his personal library.

Martín Patino, who died in 2017, three years after the release of *La décima carta*, is a seemingly frail ghost of his former self who haunts his own present in the loquacious television interview from 1982 that was rescued by García del Pino from another archive. This is a film about different, fluid and mobile, public and private archives. Martín Patino is not only a spectral antecedent—both distant and intimate—a model for García del Pino's generation of filmmakers, but also for his own. His films and the visual props, images, photos, and magazine articles that make up much of the material used in their montages (and that Martín Patino has picked up on his regular visits to the Madrid flea market, the Rastro, over the last fifty years) also constitute a ghostly archive. This alternative, subterranean record of a nondiscursive national history is far removed from the official version of either the dictatorship or the present regime.

This is emphasized in the final sequences of the film, when Martín Patino is at his most lucid. We are informed in the diary style of the film that this sequence was shot on June 19, 2014. The establishing shot from the terrace of

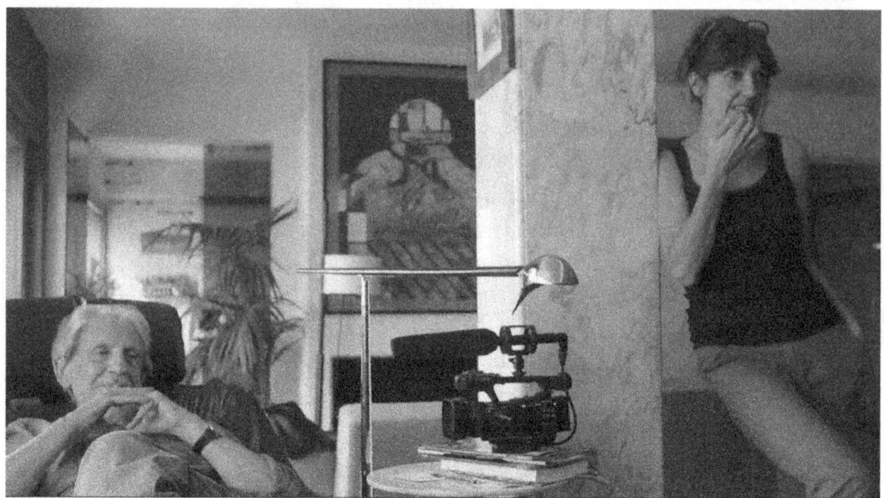

Fig. A.1 The final shot of *La décima carta*. Basilio Martín Patino and Virginia García del Pino appear together on-screen.

Martín Patino's apartment captures the midday sun as it shines on the Royal Palace below. As in the previous chapter, the date has a resonance. June 19, 2014, is the day the current king of Spain, Felipe VI, was crowned. The following shots record the new monarch's coronation speech interrupted by Martín Patino's contemptuous remarks. "This is like *Raza*," he says, referring to Franco's self-scripted and loosely autobiographical 1941 film, directed by José Luis Saénz de Heredia and widely held to be little more than propaganda. "What has this got to do with Spain? It's a complete comedy," Martín Patino snorts. Although García del Pino's voice is heard throughout the film, her physical appearance in *La décima carta* is restricted to a handful of shots of her filmed from behind or at a distance, and she is not identified. At this moment, however, as Martín Patino provides commentary on the television images, we see—as if to insist on the spectral bond linking the two generations of nonconformist filmmakers— in the very last shot of the film, the two filmmakers on-screen together (fig. A.1).

Two years before García del Pino made her film about Martín Patino, the Filipino director Raya Martín, working with a team of Spaniards, filmed what might be described as a postcolonial experiment. *Buenas noches, España* (2012) provides an interesting example of the kind of global exchange and experimentation that is explored in this book. It also points to a different set of archives that exceed the nation, or at least univocal concepts of it. While Martín's Filipino nationality points to his condition as a postcolonial subject, the film, shot largely in the Basque Country (mostly in Bilbao), was produced by the Spanish critic Gonzalo de Pedro Amatria; it stars two well-known actors from Spain, Pilar López de Ayala and Andrés Gertrudíx; and Basque filmmaker Víctor Iriate was the cinematographer. The film has no dialogue and is divided into sections of varying lengths, each interspersed—intermittently—by telegrammatic intertitles.

Condensed and poetic, *Buenas noches, España* unveils itself through its formal properties. As befits an experimental film, its discourse on the archive is more oblique than that of *La décima carta*; nonetheless, archival disruption is at its heart. The film deploys a barrage of incidental, often disconcertingly discordant, musical effects, ranging from the cacophony of screeching sounds to soothing harmonies to silence. The orchestration of these sounds gives the film the feel of a symphonic piece of work. Visually, an ever-changing array of colored filters tint the screen blue, yellow, pink, green, black, and white. Its symbolism is stressed. The actors perform a series of courtship rituals, a road trip in a car, walks in the countryside, dancing, communing with nature, and a lengthy visit to a museum. The denaturalization of the filmic process—its poetry—is emphasized in the insistent repetitions, the circular movements of the characters and the camera, the inversions and reversals of narrative logic, and the absence of linearity. In the luminescence of the filters, the translucence that seeps through the car windscreen (the silhouetted trees towering along the roadside, and the rise of the sloping country road on the horizon), there is something of a DayGlo Maya Deren to the filming.

The central section of the film is shot at Bilbao's Museo de Bellas Artes. López de Ayala and Gertrudíx peruse the works in the collection. Each imitates in comic form (and repeatedly) the poses of the subjects of Renaissance portraits. The couple and the camera dwell on the clay artifacts and sculptures. The lighting, music, and the actors' movements and performance bring to life the statues, pictures, and artifacts of the museum in ways that recall the work of José Val de Omar at the national sculpture museum in Valladolid in the 1950s that we saw in chapter 1's discussion of *Fuego en Castilla*. Although there is, perhaps, in the trance-like ritual an erotic element in *Buenas noches, España* that is absent from Val de Omar (though the element of trance is indeed there), the technical innovations of the Spanish director are present, wittingly or not, in the work of Raya Martín.

Buenas noches, España, moreover, contains a suggestion of the shaping of space that so occupied the imagination of Basque sculptor Jorge Oteiza, himself a cineaste of sorts and whose ideas on space have proved hugely influential on architects and filmmakers.[1] Oteiza was fascinated by the natural landscape of the Basque Country and particularly the rock formations of its mountains. One of the interesting features of *Buenas noches, España* is the significant use made of a particular boulder, found on a hillside and returned to again and again

by the film's two protagonists. The use of color filters and the constant iteration, the choreography of the filming itself, and its deployment of technology
mark the form of the film, the artifice, and the work it does on nature and the
archive that is the museum.

Buenas noches, España shares other features with Oteiza. The question of
form, formation, and the materiality of form is intimately connected with that
of technology. What is key to Martín's film is precisely the kind of teletechnology that so fascinated Derrida. The intertitles of film make this explicit and
tie the notion of teletechnology to the undoing of the nation. This is a film
that proclaims in its very internationalized practice the "post-nation." Located
in the Basque Country, where a significant number of the inhabitants do not
identify with Spain, *Buenas noches, España* alludes to the nation's postcolonial
status and to teletransportation as theme. Some twelve minutes into the film,
the first intertitle to appear on-screen after the initial credits (and an epigraph)
reads as follows: "Introduction to the history of teletransportation between
Spain and its colonies." The film ends with the enigmatic on-screen written
story of a soldier who went missing in Manila in the late sixteenth century only
to reappear in Mexico City. It is significant that the intertitles are references
to official archives. The formal experimentation here turns on the teletechnological mysteries—the aporias—of the national and the colonial archive that
traverse national and temporal boundaries.

Whereas the archive of Martín Patino is private, contained in the domicile of his residence, here the archive is in the anecdote of the public place (the
museum, the office of official records). The archive's authority is undermined in
the recycling of material (in ways perhaps not so dissimilar to that of Los Hijos
in films such as *Los Materiales* or *Árboles*) and the wry use of intertitles. Both
films return us to the historical past, but both confront the black holes that
link different temporalities; they open up the archive and democratize it, they
release it, and they free it from the restraints of discipline, order, and institution. They render the archive unruly.

Notes

1. Óskar Alegría who, as noted chapter 4, directed *La casa de Emak Bakia*, has
conducted remarkable research in Oteiza's own archive. Alegría has recently compiled a
book of quotations from Oteiza's comments in the margins of books that he has read and that
Alegría discovered in the sculptor's private library. Óskar Alegría, *Oteiza al margen: Notas
manuscritas sobre cine y arte* (Pamplona: Festival Punto de Vista, Fundación Museo Jorge
Oteiza, 2017). Alegría is also responsible for having created a new montage of Oteiza's Super 8
films from the 1960s.

BIBLIOGRAPHY

Alegría, Óskar. *Oteiza al margin. Notas manuscritas sobre cine y arte*. Pamplona: Festival Punto de Vista, Fundación Museo Jorge Oteiza, 2017.

Andrew, Dudley, ed. *Opening Bazin: Postwar Film Theory and Its Afterlife*. Oxford: Oxford University Press, 2011.

Arendt, Hannah. *Between Past and Future: Eight Exercises in Political Thought*. Harmondsworth, UK: Penguin, 1993.

Arregi, Imanol Zumalde. *Camino de expiación: Travesías y derroteros de nuestra reflexión historiográfica*. Madrid: Liceus, 2007.

Attali, Jacques. *Noise: The Political Economy of Music*. Translated by Brian Massumi. Minneapolis: University of Minnesota Press, 1985.

Baudelaire, Charles. *The Flowers of Evil/Les Fleurs du Mal*. Scotts Valley, CA: CreateSpace Independent Publishing Platform, 2016 [1857]. Bilingual edition.

Bazin, André. "The Life and Death of Superimposition." Translated by Bert Cardullo. *Film-Philosophy* 6, no. 1 (January 2002). http://www.film-philosophy.com/vol6-2002/n1bazin.

———. *What Is Cinema?* 2 vols. Translated by Hugh Gray. Berkeley: University of California Press, 1967.

Benjamin, Walter. *The Arcades Project*. Translated by Howard Eiland and Kevin McLaughlin. Cambridge, MA: Harvard University Press, 2002.

———. *The Origin of German Tragic Drama*. Translated by John Osborne. London: Verso, 1977.

———. *Selected Writings*. Vol. 4, *1938–1940*. Edited by Howard Eiland and Michael W. Jennings. Cambridge, MA: Harvard University Press, 2006.

Bergala, Alain. "Erice-Kiarostami: The Pathways of Creation." *Rouge* 9 (2006). www.rouge.com.au/9/erice_kiarostami.html.

Blanco, María del Pilar, and Esther Peeren. *The Spectralities Reader: Ghosts and Haunting in Contemporary Cultural Theory*. London: Bloomsbury Academic, 2013.

Bloom, Harold, ed. *Deconstruction and Criticism*. London: Continuum, 2004.

Bozon, Serge, "En Llamas." *Adolpho Arrieta: Obras*, 50–55. DVD pack. Barcelona: Edición de Intermedio.

Brown, Wendy. *Politics Out of History*. Princeton, NJ: Princeton University Press, 2001.

Brunette, Peter, and David Wills. *Screen/Play: Derrida and Film*. Princeton, NJ: Princeton University Press 1989.

Bruno, Guiliana. *Surface: Matters of Aesthetics, Materiality, and Media*. Chicago: University of Chicago Press, 2014.

Burgin, Victor. *Between*. New York: Basil Blackwell, 1986.

Butler, Judith. *Gender Trouble: Feminism and the Subversion of Identity*. London: Routledge, 1990.

Cadava, Eduardo. "Trees, Hands, Stars and Veils: The Portrait in Ruins." In *Portraits*, edited by Fazal Sheikh, 5–43. Göttingen, Germany: Steidl, 2011.

Calderón de la Barca, Pedro. *La vida es sueño*. Madrid: Catédra, 2003.

Cheah, Pheng, and Bruce Robbins, eds. *Cosmopolitics: Thinking and Feeling beyond the Nation*. Minneapolis: University of Minnesota Press, 1998.

Cohen, Tom. *Ideology and Inscription: "Cultural Studies" after Benjamin, de Man and Bakhtin*. Cambridge: Cambridge University Press 1998.

Conley, Tom. "Site and Sound." *Modern Language Notes* 121, no. 4 (September 2006): 850–61.

Cowan, Bainard. "Walter Benjamin's Theory of Allegory." *New German Critique*, no. 22 (1981): 109–22.

Cuesta, Mery. *El terrorismo doméstico de Antoni Padrós*. Girona, Spain: Editorial Fundació Espais, 2002.

Daney, Serge. "Freeze-Image/Arrêt sur l'image." *Serge Daney in English* (blog), June 18, 2009. http://sergedaney.blogspot.com/2009/06/freeze-image-arret-sur-limage.html.

———. "Portrait de Jackie Raynal." *Cahiers du cinéma* no. 334/335 (April 1982).

Deleuze, Gilles, and Felix Guattari. *Kafka, Towards a Minor Literature*. Minneapolis: University of Minnesota Press, 1986.

Delgado, Manuel. "El arte de danzar sobre el abismo." In *Imagen, memoria, fascinación: Notas sobre el documental en España*, edited by J. M. Català, Josetxto Cerdán, and Casimiro Torreiro, 221–30. Madrid: Ocho y Media/Festival de Cine español de Malaga, 2001.

Derrida, Jacques. *Aporias*. Translated by Thomas Dutoit. Stanford, CA: Stanford University Press, 1993.

———. *Archive Fever: A Freudian Impression*. Translated by Eric Prenowitz. Chicago: University of Chicago Press, 1998.

———. *Copy, Signature, Archive: A Conversation on Photography*. Edited with an introduction by Gerhard Richter. Translated by Jeff Fort. Stanford, CA: Stanford University Press, 2010.

———. *Deconstruction Engaged: The Sydney Seminars*. Edited by Paul Patton. Urbana: University of Illinois Press, 2001.

———. *Dissemination*. Translated by Barbara Johnson. Chicago: University of Chicago Press, 1981.

———. *Glas*. Translated by John P. Leavey Jr. and Richard Rand. Lincoln: University of Nebraska Press, 1990.

———. "The Law of Genre." *Critical Inquiry* 7, no. 1 (Autumn 1980): 55–81.

———. *Limited Inc*. Translated by Jeffrey Mehlman and Samuel Weber. Chicago: Northwestern University Press, 1988.

———. "Living On—Border Lines." In *Deconstruction and Criticism*, edited by Harold Bloom, 62–142 (London: Continuum, 2004).

———. *Margins of Philosophy*. Translated by Alan Bass. Chicago: University of Chicago Press, 1982.

———. *Memoires: For Paul de Man*. New York: Columbia University Press, 1986.

———. *Negotiations: Interventions and Interviews, 1971–2001*. Stanford, CA: Stanford University Press, 2002.

———. *On Grammatology*. Translated by Gayatri Chakravorty Spivak. Baltimore: Johns Hopkins University Press, 1976/2016.

———. *On the Name*. Edited by Thomas Dutoit. Stanford, CA: Stanford University Press, 1995.

———. *On Touching—Jean-Luc Nancy.* Translated by Christine Irizarry. Stanford, CA: Stanford University Press, 2005.

———. "The Other's Language: Jacques Derrida Interviews Ornette Coleman, 23 June 1997." Translated by Thomas S. Murphy. www.ubu.com/papers/Derrida-Interviews-Coleman_1997.pdf.

———. "Performative Powerlessness: A Response to Simon Critchley." *Constellations* 7, no. 4 (2000): 466–68.

———. *Philosophy in a Time of Terror: Dialogues with Jürgen Habermas and Jacques Derrida.* Edited by Giovanna Borradori. Chicago: University of Chicago Press, 2003.

———. *The Post Card: From Socrates to Freud and Beyond.* Translated by Alan Bass. Chicago: University of Chicago Press, 1987.

———. *Psyche: Inventions of the Other,* vol. 1. Stanford, CA: Stanford University Press, 2007.

———. "Shibboleth: For Paul Celan." In *Sovereignties in Question: The Poetics of Paul Celan,* 1–64. Translated by Thomas Dutoit. New York: Fordham University Press, 2005.

———. *Specters of Marx: The State of the Debt, the Work of Mourning and the New International.* Translated by Peggy Kamuf. London: Routledge, 1994.

Derrida, Jacques, and Catherine Malabou. *Counterpath: Traveling with Jacques Derrida.* Translated by David Wills. Stanford, CA: Stanford University Press, 2001.

Derrida, Jacques, and F. C. T. Moore, "White Mythology: Metaphor in the Text of Philosophy." *New Literary History* 6, no. 1 (Autumn 1974): 5–74.

Derrida, Jacques, and Bernard Stiegler. *Echographies of Television: Filmed Interviews.* Oxford: Polity Press, 2002.

Deval, Patrick. "More Light." In the pamphlet accompanying the DVD of *Ici et maintenant.* Directed by Serge Bard, 1969. Paris: Re:Voir, 2015.

Doane, Mary Anne. *The Emergence of Cinematic Time: Modernity, Contingency, the Archive.* Cambridge, MA: Harvard University Press, 2002.

Duchamp, Marcel, and Paul Matisse. *Notes.* Paris: G. K. Hall, 1983.

Ehrlich, Linda. "Letters to the World: Erice-Kiarostami: *Correspondences* Curated by Alain Bergala and Jordi Balló." *Senses of Cinema,* no. 41 (November 2006). http://sensesofcinema.com/2006/feature-articles/erice-kiarostami-correspondences/.

Expósito, Marcelo, ed. *Historias sin argumento: El cine de Pere Portabella.* Valencia, Spain: Museu d'Art Contemporani de Barcelona and Ediciones de la Mirada, 2001.

Fanés, Félix. *Pere Portabella: Avantguarda, cinema i politica.* Barcelona: Filmoteca de Cataluña, 2000.

Fernández, Vanesa, and Miren Gabantxo. *Territorios y fronteras: Experiencias documentales contemporaneas.* Bilbao, Spain: Universidad del País Vasco/Euskal Herriko Unibertsitatea, 2012.

Fieschi, Jean-André. "Slippages of Fiction." In *Anthropology-Reality-Cinema: The Films of Jean Rouch,* edited by Mick Eaton, 67–77. London: British Film Institute, 1979.

Fisher, Mark. *Ghosts of My Life.* London: Zero Books, 2014.

———. "Hauntology in Dublin." *K-Punk* (blog), December 14, 2006. http://k-punk.abstractdynamics.org/archives/008780.html.

———. "Phonograph Blues." *K-Punk* (blog), October 19, 2006. http://k-punk.abstractdynamics.org/archives/008535.html.

Foucault, Michel. "Pierre Boulez, Passing through the Screen." In *Aesthetics, Method, and Epistemology,* edited by James D. Faubion, 241–44. New York: The New Press, 1994.

Francés, Miquel, Josep Gavaldà, Germán Llorca, and Àlvar Peris, eds. *El documental en el entorno digital*. Barcelona: Editorial UOC, 2013.

Freud, Sigmund. *Beyond the Pleasure Principle and Other Writings*. Harmondsworth, UK: Penguin Classics, 2003.

Galloway, Alexander R., Eugene Thacker, and McKenzie Wark. *Excommunication: Three Inquiries into Media and Mediation*. Chicago: University of Chicago Press, 2013.

Galt, Rosalind. "Missed Encounters: Reading, *catalanitat*, the Barcelona School." *Screen* 48, no. 2 (2007): 193–210.

Galt, Rosalind, and Karl Schoonover. *Queer Cinema in the World*. Durham, NC: Duke University Press, 2016.

Grosz, Elizabeth. *Space, Time and Perversions: Essays on the Politics of Bodies*. London: Routledge, 1995.

Hammond, Paul. *The Shadow and Its Shadow: Surrealist Writings on the Cinema*. San Francisco: City Lights, 2001.

Hartog, François. *Regimes of Historicity: Presentism and the Experience of Time*. New York: Columbia University Press, 2015.

Heath, Stephen. "Keywords: *Representation*." *Critical Quarterly* 50, nos. 1–2 (Spring/Summer 2008): 87–99.

Heidegger, Martin. *Holderlin's Hymn, "The Ister."* Translated by William McNeill and Julia Davis. Bloomington: Indiana University Press, 1996.

———. *Poetry, Language, Thought*. Translated by Albert Hofstadter. New York: Harper Colophon Books, 1971.

Hernández Ruiz, Javier, and Pablo Pérez Rubio. *Yo filmo que . . . Antonio Artero en las cenizas de la representacion*. Zaragoza, Spain: Servicio de Cultura, 1998.

Hynes, Eric. "'We Wanted to Invent': Babette Mangolte on Chantal Akerman." *Village Voice*, March 30, 2016. http://www.villagevoice.com/film/we-wanted-to-invent-babette -mangolte-on-chantal-akerman-8439030.

Jameson, Fredric. *The Political Unconscious*. Ithaca, NY: Cornell University Press, 1981.

———. *Postmodernism, or, The Cultural Logic of Late Capitalism*. Durham, NC: Duke University Press, 1992.

Keller, Patricia M. *Ghostly Landscapes: Film, Photography and the Aesthetics of Haunting in Contemporary Spanish Culture*. Toronto: University of Toronto Press, 2016.

Lacoue-Labarthe, Philippe. *Typography*. Stanford, CA: Stanford University Press, 1989.

Ledesma, Eduardo. "Intermediality and Spanish Experimental Cinema: Text and Image Interactions in the Lyrical Films of the Barcelona School." *Journal of Spanish Cultural Studies* 14, no. 3 (2013): 254–74.

Ledo Cordeiro, Ramiro, *Filmar la historia a partir de Peter Weiss*. MA thesis, University Pompeu Fabra, Barcelona, September 2011.

Legendre, Maurice. *Las Hurdes: Estudio de geografía humana*. Merida, Spain: Regional de Extremadura, 2006. Originally published as *Las Jurdes: étude de géographie humaine*, 1927.

Léger, Nathalie. *Suite for Barbara Loden*. Translated by Natasha Lehrer and Cécile Menon. St. Louis, MO: Dorothy, 2016.

Leiras, Michael. *Phantom Africa*. Translated by Brent Hayes Edwards. Chicago: University of Chicago Press, 2017.

Lippit, Akira Mizuta. *Ex-Cinema: From a Theory of Experimental Film and Video*. Berkeley: University of California Press, 2012.

Losilla, Carlos. "A favor de este cine español." *Transit: cine y otros desvíos*, July 31, 2013. http://cinentransit.com/a-favor-de-este-cine-espanol/.

———, coord. "Otro cine español." *Caiman: cuadernos de cine*, no. 19 (September 2013).

Löwy, Michael. *Fire Alarm: Reading Walter Benjamin's "On the Concept of History."* London: Verso, 2005.

Ma, Jean. *Marking Time in Chinese Cinema*. Hong Kong: Hong Kong University Press, 2010.

Martin, Adrian. "The Experimental Night: Jackie Raynal's *Deux Fois*." In *Jeune, dure et pure! Une histoire du cinéma d'avant-garde et expérimental en France*, edited by Nicole Brenez and Christian Lebrat, 306–8. Milan: Mazotta/Cinémathèque Française, 2001.

———. *Mise-en-Scène and Film Style: From Classical Hollywood to New Media Art*. Basingstoke, UK: Palgrave, 2014.

Martínez, Guillem. *CT o la Cultura de la Transición*. Barcelona: Mondadori, 2012.

Marx, Karl, and Frederick Engels. *The German Ideology*. Amherst, NY: Prometheus Books, 1998.

McCarthy, Tom. "Writing Machines." *London Review of Books* 36, no. 24 (2014): 21–22.

Mendelson, Jordana. *Documenting Spain: Artists, Exhibition Culture, and the Modern Nation, 1929–1939*. University Park: Penn State University Press, 2005.

Miller, J. Hillis. "The Critic as Host." *Critical Inquiry* 3, no. 3 (Spring 1977): 439–47.

———. "Derrida's Remains." In *For Derrida*, edited by J. Hillis Miller, 72–100. New York: Fordham University Press, 2009.

Miller, J. Hillis, and Manuel Asensi. *Black Holes / J. Hillis Miller; Or, Boustrophedonic Reading*. Stanford, CA: Stanford University Press, 1999.

Minguet, Joan M. "Antoni Padrós Story." *Pensacions* (blog), May 6, 2014. http://pensacions.blogspot.com/2014/05/antoni-padros-story.html.

Mollona, Massimiliano. "Seeing the Invisible: Maya Deren's Experiments in Cinematic Trance." *October* 149 (Summer 2014): 159–80.

Mulvey, Laura. *Death 24x a Second: Stillness and the Moving Image*. London: Reaktion Books, 2006.

Nadal, Paul. "Heidegger's Critique of Modern Technology: On 'The Question Concerning Technology.'" *Be Late* (blog), July 12, 2010. ern-technology.

Nagib, Lúcia. "The Politics of Impurity." In *Impure Cinema: Intermedial and Intercultural Approaches to Film*, edited by Lúcia Nagib and Anne Jerslev, 21–39. London: I. B. Tauris, 2013.

Nancy, Jean-Luc. *Intoxication*. New York: Fordham University Press, 2016.

———. *Listening*. New York: Fordham University Press, 2007.

Naremore, James. *An Invention without a Future: Essays on Cinema*. Berkeley: University of California Press, 2014.

Nichols, Bill. *Introduction to Documentary*. Bloomington: Indiana University Press, 2001.

Oroz, Elena. "Color perro que huye." *blogs&docs*, April 7, 2011. http://www.blogsandocs.com/?p=1036.

Pagán, Alberte. "Sobre los ángeles: Entrevista con Adolpho Arrieta." April 11, 2011. http://albertepagan.eu/a-toupeira/adolfo-arrieta/.

Parcerisas, Pilar. *Duchamp en España: las claves ocultas de sus estancias en Cadaqués*. Barcelona: Siruela, 2009.

Père, Olivier. "LA/AS, Pensamiento salvaje y minimalismo grandioso." In *Todas las cartas* [Catalog]. Barcelona: Centre de Cultura Contemporània de Barcelona and Intermedio, 2011.

Pérez Perucha, Julio. "*Vivir en Sevilla* de Gonzalo García Pelayo." *Contracampo*, no. 4 (July–August 1979): 60–61.

Petrus, Anna. "In Between Days: Pequeñas revelaciones de lo íntimo, lo efímero y lo invisible." In *Todas las cartas: Correspondencias fílmicas* [Catalog]. Barcelona: Centre de Cultura Contemporánea de Barcelona and Intermedio, 2011.

Pintor Iranzo, Iván. "Queridos Víctor y Abbas." In *Todas las cartas* [Catalog]. Barcelona: Centre de Cultura Contemporànea de Barcelona and Intermedio, 2011.

Riambau, Esteve, and Casimiro Torreiro. *La Escuela de Barcelona: el cine de la "gauche divine."* Madrid: Anagrama, 1999.

Rorich, Mary. "Passing through the Screen: Pierre Boulez and Michel Foucault." *Journal of Literary Studies* 22, no. 3 (December 2006): 296–323.

Rosenbaum, Jonathan. "Barcelona Boogie and Pittsburgh Punk." *The Soho News*, June 4, 1980. https://www.jonathanrosenbaum.net/1980/06/barcelona-boogie/.

———. *Film: The Front Line 1983.* Denver, CO: Arvon Press, 1983.

———, ed. *Rivette: Texts and Interviews.* Translated by Amy Gateff and Tom Milne. London: British Film Institute, 1977.

Rottenberg, Elizabeth. "Introduction." In *Negotiations: Interventions and Interviews, 1971–2001.* Edited and translated by Elizabeth Rottenberg, 1–7. Stanford, CA: Stanford University Press, 2002.

Schöter, Jens. "The Politics of Intermediality." *Acta Universitatis Sapientiae, Film and Media Studies* 2 (2010): 107–24.

Sedgwick, Eve Kosofsky. *Tendencies.* Durham, NC: Duke University Press, 1993.

Shakespeare, William. *Hamlet.* In *The Complete Works of William Shakespeare: The Cambridge Edition.* Cambridge: Doubleday, Doran, 1936.

Sitney, P. Adams. *Visionary Film: The American Avant-Garde, 1943–2000.* Oxford: Oxford University Press, 2002.

Skoller, Jeffrey. *Shadows, Specters, Shards: Making History in Avant-Garde Film.* Minneapolis: University of Minnesota Press, 2005.

Skorecki, Louis. "Semaine des Cahiers: Deux Fois." *Cahiers du cinéma* no. 276 (May 1977): 51–52.

Solanas, Fernando, and Octavio Getino. "Towards a Third Cinema." In *Film Theory: An Anthology*, edited by Robert Stam and Toby Miller, 265–86. Oxford: Blackwell, 2000.

Stam, Robert. *Film Theory: An Anthology*, ed. with Toby Miller. Oxford: Blackwell, 2000.

———. *Subversive Pleasures: Bakhtin, Cultural Criticism, and Film.* Baltimore: Johns Hopkins University Press, 1989.

Talens, Jenaro, and Santos Zunzunegui, eds. *Contracampo: Ensayos sobre teoría e historia del cine.* Madrid: Cátedra, 2007.

Torrell, Josep. "Textos: La primera película política de estado español." *Pere Portabella*, March 2, 2010. http://www.pereportabella.com/es/textos/2010/03/la-primera-pelicula-poltica-del-estado-espanol-es.

Traverso, Enzo. *Left-Wing Melancholia: Marxism, History, and Memory.* New York: Columbia University Press, 2016.

Val de Omar, José, "Desbordamiento apanorámico de la imagen." Intervention in the IX Congress of Cinematographic Technique, Turín, September 29 through October 1, 1957. http://www.valdelomar.com/pdf/text_es/text_6.pdf.

Vila-Matas, Enrique. *Paris no se acaba nunca.* Barcelona: Anagrama, 2006.

Weiss, Peter. *The Aesthetics of Resistance.* Translated by Joachim Neugroschel. Durham, NC: Duke University Press, 2005.

Wills, David. "Post/Card/Match/Book/*Envois*/Derrida." *SubStance* 43, 13, no. 2 (1984): 19–38.

Wollen, Peter. *Readings and Writings: Semiotic Counter-Strategies.* London: Verso, 1982.

Young, Neil. "Falling Star (Stella cadente): Rotterdam Review." *Hollywood Reporter,* February 6, 2010. http://www.hollywoodreporter.com/review/falling-star-stella-cadente-rotterdam-677765.

INDEX

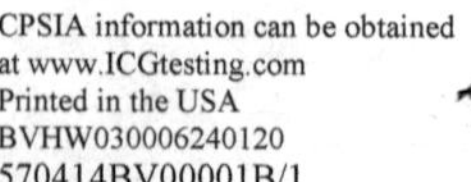
CPSIA information can be obtained
at www.ICGtesting.com
Printed in the USA
BVHW030006240120
570414BV00001B/1